FAMILY
SCHOOL
&
SOCIETY

FAMILY
SCHOOL
&
SOCIETY

in nineteenth~century canada

Edited by

Alison L. Prentice
and
Susan E. Houston

TORONTO
Oxford University Press
1975

© Oxford University Press (Canadian Branch) 1975

Cover design by FRED HUFFMAN
Photograph courtesy of Public Archives of Canada

ISBN-0-19-540246-4

1 2 3 4 5–9 8 7 6 5

Printed in Canada by
WEB OFFSET PUBLICATIONS LIMITED

Contents

Preface

This book began with our research in the history of education in nine-teenth-century Canada. As teachers we wanted to share some of our excite-ment at the wealth of documentary materials that exists in this field, as well as to provide a source book for students investigating the history of childhood and education in Canada's past. As the process of editing and organizing the book got under way, however, our excitement was occasionally destined to give way to considerable frustration. Our riches were too great; clearly there was not going to be room for all that we wanted to include. Many of the selections, furthermore, were written in the florid prose typical of an era when time for reading and writing seems to have been available, at least to some, in super-abundance. This fact resulted in two editorial difficulties. One was that to edit these works too ruthlessly was to take away much of their flavour, if not to destroy their very essence. Secondly, to eliminate parts of an argument or a series of letters seemed not only arbitrary, but sometimes seriously misleading. Although in the end we had to resort to much internal cutting of selections, our preference wherever possible was to choose between two pieces, rather than to mutilate both of them.

Such an approach, however, only intensified a second and equally serious concern, which was our desire to be comprehensive. We wanted the book to touch on as many of the major issues and themes of nineteenth-century educa-tion as possible, and at the same time to be representative geographically. Our most difficult decisions were having to choose between documents from prov-inces that were under-represented in the collection as a whole and documents that illustrated fascinating themes that would otherwise be left out. But if we were to end up with more than a collection of snippets, such decisions never-theless had to be made.

They were made with the help of Tilly Crawley, our editor at Oxford, whose keen sense of what was interesting and vital, as well as of what was not, was an essential ingredient in the process of making what at first seemed like a very random collection of materials into a book. With much patience and good humour she shepherded us through our organizing and reorganizing and finally accepted a volume that was slightly longer than the one we had origi-nally planned. For all of her efforts on our behalf, we are sincerely grateful.

We would also like to express our thanks to the many archivists, librarians, and friends who helped us by suggesting or making available to us the materials out of which this book grew. Our special thanks to Judith Fingard, Carolyn Gossage, Neil Macdonald, and David Sutherland for their ideas and interest.

ALISON PRENTICE
SUSAN HOUSTON
York University,
June 1975.

Introduction

In the history of childhood, the nineteenth century was the century of schooling. Government in most western jurisdictions took far more interest and played a much greater role in the promotion and management of schools than it ever had before, and parents and guardians seemed to look more and more to schools for the education of the young. The schoolmaster was abroad.' And 'education', construed as schooling for the multitudes, was hailed for a time at least as the great panacea that would solve many specific problems and, in a general way, bring about a better world.

Canada shared in this experience. Indeed, insofar as much of Canada was quintessentially a product of the Victorian era, one might argue that in Canada the opportunity existed to pursue Victorian ideals to a degree found in few other places. Gradually during the century schooling for longer and longer periods of time came to seem the norm for most children. Even more noticeable, perhaps, were the institutional structures that emerged to produce this schooling. In educational innovation the central provinces often led the way. Normal schools and model schools were founded to train the teachers; provision was made for assessment on property so that common schools could be supported entirely by provincial and municipal funds, and parents relieved of direct charges for the formal elementary education of their children; and in addition some jurisdictions decided that some schooling should be compulsory for all children at a certain age. As provincial departments of education and local administrative structures emerged to control the burgeoning schools and school systems, government funds were increasingly channelled only to those institutions accepting the controls, and the modern distinction between public and private education was gradually forged. Private education, either in the old sense of tutoring in domestic surroundings or in the modern sense of schooling supported independently of taxation or other government fundings, was experienced by the end of the century by very few Canadian children.

As in the course of the nineteenth century the balance shifted from voluntary means of financing schools to public and compulsory taxation for their support, important changes occurred also in the actual lives of children. The experience of apprenticeship or service seems to have been available to or desired by proportionately fewer and fewer boys and girls, and as a result, in urban centres especially, a pool of idle youth came into being. As industrialization progressed in the second half of the century, work in mills and other manufacturing establishments began to claim some of the young; some children still went into service; some continued the work of helping on the farm that had occupied rural children since the beginning of the century; yet others, like the famous newsboys, created new occupations for themselves. But increasingly schooling seems to have replaced apprenticeship, service, or work as both the ideal and actual occupation of most children. Even if they attended somewhat erratically, or did not attend for the extended number of years that became common in the twentieth century, it can be said that public schooling had become the uniform experience of the vast majority of the children of Canada by 1900.

If the nineteenth century was the crucial time, the cities of Canada were the crucial places. It was from Halifax, Saint John, Fredericton, St. John's, Charlottetown, Quebec, Montreal, Toronto, Winnipeg, and Victoria that many of the ideas in education emanated. Here were the normal schools, the departments of education, the school-book depositories, and the school-furniture manufactories, not to mention the schools and school systems that became the models for other places. Not that the experience of smaller cities was unimportant. In Ontario, Hamilton and London often seemed to be far in advance of Toronto to the most ardent promoters of educational reform. Nor can what went on in the most remote or rural regions be ignored. Indeed one could argue that many metropolitan institutions themselves were forged by migrants from rural places, whose departure from the farms and encounter with the urban environment was the catalytic experience of their lives.

Nevertheless metropolitan institutional structures seem in the end to have prevailed, for the large graded schools and school systems of cities, with their highly trained specialist teachers hierarchically arranged under the leadership of superintendents, principals, and other administrative personnel, came to be accepted as the ideal in education. And in much the same way these nineteenth-century systems seem to have set the mould for twentieth-century schooling as we know it. The small one-room schools, like the old untrained teachers, gradually came to be seen as undesirable relics of the past with little to recommend them to parents or children.

It is for these reasons that this book focuses on the experience of the nineteenth century and on those dominant provinces and metropolitan centres whose influence was so great. In order to provide documentary materials of substantial length, limits were necessary, and these seemed the logical ones. Another reason for limiting the times and places considered in this volume is the hope of moving, at least marginally, beyond the history of schools. Important as they were to the nineteenth century—and our own experience—there remains more to education and childhood than schooling. We have therefore tried to include material on families, and on surrogate schools and families as these were devised for groups excluded for one reason or another from what was gradually becoming the majority experience.

The documents raise innumerable questions. What role did families play in early Canadian education? Did the role change, and, if so, how? Why were more and more children sent to school in the course of the century? Who promoted schools and why? Why did the schools develop in the way that they did? Who were the teachers? Did their role change and if so, how and why? What was the difference in the educational experiences of girls and boys, of rich and poor, of Catholic and Protestant, of rural and urban children?

The documents in this book are a sampling of the vast materials that exist and from which historians are trying to answer such questions. We hope the documents will suggest some answers as well as the kind of questions that might be asked. We hope too that they will be suggestive not only of the important changes that took place in Canadian education in the nineteenth century, but of a number of other things as well. Perhaps they will give some indication of the roads not taken that might have been. Hopefully they will also suggest the complexity of nineteenth-century educational history: the differences in timing and approach, as educational innovation affected different classes and different parts of the country at different times. On the other hand there are also surprising continuities and similarities to be noted. School boards and principals in one place were perhaps not much different by the turn of the century from school boards and principals in another place. One wonders too how much the poor schools of the early nineteenth century really differed in purpose or method of operation from some of the overcrowded urban schools of the early twentieth century. We leave these questions and suggestions with the reader, in the hope that the documents will stimulate an interest in education in the past, as well as suggest changing interests and approaches among historians of education.

Educational history in Canada has long been obscured as a result of two tendencies in Canadian historical writing. The first was that, until recently, Canadian historians, focusing on what seemed to them the most momentous events and issues, chose to write about the national and the narrowly political, about the conquest, the winning of responsible government, or nation-building and the national economy. They ignored the history of education largely because it was simply out of their orbit. It was too local. If debates like the notorious separate school question of Manitoba attracted their attention, it was because these had become thoroughly mired in the murky waters of provincial or federal politics. The second basic fact is that historians, reflecting the prevailing intellectual and social moods of their times, tended to accept quite uncritically the conventional wisdom equating the expansion of formal schooling with progress. None of their contemporaries questioned the growth of public schools or public-school systems to any great degree. No more did they. This is true not only of the mainstream historians whose real interests were the issues of national power and/or economic development; it was also true of the several educationists, archivists, and local historians who did become more than peripherally interested in the subject, and who have written most of our traditional educational history. While much excellent work was produced by these historians, the very titles of their books suggest the one fatal flaw in their approach. From *The Development of Education in Canada*, the basic text by

Charles E. Phillips,[1] to J. G. Althouse's *The Ontario Teacher: A Historical Account of Progress*,[2] the message was the same—that the development of public-school systems and the whole idea of mass compulsory education was the desirable and indeed the almost inevitable outcome of popular need and mass demand. Nineteenth-century educational history therefore focused almost exclusively on the development and growth of school systems, and was a story of 'improvement'. The more schools there were, the bigger they became, and the greater the number of children attending them, the better everything was supposed to be getting.

Like most Whig history, nineteenth-century educational history tended to have its heroes and villains. The heroes were people like Alexander Forrester of Nova Scotia, Egerton Ryerson of Upper Canada, D. J. Goggin of the Northwest Territories, and John Jessop of British Columbia, all school administrators who were successful promoters of educational expansion and of innovations labelled 'reform'. The villains on the other hand tended to be those misguided critics who, whether permanently or temporarily, appeared to be against change and the reorganization of education under the auspices of the state.

Fortunately there were historians who were exceptions to the rule. Traditional educational historians found it impossible to ignore, for example, the developments in schooling that took place before the great mid-century era of innovation and structural change. It was equally difficult, too, to play down the long history of Roman Catholic opposition once the state started to penetrate the educational field. Thus, while sharing the tendencies described above, George W. Spragge was able to indicate the contributions made to the expansion of schooling in Upper Canada well before the free-school era, most notably by the Anglican schoolmaster and cleric, the Reverend John Strachan. Strachan's vision of an educational system for the province and his career as a teacher were revealed by Spragge as important models for later reformers.[3] Many of the discussions of the history of separate schools, insofar as they have been sympathetic to bicultural or multicultural models, have had to go even further in rejecting the 'one-path-to-progress' view of history.[4] But in spite of these and other deviations from the authorized version of educational history —that of more and better schools under the auspices of ever-growing provincial departments of education—few historians before the 1960s were able to question the fundamental assumption that educational progress meant mass compulsory schooling in some form.

The climate of the sixties and seventies has produced a more drastically revisionist mood. As contemporary critics ask penetrating questions about the schools and, more importantly, take issue with the assumption that education can only—or best—take place in schools, we are relearning something that in a way everyone has known all along, namely that education and schooling are not necessarily the same thing. And more frightening perhaps is our growing awareness that what the schools do may be much more pervasive and complex than the simple introduction of children to the basic intellectual skills required in a literate society. Even the value of literacy itself seems seriously challenged as we move into what has been called the post-literate society. These questionings are, understandably, reflected in recent work in Canadian educational history. Historians are now probing somewhat more deeply as they try to find out more about both the motives and the circumstances of educational change in the past. As a result they are asking new questions or putting the old questions in a new way. Instead of taking it for granted as an inevitable sign of progress, they now want to know, as we have suggested above, why more and more nineteenth-century children spent more and more of their time in schools. What were nineteenth-century schools really like and what did they really do? What was the educational experience that the new school systems gradually replaced?

Renewed interest in our educational past has been stimulated by the growth and increasing sophistication of local and regional history, as well as the expansion of social history generally. A new generation of historians is content to leave the giants and the somewhat larger-than-life issues of our national past aside to look at the history of more ordinary men and women, of smaller communities, and of children. Hopefully a fuller recognition of what Ramsay Cook and J. M. S. Careless have called our 'limited identities'[5] will eventually lead to a better understanding of the Canadian identity that interests us all. Comparison with other western societies in the nineteenth century should lead students of Canadian educational history not only to a fuller awareness of a shared heritage but to a recognition of what was unique to Canada in its various parts. Similar in some ways, unique in others, the power politics of Canadian education, even at its most local, was a politics that ultimately touches the lives of us all.

Notes

1. *The Development of Education in Canada* (Toronto, Gage, 1957).
2. *The Ontario Teacher: A Historical Account of Progress, 1800-1910* (D. Paed, diss. University of Toronto, 1929; Ontario Teachers' Federation, 1967).
3. George W. Spragge, 'Elementary Education in Upper Canada, 1820-1840', *Ontario History*, Vol. 43, 3 (July 1951) 107-22; and 'John Strachan's Contribution to Education, 1800-1823', *Canadian Historical Review*, Vol. 22 (June 1941), 147-58.
4. See Franklin A. Walker, *Catholic Education and Politics in Upper Canada, a Study of the Documentation relative to the Origins of Catholic Elementary Schools in the Ontario System* (Toronto, J.M. Dent, 1955); and Lovell Clark, ed., *The Manitoba School Question: Majority Rule or Minority Rights* (Toronto, Copp Clark, 1968).
5. J. M. S. Careless, ' "Limited Identities" in Canada', *Canadian Historical Review*, Vol. 50 (March 1969), 1.

1 Families and Education in Early British North America

The documents in Part I make it clear that education was not by any means equated with schooling in early British North America. The bringing up of children was pre-eminently the task of families—of mothers and fathers, guardians and masters. And the rearing of the young included, in theory at least, the duty of some formal, deliberate instruction. The catechisms, text-books, and manuals of piety and good manners that proliferated in the period were destined as much for family use as for schools, and well into the nineteenth century their titles continued to illustrate this fact.

Who was to carry out the educational function within the household? Clearly the role of the mother was not an inconsiderable one; but it was to the fathers and masters of families that clergymen and pedagogues seem to have directed their most insistent sermons and exhortations urging that more attention be paid to the education and protection of their young sons and daughters, apprentices and servants. Although some suggestion of an idealized role for mothers (concomitant with the idealization of childhood itself perhaps) may be traced to this early period, the relationship of mother and child, and family relationships in general, seem to have been less the objects of sentiment than was later to become the case. Sometimes, indeed, the relationship between both male and female parents and their children portrayed in this early period appears surprisingly formal.

Yet within the context of even the most formal family structures, one is constantly confronted by the apparent independence and authority of some youthful members of pre-industrial society. Occasionally youths away at school as well as young apprentices seem to have been granted, or to have taken upon themselves, considerable personal autonomy, even if in the case of the latter it could only be expressed in the end by running away. Ultimately one cannot help but raise the question of what youth and family life were really like in earlier times. How did it feel to be a parent or a child in an early nineteenth-century British North American household or family? What were the parameters of childhood and youth and how did they differ from what they became in the twentieth century?

Of course such questions cannot be approached in the end without some consideration of the nature and scope of 'institutionalized' schooling during these years. But here one immediately becomes aware that one of the most striking features of the early schools was their very lack of a common character. Variety in size, organization, and management was clearly a basic fact of the times. Schools, in addition, were incredibly impermanent if measured against twentieth-century standards. They tended to come and go as the teachers came and went; many, indeed, seem to have been almost entirely the creatures of the men and women who taught them. In spite of this, however, some schools did manage to survive for relatively long periods. Perhaps the grammar schools and academies were the most long-lived, sustained as they often were by the gifts of British donors as well as by the fees paid by the 'friends' of the students, but some of the charity schools founded by religious societies for the education of the children of the poor were also surprisingly stable. In the latter case too, financial support from the old country was an important aid in mitigating against the problems caused by the poverty of their intended clientele or the denominational rivalries that occasionally embarrassed them.

About the schools too, countless questions arise. Who did they serve? How much time did children spend in them? What instruction was offered and what did parents and schoolmasters or schoolmistresses see as the purposes of this instruction? Clearly there was not always complete agreement on either the goals or the techniques of formal education. But if argument about the means and ends of schooling often seems to the student of education to be one of the basic staples of its history, it is equally true that the reader of the documents in Part I should discover in them much that belongs uniquely to the particular locales or periods from which the documents come. For most regions and for most inhabitants of the colonies that were eventually to become Canada, the sermons on the duties of parents and masters, the household schools, the definitions of 'private' and 'public' in education, the catechisms and catechism-type textbooks 'for the use of private families and schools', the runaway apprentices, monitorial instructors, and part-time or peripatetic teachers, not to mention the brief and irregular attendance typical of most of those who experienced any formal schooling at all, were part of everyday experience. Gradually, as time went on, many of these features of early British North American education were altered or disappeared entirely. In many ways the differences between the ideals, attitudes, and experiences described in Part I and those that replaced them would spell the differences between the British North Americans of the pre-industrial period and their Canadian counterparts of the century that followed.

THE ROLE OF THE FAMILY

PARENTS TO BLAME FOR VICIOUS CHILDREN

Richard Cockrell, *Thoughts on the Education of Youth* (Newark, 1795; Toronto, The Bibliographical Society of Canada, 1949), pp. 1 passim, reprinted by permission.

Do not parents suffer their children to be too much in the streets? where they mix into the company of boys of every description: here they learn nothing but lying, swearing and other bad practices. Here perhaps they choose companions who are both mischievous and immoral, and never know what it was to be taught better. If the old saying be true that one rotten sheep corrupts a whole flock—what a speedy havoc must there be where there are as many rotten sheep as sound ones!

Parents would do well to keep their children, as much as possible from playing about the streets, where they seldom form any connexion but what does them more hurt than good. Loose, illiterate companions mar more than is generally supposed. By continually mixing with bad company, men as well as boys will find their ideas contracted, their judgments (about things of an interesting nature) will be found to be wrong informed, the delicate ties of amity and friendship will be corroded, and many a noble sentiment will be dislodged from the breast it loved to inhabit.

Again—It frequently happens that a boy who attends a seminary of learning, has brothers or sisters at home who do not attend; are these properly instructed with respect to genteel behaviour? If not, their conduct must have a great influence on the boy. He perhaps is one half of his time in their company, and as example works more forcibly than precept, it is much if he is not led to copy both their actions and behaviour, so that what is done by the master at school is undone at home.

Lastly. Do parents interest themselves as they ought, in this particular? Do they themselves set the example at home? In general, I am afraid it is too much neglected. They are extremely forward in censuring the schoolmaster, whenever their children are guilty of a breach of politeness, when at the same time the fault lies at their own door. What can a boy think when his father chides him for wearing his hat in the house at the same time that he has his own on? What can a boy think, when he hears his father curse and swear, and use obscene language continually in the house—or what a boy can imagine, when he sees his father come staggering home with all the majesty of drunkenness from the tavern, where he has been not only offering up a copious libation at the shrine of Bacchus, but perhaps has been engaged in its concomitant vices, such as gaming, &c. This is too frequently the case; and the effect which such conduct must have on the offspring, is too evident to need recital. Let parents therefore conduct themselves in a proper manner before their children at home, let them pay a due attention to their behaviour, otherwise the master had as well do nothing as attempt a reformation in their manners.

'Essay on the Necessity of Education, 1799', in J. G. Hodgins, ed., *Documentary History of Education in Upper Canada* (Toronto, 1894-1910), vol. 1, pp. 34-5.

By giving publicity to the following essay, through the medium of your useful paper, you will oblige one who feels for the promotion of literature in this country:—

'Tis education forms the common mind;
"Just as the twig is bent, the tree's inclined."

—Pope.

However ignorant we are of the materials of which the common mind is composed, this truth is clear, that in its infant and tender state impressions are made with the greatest ease; and those impressions which are then made are generally of a very durable nature.

It is with the greatest difficulty they are ever eradicated in any future period.

They are often the leading traits in a person's character through life.

The certainty of a person's imbibing principles in youth by which his future conduct and character will be shaped is much greater than that of any other period.

"Train up a child in the way he should go, and when he is old he will not depart from it." This being the case, the importance of an early formation of the young and tender minds of youth cannot be too often nor too forcibly inculcated. It is a matter of the greatest moment, and he who has the superintendence of the education of a family of children should consider it an employment of the greatest importance that could devolve upon him.

He is not only acting for himself, but for the community at large, and possibly for many generations yet to come.

He is forming them for the action on the great theatre of the world, where they will undoubtedly act in conformity to the precepts and examples received in their infancy.

If a parent, then, would wish to see his children possessing respect, honour and esteem of their fellow creatures, he must in their early infancy instil into their mind principles of virtue, for virtue is the foundation of every action which renders a man a valuable member of society; but if these principles are not implanted while the mind is yet young and tender, it is with difficulty their beauty can afterwards be discovered.

When the mind has become inured to vice, the practice of it becomes pleasing and agreeable, and the beauties of virtue have not a captivating power.

And I am bold to assert that it is chiefly owing to the neglect and misconduct of parents, and those whose duty it is to form and fashion the tender minds of youth, that prisons are so crowded with criminals, and courts of justice have the culprit so often arraigned before them.

Whenever I see a person receiving a punishment, inflicted upon him for a crime committed against the community, I consider him less guilty than those who had the superintending of his education; for had they, when the plants of vice were yet young and tender, suppressed their growth—had they represented vice with all its horrors and fatal consequences—it is impossible but it must have taken effect, and made it ever after appear in its true and odious light; who might otherwise have made characters of the first respectability are dragged in chains to a dungeon, there to spend a miserable and infamous life!

What, then, must be the feelings of a parent, seeing his child in this situation, when he considers himself the primary cause of the infamy and disgrace?

And what better prospect than this can those parents have with whose children our streets are thronged, who, no sooner than they are able to lisp a sentence, have their mouths filled with the bitterest curses, the profanest oaths and execrations?

It is truly a subject which requires their most serious attention.

Most of our children now, as soon as their age will admit of their passing the threshold of the doors, and they are able to articulate a word, learn the most impious language, and to practise every impiety which we should expect to find in the most abandoned character of mature age.

Whatever the parent may think of this, with however little attention he may regard it, however trifling it may appear to him, he may rest assured it is a bold beginning towards destruction.

It is the sure prelude of the child's rapid progress to infamy.

Wherefore, parents, if you wish to save your children, if you wish to make them respectable members of society, if you wish in your old age to receive consolation in their honor, stop their vicious projects and teach them virtue.

THE FAMILY AND RELIGIOUS EDUCATION

Rev. C. J. Stewart, *Two Sermons on Family Prayer* (Montreal, 1814).

Every master of a family is answerable to God for the welfare of those souls that are under his care. Nor can I well understand how a sense of religion can be maintained in a family without the exercise of daily devotion in it. Families are but little societies, as societies are larger families; and therefore religion, which is confessedly the best bond and cement of union in states and larger communities, is likewise so in little domestic governments. It is therefore incumbent upon those, who preside over a family to impress a sense of religion upon those who are beneath them. By this method we are best able to confirm and establish children and servants in the practice of their christian obligations. If ever then you would have your children to be dutiful, and your servants faithful; if ever you desire your small community here should join hereafter with the great congregation of men and angels in heaven, be sure to cultivate the spot of ground committed to your care, teach them to look up to God in every step of their conduct; impress upon them, and keep alive in them, by repeated prayers, a manly, serious, and devout frame of mind. From a neglect of doing this, it comes to pass, that our youth, as soon as they launch out into the world, fall an easy defenceless prey to those professors of iniquity, who go about seeking whom they may devour; that they become proselytes, from the best religion the world was ever blessed with, to no religion at all; and that those, who should be the flower of the nation, are too often the very dregs of it.

To acknowledge God to be the giver of all good gifts;—to put man's self, his wife, his children, his servants, and all that belongs to him under God's protection;—to ask from him, as from a father, whatever we want, and to thank him for the favours we have received; these are duties which the reason of mankind closes with as soon as they are fairly proposed. . . .

First: To begin and end the day with God, will be the likeliest way to make servants faithful,—children dutiful, wives obedient, and husbands sober, loving, and careful; every one acting as in the sight of God.

Secondly: This will be a mighty check upon every one of the family, and will be a means of preventing much wickedness;—at least, people will sin with remorse, (which is much better than with a seared conscience) when everyone knows he must go upon his knees before he sleeps.

Thirdly: This is the way to entail piety upon the generations to come. When children and servants, coming to have families of their own, cannot be easy till they fall into the same pious method which they have been long used to, "Train up a child in the way he should go, and when he is old he will not depart from it;" nor perhaps his children after him for many generations.

NOVA SCOTIA APPRENTICES

The Halifax *Journal* (July 20, 1790).

Ran-away

From the Subscriber, on the night of the 19th inst. two Apprentices to the Taylor's Business; one named

Benjamin Sullivan

aged about 20 years; 5 feet 5 or 6 inches high; stout built; swarthy complexion; black hair, which he used to wear quieued; had on a short blue coat, thickset or corduroy breeches, and had a variety of waistcoats;likewise had a long drab coat: He may change his dress.—The other named

Patt Kelly,

5 feet 7 or 8 inches high; short brown hair; had on a short drab coat, buttons covered with the same cloth; broad rib corduroy or nankeen breeches, and a green striped waistcoat.

As they went off in the night, I have reason to suspect they embezzled sundry goods, having nothing else to bear their expenses.—Whoever will apprehend the said Sullivan and Kelly, and return them to their said Master, or secure them in any of his Majesty's Gaols, so that the Subscriber may have them again, shall receive FIVE POUNDS reward, and all reasonable charges paid by

William Duffus

All Masters of vessels, and others, are hereby cautioned against harbouring, or carrying away said Apprentices.

Halifax, July 20

THE HOUSEHOLD AS SCHOOL

H. H. Langton, ed., *A Gentlewoman in Upper Canada: The Journals of Anne Langton* (Toronto, Clarke, Irwin, 1950), passim. © 1950 by Clarke, Irwin & Company Limited. Used by permission.

Wednesday, January 16, 1839. I had a new pupil to-day, a little girl of the Daniels about ten years old. I scarcely yet know what her attainments are, for she is dreadfully frightened, and though she appeared to know scarcely more than her letters at first, I shall not think it all my own doing if I find that she can read at the end of a fortnight. I hope she will get some good from me, however, for she has nearly two miles to come for her lessons. . . .

Thursday, January 24, 1839. This was school day; my new pupil is far in advance of the other children. My most distant scholars come twice a week, Mondays and Thursdays: the little ones likewise on a Wednesday, as they are close at hand, and it is worth while coming up for an hour. . . .

Tuesday, July 9, 1839. My school assembled in the afternoon, but we all felt the weather. I was sleepy, and the children were languid. I had a new scholar, a girl of ten or twelve years of age, not yet perfect in her letters. And now I think my number is up. When more come on I must turn some of the old ones off, unless I can introduce the mutual instruction system, or, as I cannot well extend my school hours, the benefit to each individual must be necessarily diminished by an increase of numbers. At present if the amount of good gained in a lesson is not very great, at any rate they are put into the way of learning, and rendered capable of improving themselves. . . .

Tuesday, December 3, 1839. I had my school today, but at present it consists only of my two oldest children. I do not regret it as these get a start from receiving more of my attention, whilst those I hope will not forget much who are at present kept away by bad roads and want of shoes. Schooling has been very light work for some time. First the harvest came, during which I had a very small attendance. Then the Regatta, which was a holiday. Afterwards potato-raising interfered a good deal, and now the roads. . . .

Thursday, December 19, 1839. This having been school day I will make it the occasion of thanking you for the little book you have for me. I have no doubt that were you, or your friend Dr. Kay, to visit my school you would find great occasion to reform it. I go on in a hum-drum old-fashioned way, teaching just reading and writing, and very little else. . . . I am quite sensible that the instruction I give goes a very small way indeed towards complete education, and I have felt a misgiving lest, in some cases, the fact of a child being sent to me for two or three hours twice a week affords an excuse for neglecting it at home. I endeavour to impress it upon their friends that I by no means charge myself with the whole education, but am willing to give a little assistance such as may be in my power. In one case, where they are very competent to teach at home, I very much question whether my assistance has not been worse than useless on this account. One individual has actually made it an excuse for not doing anything towards a schoolhouse that he could send his child to me. In other cases, however, I must do some good, though the amount of it may be small. In one neither the father nor mother can either read or write, though evidently in many respects quite better sort of people, and their children show more complete cleanliness and propriety than any others. In another case they are a very large and busy family, and have made some small effort towards instruction themselves, though they complain that the children lose in the summer what they can teach them during the winter months. They evidently value instruction, and rarely have kept their daughter at home, though she is at a very useful age. I have only to complain in one instance that the benefit afforded is not appreciated, at least that a very irregular attendance is obtained. But I should not talk of appreciating the benefit when I was just going to tell you how small it was after all. Most of my scholars have to begin from the a-b-c, and until a little reading is accomplished I scarcely think, with my limited days and hours, I can attempt anything beyond it. Writing I began with the elder ones, merely by way of occupying profitably the time in which the others were saying their lessons, but to very little profit did they use the pen until latterly, when from a smaller number I have been able to give more direct attention to it, and decided improvement begins to appear. With my readers I am at present pleased enough if they appear to take in the direct meaning of the words as they read them, without entering into any explanations or questionings that may help to open their understandings. I do not know what progress can be expected from children who say a lesson twice a week, and perhaps never look at a book at any other time. . . .

Thursday, March 12, 1840. I have been again trying to drive a little intelligence into the untutored children of the forest. I have somewhat enlarged my system of tuition, and another branch of knowledge will be added to their extensive acquirements! I get assistance from my mother and Aunt Alice; the former has taken one little scribe entirely under her superintendence, and the latter often hears one or other of the reading lessons. Mr. Fidler has twenty-eight pupils, some much more advanced in years and accomplishments than mine. . . .

Monday, February 22, 1841. I am to have two new scholars on Thursday, a boy of Powell's, our new neighbour, and one of Jordan's, the latter I daresay fourteen or fifteen years old. My mother is going to superintend the sewing department. Aunt Alice thinks that I have been very negligent to give so little attention to this important branch of education; but really, without undervaluing it, I have found since I had so many scholars that I had no time to fix work. Two days a week is not sufficient for everything, and I consider that the mothers will teach a little sewing because they derive immediate advantage from it, but with book learning it is otherwise. . . .

I was rather weary of adding, subtracting, and multiplying this morning. Being just about to lose three of my eldest scholars, I am trying to drive as much into them as I can. When they are gone I shall take my other big one only once a week, leaving one day for infant schooling. I have one or two who stick fast at their letters, and will be the better for some more particular drilling. . . .

Monday, May 3, 1841. We had a numerous school this afternoon—ten. I have had a very poor attendance for some weeks, often only two dreadfully stupid ones, and one little one. This sudden increase has called for my mother's assistance in the sewing department, and also Aunt Alice's in hearing A B C, but I think I shall now be able to form something like a class. This can only be if they are pretty regular in their attendance, however. There are too many beginners now, with whom regularity is of importance, for me to indulge in a summer holiday, as last year. Some of my pupils, I doubt not, receive good religious instruction at home, but I fear others do not. . . .

Thursday, May 20, 1841. I had an application to-day to take another scholar, but I find it quite impossible to increase my numbers. I shall however make room for the applicant soon by dismissing one who has had the benefit of more than two years' teaching, and, I am sorry to say, to but little purpose. I begin to wish we had, or could have, something more regular in the way of a school. The number of children is increasing, and my cares are much more likely to increase than to decrease. Aunt Alice teaches a little every evening; our boy, Timothy, is her pupil—not a remarkably bright one, I am afraid. . . .

AT BOARDING SCHOOL

Family History: Stairs Morrow, including Letters, Diaries, Essays, Poems, Etc. (Halifax, McAlpine Publishing Company, 1906), pp. 66 passim.

Halifax, N. S., October 1st, 1832.

MY DEAR SON,—I can scarcely yet realize that you are indeed gone so far, and to be away for so long a period from us. Your removal from the paternal roof was cause of great anxiety to me, and it rests greatly with you to allay that anxiety by a constant diligence in keeping up our correspondence, and obeying the injunctions which I shall occasionally lay upon you. I have every reason to believe that you love your whole family, and that a letter from your mother will be truly welcome. May it ever continue so is the prayer of your anxious parents. That it will I have no doubt, if you persevere in the right path. "To train you up in the way you should go" is one of the dearest objects of my heart; and feeble as my efforts in that way have been, they have been dictated by a stronger affection than you need ever expect from any other quarter. Yet your father's very strong desire to have you placed where you are, has at length overcome my scruples, and his arguments have, in some measure, brought me to the conviction that you will have superior advantages at Horton to those in Halifax.

But remember, my son, that you are now thrown into a community of little people, which is just the world in miniature, and as you acquit yourself now you lay a foundation for future happiness or misery. In the first place you must "do unto all" around you "as you would wish them to do unto you." You will think this very difficult. It is so, my son; if you attempt it in your own strength Satan will then defeat you. But you must seek aid; you must humble yourself in the dust before your Maker and earnestly entreat of His Holy Spirit to grant you the grace to keep you from sin. I mean not only at the time of prayer, I mean at all times. When at play among your young companions, you must bear about with you a sense of our own inability to do any good action, and if you are tempted to commit an improper one, I trust you will seek His grace who is all-powerful, and then you will be able to "do justly, love mercy, and walk humbly with thy God." This is a very serious letter, but I believe it is the first which I have ever addressed to you, and I wish your mind to be duly impressed with the knowledge that there is often a very short step between innocence and guilt, and if that step be once taken, nothing but the grace of God can enable any of us to retrace it. I have nearly filled my paper, and therefore must conclude; but my dear William, I will write you soon again. I leave to Catherine the agreeable task of telling you all the news. Father sends his love to his dear boy. Your brothers and sisters join me in kindest remembrances to you.

Your affectionate Mother,
M. STAIRS.

Halifax, N.S., October 8th, 1832.

MY DEAR WILLIAM,—Your father will send you to-day, by Mr. Tupper's team, the articles which you wrote for.—I had just written so far, when your letter of the 4th October was brought up to me. I am exceedingly pleased with your promise of attending to my advice, for oh! my son, what comfort would there be for me if I thought that you were to be a castaway! I feel as though I could meet any trouble but the misconduct of my children, and from that my soul shrinks.

My dear child, you must remember at all times the sacredness of truth; to tell a lie, even what some people call a white lie, is a very serious error. Lying, I consider, at the foundation of every other vice, and I think I have always, by my example, shown my abhorrence of the habit. But there are times when the whole truth need not be repeated; you are not unnecessarily to expose the faults of any person, but if questioned by those who have a right to question, never swerve from the truth. I think I need hardly expatiate upon the necessity of respecting the property of others. Surely, my dear William would never forget himself so far as to meddle with what was not his own, yet I have heard of boys who were respectably brought up, robbing orchards. Join in no such frolics! You might bring indelible disgrace upon yourself and family; and remember that He who has said "Thou shalt not steal," has not made any exception as to articles. And even admitting that we thought only of this life, I have always observed that there is much truth in the old proverb, "Honesty is the best policy."

We begin now to talk about Christmas at the breakfast table, because we expect that you will then have some holidays, and mischievous as you were, and much as you used to plague us sometimes, we would all like to see you flying up and down stairs again; and I think it would be a pleasure to you to see your brothers and sisters again for a few weeks. But you must in the meantime be very diligent at your studies, and I shall be much disappointed if I see no improvement in that way when you come down.

I wish you to write me what you are reading in, and I expect a long description of how you pass your time.

My dear child, your father and the children join me in affectionate regards.

M. STAIRS.

Halifax, 6th November, 1832.

DEAR WILLIAM,—I wish very much to receive a letter from you, and therefore I hope that you will write me by the very first private opportunity, for mother says not to write to me by the stage on account of the postage; but have your letter written ready and send it by the first private conveyance.

Catherine had a party, and I sat up till half-past one o'clock. Captain Auld has a very handsome ship. I wish you had been here to have seen her. Mother, Catherine, Joanna, Margaret and Helen all went down to look at her.

We have two new scholars since you have been away; they are William Lawson, from Prince Edward Island, and John Freeman, from Liverpool.

Some of our boys talk of going to the Horton Academy. We go now to school at 7 o'clock in the morning instead of 6 o'clock, and we remain in school till 9. I wish Christmas was come and you had your holidays. Mother says she will make a fine large frosted cake, and it shall be cut the evening you arrive.

Margaret is making you a shirt entirely by herself, and I suppose she will have it done by the time you come down. The clock is just striking nine, and mother says it is time for me to go to bed, so dear William, good-night.

JOHN STAIRS.

Halifax, November 22nd, 1832.

MY DEAR WILLIAM,—You are, I trust, persevering in industrious pursuits and looking forward to a delightful vacation spent with your friends. Let me know at what time the school will break up for the holidays, how long the term will be, and in what manner the generality of the boys will be conveyed to town. Your father has not yet determined how to get you down. I am looking out to see you in about a month, when I expect to find great improvement in your literary acquirements. I cannot too frequently urge upon you the necessity of industry, and am happy to see by your letter to John that you understand the full value of time. I hope you take the good advice which you have given him.

I was exceedingly pleased at hearing from Mr. Allan that you had been obliging enough to write him for little William, and hope you will always do these little kind offices for your school fellows.

Your father has got the wharf at Dartmouth completed, but still visits the cooperage every morning before breakfast. James and the brown horse are at work drawing building stones into town from the North-West Arm. The gray horse is sent up to Mr. Cochran's at Newport for the winter.

This is a short letter, dear William, but I am in great haste. Be a good child and believe your mother to be most anxious for your improvement and welfare.

M. STAIRS.

Halifax, N.S., February 1st, 1833.

DEAR WILLIAM,—I received your letter, from the tenor of which I suppose you had no hand in the affair between Mr. Johnston and the boys. I hope I may be right in my supposition, for it would give me much uneasiness were you to offer any insult to Mr. Johnston, for I consider him as much entitled to respect as if he were the father of every boy under his charge; you will therefore please me much by respecting Mr. Johnston. Be assured he will not require you to do anything improper.

Herewith you will receive a pair of boots, in one of which you will find 2s. 9d. for the purchase of a book. The family are all well. I remain, dear William,

Yours affectionately,

WM. STAIRS.

Halifax, N.S., February 11th, 1833.

DEAR WILLIAM,—We were all happy to hear of your being well, by your letter to your father. We have got plenty of snow, of which, I suppose, there is no scarcity at Horton. Father's new ship, the "John Porter," arrived from London a fortnight ago, is now loading, and will sail for Liverpool on Sunday. She is a fine vessel of three hundred tons, and stands letter A. No. 1, at Lloyd's; Messrs. Fairbanks and Macnab own one-half of her. I hope the Horton Academy will continue to do well. Mr. Lockerby's school is daily increasing. We have got three new scholars lately; their names are Frederick Hughes, James Kerr, and Robert Dupont.

Since you left home Joanna attempted to make some candy for you, but did not succeed. She intends trying it again. I hope she may be more fortunate, for I think a lot of good white sugar candy would be very acceptable to you and your cronies. Mother desires me to say that she intends writing to you very soon, and is very happy to understand that you were not one of those who behaved with disrespect to Mr. Johnston. The watchman has just cried "half-past nine." Joanna is preparing a Welsh rarebit. I wish you were here to partake of it. Our sisters are all well. Anna is much improved, but she cannot walk. Mr. Ford, a gentleman from the States, has commenced giving lectures on Astronomy in the Acadian School at eight o'clock in the evening. We have got a family ticket; the lectures are given on Tuesdays and Thursdays. Father, mother, Joanna and I went last Tuesday. Father and I are going on Thursday. I was very much pleased with Mr. Ford's lecture.

Helen and Margaret request me to give their love to you. They are very well, but Helen hurt her hand a little on the stove to-day. I must now conclude.

Your affectionate brother,
JOHN STAIRS.

Halifax, N.S., February 17th, 1833.

MY DEAR WILLIAM,—Your letter to your father of last week gave both him and me a little uneasiness. We are sorry to hear that you are not agreeably situated at Mr. Johnson's, and the idea of your changing your place of residence, and being from under the care of the assistant teacher (for Mr. Pryor will surely soon procure one), is matter of anxiety with us. You have at present, as far as I can understand, the advantage of some religious instruction in the family where you are placed. Will it be thus at Mr. DeWolf's? And the additional expense of 2s. 6d. per week should be an object of consideration, although not of the first importance. After a good deal of thought on the subject your father has come to the determination of allowing you to act for yourself in the affair, trusting that you will not let a feeling of caprice induce you to make the change; but if, after weighing the matter well in your own mind, you think that it will be for your ultimate benefit to remove to Mr. DeWolf's, you have liberty to present the enclosed note.

My dear boy, think well on the subject, and do not study your present comfort so much as your advantages as to instruction, and the facilities for improvement which you may have. Remember that all our anxiety is that you should acquire knowledge. I hope you persevere in the study of Natural Philosophy. You will find if you now go through the drudgery a little, that hereafter you will have a wonderful deal of pleasure in the science. Let me know if you still go on with Greek, or if you have discontinued it and fill up the time by a closer application to Arithmetic. Write me a long letter all about your studies, and if you go to Mr. DeWolf's, describe to me how you are situated, tell me the names of the boys who are in the house with you, and also write to your father respecting your removal. Be very particular in ascertaining that the charge will not be more than 10s. per week, for it would be a sad trial to find that your father was saddled with a still greater expense than he contemplated. He would have written himself, but is greatly engaged to-day with business, and begged of me to acquaint you with his sentiments.

John has written you a letter, but I must acknowledge that it is not altogether his own diction. However, I hope that you will take pleasure in answering it. The children all join your father and me in the warmest love to our dear William.

Your affectionate mother,
M. STAIRS.

November, I mean March 15th.

MY DEAR PARENTS,—I received your letter last Sunday, and I would have answered it before, only I had nothing particular to say. I believe we are going to get another boarder soon, but I am not certain. They still keep crowding into Mr. Johnson's. There are at present 26 boarders, besides 12 in the family. At Mr. D——— they are the most cleanly people I ever saw, and if it could be, neater than at home. They take great care of my clothes and mend them whenever they want it. I have got my boots mended, and Mr. DeWolf paid for them. I wish you would send me about one dozen buttons, the same size as one I will send down, and about 1-16th of a yard of blue cloth to mend my clothes. Joanna's candy was very acceptable. I saw Mr. Roy last Wednesday and gave him the letter. I could not give him it before, because he lives up the road nearly eight miles. The weather still keeps very cold, and we have had not above 12 fine days.

W. STAIRS.

MY DEAR BROTHER,—As you are so anxious that I should write to you in particular, I will; but you must remember that when I write to one I write to all the family. I was glad to hear Mr. Lockerby's school was increasing. We have fine fun up here every morning. We have about a mile to go to school, and we have rigged up a sled to take to school. We have four boys for horses, and we ride by turns. I had my ride this morning, and if you were up here you would have yours too. Give my love to all the family.

W. STAIRS.

John Stairs in particular————

MY DEAR SISTERS,—I wish you would write also.

W. STAIRS.

Halifax, N.S., March 27th, 1833.

MY DEAR SON,—Not hearing from you more frequently makes me exceedingly unhappy. How can you be so ungrateful as never to think of home?

I can assure you I am very dissatisfied with your conduct; it is your duty to sit down and write to us at least every week, not to leave it to the last minute, but to take time and write a good, long, well-spelt letter. If you begin so early to neglect your family, I know not what we may expect in future.

I have had a narrow escape for my life, and am indebted to your little brother for my preservation. Your father and sisters being out, I was sitting here alone on the evening before last. I got up and went to the closet in John's room and stooped down, and by some accident my cap took fire from the candle. In less than an instant my cap, collar and pocket handkerchief were all in flames. In an agony of terror I threw myself on my face on the carpet, thinking to drag it about me; but it was tacked down, and I received no benefit from it. John, who saw my danger, sprang out of bed and threw a basin of water, out of the wash-stand, over me. The flames began to revive again, but he smothered them out with his hands. I received no further injury than being burnt about the size of my hand on the back of my neck. It is getting better.

I send you by this opportunity a pair of new trousers. I wish you to write me if they fit well. If they are too long you must get somebody to tuck them for you. You will also receive some magaines, which were given to me by the captain of the "John Porter."

I must add that you do not deserve such indulgences, and that I am by no means satisfied; your brother and sisters, I am afraid, will forget you.

Your truly anxious mother,

M. STAIRS.

Halifax, June 2nd, 1833.

MY DEAR WILLIAM,—We were all very sorry to hear of your sore hand, and I should like to know something further about it.

The time is now drawing near when we shall have the pleasure of your being with us. Your father has been keeping very close to business, for trade has been so dull lately and so many people have failed, that his ideas respecting commerce have become very gloomy. I hope you will come home with the determination of putting your shoulder to the wheel. All that you can do is to give a cheerful and steady obedience to your father's commands. I had hoped that you would have been put into the counting house of a stranger, but matters have gone so wrong with the commercial part of the community that your father cannot afford to spare your services, but must make use of you in the place of some one that in better times he might have hired; therefore you must make up your mind to going into our own store, and I hope, my dear son, that you will be a pattern to those who are already there.

John Craigen has set up in business for himself, and we have now only Richard and Andrew. They are much older, and of course understand their duty much better than you, and you must expect to be quite under them; but you can show them an example of steadiness and attention. I never saw such a time of necessity in my life as there is in general over the town. We are going on with the house, but everything is so gloomy that I cannot take any pleasure in it. We must hope that it will draw us to place our affections on things above.

I have great reason for thankfulness in having my children all well, and I endeavour to be always conscious of this, but I cannot conquer my lowness of spirits. I hope, my son, that you will be my comfort.

Your father, brothers and sisters join me in love.

M. STAIRS.

We sent you something for making trousers. Let me know if you have received it. I will try to procure you a cap.

Halifax, July 2nd, 1833.

MY DEAR WILLIAM,—You must have observed how seldom I have written to you lately. My heart has been at Horton, but my mind has been in a most anxious, unsettled state owing to the calamitous condition of the community. When I see so many of our old acquaintances suffering, I cannot but feel sorrow for them and dread for ourselves, and therefore I have desired Catherine to write instead of doing so myself. I see where the error of the people here has been—the women have been extravagant, the men too speculative. Heaven grant it may prove a warning to us all.

My dear child, you are about entering the shop and office at a time of great scarcity. I think it will be for your ultimate benefit. The present season of suffering will impress your mind with the necessity of keeping out of debt. If men would be satisfied with small things and regulate their house expenses accordingly, it would be much better for us all. Your father's plan at present is to contract his business, and I hope that you will commence with a firm determination to be proud of industry. Some men in this town have been ruined by their sons' indolence and pride. If you have formed any foolish notions as respects the kind of work you would do, they must be given up. These notions have been the ruin of Halifax. Oh, William! it is melancholy to relate, but many families in this town who lived as comfortably as ourselves have not now the means of going to market. Yes, my son, they are at this moment suffering for food.

I have said much respecting the disastrous state of affairs here. It is to impress on your mind the necessity of industry. But there is one thing which I would urge still more strenuously, that is, "To seek first the kingdom of God and His righteousness, and all things shall be added thereto." My child, ponder over this text well; let it not be driven from your thoughts. Oh! may the Holy Spirit assist you and enable you and us all to commit our affairs for time and for eternity into His hands.

Your last letter was cause of sorrow to me for the loss you had met with, but I was consoled by the method you took to extricate yourself from the difficulty. If you had delayed acquainting us the affair would have been worse. Your father was not very angry; he rather pitied you, but money is very scarce with us.

Be careful of your clothes, but when you are leaving Horton, if you have any which you have outgrown and you think they will not answer for John, you can get Miss DeWolf to dispose of them as she did some before.

I wish you could procure some kind of a cheap straw hat at Horton. I would send you the money to pay for it. We do not know how to fit your head. Be careful of the money which I enclose in this letter. Pay all the people immediately. Write me soon. I am,

Your affectionate mother,
M. STAIRS.

Wolfville, N.S., July 10th, 1833.

DEAR MOTHER,—I received yours on the 7th, and I have paid all my bills in Horton. I have taken your leave and bought myself a straw hat. If I had not done so, I don't much think that you would see me in Halifax this vacation. I have lost more flesh just by wearing that cap on those hot days this summer than I gained all winter. It is so warm now that I can scarcely manage to write, although I am sitting by the window with a breeze blowing in, and my jacket off. Several of the boys are going to Halifax to-morrow, although the vacation does not commence till this day week. I wish you would forward me by the first opportunity 14 shillings to take me to Halifax, and 3 to pay for my hat. The stockings fitted admirably. I shall be glad to get to Halifax; it is so much cooler there than here. I never felt it so hot. I have been making calculations, and find that I can go to town by a private conveyance 11 shillings and 10 pence cheaper than in the coach, so I think that I had better try to save that much money. I have not much more to write. All I have I can soon tell you by words. The boys are all very impatient to get home, as you may suppose that I am.

Give my love to all the family.

I am, your affectionate
W. J. STAIRS.

Halifax, Saturday, Aug. 1833.

MY DEAR SON,—It was my intention to have written soon after your return to Horton; but feeling that what I had to say would be disagreeable, I have deferred it until now.

During the Christmas vacation I was much pleased with you. I believe I had not occasion to find fault with you once all the time you were with us; but the last time you were down there was such a degree of carelessness and indolence in your conduct, that I was glad when the time came round for you to go to school, and it was, I can assure you, the first time your mother was glad to have you leave the house. Heaven grant that it may be the last time I shall find pleasure at your departure; but my son, you cannot expect your father and mother will continue to love you if you give your time entirely up to play and show no disposition to improve your mind when with them, by reading, or accomplishing any little work which they may put upon you. I cannot forget the indolence you showed respecting clearing out the walks.

Mr. Johnston told your father that he knew nothing of your intention to leave his house until he missed you out of it. What an improper way of leaving! Why did you not acquaint him with your intention before you went? It was insolent in the extreme.

Your last letter to Catherine was cold and unsatisfactory: It was written in the most careless manner imaginable. You do not pay the slightest attention to a paragraph in hers in which she acquaints you with John's having burnt his face very much with gunpowder. It has now got pretty well, but you might have noticed it. The fact is, William, that you must become industrious; you must write letters, and longer letters, to your family, or depend upon it, my young gentleman, you will come off by the worst. Pray did Mr. Pryor give you a receipt, and why did you not send it to your father?

I hope that I shall soon receive a long letter from you, in expectation of which I still subscribe myself,

YOUR AFFECTIONATE MOTHER.

THE BRITISH CONSTITUTION FOR EVERY BOY

The Every Boy's Own Book, or a Digest of the British Constitution, Compiled and Arranged for the Use of Schools and Private Families by John George Bridges (Ottawa, 1842), pp. 5-9.

"GREAT BRITAIN—a power to which Rome in the height of her glory is not to be compared, which had dotted the whole earth with her possessions and military posts,—whose morning drum follows the Sun, and keeping company with his beams, circles the globe daily with one continuous and unbroken strain of the martial airs of England."—Daniel Webster.

LESSON 1st.

Adam, the first King, as well as the first man, was the father of his own subjects, and when the eldest son succeeded to his father's authority, he succeeded also to his title of father, and hence the style of father is given to this day to all Kings, which points remarkably to the original of Government, or Kingship, in the time of man's innocency in Eden, which God first instituted there, both in nature and by positive command. And therefore we owe to our Sovereign the same obedience, which Adam's children or subjects paid to him, for God's commands and institutions descend through all ages to the end of time, and Government is of the same necessity and obligation now, as it was when it was first imposed by God, and it is equally "his ordinance" now, as it was then.

If Government and its succession was ordained by God himself,—then it is as natural that it should succeed in the same track as for the sun to proceed in his diurnal course.

There are but three kinds of Government. When the sovereign power is vested in one person it is called a Monarchy: if in all the nobles it is called an Aristocracy, or an Oligarchy if confined to a few of these: if an assembly of the people have the chief authority, it is called a Democracy or a Republic.*

Of all the different species of Governments, the Monarchical is the most ancient and natural, originating at first in parental authority, hence Kings are called the fathers of their people.

The Assyrian and Egyptian Monarchies are the most ancient that we read of, but, there are several Kings mentioned in the Scriptures, in the early history of the Patriarch Abraham. The Jews were governed by God himself 'till Sauls' [sic] time, from whence it has been called a Theocracy—taken from the Greek word signifying GOD. After his elevation to the Throne of Israel by Gods' [sic] appointment, the Government continued Monarchical till the destruction of the temple.

Some Monarchies are despotic, where the subjects are slaves at the arbitrary power and will of their Sovereign; such as the Turks and most Asiatic nations; others political or paternal, where the subjects like children under a father, are governed by equal and just laws, consented to, and sworn by all Christian Princes at their Coronation. Some Monarchies are hereditary, where the Crown descends either to male heirs only, as in France, or to the next of blood, as in Great Britain, Spain, Portugal, &c. Others, elective, where upon the death of the reigning Prince, without respect to their heirs or next of blood, or by expiration of their time of limitation of rule, another by solemn

---

* *Note.* —In strictness of language, a great difference exists between a Republic and a Democracy. Properly speaking, the term Republic, is more justly applicable to Great Britain than to any other nation on earth, for although it may be objected, that one of its pillars is Monarchy, yet, it is very evident, that the whole tendency and practice of the British system is Republican, that is impartially respective of the general good.

Democracy on the other hand, is that form of Government, which irrespective of the obligation of law and custom, places the present will of the populace above all restraint, and of course leaves the general weal entirely at the mercy of that, which is more fickle and capricious, than the winds of heaven.

The ancient Lacedamonian Republic was likewise provided with hereditary Monarchs, who reigned in a direct line for 700 years.

370.971 F21a

c.1

election is appointed to succeed them. This used to be the system in Poland before its partition, and formerly also in Denmark, Hungary and Bohemia, and is still practised in the United States of America, for although their Chief Governor is called a President, still he is their Sovereign, and is elective.

QUESTIONS AND ANSWERS
EXPLANATORY OF LESSON 1st.

Q.—Why are Kings called the Fathers of their people?
A.—It originated in the parental authority of Adam the first man, who ruled over his own descendants.
Q.—When was rule or Kingship first instituted?
A.—In Eden,—in the time of man's innocency.
Q.—By whom was it ordained?
A.—Of God,—both in nature and by positive command.
Q.—What is due to our Sovereign?
A.—Obedience.
Q.—Whose commands enforce obedience to the end of time?
A.—God's.
Q.—How many kinds of Government are there?
A.—Three.
Q.—What is meant by a Monarchy?
A.—When the Sovereign power is vested in one person.
Q.—What is understood by an Aristocracy?
A.—When the power is vested in all the nobles.
Q.—How is an Oligarchy constituted?
A.—When the power is confined to a few nobles.
Q.—What is a Democracy?
A.—When the Chief authority is exercised by the people.
Q.—What applied to a Republic?
A.—The same as a Democracy.
Q.—What are the most ancient Monarchies that we read of?
A.—The Assyrian and Egyptian.
Q.—By whom were the Jews governed till Saul's time?
A.—God.
Q.—What is the derivation of the word Theocracy and its meaning?
A.—When God ruled the Jews it was called a Theocracy, and is derived from a Greek word signifying God.
Q.—Who ascended the Throne of Israel by divine appointment?
A.—Saul.
Q.—What is meant by a despotic Monarchy?
A.—When the subjects are ruled at the will of their Sovereign.
Q.—What is understood by political or paternal Monarchy?
A.—When subjects are governed by equal and just laws; which are sworn to for strict observance by the Sovereign on receiving the Royal investiture.
Q.—What is meant by hereditary Monarchy?

A.—Where the Crown descends to the lawful heir.

Q.—In what right of succession does the Crown descend in France?

A.—To male heirs only.

Q.—What is the right of succession in England?

A.—The Crown descends to the next of blood male or female, in Great Britain, Spain and Portugal.

Q.—What is an elective Monarchy?

A.—Where the Kingly power is for life, and on the death of the Sovereign, his successor is elected by the people.

Q.—In what countries used this elective right to be exercised?

A.—In Poland before its partition, and also in Denmark, Hungary and Bohemia.

Q.—How is the elective power exercised in the United States of America?

A.—In an election of a President by delegates chosen by the people, whose Reign expires with the time of limitation of rule of four years. . . .

EARLY SCHOOLS AND SYSTEMS OF INSTRUCTION

EARLY VIEWS ON TEACHING

Richard Cockrell, *Thoughts on the Education of Youth* (Newark, 1795; Toronto, The Bibliographical Society of Canada, 1949), pp. 1 passim. Reprinted by permission.

The education of youth is of such an important and interesting nature to society, that the man who embarks in so glorious a cause benefits a community as much as he possibly can, provided his abilities are adequate to the task; he is not only serving the present, but is also rearing on a firm basis, the pillars of the succeeding generation.

It is certainly necessary for every person who undertakes the arduous task of a tutor, that he be a man of sound learning and an irreproachable character.

By a man of sound learning, I mean one who understands well the fundamentals of those branches which he undertakes to teach; this enables him to open the minds of his pupils with facility, and convey his ideas in a clear and masterly manner. Then not being reduced to the miserable necessity of having recourse to old manuscripts for the questions and solutions which he proposes to his scholars, he performs the duty of the day with chearfulness, lectures his scholars into a knowledge of what they are about, and by thus exhibiting causes and effects, he furnishes the tender minds with something more than superficial.

The expression, an illiterate tutor, would in ancient times, I dare say, have been thought a solecism. But alas! how frequent do we find, now-a-days, persons filling the places of tutors, who have neither abilities nor address to recommend them, scarce knowing B from a bull's foot. It is evident this description of men do not act pro bono publico, but for their own private ease and emolument. Hence we daily behold tailors, blacksmiths, cobblers, worn out livery servants, &c. &c. turning schoolmasters, and, Isaac Factotum like, can do every thing.

O YE mushroom gentry! do you sincerely reflect on the consequences of your conduct? Children placed under your tuition at a time when their minds are free from care, and their memories at the highest pitch of perfection, and you by your unwarrantable licence deceive their parents, and instead of cultivating their geniuses, nip the embryo blossom and crush to nothing the prolific source of their future happiness.

The moral conduct of a tutor, as I observed before, should stand unimpeached; his behavior, particularly in the presence of his pupils, should be in exact conformity with the "rule of right:" he should warmly encourage virtuous actions, and use every effort to suppress vicious ones. No master ought to be addicted to drunkenness, lying, swearing, obscene language, &c. &c. for these vices cannot fail of acting in some measure on children whose minds are susceptible of every impression; for as the celebrated Dryden observes,

> Children like tender oziers take the bow,
> And as they first are fashion'd always grow;
> Hence what we learn in youth, to that alone,
> In age, we are by second nature prone.

It behoves every master of a school to become acquainted as early as possible, with the disposition of his pupils: soft words are sufficient in order to induce some boys to diligence, some will not do without threats, and others will never make any progress without now and then being brought to the birchen altar.

The passionate man is a very improper character to have the care of children; for when under the influence of passion, he will use such a degree of severity as oftentimes produces very serious effects. I have frequently experienced the bitterness of it myself when a boy. . . .

If masters would also use proper means to gain the affections of children, I am sure they might be successful and more happy in their situations; for I am convinced from experience that it is possible to win the children so far as they shall both respect and fear you: they are reasonable beings, and in general can be wrought upon best by argument. I do not like the idea of stripes, and would never recommend them but when the strictest necessity required it. . . .

I will now say a few words with respect to the manner of teaching.

That master who does not observe method in teaching, will find himself continually in confusion, and the business of the school not half done. Some masters will teach fifty scholars with more ease than others will twenty, and this difference arises merely from classing them. The master who classes his scholars in a proper manner, will not only find the business of the school performed with greater ease, but will also have the pleasure of seeing his pupils make a greater progress, for whether it be in reading, cyphering, or mathematics, observations can be made and instruction given unto half a dozen boys, with as much ease and success as to a single one. Besides it has a tendency to create a spirit of emulation among them.

I believe, if masters would ground their scholars well in spelling, they would find them make a greater proficiency; as soon as children can tell their letters, they are generally put to reading, and spelling is totally neglected. Hence we find so many persons who can read a chapter in the bible or paragraph in the newspaper, in a tolerable manner; but with respect to spelling, they are entirely ignorant. I do not approve of children spending so much time, as is commonly the case, in reading the old and new testaments; and indeed I do not know but it would be full as well if the bible was not introduced at all into schools, for if children can read the lessons which are to be found in spelling books tolerable well, I am sure it will answer little purpose to put either the old or new testament into their hands, for, (excepting some Greek or Hebrew words, which by the by, oftentimes puzzle the clergy to pronounce right) the language is so plain and easy, that little improvement is to be reaped. The truth of what I have asserted is evident to a demonstration; put a newspaper, magazine or any other book into the hands of a boy who can read a chapter in the bible tolerable well, and see what a figure he will make; you would be almost led to think that he had never applied himself to reading, or that he had been neglected. There are several books extant which boys might be put into as soon as they can read the lessons properly, which are in the spelling books, viz. such as Enfield's speaker, Scott's lessons, &c.

The scarcity of books in this Province is to be regretted by all lovers of learning. I am clearly of opinion that if any person would send into the States, or to England, for a collection not only of school books but of others, he would greatly benefit himself, and the Province also.

By what I have written, I hope no one will accuse me of depreciating the holy writ; it is far from my intentions; I revere it, and would exert myself as much as any one, in order to promote a more general knowledge of it; but at the same time, when put into the hands of a school boy at a time and in a manner which I have already mentioned, I look upon it as almost useless.

In teaching arithmetic the master should thoroughly explain and give a demonstration of every rule as the scholar enters it, shew what dependance it has upon former ones and never to let any of the scholars fret and stew over a question, a day, two or three days or perhaps a week, as I have known to be frequently the case.

In teaching mensuration either of superficial or solid bodies, the master may give ocular demonstration of several of the rules, by cutting out the figures of the former in paper, and the latter out of apples, turnips or potatoes; it will be found to be of infinite service to the scholars. In such like manner, the master ought to proceed throughout the mathematics, whenever opportunity served.

One thing I would wish to observe, before I dismiss this part of the subject, and that is, I am no advocate for giving children tasks at the time of vacation; if you give holidays, give them, and not set a scholar, perhaps as much more for a task, as he would have had to learn had he been at school; I do not like to see any thing given by halves; no master ought to be too profuse in giving holidays, but I would recommend to them that when they do give, to give chearfully, and let them be free from the incumbrance of school duty.

I could wish that the noise which is so customary in school hours, was entirely suppressed; I mean that which arises from the scholars getting their lessons; many masters I know give encouragement to this way of proceeding, but I am clearly of opinion that it impedes the business of the school, rather than any thing else, for those scholars who are studying over questions, or committing any thing to memory, and not being of quite so vociferous a cast as the others, must certainly be much incommoded by this noise; a noise which I can compare to nothing but the aggregate hum of a bee-hive. . . .

It undoubtedly is a duty incumbent on every master to teach his scholars the rules of politeness; he should be cautious and check them whenever he sees a deficiency, and at all opportunities be careful and set the example himself. But is it frequently the case that children seem to leave behind them at school what degree of politeness they have attained to, and take it upon their return, forgetting in the master's absence, to put into practice the precepts delivered by him. The parents are apt to raise a hue and cry that the master teaches his scholars no manners; they complain of his wearing his hat in the house, or omitting the little monosyllable, Sir, &c. But if we examine into the cause of this behaviour, I believe we shall find it not to rest with the master. . . .

To conclude, by the observations I have made respecting the qualifications of a tutor, I hope the reader will not accuse me of endeavoring to raise my own reputation at the expense of others. It is far from my intentions. I envy no man. But I must again say, that if masters were put under proper examination, before they were permitted to take upon them the care of a school, it would be attended with the happiest success.* This plan they strictly adhere to in the United States; no master is there permitted to open a school, without he appears, by a proper scrutiny of his abilities, to be a qualified person. If this plan was proposed here, it would, I think, meet with encouragement, and I for one would raise my voice and loudly exclaim

A M E N

---

*Does not experience justify the truth of this observation? There are three very recent occurrences, which cannot possibly be yet obliterated from the minds of the public.

The allusion is this—within the course of these two or three last months, three men, who acted in the capacity of schoolmaster in this Province, were obligated to flee into the States, on account of their bad conduct, viz. one for robbing a gentleman of some dollars, another for . . . and a third for embezzling a certain quantity of wheat, &c.

ON PUBLIC VERSUS PRIVATE EDUCATION

A Sketch of the System of Education and Course of Study pursued in the Montreal Academical Institution under the Direction of the Rev. H. Esson (Montreal, 1827), passim.

...The much agitated question, of the comparative merits of a Public and Private education, may be discussed in few words. If the object of Education were, to fit men, merely, for a life of contemplation and seclusion, a private education might have some claim to a preference. But, since it is the end of Education, to fit youth for business and action, to prepare them for the warfare of life, the competitions and collisions of the world—it is obvious, that a public school, exhibiting, as it does, in miniature, an image of the world, furnishes, precisely, that kind of discipline, which is the best preparation, for the duties and exigencies of life. As to the dangers to which a boy is exposed, in a public school, whether they be alleged to affect his person or his morals, it is conceived, that they have been greatly exaggerated, and admitting, that they are as great, as they have been represented, the sooner a young person is accustomed to meet the trials and hazards, which he must encounter in life, the sooner will he acquire that intrepidity and fortitude, which form his best security, personal and moral, in future years. In a public school, the character of a boy acquires, a firmness, a manliness, a hardihood—by competition and collision with his fellow-pupils, and by having his self-will checked and opposed by that of others. Thus he grows up, like a hardy plant exposed to the external air, and to all the varieties of the weather—whereas, the pupil of private education, like a hot-bed plant, neither in the constitution of his mind or body, is fitted to bear the asperities and adversities of life. Indeed, if a just view be taken of the circumstances of the case, it will appear, that the objections, urged against a public school, are without any substantial foundation— or, if they have any application, it is, only to the case of a youth, who, in attending a public Seminary, is left, without any private or domestic superintendence. When the pupils, as in the present instance, are, almost without exception, placed either under the protection and guardianship of parents and friends, or, as in the case of the boarders, under the immediate eye of the masters it is evident, that all the advantages of a private Education, are combined with those of a public.—And when those, who preside over the domestic education, enter heartily into the views, and co-operate steadily with the endeavours of the public teachers, the utmost that the power of Education can effect, on the minds and morals of youth, may be reasonably expected from their united exertions.

As connected with this subject, it may be proper to mention, that, in the government of this Seminary, measures of coercion and severity are employed, only, when the influence of milder methods is found ineffective. The principle of fear and terror, in its operation on the mind of youth, is, if not less powerful, at least far less salutary and generous, in its influence, than emulation, and motives of honour and shame. For this reason, it is the object, in the discipline of the Seminary, as much as possible, to treat the pupil, as a rational and moral being—to work upon his mind, by the influence of honour and shame, —of hope and generous ambition, and to govern him by the power of reason, —by conviction and persuasion. And with a view further to awaken and to strengthen moral feeling in the youthful mind it is the object, to encourage these to exercise a kind of moral censorship over one another, to cherish and cultivate a spirit of honour and generous pride, and hence, when any offence is committed, against good feeling, or good morals, an appeal is directly made, to their own sense and judgment—and a sort of public opinion is thus established and made to operate, in school, as in the world; a much more effectual means, of checking every thing, that is unworthy or immoral, than the utmost rigour of discipline, or the most unremitting vigilance and circumspection, on the part of the masters. . . .

TERMS

Board and Lodging per Annum, ...	£30—"—"
Washing and Mending, ...	4—"—"
Education per Annum, viz:	
English Reading, Spelling,	
Grammar and Writing, ...	6—"—"
Arithmetic and Book-keeping, ...	8—"—"
Greek, Latin and Mathematics,	
Geography Chronology and History, ...	10—"—"
French, ...	3—"—"
Drawing, ...	
Dancing	
Music, ...	
Fuel during winter months	"—7—6

Boarders are required to furnish their own beds, bedding and towels. School fees and Board wages, are paid at the end of each quarters.—The quarter days are 1 Nov., 1 Feb., 1 May, 1 August and the day scholars are required to bring their fees to school on these days.

ON THE MANAGEMENT OF GRAMMAR SCHOOLS

John Strachan, *A Letter to the Rev. A. N. Bethune, Rector of Cobourg, on the Management of Grammar Schools* (York, 1829), pp. 1 passim.

> York, Upper Canada,
> 6th October, 1829.

DEAR SIR,

You have frequently requested me to give you my thoughts on the management of Grammar Schools, and in doing so to have particular reference to those which are already established in the Province. As several other of my friends, who, as well as you, are Trustees of District Schools, have at different times made the same request, I have felt it my duty to take the matter into serious consideration, and in the hope that my practical experience may be of some use, I send you the following detail. . . .

GOVERNMENT OF THE SCHOOL

The management of every well regulated school, resolves itself into the two great departments of Government and Instruction.

The government was lodged in the Teacher and Censors.—The latter consisted of from twelve to sixteen of the oldest and most advanced boys. They were especially interested in the reputation of the School, and from their office perpetual conservators of the peace.

Out of the whole body, two Censors were appointed in rotation for each week, who had various and important duties to perform. It was their business to keep the daily and weekly Registers—to take charge of the property of the School—to mend the pens, and prepare the Writing-Books—to act as Monitors or Teachers, and to report absentees and delinquents.

The daily Register contained a minute detail of all the transactions of the day—the various lessons that were examined—the names of the boys at, and next the head, and of those at the foot of every class—the offences that were inquired into, and in fine every thing worth notice.

The weekly Register was an abstract from the daily. There was likewise a monthly Register, which was also called the Book of Merit, kept by the Master. Into it were transcribed the names of the boys oftenest at and next the head of their respective classes; the names of such as had distinguished themselves in any extraordinary manner—such as performed voluntary tasks, which, if well done, were inserted, and the names of those whose good behaviour reflected credit on the School.

The rewards consisted of a few prizes at the end of the year, and one great advantage of the Register consisted in furnishing infallible evidence of those who best deserved them. About a month before the vacation, a Committee of boys was chosen by the whole School to inspect the Registers and to report the names of those who had excelled in the different departments throughout the year. This list, when completed, was hung up in the School, and any boy had a right to appeal and to have another Committee and a new inspection if he thought himself aggrieved. This right was only exercised in two or three instances, and resulted in confirming the Report of the first Committee, for as the Register of the transactions of the preceding day was publicly read every morning and was open to all—inaccuracies, if any occurred, were immediately corrected, so that few or no errors entered into the Weekly Register far less reached the Book of Merit. The rewards, therefore, were not for excelling during a few days or a few months but through the whole year. A boy must have been the best Latin or Greek Scholar in his class—the best Arithmetician—the best Civil Historian—the best Geographer—the best behaved, &c. for the season before he could be entitled to a prize for excelling in any of these respects, and all this must be proved by records regularly kept during the whole period. This plan not only kept up a great degree of harmless emulation, but effectually prevented any heart-burning or suspicion as to the justice of the reward, and altogether relieved the Master from the personal responsibility.

The punishments in a day-school cannot be so completely modified as where all the pupils are under the immediate superintendence of the Master, and at a distance from their Parents.

In the latter case, corporal punishments may with good management be entirely dispensed with; but this can scarcely be effected when the scholars are much at home, and neglected or indulged by their Parents. It is, nevertheless, certain, that by making a boy's rank depend on his behaviour and acquirements and keeping up a constant exertion and watchfulness it may be nearly accomplished. The punishments most in use were to commit lines to memory —double tasks—confinement, (but not in the dark) when it could be enforced.—For great perverseness—habitual negligence of school business or immoral acts—swearing, lying or pilfering, corporal punishment was sometimes inflicted.—This being the most painful duty of the Teacher, and it having been long his opinion that under favourable circumstances such punishments might be laid aside, every precaution was taken to avoid them or lessen their number. The most effectual remedy was found in the institution of regular trials.

When a boy was accused of any offence not apparent to the Master, a minute investigation took place in the face of the whole School—A Jury was sometimes formed, and no punishment followed till after the clearest conviction.—To punish arbitrarily is not only frequently unjust on the part of the Master, but is attended with the most pernicious effects on the pupil.

Sometimes security for good behaviour was exacted, and if a boy happened to be very much addicted to the fault of which he had been convicted, he found great difficulty in procuring sureties, because his subsequent default would bring upon them a punishment of tasks, lines, &c., and frequently none of his school-fellows would risk themselves in his favour.—This commonly produced a most salutary effect. Boys were seen going round the School begging their School-fellows to become security for their good behaviour, and when refused, pleading for this once and promising never again to be guilty.— Such a process could not fail of being useful, and had far more influence than any thing the master could say, as they heard from their fellows in the plainest language the opinion entertained of them by the whole School.

In extraordinary cases, but of rare occurrence, and when the fault was aggravated, the guilty boy was put in coventry for a few days—never longer than a week.—During this time, no boy was to speak to, or play with him, or have any communication with him during the play hours. This punishment never failed of having the desired effect.

By having recourse in this manner to the boys themselves in the regulation and government of the School, the Master was relieved from much painful responsibility—the patient investigation of facts interested all the boys and brought them to the same conclusion—the culprit was satisfied by the fairness of his trial, of the justice of his sentence, and the pain which he experienced during the inquiry was very often considered a sufficient punishment. . . .

Notwithstanding the variety of the branches taught, the Master's labour, exclusive of unremitting attention, was not so great as may at first be supposed, and he seldom had occasion for more than one assistant.—In all well regulated Schools there very soon arises a sort of traditionary knowledge, which is continually accumulating. Besides when a new class is formed there are commonly some boys remaining who were in the former and who join again, either because they have not acquired so perfect a knowledge of the subject as was desirable, or because they were so young when first introduced, that a repetition is considered advantageous. In either case they become very useful auxiliaries to the Teacher, by explaining to their companions the general method of proceeding, and many little matters which the Master might overlook, or find tedious and irksome to dwell upon with the necessary minuteness.

It is farther to be observed, that in such Schools, the younger boys by witnessing daily the higher classes proceeding in their studies, acquire imperceptibly a number of preliminary ideas and conceptions, which greatly facilitate their future progress when they come to the same branches of knowledge.

It is in this that the advantage of a public over a private education is most easily and strikingly illustrated. A boy in a large School becomes familiar with numbers—with angles—triangles—squares—circles—rectangles, &c. long before he is admitted into the classes where they become an object of study: while a boy of equal capacity, taught privately, having neither seen nor heard any thing about them till he is called upon to study them, has many preliminary difficulties to overcome, which in the case of the other have been already removed. In the one case the Teacher is relieved from much tedious detail, and in the other the boy may take a dislike at a science on the outset, which under more favorable circumstances he would have liked and excelled in. . . .

GENERAL REMARKS

An advantage of no small importance was found to result from the variety of the things taught in the School, namely, that there was hardly any boy that did not appear with credit in some one class. At an early period of the School a boy was sent whose parents were poor but whose uncle had sufficient interest to place him at Woolwich if he could be prepared before sixteen to stand the necessary examination. He had been with different teachers, and was pronounced too stupid to learn any thing and was already fourteen.—On examination, he was found exceedingly deficient—he could neither read nor write with any propriety—yet as his all depended upon his progress, and as he had hardly two years to prepare himself the master was exceedingly anxious to do something for him. After several attempts he began under the system adopted to comprehend Arithmetic, and although it had been declared that he never could be made to understand Addition, he very soon grasped the whole Science.—He was tried with Euclid, and succeeded.—The Elements of Algebra were attempted, and with profit, and though naturally sluggish, it was found that he had some turn for Mathematics. Encouraged by the progress which he made in these branches, he began to grow ashamed of his writing and English reading, in which he had hitherto made no improvement, and soon made fair progress in both; and although he was still very slow in acquiring a knowledge of Latin, he attained a considerable accuracy in the Grammar before he left School and could read a little in Caesar. The consequence was, that he passed the Mathematical part of his introductory examination at Woolwich with great commendation; and the Latin part, which is I believe easy, without censure, and in a period unusually short received a Commission in the Artillery.

Another boy had been at School upwards of two years and given indication of no disposition to learn. His progress was hardly perceptible—younger boys were daily leaving him behind—he was tried in various classes without success, and the Master almost despaired. Though by no means qualified for the Civil History class, he was placed in it as a last resort—he got interested—he brought his questions better written than ever he had done any thing else—he gained two or three places—he was roused as from a lethargy and soon reached half way up the class. The Master relieved from the pain which his former backwardness had given him, spoke to him privately, encouraging him to try in his other classes—he next began to excel in Arithmetic—then in Geography, and at length he left the foot of his Latin classes, where he had remained almost immoveable for years, and although never a first rate Scholar, he left School with considerable attainments. . . .

It will be seen that in the system pursued the boys in a great degree taught themselves, the teacher acting in many instances merely as a director. This circumstance has induced a minuteness of detail which may appear trifling to those who are not in the habit of appreciating the magnitude of the interest confided by Parents to Teachers, as well as to such (and the number is very great) who consider themselves adepts in the science of education, and who commonly declare that their only reason for sending their children to School is the want of time to instruct them at home. But we who are still wedded to the opinion that it is one thing to be able to learn and another to be able to teach, think that much yet remains to be done to facilitate the communication of knowledge; and if it appear that something in this way has been accomplished in the foregoing detail, it will not be deemed of small importance by those who believe that it is very possible to possess vast stores of knowledge without being able to impart them even to the willing and anxious pupil; and that to fix the volatile, stimulate the sluggish, and overcome the obstinate, demands an acquaintance with the human mind not quite innate, nor likely to be gained without some experience. . . .

Silence was strictly enforced, for no fixed medium can ever be found between that degree of silence which may be sufficient for all useful purposes and noise and disorder. No boy was therefore allowed to speak except on the business of the class, nor to move from his seat except at the pleasure of the Teacher.

In hearing the classes care was taken to make the business as interesting as possible.—For this purpose the lessons were always short and minutely examined, and never passed till thoroughly understood. During the preparation of the lesson, or before it was called up, the boys were encouraged to ask explanations of difficult passages, and to put questions about matters which they did not fully comprehend, all of which were listened to with patience and answered with candour, even when they were not very pertinent.—From the regular routine of lessons it is evident that much depends upon punctual attendance. So much inconvenience was felt even from the interference of the usual Holidays that they were given up except now and then that an afternoon was granted for a good copy of verses. But if a single play day was felt injurious how much more the irregular attendance of individuals. Besides the loss of time to the absentees themselves, the greatest inconvenience is incurred by the classes to which they belong. Their progress is impeded; the equality between them and their fellows is rendered less complete, and much trouble becomes frequently necessary to investigate the cause of absence. Indeed the boy's taste for learning may be deeply injured in a very little time when they find on their return that they have lost ground; and in a large School where every one is advancing a very short absence may leave them irrecoverably behind.—So deeply convinced am I of the great importance of boys attending with punctuality and good will, that notice has frequently been given to those Parents who were apt to indulge their children in holidays, that the Master would not be responsible for their progress and would much prefer the withdrawing them from the School than any longer permit irregular attendance. Indeed such parents have much to answer for, as we have known instances where this injudicious indulgence has altered the character of their children and their usefulness and happiness for life. . . .

They who take the trouble to glance over their years at school, will call to mind the difficulty which they found in discovering the practical use of many things which they were obliged to learn. The business of the School seemed to be totally different from any thing out of doors, and to have no connection with the business of common life. To remove this as early as possible was one of the advantages aimed at in this system. Mental Arithmetic was applied to objects around us and in our hands. Geography to the local knowledge of the learners; figures were made of the School premises and the play ground; these were so extended as to take in the town, the roads leading to it, the Lake, &c. Geometry commenced by familiarizing them to the figures formed by the walls, flooring and ceiling of the rooms, or furniture, and the comparing them with diagrams, and the definitions. This method is capable of being carried a great length, and of rendering the use of almost every branch sufficiently plain to be comprehended by very young boys: for all the sciences have been discovered by practical men, and were first studied for their immediate use in the business of life; thus Botany, for the medical value of plants; Astronomy, for the use of Husbandry, Navigation, &c. . . .

The arrangements detailed do not seem to provide for what is called a mere English or Commercial education, but experience hath taught us, that with boys of ordinary capacities, all the branches pointed out for the different periods may be carried on together, and that by lessening their number we expose the pupil to idleness, without obtaining any countervailing advantage. Boys advance faster in any one study by having several occupations than by confining their attention to that alone, and I feel convinced that a boy by the time he is sixteen may acquire as much classical knowledge, together with all the branches recommended, as if he had been entirely confined to Greek and Latin, and vice versa. And I know from facts, that the boys who remained the usual time at School, and took the full benefit of every thing taught, instead of being inferior to those declining to study the classics and who confined themselves to what is called a business education, were far superior in their knowledge of Arithmetic and keeping accounts, &c.

CONCLUSION

We had only one annual exhibition when the friends of the pupils were invited. The first day was employed in examining the boys in their Classical and Scientific acquirements. The Latin and Greek Classics were examined by the Master, in exactly the same manner as they daily were in School, after which the visitors were requested to ask them any questions that they thought proper. After this the Mathematical classes presented themselves. One was prepared to demonstrate any proposition within certain books of Euclid's Elements; or to solve equations in Algebra, within a certain scope. Another performed trigonometrical operations; and the younger boys were exercised in mental and mixed Arithmetic, the spectators being invited to propose questions.

The second day was taken up with debates, a variety of recitations, and exhibiting the mode of examining the classes in Civil and Natural History, Geography, &c. It was also usual on this day to recite one of Milman's, or Miss Moore's Sacred Dramas, in which the boys acquitted themselves, on most occasions, with great success, and much to the delight of the audience. But the most interesting business of the day was the opening of the Book of Merit, and the distribution of the prizes. This was done by the committee which had been appointed by the boys themselves to inspect the Registers and make out a list of the successful competitors. The names were read one by one by a member of the committee, on which they came severally forward and received the prizes, the Master mentioning that it was for their excelling in such a class; for extraordinary tasks, or for good behaviour. What was peculiarly delightful, their success, so far from producing envy, was accompanied with universal satisfaction. Their fellows looked upon them as an honour to the School, and secretly cherished the hope of being next year among the happy number. . . .

I remain,
Dear Sir,
Your most Obedient Serv't.
JOHN STRACHAN.

ADVERTISING NEW SCHOOLS

J. G. Hodgins, ed., *Documentary History of Education in Upper Canada* (Toronto, 1894-1910), vol. I, pp. 131-2.

MR. AND MRS. WOOLF'S BOARDING AND DAY SCHOOL.

Mr. and Mrs. Woolf beg to inform the public that, on the 12th instant, they purpose to commence a boarding and day school, (in the house recently occupied by Dr. Macaulay,) for the instruction of young ladies in the different branches of female education.

Cards of terms, and every other requisite information may be had on application.

Kingston, 3rd of May, 1817.

MRS. HILL'S KINGSTON SCHOOL FOR YOUNG LADIES, 1818.

Mrs. Hill, most respectfully, informs the inhabitants of Kingston and its vicinity that she has taken the house, lately occupied by Messrs. Johns and Finkle, where she intends commencing a boarding and day school for young ladies, on Tuesday, the 22nd of October, and hopes, from the attention which she will pay to the improvement, morals and comfort of her pupils, to merit the approbation of the parents, who will entrust their children to her care.

She will teach reading, writing, arithmetic, grammar and geography, with plain and fancy needle-work. Embroidery will also be at the option of the parents.

The following are the terms, viz.:—

Small children, Reading only	15 s.	per quarter.
Reading, Writing and plain Needle-work	20	do
Grammar, Arithmetic, Geography		
and fancy Needlework	30	do
Embroidery, extra	15	do

Mrs. H. will take boarders at the most moderate rate.
Kingston, October 3rd, 1818.

MR. HARRIS' PRIVATE SCHOOL FOR YOUNG LADIES, ETC., 1818.

Mr. Thomas Harris, late teacher in one of the most respectable schools in Quebec, intends opening a school on the 14th of September, at the residence of Mr. R. Johnston, teacher of the Lancasterian school, in which the following branches will be taught, viz.:—Reading, writing, arithmetic, English grammar and geography.

The young ladies will be superintended in the different branches of needle-work by Mrs. Johnston in a separate apartment.

A few young gentlemen may be accommodated as boarders on reasonable terms.

Kingston, September, 1818.

ERNESTOWN (BATH) ACADEMY, REOPENED, 1818.

The Trustees of the Ernestown (Bath) Academy hereby give notice that they have appointed the Reverend Alexander Fletcher, Preceptor of that academical Institution, which will be opened in a few days, after having been closed for some time.

The Rev. Alexander Fletcher and Mr. McIntosh have commenced teaching in Ernestown Academy, viz., the English language grammatically, writing, arithmetic, book-keeping, geography with the use of globes, mathematics, recitation, composition and history with the Latin and Greek languages.

Mr. Fletcher attended a complete course of classical studies at the Colleges of Glasgow and Edinburgh; Mr. McIntosh received a liberal education at King's College, Aberdeen; and from their combined experience in, and adoption of, the most successful and approved modes of tuition, they hope to merit the approbation of their employers.

Boarders can be accommodated in respectable private families on the most reasonable terms.

Ernestown, October 6th, 1818.

RULES AND REGULATIONS FOR A NEW SCHOOL

Rules and Regulations for the Montreal Union School (Montreal, 1820), pp. iii-vii and 8-16.

PREFACE

The difficulty of procuring a respectable Education for their Children, on such terms as they could afford, is an inconvenience to which a large portion of our most deserving Citizens in this Country have been long subjected, and have often expressed an anxious desire to see remedied, by some plan calculated for the purpose. It has however happened in this case, as in many others, where the change must be the work of the public; although the injurious consequences of the present state of Education, have been privately felt and publicly reprobated, until the present day, no decisive steps have been taken to remove the obstacles complained of, or to facilitate the attainment of knowledge for the juvenile members of our society. . . .

Viewing with regret the tardy progress of Tuition in the Canadas, and anxious to place it within the reach of all who wish to participate in its benefits, by a removal of those obstacles which have hitherto militated against its advancement; and being desirous that some plan of education should be adopted, wherein the parents and natural guardians of the children should have a voice in the arrangement of their education, a few Gentlemen in this city have agreed to form a Seminary for the Education of Youth in this place, to be designated by the name of The Montreal Union School. This Institution is to be devoted to the instruction of Youth in those branches of Education usually taught in Grammar Schools in Great Britain; and also in such other branches as may be deemed conducive to the benefit of society at large, and adapted to the views of the different Pupils who may attend it. The whole will be placed on such a footing with regard to expense, as to render the advantages it holds forth accessible to all who wish to share in them; and the School will be conducted agreeable to such rules as are deemed best calculated to ensure its success, and meet with the approbation of the Public.

Montreal, 10th March, 1820.

RULES
AND
REGULATIONS
FOR THE
MONTREAL UNION SCHOOL

1st. Every Person sending one or more Pupils to the Montreal Union School, or giving an annual donation of not less than Ten Pounds, shall, for the time being, be considered as a Subscriber to the Institution . . .

3d. At the General Annual Meeting, there shall be chosen by a majority of votes of the Subscribers to the Institution, a Committee of Seven Members, who shall appoint a Secretary and Treasurer to the School, of which Seven Members, Five shall be a quorum, for transacting business. Those members so elected, shall be denominated the Managing Committee, and shall have the sole direction and charge of the affairs of the Institution. . . .

10th. The Managing Committee shall appoint fit Teachers, and fill up vacancies among them according to the following rule, viz. when a Teacher or Teachers shall be wanted, an advertisement shall be inserted in at least two of the public papers of this City, at least three weeks before, specifying the department for which such Teacher or Teachers are wanted. . . .

12th. The Members of the Managing Committee shall take in rotation the duty of visiting the School, one Member being appointed every month for that purpose, who shall call and see the method of proceeding by the Masters, as often as he can conveniently do so, and report the proceedings to the Secretary for the inspection of the Committee. . . .

15th. There shall be in all cases an appeal from the decision of the Managing Committee to the General Meeting, and the Committee and all those connected with the School, shall be amenable to the general meetings for their conduct in all respects, unless where the contrary is provided for by the rules.

16th. Whenever any Teacher is guilty of any impropriety of conduct, either in the omission or discharge of his duty, it shall be in the power of the Managing Committee to suspend, reprimand or discharge any Teacher so acting, it being understood that their proceedings in this respect shall not infringe the privilege given in rule 15th. . . .

37th. The following branches of Education shall be taught at the Montreal Union School:

English & English Grammar,
Writing and Arithmetic,
Book-Keeping,
Geography,
Mathematics,
Drawing & Surveying,
Navigation,
French,
Latin,
Greek.

38th. As soon as twenty female pupils shall be obtained for the Institution, and who together, with the above mentioned branches of Education, are desirous of learning those taught by females, an Instructress shall be procured for their tuition in these branches, it being understood that she is not to teach any branch of Education provided for by the foregoing rules. . . .

IMPROVING THE POOR THROUGH EDUCATION

Reports of the Society for Improving the Condition of the Poor of St. John's (Liverpool, 1809-11), pp. 4-7.

From the 31st July, 1808, to the 31st July, 1809.

The Committee have peculiar pleasure in laying before the numerous friends of the Society, the present report, as it evinces the improvement and utility of the Institution in a very striking manner.

The Society, at the last anniversary, appeared to be in an improving way, and its friends so sensible of it, their subscriptions were unusually liberal, in order to liquidate the claims on the Society, and place its funds in advance, but such has been the inclemency of the past winter, the extreme scarcity of the principal necessaries of life, and the unhealthy state of the community, their benevolent intention has, in some degree, been rendered ineffectual, by the increased and prolonged calls upon it. The Committee had, however, the satisfaction to find exertion increase with the pressure of the season, and have to express its thanks to the Ministers of the respective establishments, who, with the utmost readiness, exerted their abilities in behalf of the suffering poor.

The present state of the account, the Committee trusts will be considered favorable, bearing in mind the astonishing price of bread and flour, during the winter (which more than doubled the expenditure of those articles) and the expence of a passage for Mr. Marshall, a Schoolmaster, to succeed Mr. Brake, who declined continuing longer than October next: With the salaries as usual, calculated up to the 20th of October next, the Society appears to be £82. 7s. 4d. in debt, from which may be deducted stock on hand for sale £27. 4s. 1d. and provisions left, value £7. 17s.

Owing to the severity of the weather at some periods, and the sickly state of the children at others, the Girls' School had very few attendants during the months of December, January, and February, since then it has been visited regularly by a Committee of Ladies, through whose attention and exertion the school has been more fully attended than at any former period, the number being from 70 to 90 each day,—they are mostly under 12 years of age. Since the last Anniversary, 74 have been admitted, one has been apprenticed, and several gone out to service. A great deal of plain work has been done, and a price affixed by a Committee of Ladies.—

36 lbs. of Wool have been dressed,

19 lbs. of Yarn spun,

30 pair of Hose,

84 pair of Socks,

68 pair of Cuffs,

and a variety of other articles have been knit.

The sum of £9. 14s. 5d. has been received in the Girls' school for articles sold and work done, and sundry articles remain for sale, valued at £3. 4s. 1d. the sum of £8. 6s. 3d. has been paid for labour, Skins, Cards, Wool, Soap, and other articles, which leave a balance in favor of the Institution of £4. 12s. 2d. The whole number of Girls admitted to the School, has been 378.

The Boys' School has been very fully attended, and their improvement regular, many of them are adepts in making and mending nets. The sum of £10. 1s. has been received for work done and articles sold.—Nets and Twine valued at £24. remain on hand; there has been £19. 19s. paid for labour, twine, quills, and other articles, which leaves a balance in favor of the society of £14. 2s. 4d. 44 Boys have been admitted since the last anniversary; 24 have gone out to the fishery, most of them could make and mend nets.—One has gone to England, 3 apprenticed to Coopers, 2 to Carpenters, 1 to a Shoe-maker, and 5 to the Fishery. The whole number of Boys admitted to the School is 247, and from 80 to 100 attend daily.

Annastacia Brown, one of the orphans brought up by the Society, is apprenticed to William Percy, of Brigus.

Lambert, the child reported last year as deserted, has been taken under the care of his Grandfather.

Edward Monahan and Joan Brown, two orphans, continue to be provided for by this Society.

Ninety-four persons have been relieved, and one fourth the passages provided for twelve others, sent to their native country in a disabled and feeble state. Three persons under relief of the Society have died, and three have been apprenticed under its regulations.

	£	s.	d.
The expence of the Boys' school this year, deducting the profits from labour and amount of coals	101	6	7
Of the Girls' school	69	18	11
Of the Institution in general	16	4	0
Relief issued to the poor	266	1	11

To relieve the objects at present on the list, and maintain the orphans up to the 20th of October, will require about £40. It will be necessary for some Spelling Books, and other articles to be provided.

From 31st July, 1810, to the 31st July, 1811.

The Committee are happy to have it in their power to congratulate the friends of the Society on the very favourable Report they are able to communicate.

The state of the poor has been greatly ameliorated, the number of applications have been considerably reduced, and such have been the improvements in the method of administering the most prompt relief, that it has been impossible for any real object of distress to be destitute of the benefits of the Institution, or to make any application in vain. . . .

The Ladies who have visited the Girls' School continue to make favourable reports to the Committee of that Branch of the Institution, both as they respect the improvement of the children, and the attention paid by the matron and her assistant to their duties; they however, regret very much that the parents and relations of children do not oblige them to attend the School more regularly; they have also to lament that some of them have little or no attention paid at home to their cleanliness. A considerable quantity of plain work has been performed much to the satisfaction of the employers; there has also been the usual attention paid to the carding, spinning, and knitting. Several girls have gone out to service, the daily number which attend is about fifty; there have been fifty-six admitted since the last anniversary, and the whole number admitted since the commencement of the Institution is four-hundred and sixty-one.

Mr. Marshall has continued to improve the Boys' School under his management; the Committee therefore have considered his particular attention to be deserving of every encouragement, and in consequence of the increased number of Boys, which required a greater portion of his time, added to the high price of provisions, have thought proper to add £20 per annum to his salary; and they beg leave to recommend to the friends of the Institution their remembrance of Mr. Marshall's good conduct, and to entreat their general and individual endeavours to make his situation as eligible and comfortable as possible. The Committee are happy to say, that making and mending of Nets has been revived in the School to general satisfaction, both for improvement in so useful a branch, and of profit to the Institution. Fifty-eight Boys have been admitted since last year. Several have been apprenticed by their friends, but none have been placed out under the patronage of the Society. There are about seventy Boys attend [sic] daily, and three-hundred and forty-one have been admitted since the commencement of the Institution.

Edward Monahan has been provided for by Mr. Lionel Chancey.

Joan Brown, an orphan, continued under the care of the Society.

Margaret Dulhanty, and Richard Mulcahy, the Society also continue to provide for.

Two persons, relieved by the Society have died, and part of the passages have been paid for six persons to their native country.

	£	s.	d.
The Expence of the Boys' School this year, exclusive of Coals has been	61	3	3
Ditto of the Girls' School	66	16	8
Ditto of the Institution in general	24	10	4
Relief issued to the Poor	183	15	0

The Society last Year was £95 12 6. in debt, at present, the debts are all discharged, and £47 1 8. remains in the hands of the Treasurer.

Proceedings of the Society for Educating the Poor of Newfoundland, Third year, 1825-6 (London, 1826), pp. 5-7.

Your Committee have much satisfaction in presenting the Report of their Proceedings during the last twelve months; a period in which they have been favoured by a gracious Providence with such a measure of success, as fully justifies the hope, that the NEWFOUNDLAND SCHOOL SOCIETY may be permitted to accomplish in due time the important Objects for which it has been instituted.

In the summer of last year, three additional Masters with their wives, and George Browning, an Apprenticed Monitor, having duly qualified themselves at the central National School in Baldwin's Gardens, sailed for Newfoundland, where they arrived in safety, in the month of August, and immediately proceeded to their respective destinations, viz. Mr. and Mrs. Kingwell to Harbour Grace, Mr. and Mrs. Teulon to Carbonnierre, Mr. and Mrs. Martin to Petty Harbour, and George Browning, to Quidi Vidi. . . .

"The little dears evince so strong an attachment to the School, that after they leave it in the evening, many of them will meet again after supper in a certain place, generally the porch of some door, and repeat together what they have been engaged in during the day; one will be chosen as a teacher for the purpose of rectifying mistakes, they will then go on with their respective lessons, not leaving off till the whole are finished. . . .

"It is with peculiar satisfaction and gratitude to Almighty God, the Author of all good, that I am enabled to say, that our schools continue to increase. Our number now, in the Sunday School, is 130, viz. 62 Boys, and 68 Girls, who take great delight in the School; and in the Day School 118: viz. 49 Boys, and 69 Girls, including those admitted this morning. It was truly gratifying to witness the pleasure manifested by the children in their returning to school after their fortnight's vacation; but to see their untutored habits giving way to a more steady and regular deportment, is much more so. One instance, especially, of this nature, I think worth communicating to you.—Swearing is a very common sin here among children. One of our boys, aged 12 years, was much addicted to it, of which, of course, we endeavoured to break him. We had talked to him at various times, prayed with, and for him; yet he would not give it up, and appeared to consider it a matter of indifference. One day he so far forgot himself, as to blaspheme in a most shocking manner before me. This I considered demanded some decisive measure; and after a suitable reproof, according to our judgment, we came to the painful resolution of forbidding his attendance at School until he had left off the habit, lest his example should prove prejudicial to the other children. He was accordingly dismissed: but about five weeks after, on a Sunday evening, as we were about to go into the School, he came up to us weeping, and very frankly confessed he had been a very wicked boy; and begged to be permitted to come with us again. After having had some close conversation with him, during which he told us he had prayed to God to forgive him, we consented, exhorting him to pray to God to change his heart. Since his return, he has given us no cause to regret taking him back."

By a subsequent letter Mr. Kingwell writes as follows:—

To the following passage in the same Letter, the attention of the Meeting is particularly requested.

"You must have seen by my last, how likely it was, that we should be straitened for room: though we now have 118 children, not above 100 can be accommodated at one time, the boys and girls being necessarily classed together, which is not at all as it should be. If the Committee think proper to build here next spring, much help may be expected from those interested, according to their ability. Already are given as many beams, and as much clap-board as will make the frame, and close in a building of 42 feet by 20 feet; in addition to which, some who cannot go to the woods, have bound themselves for, some three, some five and others six days work, to hew the beams, and fit them for the carpenters' use. Our Subscription list is not yet much; we may hope to receive this season about £10, but have as much as £20 subscribed for next year:—with the assistance the inhabitants would render, the Committee might build a Dwelling-House, and two commodious School-Rooms for about £250.—We hope, and pray, that the Lord may so bless the pecuniary department of the Society, that the work may not be hindered."

A MONITORIAL SCHOOL

Joseph-François Perrault, ed., *Cours d'éducation élémentaire à l'usage de l'Ecole gratuite, établie dans la Cité de Québec en 1821* (Quebec, 1822), pp. 1 passim. Translated by Janna Best.

INTRODUCTION

For several years the lack of education in this country has been a subject of continual controversy and criticism and has often given the opportunity for disagreeable reflections, as much against the Clergy, who are gratuitously accused of being against all education, as against the Government for seizing the possessions of the Jesuits in this country; unlike European powers, after the dissolution of this Society (of Jesus), they did not keep on those who were particularly gifted in improving education.

Whatever the case may be, several educated citizens of the City of Quebec were very much aware of the total lack of education in the poorest class and felt that this was one of the causes of insubordination and disturbances which seem to have increased for quite some time. They thus called a meeting of the citizens of Quebec to consider what means could be used for providing the advantages of a Christian education to the poor Catholic children of the City, who in effect are the only ones who lack instruction. This would be until such a time as the Legislature should pass a bill on this subject.

Many people, both Clergy and Laymen, attended the meeting and unanimously passed several resolutions. These were to try and provide for the children of this class a knowledge of the true God, to fill their young hearts with the need of all men to love him and serve Him, and to give them an elementary education, that is to say: to teach them to read, write and do arithmetic.

A committee of 21 members was chosen to study this worthwhile work and a subscription was started to cover expenses.

ELEMENTARY EDUCATION COURSE

A little later this committee made a Report on the rules which they considered necessary for the government of schools and the instruction that would be given there. It is a summary of these rules and the teaching methods, modelled on those of Lancaster, Bell and others, which form the subject of this little work. It was thought important to have it printed in the hope of giving some uniformity to the elementary education courses and thus to help students when they are admitted to the seminaries to pursue higher studies.

The success of the Free School in Quebec and the progress that the children have made there are the best recommendations one can make to the public for adopting the teaching methods which are fully outlined in this little volume.

It has this special advantage that one man of ordinary education, with a little intelligence and application and using the adopted method, can run, on his own, a school of several hundred pupils with less difficulty than with fifty pupils under the old method. Besides, the progress of the pupils is much more rapid, as experience has already shown here, and the expenses are considerably less.

In addition, this work was undertaken under the scrutiny of devout Churchmen and learned lay people and has earned their approval.

All these advantages lead one to believe that it will be favourably received by the public and generally adopted in the elementary schools of this province.

RULES FOR THE ESTABLISHMENT OF SCHOOLS
Passed by the General Committee, 30 August, 1821
Aim of the Establishment
1) The children, who are admitted to schools established by the Society, must be persuaded that the main reason for their having been accepted is to learn to know God, to love Him and serve Him, and thus to become respectable men and useful citizens. In order that they do not lose sight of these two aims, and to make sure they are familiar with rules concerning them, the Master will read them out once a month.
Duties of the Pupils
2) They will respect the Master and obey him when he asks them anything concerned with their instruction and education. They will accept quietly the reprimands or punishments which he thinks suitable for them; the same will be true of them with the Assistant Masters and the Monitors.
3) They will avoid calling each other names, hurling insults or quarrelling; they must love each other and mutually help each other to do their duty.
4) Near to the School they will never make any noise or play a game that might inconvenience passersby or the neighbours; they will go quietly into class and come out again in like manner.
5) Throughout school hours they will be silent and will be most attentive to all that is said or taught them, not talking except when it is absolutely necessary.
6) They will not leave their seat without obtaining permission.
7) If they arrive late for class, they will explain to the Master the reasons which have prevented them from coming earlier.
8) Several at one time can never be permitted to go out of the class to satisfy their natural needs.
9) They will behave decently and nicely during class and at the end they will wash their hands and faces, also their feet if they are bare.
10) They will bring in the firewood to the classroom when the Master asks them to.
11) After each class, the Master will name one or two pupils to straighten the benches and tables, to sweep out the school rooms, to wipe and dust and to make everything very neat and clean.
Classes
20) 1. The children who are learning their A, B, C, will be on the benches nearest the Master.
   2. Those who are beginning to spell words of one syllable, next.
   3. After them, those who are spelling words of two syllables.

4. Then those who are spelling words of three syllables and more.

5. Next those who are reading whole words, sentences and lessons.

6. Finally those who are learning the rules of arithmetic.

Publications

21) In order to avoid the expense of buying A, B, C,s and other books, there will be several boards with the alphabet printed in big letters; on others, words of one syllable; then some with two syllables and others of three, four, five and six syllables; some boards will have whole words; others phrases and sentences, and others whole lessons, figures, arithmetic tables and rules.

22) These boards will be put up in full view of the pupils of each respective class to be read, re-read and written by each class without moving them around. . . .

Writing

24) In order to dispense with the purchase of paper, ink and pens for the pupils, shelves will be made in front of the first benches, with a rim to keep in white sand and the base painted black. The beginners will write, with their fingers or with wooden pointers, the letters, words and figures which will be shown them. Slates will be provided for those who are more advanced.

Monitors—Teaching Methods—Moving Up and Down in the Class

25) The Master will name and place at the head of the class a *Monitor*, whose duty will be to see to the good behaviour of those on his bench, to point out the letters on the board to be named by each of them, and the syllable to spell, the word to read the sum to do, etc. . . .

Distinctions

26) The Monitors will have marks of distinction such as Monitor First Class, Second Class, Third Class, Fourth Class, etc.

27) The first in each Class will also have a mark of distinction, such as the First of the First Class Monitors, Second Class, Third and Fourth, etc.

Admission

28) A pupil may only be admitted on the order of the Committee for the Supervision of Schools, by means of a written recommendation from a Member of the General Committee, which will give the first name and surname of the child, his age and the area where he lives. This permission the Master will keep with him so that he can produce it if necessary.

Age for Admission

29) No pupils will be accepted under the age of seven or over the age of fourteen, except in certain special cases for which the Supervision Committee will be the sole judge.

Punishment

33) The Masters appointed by the Society will not be able to expel any pupil, nor inflict any punishment other than those laid down by the Supervision Committee.

THE BASIS OF MUTUAL TEACHING

The adoption of the method of mutual teaching by the most civilised peoples in Europe is a certain proof of its superiority over the ancient methods of teaching; not only is this method preferred at the present time in the elementary schools, but they are still trying to introduce it in the colleges and academies for teaching more advanced studies.

Its superiority is not therefore a problem; but one mustn't be so blind as to think that as soon as this method is used there will be instant success. It has, like every system, its principles; and if these are not well understood, or if they are not properly utilised, only a moderate benefit can be drawn from them.

The main point in the method of mutual teaching is to keep the pupils constantly alert, to never let them be idle, without however keeping them at long and difficult lessons. For that it is necessary to put before their eyes something that continually focuses their attention. . . .

He who is placed at the head of such a school must be well versed in the knowledge and execution of these different exercises, giving to them all the variety and activity that they can afford according to available time and opportunity. But since it is not possible for one man alone to utilise these different incentives, he must make use of the help of the best educated and most intelligent young people in the school.

It is from this that the term *mutual teaching* comes, which is given to this method of instruction. The success of the school and the progress of the pupils depends therefore on the choice that the Master makes. He will have to be most careful in the selection from amongst these young people of some to make Monitors and others to make Assistant Monitors.

The Master must insist that they arrive the first in the classroom to put up the letters, words or lessons which each class must read from the large boards; they must also be the last to leave so that they can put back all the letters, words or lessons in their place, also all the other boards and the slates; then they must make their reports to the Master on absences, behaviour and the progress of the pupils in their respective classes, so that he himself can make the general report which must be ready to present to the members of the Society when required, so that the latter can decide on rewards or punishments for the pupils with a full knowledge of the background of each case.

The Master must never forget to make each class go over what has been shown them in the course of the week. this should be every Saturday morning. Then he should question the pupils on grammar, according to the standard of each class, and to make them learn the answers by heart.

He should begin with the class of children who are learning the alphabet. While they are doing their exercises out loud, the other classes must be kept busy doing theirwork in silence, either writing or doing sums until their turn comes to do their exercises out loud.

With these fundamentals established and carefully carried out, we must go on to the following exercises and commands:-

Words of Command
On entering the classroom, the pupils, wearing their hats, must take their

places where they were the last time they were there. When they have done that the Master says in a loud voice ATTENTION! at which the pupils all together at the same time let their arms fall to their sides. Then the Master says HATS OFF! Immediately the pupils must put up their hands to their hats or bonnets and let the hats fall back on their shoulders where they will remain throughout the school day, hanging on a cord around their necks. Then the Master calls out KNEEL! and at this command all the pupils must kneel down. At the words CROSS YOURSELVES! each one makes the sign of the cross, and at FOLD YOUR HANDS! they all will put their hands together in front of them and keep them there throughout the prayer, without leaning back against the benches. When the prayer is over, the Master says STAND UP! whereupon all the pupils will stand up and sit down on the benches behind them at the word SIT! and here they will remain while awaiting the order that each Assistant Monitor, at the top of the bench, will give them. Each Assistant Monitor must give out to the pupils on his bench the lesson that they have to study.

1st Class

GET READY! The Monitor of the First Class, standing on his stool near the large board, calls out to them GET READY! At this order the children must stand up and hold their boards and pencils at chest level, with the board in the left hand and the pencil, between the thumb and first two fingers of the right hand.

LOOK! Soon after the Monitor points with his long stick at the letter A, which is hanging on the large board where there must not be more than three or four letters, and he says to them: "Look closely at this letter, it is called A. It is formed by a line sloping to the right, another to the left and cut across the middle by a horizontal line. To write it begin by making a line to the right and then to the left. At the bottom of each of these lines there is a small straight line. After that put the line across the middle." (The Monitor must show with his stick how the letter is made and how it must be written.)

WHAT IS THE NAME OF THIS LETTER? After this introduction the Monitor turns to the first pupil on the bench and asks him "What is the name of the letter?", while pointing out the letter A on the large board.

If the pupil doesn't remember it, he keeps passing on to another until he finds one who names the letter correctly. The one who names it takes the place of the first pupil who couldn't name it; he also gets his mark of distinction and the first one goes down and takes the place of the one who corrected him. The Monitor continues to have the letter named by all the pupils in the class and moves around the ones who make mistakes.

When this letter has been named by the whole class he passes on to the second letter, B. He points out that it is formed by a straight line with two curves on its right; he shows them with his stick how it must be written and proceeds as above for the letter A. He does the same for the letter C and so on for all the other letters of the alphabet, on succeeding days.

POINT! EXAMINE! When this is done by the whole class, the Monitor begins again by pointing out the letter A and without naming it or describing it, he orders the class to point to it on their cards, and at the word POINT!, each pupil must look for it on his board, and hold his pencil above it until the Assistant from each bench has examined (by passing behind the bench and looking over the right shoulder of each pupil) and seen that it was correctly pointed out. At the word EXAMINE! he will point out to those who were wrong the letter which they should have pointed to.

WHAT IS THIS LETTER CALLED? When the Assistants have returned to their places with their pointers upright to show that the examination is completed, the Monitor questions whichever pupil he thinks he should, asking him (while pointing out the letter on the big board) "What is this letter called?" If he replies correctly, he questions another pupil on another letter, which he also makes him point out on his board, and so on. He chooses letters from the right and the left until all the pupils in the class have been carefully examined on all the three or four letters hanging on the large board, at the same time taking care to move down those who are wrong, or who have hesitated, and moving up those who have replied correctly and quickly.

SLATES. When the Monitor thinks that the pupils are familiar with all the letters shown on the large board, he orders the Assistants to distribute the slates. This they must do at the word SLATES! They go and get them from the place where they have been put away and give one to each pupil on his bench, along with a pencil which each pupil will hang around his neck on a string.

TO THE DESK! GET READY! When this is done and the Assistants have returned to their places with their pointers in the upright position, the Monitor orders the children on the first bench, who have not been given slates, to come up to the desk by calling out TO THE DESK! Immediately, the pupils from this bench come forward together to the desk and rest their left arms on the small shelf in front and bring their right hands onto the upper shelf where the sand is, with their pencils held firm between their thumbs and first two fingers. At the words GET READY! those who have slates hold them in their left hands, their pencils in their right hands between their thumbs and first two fingers. When this is done, the Assistant Monitors go up and down the rows to see if the pupils are holding their slates and pencils properly. Then having seen by the upright pointers that all is ready, the Monitor says WRITE the letter A like this. Then he shows them with his pointer where to begin and finish the letter.

EXAMINE! When it seems that this letter has been written by all the pupils, the Assistant Monitors go up and down the rows to examine and correct on the order EXAMINE!

CLEAN YOUR SLATES! When they have returned to their places and having given the signal, the Monitor calls out "Clean your slates!" At which the pupils must put their right hands to their mouths and take some saliva with which they clean off the letter written on their slates. The Assistant from the first bench smooths out the letters which were written in the sand. The Monitor carries on in the same manner having them write all the other letters hanging on the large board.

BEGIN AGAIN! When the Monitor thinks that the pupils have written and know sufficiently well the letters on the large board, he orders the whole class to write them again in silence, saying "Begin again!"

It is on this second test of writing that the Mark of Distinction of First in the First Writing Class must be given.

As soon as the Master and the Monitor of this class are satisfied that all the capital letters of the Roman Alphabet are thoroughly familiar to the pupils, in the same manner as outlined above they will proceed to show them, and trace and make them write on the sand and on their slates the letters printed on the other side of the Roman alphabet (that is, the small letters). When these have been duly taught, repeated and written, they will show them a third alphabet of large and small italics. Finally, fifth and sixth alphabets made up of large and small letters in writing. These alphabets will be shown to them in the same way as the first ones and they will have to write them for longer so that they can form a good hand before they go up to a higher class where they will make constant use of writing.

1.2.3.4.5.6.7.8.9.0. It must not be forgotten to show them, before they pass on to another class the names and the shapes of the numbers 1,2,3,4,5,6,7,8,9,0, and to have them add them in every way, asking them: how much is one and two; to which each pupil should reply, it is 3; and 3 and 3 are 6, and so on, taking all the figures and adding them in every direction. Every Saturday morning without fail, and sometimes during the week when all the exercises are finished early, the Master will ask the students of the First Class the following questions, to which they must give the answers given below, until they know them all perfectly.

Q. What do you call the figures shown on the large board?

A. They are called letters.

Q. How are letters formed?

A. They are all formed from three lines: straight, slanting or curved. Some letters are formed by only one of these lines, others by two, and in still others we see all three used as in the letter R.

Q. How are the letters divided?

A. They are divided into VOWELS and CONSONANTS, or VOICES and ARTICULATIONS.

Q. How many vowels are there?

A. Generally speaking, there are five.

Q. What are they?

A. A, e, i, o, u, and also one can include y.

Q. Why are they called vowels or voices?

A. Because by themselves they form one voice or sound.

Q. How many consonants or articulations are there?

A. There are nineteen.

Q. Name them.

A. B, c, d, f, g, h, j, k, l, m, n, p, q, r, s, t, v, x, and z.

Q. Why are they called consonants or articulations?

A. Because they only can form a sound with the help of vowels or voices.

Q. Are there not also double letters?

A. Yes there are some amongst both the vowels and the consonants.

Q. What are they?

A. Those from amongst the vowels are *ae, eu, eau, ieu, oe, oi, ou*; and amongst the consonants there are *ch, ft, ff, ph, sl, ss, st*, w.

Q. What are letters used for?

A. To form words.

As soon as the oral exercises of the First Class are finished and the order to begin again has been given to the pupils and they are writing in silence, the Second Class, made up of those who are beginning to spell word of two letters and more, must start . . .

PROBABLE TIME TAKEN BY PUPILS TO DO A COMPLETE COURSE OF THE ELEMENTARY EDUCATION CONTAINED IN THIS VOLUME.

(It must first be noted that a week of six days only gives four days of school, since one day has to be taken off for a holiday and two half days for Catechism.)

ALPHABET—First Class

The Capital letters of the Roman Alphabet are 24 in number. By
learning 3 in the morning and 3 in the afternoon, there are 6 a day;
therefore for the 24: . . . . .4 days
The same for small Roman letters . . . . .4 days
Since the large Italic letters are very similar to Roman capitals, they
will be easily learnt with 6 in the morning and 6 in the afternoon,
total . . . . .2 days
The small letters will require . . . . .4 days
Since the large letters for writing are more difficult to learn, they will
take the same time as Roman capitals . . . . .4 days
The small letters in writing will take the same time as the small italics . 2 days

20 days

Thus the likely time taken to learn the six alphabets will be twenty teaching days, which, at the rate of 4 days per week, will require 5 weeks.

This doesn't allow separately time for learning the numbers and the twelve replies to the questions on the letters, since these are learned in the 20 days already calculated (as well as learning to count and to write all of it) while the other classes are having their oral exercises.

SPELLING—Second, Third and Fourth Classes

To spell 45 words of 2 letters, shown in the first table, and 150 words
of 3 letters, at 8 words per day, 4 in the morning and 4 in the
afternoon, will take . . . . 24½ days
To spell 275 words of 4 letters from the second table, and the 132
words of 5 and 6 letters from the third table, at 10 words per day
will take . . . . 40½ days
Fwd . . . . 65 days

To spell the 657 words of 2 syllables on the first table, the 837 words of 3 syllables from the second table, the 597 words of 4 syllables from the third table, the 132 words of 5 syllables from the fourth table and the 66 words of 6, 7 and 8 syllables from the fifth table: total 2,289 words at 12 per day . . . . 190½ days

255½ days

These two hundred and fifty-five days of class at 4 days per week will require 63¾ weeks, during which time the pupils will perfect their writing on their slates, learn by heart the words which they have spelled so they know how to write them. They will also know the 51 replies on grammar. They will learn also the small multiplication table and begin to do a little addition.

READING—Fifth Class

To learn to read correctly the 15 lessons of 1, 2, 3, and 5 syllables as well as those in verse, with one week for each will require 15 weeks or . . 60 days

During the sixty school days the pupils will learn by heart 88 replies on grammar, to write on paper and to learn some rules to prepare them for special study of Arithmetic.

ARITHMETIC—Sixth Class

For a perfect knowledge of the four principal rules of Arithmetic shown on the last 38 signs in the book, it will be necessary to have 12 exercises on each one, which at two per day, will take a week and a half for each rule, in all 57 weeks or . . . . 228 days

During this time the pupils will learn the conjugation of verbs, the long multiplication table and they will read books.

SUMMARY OF TIME REQUIRED

Alphabets	20 days, making	5 weeks
Spelling	255½ days, making	63¾ weeks
Reading (15 lessons)	60 days, making	15 weeks
Counting & Reading	228 days, making	57 weeks
Total	563½ days, making	140¾ weeks
Allowance for holidays and absences		9¼ weeks
TOTAL		150 weeks

To complete the course of Elementary Education contained in this volume, consisting of READING, WRITING and ARITHMETIC, will take three years. They will have had to learn the spelling of 2897 words included in the different tables, and the 151 replies to the questions on grammar; the principal parts of verbs and their conjugations; also their prayers and the Longer and Shorter Catechism.

Note: I have translated *Télégraph* as "Large Board". It really was a stand on which previously prepared signs could be hung. These signs could easily be removed and replaced with other signs. jrb

2 The Campaign for Universal Education

Dissatisfaction with existing standards of education could almost be called a universal in North America. Critics there have always been and no doubt always will be, and early and mid-nineteenth-century British North Americans were no exception. But their vision of what could be accomplished by educational reform has perhaps never before or after been paralleled. They were the original believers. Universal education, by school reformers at least, was hailed as a universal medicine, the one basic cure for many, if not all, of the ills of nineteenth-century society.

The ills that British North American reformers perceived were myriad. Periodic economic collapse and a sense of helplessness in its face, caused by dependence on the trade of two great and somewhat unpredictable imperial powers, were endemic to their times. The problem was often seen in terms of North American competition: would the British Maritime and Canadian provinces ever be able to match the neighbouring American states in enterprise and wealth, or were they destined always to be economic backwaters, doomed forever to a state of stagnation? Of equal concern were the poor, and the apparently ever-increasing crime rates in the colonies. Both individual and collective moral health, as well as individual and collective fortunes, seemed to mid-century educators to be very precarious commodities indeed.

Universal schooling was the proposed answer to these and many other problems; it was the panacea that was to produce the 'mighty revolution to come'. To accomplish the goal of educating every child, reformers believed first of all that schooling had to be made free. They thus proposed that the common or parish schools that had gradually emerged in many communities, and had been partially subsidized by government grants in most provinces, be entirely sustained by a combination of provincial grants and assessment on local property. The abolition of any kind of assessment on the parents or guardians of common-school children, it was argued, would remove the last stumbling block that still prevented many families from sending their dependents to school. Free common or parish schooling, of course, was by no means the only reform proposed by educators. Bigger schools, graded classes, teacher training, better advice to, and more supervision of the children, teachers, parents, and local educational authorities connected with the schools were all considered essential aspects of the campaign for educational improvement.

Why did these reforms seem so necessary? How were they put into practice?

Why were they criticized? What, in fact, were the internal contradictions that emerged as a result of the conflicting goals of nineteenth-century educators? At least partial answers to these questions will be found in the documents in this section on the ideology of educational reform and some of the early debates surrounding it.

As the debates on both means and ends continued in all provinces, the machinery to put reform into effect gradually emerged in the form of provincial and municipal education 'systems' with their ever-burgeoning boards, offices, and supervisory personnel. These administrative systems emerged essentially in response to three basic requirements of nineteenth-century educational reform. One was the desire for the orderly and systematic provision of the various educational institutions and materials that embodied school reformers' goals. Another was the hope that the advent of relatively distant authority might alleviate much of the bitter conflict that schooling often engendered on the local scene. Finally, and perhaps most basic, was the belief in the necessity of fiscal control. If provincial or municipal money was to be lavished on the schools, then responsible governments, it was argued, had the right and in fact the duty to see that it was properly spent.

The crux of the matter lay in one's definition of what constituted proper spending. Through their boards of school commissioners, councils of public instruction, superintendents, and inspectors, nineteenth-century provincial and municipal governments attempted to define the goals and promote the means of educational improvement, to inspire, cajole, and if necessary coerce the authorities under them to accept and put them into practice. Ways to get better teachers and books, plans for better school buildings or furniture, methods of better organizing, managing, or motivating children became the stock-in-trade of education departments as they strove to exercise their mandate for improvement. Equally important was the drive for information. Schools, pupils, books, and teachers had to be counted, statistics analysed and disseminated. The information once gathered and processed, reform could proceed more effectively on the basis of the knowledge gained. Legislatures could pass the necessary laws, while boards of education and chief superintendents of schools generated the propaganda and new regulations that justified them and would make them work.

For the critics of state intervention in education there were two fundamental issues. First of all, reform from the top down could be criticized on the basis of its content, for being quite simply wrong about the nature and needs of schools. What one person saw as improvement, another might easily see as the ruin of both the schools and the children. Even more basic perhaps were the criticisms that focussed on the principle of state intervention itself. The state did not belong in the classrooms of British North America, according to this school of thought. Whether the debate was about content or about the principle of government involvement in schooling, it tended to focus on the costs and on the proliferating personnel of educational reform. Should teachers be trained? If so, how and at whose expense? Would they be graded in any way, and if so, by whom? What were the rights and the responsibilities of principals and superintendents? Were they even necessary? Was educational reform worth all the trouble and expense involved?

Answers to these questions varied from province to province and from region to region, as did the style and content of educational debate. The documents in Part 2 by no means cover all the issues that were raised or the ways in which they were resolved, but hopefully will give some indication of both the kind and the intensity of nineteenth-century educational argument. More difficult for the historian to penetrate is the question of the sources of conflict. Why were certain individuals and groups of people so strongly opposed to free schools or to centralized administrations, and who were the people who tended to favour these innovations? What were their reasons for choosing one side or another, and how serious was their commitment in the long run? What, finally, was the function of the new educational systems in Canada in the second half of the nineteenth century in terms of the larger society?

THE QUEST FOR IMPROVEMENT

INVESTIGATING THE STATE OF EDUCATION

Report of a Special Committee of the House of Assembly Appointed to Enquire into the State of Education in this Province (Quebec, 1824), pp. 29-47.

ANSWERS of the SEMINARY of QUEBEC to the Questions of the Chairman of the Committee appointed to enquire into the present state of Education in this Province.

Q. What is the present state of Education in this Province?

A. If by Education is understood the knowledge, even elementary, of Letters, it must be admitted that it is reduced to but little, particularly in our country parts. There are unfortunately several Parishes where there would hardly be found five or six persons capable of expressing their thoughts tolerably in writing, and of performing the most common rules of arithmetic. From the knowledge we have, we should be inclined to think, that in our country parts, upon an average, about one fourth of the Canadian population can read tolerably; that there may be one tenth who can write their names, poorly enough in truth. In this humiliating enumeration, we comprise only the cultivators of the earth, and not persons of certain professions which require more extensive knowledge.

Although Education be but little advanced in this country, it would have been much less so, had it not been for the zeal of a good number of the gentlemen of the Clergy, who have made great exertions for the purpose of procuring Education for the Children of their particular Parishes, by building School Houses and maintaining Masters. Their success would have fully corresponded with their generous exertions, if a law in force in this country had not prevented them from endowing those Schools, and thereby perpetuating the good which they commenced. . . .

Q. What are the causes which may have retarded its progress?

A. Amongst the different causes which may have retarded the progress of Education in this Province, one may consider the following as the principal: —

1st. The want of pecuniary means with a very large number of parents.

2nd. The difficulty of procuring School Masters of irreproachable morals.

3rd. Finally the want of good Elementary Schools in our country parts. The greater part of the Schoolmasters found there, particularly those established under the 41st Geo. III. are not of a kind to obtain the confidence of the country people, because . . . the Gentlemen of the Clergy have no right to superintend their conduct, and they are named without the participation of the principal Inhabitants of the place.

Q. What are the most proper means to diffuse it?

A. In our humble opinion the most effectual means would be, to establish in each Parish Elementary Schools, to be under the immediate direction and superintendence of the Curate, Church Wardens and principal Members of each Congregation. The Curates having it then in their power to superintend the Schools, and to know the morals, and religious and social principles of the Masters put in charge of them, would induce their parishioners to send their children to School, and we are intimately persuaded, that with time these Schools would end in being very well attended. To establish these Schools in a fixed and permanent manner, it would be necessary for the Legislature to authorize the *Fabrique* of each Communion to acquire sufficient funds for the maintainance of those Schools. If such a law were passed one would soon see rising in all the Parishes permanent Schools, which hereafter would be endowed by the different Curates and by rich Individuals, who now make daily complaints that the obstacles are not removed which prevent them from doing the good which they desire to do in respect to the elementary education of children. With Schools thus founded and endowed, a respectable Salary might be provided for the Masters, whereof the choice would be by so much the more easy as the means of subsistence to be offered them would be greater.

Q. What is the number of Scholars in that part of the Seminary of Quebec, which is called "*Le Petit Seminaire*"?

A. There are about one hundred and sixty.

Q. Could a greater number be received into the said Seminary?

A. When the repairs of the *Petit Seminaire* now commenced are completed, there could be received therein about one hundred and fifty Boarders, and as many day Scholars at the least.

Q. Why do not a larger number of Scholars request admission to study in the Seminary of Quebec?

A. That a larger number of Scholars do not request admission to our Seminary may be attributed:

1st. To the want of Elementary Schools, where young people prepare for a course of studies, and where they usually acquire a taste for them.

2nd. To the want of pecuniary means. Although the charge for boarding and lodging is small, and the Scholars pay nothing for tuition—the Seminary itself paying the Professors—nevertheless, the number of parents whose means permit them to place their children at the Seminary is small. The charge for the boarding and lodging of the Scholars is twenty pounds currency for twelve months. If they are sick, or the Seminary does not take them to where the Vacations are usually passed, a proportionate deduction is made to the parents.

The day Scholars pay one pound currency for fuel, sweeping the school rooms and bringing in the wood. With these two last articles they were charged previous to the beginning of the repairs of the *Petit Seminaire*.

3rd. To the indifference, unfortunately too general, of parents; who not having themselves any idea of education, are little inclined to confer it upon their children.

Q. Is it not essential that before being capable of admission to the Seminary, it is necessary for the Scholars to have gone through a course of elementary instruction elsewhere?

A. Before a boy be admitted to commence his course of study in our Seminary, we require that he should be able to read Latin and French, and know how to write.

Q. Would you be pleased to state to us, what is the course of studies through which scholars are put in your Seminary?

A. Our course of studies consists in teaching the French, Latin and English Tongues, Geography, Mythology and History; after these comes a course of Literature, Rhetoric and Philosophy; this last consists of Logic, Metaphysics, Morals, Natural Philosophy and Mathematics, in all their branches. Besides this our young scholars, of late years, begin, in the lower classes only, a systematic course of Arithmetic, which they continue during the following classes.

Q. What aptitude for the sciences have you observed in the youth in general, including that portion of them which studied with you?

A. We think that the Canadian Youth have as great an aptitude for the Sciences and the Fine Arts as is usually met with in the Youth of other Nations, and we believe also that we may assert without fear of violating the truth, that the greater number of the Young men who have studied in our Seminary have shewn sufficient talents to succeed, and we are proud to be able to count amongst those who exercise honorable Professions, as well in the City as in the other parts of the Province, and who distinguish themselves therein, no small number of Pupils of the House, who eminently succeeded in those courses of study. . . .

The Revd. DANIEL WILKIE, Clergyman of the Church of Scotland and

Teacher in this City, answered as follows:

Q. From your experience as a Teacher and knowledge of the country, can you furnish the Committee with any information on the general state of Education in the Country, the causes of its retardment and the means of promoting it?

A. I have been a Teacher in this City for about twenty years; from the experience and knowledge I have had, I consider that the state of Education in this Country is considerably lower than it might be. I can assign no other cause of this, than the want of Parish Schools in the Country parts, and that of a University in the Province. The number of Scholars now attending my School is thirty. To be admitted in my School they must be first able to read English. The Sciences taught are, the English Grammar, the French, Latin and Greek Languages, Arithmetic and Mathematics:—the rate of Tuition is £12 a year. About the fourth or fifth part of the Scholars are Canadian boys. As far as my experience goes, I have remarked the same aptitude in the youth of this country for learning as that of the youth in Europe, having been a Teacher during five years in Scotland.

Q. What would be the beneficial effects which you would anticipate from the establishment of a University in the Province?

A. It would take a long time to detail all the advantages which might be expected from the establishment of a University in the Province; but it may be said generally, that there would be a more general diffusion of knowledge, a much greater number of persons fit to instruct others, and a greater ambition to excel in learning. Such a University should necessarily be endowed with Public Funds, in order to support the Professors and Teachers in all the different Arts and Sciences, as also to procure Apparatus and Libraries, which could not be done by the efforts of Individuals.

Q. Had your School the advantage of any support from Government?

A. My School never enjoyed any advantage of this kind, beyond that protection in which all the subjects of Government equally share. On the death of the late Mr. Tanswell, in 1819, who enjoyed a Salary for teaching classical learning, I applied to His Grace the Duke of Richmond, then Governor in Chief, to be allowed that Salary, but was answered that it was already disposed of.

Q. What is the number of young gentlemen who have been educated at your School, and what are the branches of science in which they have been taught?

A. To the first part of this question I answer, that since my establishment in Quebec, about a hundred or a hundred and twenty young gentlemen have left my School to enter upon their respective professions. This may therefore be considered as the number of young gentlemen educated in my School. There is a much greater number of pupils who from change of residence, change of opinion, and various other causes have discontinued their attendance, and left their education unfinished. The branches of learning taught at my School are, the Latin, Greek and French Languages, Arithmetic and Mathematics. I have been obliged to engage in this extraordinary multiplicity of business, on account of the want of separate Institutions and separate Professors, where and by whom these various departments of education might be individually conducted. For the same reason I have been obliged to devote part of my time to the instruction of my pupils in various minor branches, such as Geography, History, English Grammar, and several other subjects in which Instruction cannot be had separately in this Country. The want of separate Professors for the different branches of knowledge, is one of the chief causes, in my humble opinion, which contribute to retard the progress of education in this Province. The want of Classes and Institutions for conducting the subsidiary branches of Education is also severely felt. When a Teacher has his attention divided among such a multiplicity of objects, it is impossible for him to treat of them in that interesting and zealous manner, which is calculated to kindle and keep alive an ardent love of knowledge in the youthful breast. The present desultory mode of conducting education in this Country is extremely laborious to the Instructor, and far from being attended with proportionate advantages to the Learner. Another evil arising from the want of any publicly authorized course of education, is, that the degree of instruction deemed necessary for any of the liberal professions depends in every instance almost entirely on the ever varying foundation of private opinion. I say nothing here of the great disadvantages we suffer from the want of suitable apparatus for illustrating natural Philosophy, Chemistry and other Sciences depending upon experiment, and without which they cannot be understood.

Q. Was there any, and what number of Schools in Quebec at the time of your establishing yourself there, wherein Mathematics and the Classics were taught, and what Schools of the same description now exist in Quebec?

A. Besides the Seminary, which is a permanent establishment, the Rev. Mr. Jackson taught a School of this nature at the time of my commencement. Mr. Farnham and the Rev. Mr. Spratt subsequently opened Schools of this description. At present, the most frequented School of this kind, is conducted by the Revd. Mr. Burrage.

CONCERN FOR REFORM IN NOVA SCOTIA

D. C. Harvey, 'A Documentary Study of Early Educational Policy', *Bulletin of the Public Archives of Nova Scotia* (Halifax, 1937), vol. 1, no. 1, pp. 9-13. Reprinted by permission of the Public Archives of Nova Scotia.

REPORT OF THE SPECIAL SCHOOL COMMISSIONERS
WESTERN DISTRICT, 1824

Answers to the queries respecting the state of Schooling and School Masters—
To the first—

There is no permanently established school in the Western District of Annapolis—In some neighbourhoods, particularly in the Town plot of Digby and at Sissibou River, there has been a school kept, with few intervals of omission, since the early settlement of the country—At the former place there is a rough school-house erected on the *Church*-ground, in which, a Catechist of the Venerable Society teaches reading, writing and common arithmetic *gratis* to a certain number nominated by the Rector, and to all other applicants, at the current price of tuition—There are other small slightly-built school-houses in various other places, of which a list is subjoined—These have been erected by local contributions—The perplexed right of property in them is frequently matter of dispute and sometimes of contention—Transient schools generally find accommodation in them but sometimes are refused it.— *To the second*—

We add a list of such Masters as we know of being licenced, and also of such others as are general residents—None of these are constantly employed —At some periods, their respective neighbourhoods are scant of a *sufficiency of uneducated children* to form a school,—At other times, our resident masters are *undervalued* and *underbid* by itinerant strangers who offer to teach— Of these latter, some few have proved abandoned characters, *sufficiently specious* to deceive the ordinary class of settlers, though, without any one solid literary qualification—Male and female instructors (not making teaching their steady profession) are occasionally engaged in neighbourhoods for a single season—These are often of the friends or relations of such neighbourhoods, disengaged (for the time) from more profitable employment— *To the third,—fourth and fifth*—

The number of scholars attendant upon a school is very fluctuating—In the closest neighbourhoods, that, would be a very full school, which, should embrace, *during the most favorable seasons of the year*, from thirty five to forty scholars, including both sexes—, and *during some parts of the year* it must be expected to dwindle down to ten or fifteen—Children dwelling more than three miles from the school-house cannot well attend—Children of the poorer, —and perhaps those of the next rising class of settlers, after the age of ten or twelve years cannot well be *spared from work*—If such improve in learning after that age it is, by means of *Night-Schools*, kept *in time of Winter*—One or two neighbourhoods of our thickest settlements, may afford, within a sweep of three or four miles from a common centre, a constant annual list of sixty children (including both sexes and all ranks and degrees) between the ages of four and twelve,—But, inferior health,—or the occasional want of decent cloathing are drawbacks from the school,—And so also are indifference, unsettled views,—domestic bustles, prejudices,—as well as, in some cases, *real poverty*, and in others, covetousness—subject, as every school is, to these deductions and considering that, the *maximum* of learning sought by the *generality* is no more than to read and write *indifferently*, and to cypher so far as to cast up pounds shillings & pence, it is not to be expected that, our best settled neighbourhoods could enable a school to average more than thirty scholars (boys with girls) by the Year. . . .
To the eighth and ninth

As before observed, none of our neighbourhoods have a constant or permanently established school—The settlers in the Town plot of Digby and at the mouth of Sissibou River come nearest to the accomplishment of this end—The whole Western District of Annapolis County might be cast into eleven school circuits of nearly equal magnitude and population—Each of these eleven would embrace an *extent of land* sufficient for a *very large* parish or township—In the present state of our settlements each one affords some central spot that is moderately populous—A regular school in each of these central positions would prove *more or less* beneficial to all the settlers, but least perhaps to the poorest—for our poorest settlers are nowhere to be found in a body, but detached and scattered on the out skirts, upon new or barren tracts —The constant residence however of a sober, moral and orderly schoolmaster, though possessing but slender literary qualifications, would be advantageously felt throughout the circuit—The decease of most of *our elders* has left the *present race* of our inhabitants without any means of *benefiting by example,*—But, *one correct stationary man*, aided by the occasional visits and correspondence of the District Clergy, might strengthen the influence of the well disposed, and preserve something of just moral sentiment alive—

To support such a school-master in a *decent state of life* would require thirty pounds by the Year over and above all he could expect to derive from the settlers for, perhaps, ten years to come—If the place and times for holding his school, the ages at which he should receive scholars,—the number to be taught gratis,—the rates of tuition money for the rest,—the school books to be used, and other matters of regulation were to be *peremptorily* settled and made public by *his* and *their* superiors, the people would soon fall quietly into the habit of sending their children to the full of their ability,—And the result would probably yield to the Master a *steady product* of from thirty to forty pounds—with an income of Sixty pounds or, a little upwards, aided by the industry of his own wife and family, a School-Master could live, in a *country neighbourhood*, with tolerable comfort and suitable decency.

We are well aware that, the money now at His Excellency's disposal is inadequate to the supporting this proposed system,—and perhaps, *considering the peculiar circumstances of this district,*—is insufficient to effect any important benefit to the children of our *extensively scattered* poorer class—Our endeavor is to give His Excellency a clear exposition of the present state of this part of the province as respects education, so that He may judge of the practicability of extending it to more or less of our poor—And, whatever course His Excellency may prescribe we will with great satisfaction support, according to the best of our abilities—

We further beg leave respectfully to add that, It has been suggested as a sure method of preserving and *gradually diffusing* useful knowledge through this District, to *aim first* at the establishment of *one good english* [sic] *school* that should afford tuition *freely*, to a limited number of the decent poor, and, at *a moderate price*, to all other children—It is said that, such a school might steadily hold up *one correct example*, and become (*at the least*) the nursery for a better class of minor teachers of our own growth, if it did not prove the mother of a sufficiency of similar schools where circumstances invited—The Kind of School proposed, to consist of three classes—In the first class, to be taught reading and *neat handwriting*,—In the second, common arithmetic,—In the third, compound arithmetic with as much of geometry as is applicable to ordinary mensurations—

It might be unjust to force,—And it would otherwise be impracticable to unite *the generality* of this District in a scheme of this kind, because, to all but a few, the advantages would appear discouragingly remote and contingent—There are a *very few* liberal minded persons, in various parts of our Townships, who would probably aid any spirited neighbourhood that should undertake such a project—But all the means they could afford would not enable such neighbourhood, *without foreign assistance*, to effect it—Our country has, for a long time, gone backwards as respects intelligence, a suitable teacher therefore must be sought *with care and expence* from a distance—Such an one would not come without the assurance of a competent salary secured for a considerable term of duration—Now it is expedient that, a respectably settled school-master should be a married man—as such, he should be furnished with a dwelling-house and school-house *rent free*,—Be exempted from, or indemnified against personal taxation, and have a certain clear annual stipend of not less than one hundred pounds—Short of this provision no *properly qualified* man could be obtained,—and considering the great expenditure of fuel and cloathing in this climate, and the high price of the latter article, no schoolmasters [sic] family could subsist with comfort and the requisite decency on a smaller allowance—It is just barely possible that, some one settlement within this District could make provision for such a school & master with a foreign assistance of not less than Sixty pounds pr. annum.

1.—LIST OF SCHOOL HOUSES

		Miles
In the Town-plot of Digby	one Dist from Digby	0
At the Grand Joggin	one Dist from Digby	4
Marshal Town ridge	one Dist from Digby	6
North side St. Marys Bay	one Dist from Digby	12
Sissibou River	one Dist from Digby	18
Gullivers Hole	one Dist from Digby	10
Sandy Cove	one Dist from Digby	15
Grand Passage	one Dist from Digby	40
Clare	one Dist from Digby	30

2.—LIST OF SCHOOL MASTERS

JESSE HOYT—aged about 60—married—licenced and employed in Digby as the Society's catechist—A sober orderly man—

JONATHAN RANDALL aged about 70—licenced and usually employed about the Grand Joggin, but sometimes 15 miles distant, on the Neck—

JOHN MORFORD—aged about 65—married, usually employed between Digby & Sissibou—licenced—

J. DALTON—licenced—employed sometimes at Sissibou and sometimes on the Neck—aged about 50—

JOHN B. GREGG—aged about 30—single, employed sometimes at Grand Passage & sometimes at Sissibou—

EDWARD FOWL—employed with his wife in a little school on St. Marys Bay road—

PIERRE LOUIS BUNELL and LOUIS DUBOUILLON are two teachers in Clare of competent ability—Natives of old France and resident here, the one, 30 years, the other about 10 years

3—SCHOOL CIRCUITS—for the Western District of Annapolis, each comprising nearly an equal number of settlers—

1—The country included between Bear River and the Joggin road towards Shelburne—

2d—Digby Town plot and the vicinity—3d—North shore of St. Marys Bay from the Marsh to Oldmans point—4th Weymouth and the vicinity—5th—6th—7th—the upper, middle and Mentegan Districts of Clare—8th—Grand Passage including Long & Breyer Islands—9th Little River and Sandy Cove—10th—Trout Cove & Gulliver Hole—11th Broad Cove and Mountain settlements—

N.B.—Whole population about 5,000 souls—

HOPES FOR THE FUTURE

Essays, on the Future Destiny of Nova Scotia, Improvement of Female Education in Nova Scotia, and on Peace (Halifax, 1846), pp. 2-7.

This is the age of improvement;—and it is not improbable that in a short time, not only shall a railroad connect Halifax with the Canadas, and consequently the United States with Nova Scotia, but that it shall wend its way through the Rocky Mountains to the Pacific Ocean, there to meet Steam navigation connecting the New World with China, thence to be continued through Asia and Europe to the Mediterranean, united again with England by Steamers, and by the Cunard line complete the entire circumference of the globe! This would be a *noble enterprise*. It is certainly not beyond the bounds of possibility. The whole route might be passed over in a very few weeks. The vacation of a student would be quite sufficient for the entire journey. Should such an enterprise as this be undertaken, the character of Nova Scotia would at once be redeemed from insignificance, and its resources prove that it is destined to become a flourishing and rich country.

We should not regard public works like these as impracticable: it is a mistake. The term "CANNOT," *should be laid aside in a country like this.* See what others have done in redeeming the trackless forests of America from their native state! With them there is no cannot—not even tarrying in their course. Their motto is *"go-ahead,"* and this they fully exemplify in practice. We have all the materials for railroads at our doors; iron and coal in abundance; stone of the best quality for canals; and timber for shipping, and all the purposes of commerce without importing from the Baltic. . . .

. . . *We have the germ of national prosperity;* but whether it is to be developed in our genial soil, and like the acorn become enlarged until its roots shall take deep hold therein and its green foliage spread over the face of the country, affording a healthful shade, or not, is for us now to determine. Here is a wide field for the enterprising youth of our land, where they may put forth their exertions with a prospect of certain success. Such a policy as we have proposed would draw men of capital and influence to the country and afford both labor and wages to an immense population. As matters are at present no man of talent and capital would think of establishing himself in Nova Scotia. There are no public works, nothing to engage the attention of the enterprising. But the work once begun, and set in full operation, manufactures would be established, arts advanced, and all that can make a free and prosperous people happy, enjoyed. . . .

What is the main spring which is to set the whole machinery in motion? It has been already named at the commencement of this essay. And here we would gladly pause and ask our reader, nay trumpet-tongued, were it possible, re-echo the question, vivà voce, to every village and hamlet in the Province, not passing by some of its *chiefest patriots; what is the main spring of Nova Scotia's future greatness*? Some might answer "Responsible Government," others another policy. I answer with the history of nations in my hand, *Education.* "Knowledge is power;" and *the power* which alone can set in motion all the multifarious machinery upon which our Provincial interests depend. If this be correct, knowledge should be cultivated; nay it is impossible any longer to conceal this fact from our countrymen, however vigorously such a principle may attack the narrow policy of those who act upon the principle that *"the popular passions are the imps and demons of a political conjuror, and that he can raise them as other conjurors affect to do theirs, by terms of gibberish."* If knowledge be the foundation of our future prosperity, what lover of his country, with the least spark of a Briton's pride glowing in his bosom, while he sees the thousands of his fellow countrymen ardently striving to obtain that boon which alone can truly ennoble the mind and establish the firm basis of our real interests, would shut up the sources of knowledge; nay, glory in beholding the wreaths of flame and smoke ascend which might raze to their foundation all institutions of sound learning!

And here let none in their course of political jugglery add insult to injury by shouting in the ears of the populace; "Down with Colleges," "give us common schools!" The man, who at the present day, in the face of his country avows principles like these, is either a fit subject for a lunatic asylum or is goaded on to political madness, which is a still greater misfortune. Alas! that the private interests of *defeated demagogues* should prompt them to touch with unhallowed hand the sacred seats of Learning; to darken with opaque clouds, our Literary atmosphere! But these clouds must soon pass away, and the light of truth shine more brightly and in all its effulgence forever dissipate the pestilential vapor. Yet these are their country's patriots, who endeavour to render turbid the fountain of science, or forever to seal it up; and these are the men who seek to have their names emblazoned on the page of history, endeavouring to the utmost of their ability to stay the tide of knowledge which is spreading over the land. Their names may live in connexion with the educational history of the country, in the memories of their injured countrymen, but only to be execrated. And here we appeal to our readers to answer on behalf of those in whose political pathway the light of science presents such an insuperable obstacle that they would annihilate all our higher institutions of learning, *what have they ever done in any form for Education? Have they toiled indefatigably to develop* ANY *system for the improvement of Schools?*

No! they have done nothing but snarl at those who have given their time and best efforts to improve the system of education in all departments. *They talk* of common school education for all, as the only substantial good,—while *they* themselves *know they are endeavouring to deceive the people.* We need not however, press facts which are so notorious.—The truth is that as men in past ages have sacrificed their country at the shrine of their ambition, so at the present day there is nothing too gross to attempt in accomplishing private purposes. Far distant be the day when men of such principles will hold the reins of state to bind our country with the galling chains of ignorance and oppression.—But we fear not such a doom, so long as Britain's flag waves on our shores. Education must advance—the light of science even now sheds its steady rays in the midst of opposing darkness and will continue to radiate till it shall mingle with the light of other lands to bless and save from ignorance and superstition the benighted millions of our race, who now sit in darkness. Nova Scotia as a new country is proudly elevated in an Educational point of view, and her advantages in this respect warrant the conclusion that she is yet to be a bright star in the literary firmament. Unlike countries emerging from barbarism she in her infancy has received from the hand of the Parent State, the refined results of science where they are found in the manhood of old age; and as there are heights, and depths, and breadths, in science, which are yet to be explored, why shall not Nova Scotia be the victor in scaling those sublime heights and descending to those profound depths, which are yet beyond the reach of mortal ken, and be crowned with the laurels of literary and scientific fame?

Do any ask when is this bright day to dawn? We reply, it has already dawned. King's College was established at an early period; and some of those who have graduated in its halls, are now our brightest luminaries.—Since that time, other literary Institutions have been raised up by the well-understood wishes and efforts of the people. And here we ask those who stand opposed to such a policy, are not the dearest interests of our country connected with their vigorous operation? Yes, answer the thousands who have aided in the erection of those seats of learning! Yes, reply the youth who attend the classic halls of Nova Scotia! Yes, re-echoes the genius of our country's prosperity! Let Novascotians who inherit the talent and mental energy of their forefathers arise with the spirit of free men in supporting their educational establishments, that they may leave a rich inheritance to their sons, and future generations embalm their memories in grateful hearts. EDUCATION! What is it? It is knowledge —it is power—it is the chief agent in the founding of empires, their bulwark of defence—it is the mighty lever which moves all the machinery of the Globe. In what does it consist? In comprehending a part of Dilworth's spelling book, and ciphering to the rule of three? No, but in that mental training which discovers the hidden relations between causes and their effects,—that deep digging and labour required fully to develop the powers and capabilities of the human mind. Let our countrymen who feel all the wants of the key of knowledge see well to it that their places of education both high and low are properly sustained, each bearing that relation to the others which a prudent policy would dictate.

We should be stimulated to diligence in this matter by the noble examples of classic lands, such as Greece and Rome. The remembrance of their illustrious dead awaken feelings strangely interesting. Let us in imagination for a moment transport ourselves to Rome and visit the place where Cicero in the full Senate House under the most impassioned spirit of eloquence strongly inveighed against the atrocities of the haughty Cataline, having accused him of treason against the State; and the soul at once becomes riveted to the spot in reflections deep and vast. The mind in deep contemplation conjures up the master spirits of those, whose counsels in the Senate, and whose exploits in the field, were the wonder and terror of the world, while we tread with solemn and reverential awe upon the ruins of a people now no more. Is it their antiquity that calls forth our feelings of veneration? No! it is their *literary character.*— In like manner the mind of the traveller in visiting the ruins of Greece becomes deeply affected. The reminiscences of her once flourishing republic rise thick and fast, and he involuntarily and with deep emotion exclaims—Where are thy Wise men and Philosophers who once taught in these hallowed groves the pure principles of science which scattered the ignorance of those remote ages as the rays of the rising sun do the shades of night? Where are thy Statesmen, whose eloquence reverberated from the inmost recesses of the soul, producing the most magic effects upon popular assemblies? Where are thy heroes? Where thy proud magnificence and boasted glory? Alas! nought remains but fragments of her ancient sculpture and architecture.—Athens has become a prey to the spoiler, the despot, and stranger. All these feelings are an involuntary tribute, which none can refuse, to the Genius of Science. Nova Scotia has every facility for making rapid advances in a literary and scientific course, and no doubt the generations to come will look back upon her Orators, Philosophers, and Statesmen, with like feelings of profound veneration.

THE PURPOSES OF REFORM ACCORDING TO THE EXPERTS

Egerton Ryerson, 'Report on a System of Elementary Public Instruction for Upper Canada' (Montreal, 1847), in J. G. Hodgins, ed., *Documentary History of Education in Upper Canada* (Toronto, 1894-1910), vol. 6, pp. 143-6.

A system of general education amongst the people is the most effectual preventative of pauperism, and its natural companions, misery and crime.

To a young and growing country, and the retreat of so many poor from other countries, this consideration is of the greatest importance. The gangrene of pauperism in either cities or states is almost incurable. It may be said in some sort to be hereditary as well as infectious,—both to perpetuate and propagate itself,—to weaken the body politic at its very heart,—and to multiply wretchedness and vice.

Now, the Statistical Reports of pauperism and crime in different countries, furnish indubitable proof that ignorance is the fruitful source of idleness, intemperance and improvidence, and these the fosterparent of pauperism and crime. The history of every country in Europe may be appealed to in proof and illustration of the fact,—apart from the operation of extraneous local and temporary circumstances,—that pauperism and crime prevail in proportion to the absence of education amongst the labouring classes, and that in proportion to the existence and prevalence of education amongst those classes, is the absence of pauperism and its legitimate offspring.

To adduce even a summary of the statistical details which I have collected on this subject, would exceed my prescribed limits; and I will only present the conclusions at which competent witnesses have arrived after careful and personal inquiry. F. Hill, Esquire, Her Majesty's Inspector of Prisons in Scotland, at the conclusion of a statistical work on National Education in Great Britain, Prussia, Spain and America, states the following amongst other inferences, as the result of his investigations:

"So powerful is education as a means of national improvement, that, with comparatively few exceptions, the different countries of the world, if arranged according to the state of education in them, will be found to be arranged also according to wealth, morals and general happiness; and not only does this rule hold good as respects a country taken as a whole, but it will generally apply to the different parts of the same country.

Thus in England, education is in the best state in the northern Agricultural District, and in the worst state in the southern Agricultural District, and in the Agricultural parts of the Midland District; while in the great Towns, and other manufacturing places, education is in an intermediate state; and at the same time, the condition of the people and the extent of crime and violence among them follow in like order."

J. C. Blackden, Esquire, of Ford Castle, Northumberland, England, in concluding his evidence before the Poor Law Commissioners, expresses himself thus; "In taking a short review of my answers to the Commissioners'

Queries, the advantageous position of our labouring population, when compared with the position of those in the more southern districts of the country, must be manifest. It is impossible to live among them without being struck by their superior intelligence, and their superior morality. I am fully justified in this assertion by the Parliamentary Returns of criminal commitments in the several Counties of England, which prove Northumberland to be very much more free from crime than any other County. A principal cause of this I have no doubt arises from the education they receive at the Schools scattered over the country."

The Reverend W. S. Gilly, Vicar of Norham Parish, Northumberland, states the following facts in evidence before the same Commissioners:

"I scarcely know an instance in this Parish in which the children of an agricultural labourer have not been sent to School, for the most part at their own expense. I believe the parents set a greater value on that education the expenses of which they defray themselves; they watch their children's progress more narrowly. From prudence and education results the prosperity of this District; and it is not here as in some places, that the absolute plenty of the land, and the relative poverty of the people who live in it, keep pace one with the other! A high standard of character has raised the standard of comfort here: and for many years useful education, combined with Christian education, has been diffusing its blessing."

The same causes have produced the same effects in other countries. Prussia is a conspicuous example. The following is the statement of Thomas Wyse, Esquire, Member of the British Parliament, and author of an elaborate work on Education Reform, who has made extensive tours of personal inspection on the Continent. Personal observation enables me to attest to the correctness of that part of Mr. Wyse's statements which relate to the recently acquired Prussian Provinces on the Rhine. Mr. Wyse says—"What is the real social result of all this?—How has it affected the population for good or for ill?—How is it likely to affect them in future?—The narratives given by Pestalozzi, De Fellenberg, Oberlin and the Père Girard, of the singular revolution, mental and moral, and I may also add, physical, effected by the application of their system of teaching on a hitherto ignorant and vicious population, though admitted to be isolated experiments, ought not the less to be considered evidences of the intrinsic force of the instrument itself, and of its power to produce similar results, wherever and whenever fairly tried, without reference to country or numbers; that is, whenever applied with the same earnestness, honesty and skill in other instances as in theirs. And of this portion of Prussia —of the Rhenish Provinces—it may surely be averred, that it has now been for some time under the influence of this system, and that during that period, whether resulting from such influence or not, its progress in intelligence, industry, and morality, in the chief elements of virtue and happiness, has been steadily and strikingly progressive. In few parts of the civilized world is there more marked exemption from crimes and violence."

A judicious American writer observes, that "nearly nine-tenths of all the pauperism actually existing in any country, may be traced directly to moral causes; such as improvidence, idleness, intemperance, and a want of moderate energy and enterprise. Now it is hardly necessary to add that education, if it be imparted to all the rising generation, and be pervaded, also, by the right spirit, will remove these fruitful sources of indigence. It will make the young provident, industrious, temperate and frugal, and with such virtues, aided by intelligence, they can hardly fail in after life to gain a comfortable support for themselves and families. Could the paupers of our own State be collected into one group, it would be found, I doubt not, that three out of every four, if not five out of every six, owe their present humiliating position to some defect or omission in their early training."

What has been stated in respect to agricultural labourers, and of the labouring classes generally, is equally and specially true of manufacturing labourers. From the mass of testimony which might be adduced on this point, one or two statements only will be selected. The first is from the evidence before the Poor Law Commissioners, by Mr. A. G. Escher, of Zurich, Switzerland, who has been accustomed to employ hundreds of workmen. In reply to the question, as to the effects of a deficiency of education on success in mechanical employments, Mr. Escher says: "These effects are most strikingly exhibited in the Italians, who, though with the advantage of greater natural capacity than the English, Swiss, Dutch or Germans, are still of the lowest class of workmen. Though they comprehend clearly and quickly any simple proposition made, or explanation given to them, and are enabled quickly to execute any kind of work when they have seen it performed once, yet their minds, as I imagine from want of development by training or School Education, seem to have no kind of logic, no power of systematic arrangement, no capacity for collecting any series of observations, and making sound deductions from the whole of them. This want of capacity of mental arrangement is shown in their manual operations. An Italian will execute a simple operation with great dexterity; but when a number of them is put together, all is confusion. For instance: within a short time after the introduction of cotton spinning into Naples in 1830, a native spinner would produce as much as the best English workman; and yet up to this time, not one of the Neapolitan operators is advanced far enough to take the superintendence of a single room, the Superintendents being all Northerns, who, though less gifted by nature, have had a higher degree of order and arrangement imparted to their minds by a superior education."

In reply to the question, whether Education would not tend to render them discontented and disorderly, and thus impair their value as operatives, Mr. Escher states: "My own experience and my conversation with eminent mechanics in different parts of Europe, lead me to an entirely different conclusion. In the present state of manufactures, where so much is done by machinery and tools, and so little done by mere brute labour, (and that little diminishing), mental superiority, system, order, punctuality and good conduct,— qualities all developed and promoted by education,—are becoming of the highest consequence. There are now, I consider, few enlightened manufacturers, who will dissent from the opinion, that the workshops, peopled with the greatest number of well informed workmen, will turn out the greatest quantity of the best work, in the best manner. The better educated workmen are distinguished, we find, by superior moral habits in every respect.

"From the accounts which pass through my hands, I invariably find that the best educated of our work people manage to live in the most respectable manner, at the least expense, or make their money go the farthest in obtaining comforts.

"This applies equally to the work people of all nations, that have come under my observation; the Saxons the Dutch, and the Swiss, being however decidedly the most saving without stinting themselves in their comforts, or failing in general respectability. With regard to the English I may say, that the educated workmen are the only ones who save money out of their very large wages.

"By Education I may say, that I, throughout, mean not merely instruction in the art of reading, writing and arithmetic, but better general mental development; the acquisition of better tastes, of mental amusements, and enjoyments, which are cheaper while they are more refined."

The same Report contains the evidence of many English Manufacturers to the same effect, and also the Report to the Secretary of State for the Home Department on the Training of Pauper Children, 1841.

The same causes produce the same effect among the labouring population of the manufacturing towns in the United States.

In 1841, the Secretary of the Massachusetts Board of Education made a labourious inquiry into the comparative productiveness of the labour of the educated and uneducated manufacturing operatives in that State. The substance of the answers of the manufacturers, and business men to whom he applied, is as follows: "The result of the investigation is the most astonishing superiority in productive power on the part of the educated over the uneducated labourer. The hand is found to be another hand when guided by an intelligent mind. Processes are performed not only more rapidly, but better, when faculties that have been cultivated in early life furnish their assistance. Individuals, who, without the aid of knowledge, would have been condemned to perpetual inferiority of condition and subjected to all the evils of want and poverty, rise to competence and independence by the uplifting power of education. In great establishments, and among large bodies of labouring men, where all services are rated according to their pecuniary value, there is it found as an almost invariable fact, other things being equal, that those who have been blessed with a good Common School Education, rise to a higher and higher point in the kinds of labour performed, and also in the rate of wages paid, while the ignorant sink like dregs to the bottom."

From the preceding facts, may be inferred the importance of a sound Common School Education, among even the lowest class of agriculturalists and mechanics, in respect both to employers and the employed.

'PROGRESS' DEBATED AND THE COSTS OF REFORM ASSESSED

ON TEACHERS AND THE COSTS OF IMPROVEMENT

'Memorial to the Legislature of the Gore District Council against the Common School Act of 1846', in J. G. Hodgins, ed., *Documentary History of Education in Upper Canada* (Toronto, 1894-1910), vol. 7, pp. 114-16.

TO THE HONOURABLE THE LEGISLATIVE ASSEMBLY, IN PROVINCIAL PARLIAMENT ASSEMBLED:

The Memorial of the Gore District Municipal Council: Respectfully sheweth:

That, from the great dissatisfaction manifested throughout this District with the new School Act of 1846, and feeling deeply sensible of the importance of a system of Elementary Instruction suited to the wants of the people, Your Memorialists are induced to bring the subject under the notice of Your Honourable Body, with a view to obtain, by legislative enactment, such modification of the said Act, as will simplify its provisions and render it less expensive in its operations, or otherwise, the substitution for it of the Act repealed by the Act of 1843, i.e., that of 1841:—4th and 5th Victoria, Chapter XVIII, with such amendments, as will, in conformity with the Municipality Act, secure these results. . . .

4. Your Memorialists would . . . beg leave to represent that the sums required to pay a Provincial Superintendent . . . a Clerk and the contingencies of his Office, amounting, as is supposed, to some Eight or Nine Hundred pounds (£900) as well as those paid to twenty District Superintendents of Schools, which will, if all are paid in proportion to that Officer in this District, amount to Three Thousand pounds (£3,000) more, making the whole fall little short of Four Thousand pounds (£4,000) per annum, would, in the opinion of your Memorialists, be more profitably employed in the payment of Common School Teachers.

5. With reference to a Normal School, containing one, or more, Elementary Model Schools, established by the Fifth Section of the School Act of 1846, Your Memorialists find, that the sum of Fifteen Hundred pounds (£1,500,) are appropriated to procuring and furnishing the necessary Building, and a like sum for the payment of Teachers' salaries, and other contingent expenses; besides which, it is stated by the Chief Superintendent, in the Special Report already alluded to, that "the experience of other Countries, similarly situated to ours, sufficiently shows how much the current expenses of such an Establishment must exceed the sum granted to aid in defraying them,"—thus showing, that the large sum of Three Thousand pounds (£3,000,) are taken from the Common School Funds for the current year, and the sum of Fifteen Hundred pounds, (£1,500,) with as much more as the current expenses will exceed the latter amount, will be required, annually thereafter, for the maintenance of this department of tuition, without, as Your Memorialists most seri-

ously believe, any benefit being derived by the community from an outlay of such magnitude.

6. With respect to the necessity of establishing a Normal, with Elementary Model Schools, in this Province, Your Memorialists are of opinion, that, however well adapted such an Institution might be to the wants of the old and densely populated Countries of Europe, where services in almost every vocation will scarcely yield the common necessaries of life, they are, (so far as this object expected to be gained, is concerned) altogether unsuited to a Country like Upper Canada, where a young man of such excellent character, as a candidate is required to be, by the National Board of Education in Ireland, to enter a Normal School, (page 56 of the Special Report,) and having the advantage of a good education besides, need only turn to the right hand, or to the left, to make his services much more agreeable and profitable to himself, than in the drudgery of a Common School, at a salary of Twenty-nine Pounds (£29) per annum, which is the average amount paid School Teachers in Upper Canada for the year 1845, as set forth in Appendix Number 2, to the Special Report, nor do Your Memorialists hope to provide qualified Teachers by any other means, in the present circumstances of the Country, than by securing, as heretofore, the services of those, whose Physical Disabilities, from age, render this mode of obtaining a livelihood the only one suited to their Decaying Energies, or by employing such of the newly arrived Emigrants, as are qualified, for Common School Teachers, year by year as they come amongst us, and who will adopt this as a means of temporary support, until their character and abilities are known, and turned to better account for themselves. . . .

8. Your Memorialists would, therefore, pray, that Your Honourable Body would be graciously pleased to take the premises into consideration, and adopt such mode of relief, as to Your Honourable Body may seem fit; and your Memorialists, as in duty bound, will ever pray.

JAMES LITTLE, Chairman.

JOHN WHITE,

Hamilton, 10th November, 1847   FRANCIS CAMERON, Councillors.

THE DISTRICT OF COLBORNE REPLIES

Extracts from the Minutes of the Municipal Council of the Colborne District, passed on Tuesday, February 8th, 1848, *Education Papers*, RG 2 C-6-C, Public Archives of Ontario.

The Standing Committee on Common Schools, to whom was referred *"The Memorial of the Municipal Council of the Gore District to the Legislative Assembly, on the Subject of Common Schools."*

Beg leave to report: —

"That Your Committee, having maturely considered the objects contemplated in the memorial of the Municipal Council of the Gore District, and the reasons offered therein for the alterations in the present school law, desired by the Memorialists, are of opinion that it is not expedient that your Honourable Council should commit itself to the course recommended by the Memorialists; namely, to co-operate with the other District Councils throughout the province, in endeavouring to procure the repeal of the existing School Act, and the revival of the Acts repealed by the 4th and 5th Victoria, Chapter 18."

"Your Committee beg leave respectively [sic] to add, that they conceive the provisions of the Acts proposed to be revived so inapplicable to the present circumstances of this Province, the powers conferred by them so inadequate, and the means they provide as agents or instruments for carrying on the great work of popular Education so disproportioned to the results expected and needed by the people, that the amendments which must be either now introduced into them, or which a very short practical experience of their working would show to be indispensable, would produce a mass of Legislation much more "unwieldy and complicated" than the law for which it is proposed to substitute them."

"However desirable it may be to have "Simple and cheap" enactments for the conduct and support of Schools, it is much more essential that these enactments should also be efficient; and that they should so provide for the control and expenditure of the public money, the supervision of the schools, and above all, the adequate supply of competent and well-trained *Teachers*, as that the rising generation of Upper Canada may be prepared at least to make some near approach to that place in the social scale which their more intelligent, because better educated neighbours now threaten to monopolise. That the youth of the rural districts of this fine Province are much behind the age, and that this inferiority is *solely* owing to the defective systems of public instruction with which the people have been urged to remain content, are mournful facts which no one can deny, and which read but a sorry comment on the Laws the Memorialists propose to revive."

"That the moneys required to pay for the establishment and support of Normal and Model Schools are little less than a waste of so much of the Legislative Grant," is an opinion in which Your Committee are so far from concurring, that they believe it is from these sources must mainly arise the instrumentality through which the friends of education can alone hope for the first considerable amelioration of the evils they lament, and they can only regret that the great benefits they anticipate from these institutions must necessarily be tardy in their operation. Nor can Your Committee reconcile it either with their just expectations, or their sense of duty, to rest satisfied with "the services of those whose physical disabilities from age and decaying energies" render them unfit, or of those "newly arrived emigrants" whose unknown "character and abilities" render them unable to procure a livelihood by any other means than by becoming the preceptors of our children, the dictators of their sentiments and manners, the guardians of their virtue, and in a high degree, the masters of their future destinies in this world and the next."

"Your Committee are of opinion, from the best information they have been able to collect, that "the dissatisfaction manifested throughout the Gore District with the new school Act," is far from being general in other parts of the Province, and that on the contrary, as the existing Law becomes better understood; as the difficulties in most cases imaginary, which at first interfered with the proper discharge of the duties of Trustees, are explained or dispelled; as an enlightened public opinion shall gradually be brought to bear on the parts assigned to visitors and District Superintendents, impelling them to a more vigorous and effective discharge of the important trust confided to them; as the Normal and Model Schools begin to yield their legitimate fruits; and as the blighting effects of employing men as School Teachers who are neither in manners nor in intellectual endowments, much above the lowest menials, shall press less and less heavily upon the mental and moral habitudes of the rising generation, the great benefits to be derived from the present Common School Act, and its immense superiority over all former school laws of Upper Canada, will become more and more confessed and appreciated. Already that public apathy which is the deadliest enemy to improvement, is slowly yielding to the necessity imposed by the present law upon Trustees and others of acquiring extended information; of entering with a deeper interest into all matters connected with Common Schools; and of joining with visitors, superintendents and Municipal Councillors in a more active and vigilant oversight of them. It should not be considered a too sanguine anticipation to look confidently forward to a period not very distant, when the admirable machinery of the present law,—its active and zealous Chief Superintendent, its Normal and Model Schools, its District and Township School Libraries, its visitors and Trustees, shall begin to produce in Upper Canada the mighty intellectual and moral reformation which similar institutions have already effected in other lands: but it is quite too much to expect that in an existence of little more than one year, with many of its most important agencies yet in embryo, and others totally inoperative, in the face of prejudices, against much ignorant and some wilful opposition, amongst a population in many places as unprepared to comprehend as to accept its advantages, that under such circumstances it could already have produced results at all commensurate with the pecuniary expense of its first introduction. . . .

all which is respectfully submitted.

Municipal Council Chamber,	(Signed) Thos. Benson
8th February 1848.	Chairman.

TEACHERS ON THEIR OWN IMPROVEMENT

D. P. Macdonald to Egerton Ryerson, July 1850. *Education Papers*, RG 2 C-6-C, Public Archives of Ontario.

The second part of the Resolutions adopted by the School Association of the Eastern District.

Resolved ...

2nd.—That the present distribution of the School Fund does not give general satisfaction; for the reasons that large Schools, though less in need get greater sums, while small Sections and remote Schools receive only a few dollars: the Government Grant wherefore, should be equally divided among Schools, in proportion to the length of time each School being kept open; and the Amount of School tax raised in each Section, should be paid by the Collector to the Teacher of the same on the Trustees' order.

3rd.—That the Conferences to be observed by the School Association, are intended for the good of Education; the necessary time therefore required to attend such conferences or Quarterly Meetings should be allowed to Teachers by Law, as the Vacations are now granted them; and the Officers of the Committee should be allowed some compensation, for attending the same in the discharge of their official duties.

4th.—That in this part of the Country there are always more pains and trouble taken in order to make warm and comfortable stables for horses than to see if School Houses are fit for the purpose, because it is a general belief that all the necessary furniture required for a School House consists in a few stools, a desk or two nailed to the wall without any regard to the size of the children, and a stove. It is visible that no order can be observed in a school room furnished in that manner; and that the progress shall be equally defective: consequently, no public money should be granted to any School Section, without having a School House furnished according to a plan adopted by Government and a dwelling house for the Teacher.

5th.—That the local Superintendent of Schools should act in the administration of the duties of his office, without any distinction of either high or low, rich or poor, radical, tory or any one else, with the same independence and impartiallity [sic] which are required of the Judge on the Bench, and that it is not to be expected that an Officer appointed on a political test, (as all the Officers of the District Council are) whose tenure of Office depends upon his acting in compliance with the whims and fancies of his superiors, can act, let him be ever so well disposed, with that manly upright integrity which is so indispensably required of a Superintendent of Schools. In order to be clear of these impediments, the Local Superintendent should be appointed by Government; and a suitable salary granted him, independent of both the people and the Council.

6th.—That the average of Scholars attending each School in this District is about 34; and that it is proved by experience that the more children there are in one School the easier it is to keep up emulation which is also proved to be the soul and essence of teaching; the School Sections therefore, should be enlarged: by following the Rules of the School Association 50 or 60 Scholars in each School would not be too many.

7th.—That the average salary, now allowed to each Teacher in this District, is about £23. per annum—; and that a Lumber-Man could not get a cook to hire in his shanty for less than that wages: it is therefore plain, that . . . something must be done by the present Ministry in order to better the condition of Teachers. If the salary of School Masters is left as at present at the discretion of foolish Mothers, and ignorant Parents in general, it is in vain to establish Model Schools or School Associations, and in particular, it is the greatest folly to grant any public money for the use of Common Schools; and it is equally useless to lose time in passing Laws for general Education: therefore, the annual salary of Teachers should be stipulated by Government at £50." for the lowest and higher according to merit.

8th.—That dupes and dunces cannot carry out the benefits and improvements contemplated by the School Association; and that those possessing the necessary talents cannot be had, unless a suitable provision is made for them by Government; and that no Teacher can do his duty properly without having both his whole soul, mind, and body, present in the School room during school hours, unmolested by any care or trouble: for these considerations, and in order that the country should receive the full benefit of general education, Common Schools should be established, as regarding their pecuniary affairs, on a plan similar to that of the Parochial Schools of Scotland, which could be easily effected by adopting Doctor Ryerson's plan of supporting Schools according to property—or by setting aside a tract of the wild lands of the country, in order to do away entirely with the existing School Tax.
Revd Doctor

The Resolutions of which the annexed are copies were duly adopted along with the Constitution of the School Association; I am therefore ordered by the Committee of the same to submit them to your discretion.

Rev.d Sir,

St. Raphaels July 9th, 1850   with the greatest respect,

D. P. McDonald,

Chairman of the School

Association

EGERTON RYERSON ON THE NEED FOR CENTRAL CONTROL

Egerton Ryerson to Members of the Government, 14 July 1849. 'The Abortive School Legislation of 1849' in J. G. Hodgins, ed., *Documentary History of Education in Upper Canada* (Toronto, 1894-1910), vol. 8, pp. 235-43.

. . . 3. It has been my endeavour, from the beginning, to increase the powers, and render more simple and easy the duties of Trustees, and more certain and prompt the payment of Teachers' salaries, as is evinced in each of my three and unpublished Reports, or Communications, sent by me to the Provincial Secretary for the consideration of the Governor General-in-Council, on the Common School Law for Upper Canada. The provisions of the Cameron Bill are of a directly opposite character.... Indeed, so discouraging is the future, presented to Teachers by the provisions of this new Bill, that an old and experienced Teacher called upon me, a short time since, to know on what terms his son could be admitted for a short period to the Normal School as a paid pupil,—stating that he had intended to prepare his son for his own profession of teaching and had intended to send him to Normal School for that purpose; but so dark were the prospects presented to Teachers by the proposed new School law, that he intended to qualify his son for business. In each of my School Law Reports and Communications, I have remarked upon the hardships of Trustees under the present law, and pointed out the means and necessity of lessening them; but the new Bill increases them. And it appears to me unjust to impose upon certain men the obligation, under a penalty, of assuming the duties of Trustees, allowing them no remuneration for their trouble, as are Municipal Councillors, and yet, restricting their powers and burdening them with additional forms and conditions, in the performance of their duties....

4. The proposed new Bill abolishes the present Boards of Trustees for Cities and Incorporated Towns,—annihilates the system of Schools commenced in several Towns, and re-establishes the old system, which the entire experience of America has shown to be incapable of establishing any more than the lowest class of isolated Common Schools,—making no provision whatever for a system, or gradation, of Schools in any Town, or City, as primary, intermediate, and high Schools, such as are founded in every City and considerable Town in the neighbouring States. It is true, that little has been done in our Cities and Towns in comparison of what might, or ought to, have been done; but it is also true that much more has been done in all the Cities and Incorporated Towns in Upper Canada, (Toronto alone excepted,) under the School Act of 1847, than under any former law, notwithstanding the omission of a provision to impose Rate-Bills,—the cause of which I explained to you when in Montreal last Autumn. It is also to be observed, that Corporations of several Towns have made a noble commencement in the erection of proper School-Houses, and establishing a proper system of Schools. In Hamilton, fourteen school-lots have been obtained in different wards of the City, and steps have been taken to erect as many fine School-Houses. In St. Catharines, I understand, the erection of a large Central School, with several departments, has been projected. In Brantford, such an erection has been determined upon; and a Member of the Corporation was lately deputed to come to Toronto and procure from me suitable plans, which I was enabled to recommend. In the Town of London, such a Building, capable of accommodating 600 children, in different departments, under different Teachers, but the whole under the

direction of a Head Master, has already been commenced. The apportionment of the Legislative Grant to the Town of London for the current year, is little more than £100, but the voluntary, self-imposed School-tax exceeds £700— One or Two Hundred pounds more than the amount of the School assessment of the large City of Toronto! These facts are presages of better times for the youth of our Towns, if such noble efforts are not crushed in the bud by the introduction of this new School Bill, which, without a single Petition from any quarter, and without a single word of notice, or explanation, in the Legislature, sweeps the present City and Town School Law of 1847 from the Statute-Book, and dooms the friends of improved Education in our Cities and Towns to disappointment, defeat and disgust.

5. The new Bill abolishes all that has been done under the present Act to introduce an uniform series of excellent Text-Books into the Schools,—annuls the authority of the Provincial Board of Education to recommend Text-Books for the Schools, and places that authority in a great number of County Boards, to be appointed by the Crown. The use of an uniform and suitable series of Text-Books is one of the most important features of a good School System, and the most difficult of establishment. Yet, in less than three years, has a series of Text-Books, unrivalled for excellence and cheapness, been introduced into a considerable majority of the Common Schools of Upper Canada, and that, without the prohibition of other Books, or the exercise of arbitrary authority, but, by simple recommendation, and providing facilities to make them known and accessible to all parts of the Province. I know of no instance of such success on this point, even during the period of five years, in any State, or Province, of Europe, or America. But the Cameron Bill, not only denudes the Provincial Board of Education of the power thus so beneficially exercised, but does not provide for the continued authorization of the Text-Books already recommended, until others are authorized. To the proceedings of the Board of Education for Upper Canada, in regard both to the Normal School and Text-Books for the Common Schools generally, I have heard not one whisper of opposition, or dissatisfaction, from any part of Canada, yet, without a petition, without a single reason assigned in the Legislature, are the two years' labours of the Provincial Board in regard to Text-Books, dashed to the ground, the Schools throughout Upper Canada, on the first day of January, 1850, are left without an authorized Text-Book, and are opened to the introduction of every kind of book-trash, which itinerant vendors, and their dupes and agents, may supply until the contemplated local Boards become organized and prepared for action,—which will not be much before the end of the year. Besides, no provision is made in this Bill to defray the expenses of these projected Local Boards. Not a farthing is provided to enable them to procure specimen Text-Books, to conduct their proceedings, or give effect to any of their recommendations. They are to make bricks without straw.

The idea, or hope, of having an uniform series of Text-Books in the Schools, when their use is dependent on the sanction of twenty-five independent Local Boards is, of course, preposterous; and I have sufficiently explained, in my last interview with you, how inferior are the advantages of any Local Board for ascertaining, and recommending and providing facilities for procuring suitable Text-Books, in comparison of what are possessed by a Provincial Board, and the Chief Superintendent of Schools. I have also explained to you the great importance of the principle acted upon in other Countries, that the authorities managing the Normal School, or Schools for a State, recommend the Books used in the Schools of such State, and, for the obvious reason, that the Books used in the Normal, and its Model, School, ought to be used in the Common Schools, and that it is of great advantage for Teachers to be trained in the proper mode of using such Books, as well as to have some knowledge of the character of the Books composing the Common School Libraries,—copies of which should, of course, constitute part of the Library of the Normal School, and characteristic notices of which should be given in some of the Normal School Lectures.

6. The only way in which a State, or National, System of Schools can be established and maintained in connection with local popular institutions, is, by the Executive authority making the General Regulations, and being able to secure their observance by means of the distribution, and a veto power in the application of the Legislature School Grant, or State Fund, in aid of Schools. This is provided for at every point, and, in the most efficient manner in the School Law of each of the neighbouring States, where there is a State System of Schools. This is completely provided for in the National School System in Ireland. It is provided for, to a limited extent, in the present School Law of Upper Canada; but the new Bill, as is shown in a previous Communication, precludes, by its financial provisions, all possibility of a Provincial School System, and appears to render the office of Provincial Superintendent, to a great extent, nugatory. Indeed I am credibly informed, that the original Draft of the Bill provided for the abolition of that Office; and the whole Bill seems to have been constructed with that view. . . .

9. There are yet two other provisions of the new Bill to which I must direct your particular attention: Both of these provisions were introduced, as amendments, at the last moment, and without any previous notice, when the Bill was being passed through the Committee of the House at a galloping speed. The one places the duties of my Office under the direction of the Provincial Board of Education; the other proscribes all Books from the Schools containing "controverted theological dogmas, or doctrines." If the provision to make the Superintendent a Servant of the Board of Education, is not designed to be practical, it must then be intended merely to gratify the enmity of certain individuals against the present Incumbent, by placing him in a comparatively humiliated position, and denuding his Office of the standing and influence which it now possesses. But if this provision is designed to be practical,—as I think it must be assumed,—then, it is liable to the following additional objections:

(1). It subjects every decision, every Letter, every act, every part of the proceedings of the Superintendent to the embarrassment, delay, and perplexity of a discussion in a Board. I know the operation of this system in the comparatively limited Correspondence and local matters relating to the Normal School,—where, I think, it is unavoidable and necessary. In such a Board of weekly meeting and discussion, one unfriendly person can render the official life of a Provincial Superintendent disgusting and miserable, and no situation can afford better opportunities for intrigue against him. If he gives any advice, or performs any mission, or duty in any part of the Province, there will not be wanting persons to assail him in private letters to individual Members of the Board,—especially to any individual Member known to be unfriendly to the Superintendent; and, thus, the whole course of his labours may be embittered as well as embarrassed. I speak on this point from experience, in the more limited affairs of the Normal and Model Schools.

(2). It is at variance with all precedent. There is not an instance in any State in America, much less in Europe, of a State Superintendent, or Commissioner, of Public Schools, or Minister of Public Instruction, being placed under a Board of unofficial, and, therefore, of irresponsible persons. . . .

(3). This feature of the Cameron School Bill withholds from the administration of the Common School System the application of the principle of responsibility, which is applied to every other Department of the Public Service in Canada. An unsalaried Board is not a responsible Body; nor can its Members be supposed to devote, without remuneration, the requisite time and study necessary to become acquainted with all the interests and questions involved in the administration of so important a system. A salaried Superintendent is responsible, like that of any other Government Officer. He has the stimulus of such responsibility, on the one hand, and the protection of a responsible Government, on the other; and the principle of "Responsible Government" is applied to him and to his Department, the same as to other Public Officers, and their Departments. . . .

These [criticisms] appear to have been the anticipations of extreme partizans, in respect to myself, and my labours. . . . But they are a little too late, as it respects myself. Had they acted twelve months sooner, they might have realized their wishes. At that time I had no statistics, no official facts whatever, to prove that my plans were not the vagaries of a "visionary schemer." But, since that time, not only have the pages of the *Journal of Education* developed my views to a large portion of the public, but two Annual Reports have been prepared, and are within the last week in print; and, to the numerous facts and testimonies contained in these documents, I now fearlessly appeal as to the practical character and success of the School System and Measures which I have adopted and recommended. To the statements and opinions of several District School Superintendents,—as given in my School Report for last year, 1848—as to both the acceptableness and efficiency of the general provisions of even the present School Law in the estimation of those who have had most experience of it,—I appeal, as of more weight than the notions of the projectors of the new Bill. . . .

It is neither my right, nor wish, to presume to dictate to the Government as to its Measures, or proceedings. But, I think it is my right, and only frank and respectful on the earliest occasion, to state, in regard to my own humble labours, whether I can serve on terms and principles and conditions so different from those under which I have, up to the present time, acted; though I cannot, without deep regret and emotion, contemplate the loss of so much time and labour, and find myself impelled to abandon a work on which I had set my heart, and to qualify myself for which I have devoted four of the most matured years of my life. All that I have desired of the Government is that which I have respectfully suggested in the first remark of my Communication of the 12th May last; namely, that, before demolishing the present Common School system of Upper Canada, the Government would inquire into its character—its working and results, by a Commission, or otherwise, and hear the statements and opinions of different men and parties of much experience and varied information on the subject.

The reasons why the spirit which originated the Cameron Bill dreaded the light of such investigation, are quite obvious. But, if the convenience of the people and the Common School interest of the Country are not worth so much attention and trouble on the part of the Government, I grieve for the educational future of Upper Canada. Had the Government thought proper to institute such an inquiry, either before, or during, the last Session of the Legislature; or, had it seen fit, (seeing that it, declined adopting the short School Bill submitted by me in) to defer legislation altogether on the subject until the next Session, as the present School Act could be administered for six or nine months, under the new Municipal system, as well as under the present, and, in the mean time, have instituted an inquiry into the principles and working of the present School Law, and the changes necessary to amend and perfect it, I believe the result would have been as honourable and gratifying to the Government, as beneficial to the country.

Having now fulfilled my promise, to communicate to you, in writing, my views on this important and extensive subject, I leave the whole question in your hands.

ADVOCATES OF LOCAL CONTROL REPLY

Newspaper Clippings, *Education Papers*, RG 2 T, Public Archives of Ontario. *Examiner*, 26 December 1849.

What are Mr. Ryerson's objections to the new bill? Why, that it places in the hands of the people the power to manage their school affairs; that it knocks on the head the system of centralization, which enabled Dr. Ryerson, under the shadow of two or three stool pigeons dignified with the name of the "Provincial Board of Education," to dictate to the whole of Upper Canada what books should be used in the schools, and prohibit the use of any that did not chime in with his whims, taste, prejudices, bigotry, or superstition. A high and mighty crime has the introducer of the new school bill committed against his Imperial Mightiness, Egerton the Great. That it abolishes the visitorial system; permits Township Councils to assist schools, in poor sections, by pecuniary aid; gives no power to Municipal Councils to establish common school libraries; are some of the grave objections urged against the measure by Mr. Ryerson. But we suspect that the greatest objection, after all, is, that it gives the Superintendent only $420, instead of £500, a year, as under the present Act. The modesty of the meek Superintendent prevented from including this in his list of objections. We shall examine his objections seriatim, and endeavour to find out their exact gravity and force:

1.—"The new law repeals the very law by which Legislative aid is now granted to Common Schools in Upper Canada."

The "Legislative aid" depended upon parliamentary vote, and if it was omitted last session, the omission was wholly independent of the new School Act. The new School Act did not take from Parliament the power to vote the appropriation.

2.—"It makes no provision whatever for enabling Municipal Councils to establish Common School libraries."

The Act empowers the Trustees to "select from a list of books which shall have been made out by the Board of Education for their County, the books that shall be used in their school." This, of course, includes all the books necessary for common school purposes. What does the Dr. want more? The establishing of libraries in Townships is a matter altogether apart from supplying the schools with books. If the Municipal Councils have not power to establish them, it is an omission of the Municipal Act. And the establishment of such libraries is entirely a new question. No previous school bill contained any provision of the kind; and although Mr. Ryerson has picked up the notion that we must have them just now, a whole people may not be ready to take up his crotchets at a moment's warning.

3.—"It makes no provision whatever for enabling the contemplated County Boards to perform the duties imposed upon them."

So Mr. Ryerson says. What are the facts? The Act authorizes the County Boards to examine candidates for the office of Teacher, and to grant certificates authorizing them to teach; to annul certificates given by any former Board, or by the Master of the Normal School, if just cause appear for doing so; to select and recommend proper books for the use of schools in the Country, and to cause a list of the books they select to be sent to each Township; to keep a record of their proceedings, and to report annually in the month of July to the Superintendent for Upper Canada, giving a statement of their proceedings and such suggestions as they think proper. These powers are conferred and duties enjoined by the Act. What higher authority or supplementary "provisions" they require, the learned Superintendent has neglected to specify; and yet he tells us there is no "provision" to enable them to perform their duties.

4.—"It provides no security or means by which the diversion, in any case, of any part of the Legislative school grant from the object contemplated by the Legislative can be prevented."

This objection is a pure, and withal a very ridiculous invention. If the money should be applied to any other purpose than that "contemplated by the Legislature," the parties so diverting the fund, would be guilty of a breach of trust, and liable to the penalties of the law for the offence.

5.—"It provides none of the means essential to acquiring the needful information in regard to any matters relating to the operations or administration of the law, or the expenditure of monies, in particular cases in any Township in Upper Canada,—as it does not authorize even the slightest correspondence on either side between the Provincial Superintendent and any Township Superintendent, leaving the Provincial Superintendent no means whatever of acquiring local information of any kind, except by application to the Clerks of the County Council."

There is no particular law authorizing a Highlander who has emigrated to Canada, to correspond with his grandmother; but he never thinks of asking for such "authority;" nor does the want of it give him any trouble. If any Township Superintendent should ask the Chief Superintendent for "needful information in regard to any matters relating to the operations or administration of the school law;" does Mr. Ryerson tell us that he has no "authority" to reply? Would he violate the law or overstep the bounds of his duty by replying? "No essential means of acquiring information." Why, the Township, Towns, and City Superintendents are all required to report annually on nearly every matter connected with the schools, to the local Municipalities; the County Boards have to report annually to the Provincial Superintendent; and every Teacher has to report to the Township, Town, and City Superintendent in the form prescribed by the Provincial Superintendent. The Trustees are also required to report fully every year, in forms prescribed by him.—Penalties are attached to the non-performance of this duty. Does all this machinery afford "no means of acquiring information? What would Mr. Ryerson have? Almost every one connected with the schools, except the children has to report; and yet one of the greatest complaints he can trump up against the bill is that it affords "no means of acquiring information!"

This is the whole catalogue of omissions complained of by Mr. Ryerson. That they are the merest trumpery may be seen at a glance.

Then comes a further list of objections from Mr. Ryerson, which he classes as 'injurious provisions.'

The first of these is, to our mind, the great recommendation of the Act. It decentralizes the whole system, takes the absolutist power out of Mr. Ryerson's hand, and distributes the authority equitably and fairly amongst the people. It substitutes for the Central Board of Education, of which Mr. Ryerson was virtually body and soul, a Board in every County, and places in the hands of each Board the power of choosing books for their County. The loss of this dictatorial power, and of £80 salary, are severe afflictions that have sunk deep into the soul of the Superintendent. It is of this popularizing, this un-Prussianizing of the system that Mr. Ryerson complains. The pedagogucic [sic] despot is dethroned. To the people their suspended rights have been restored. Hinc illae lachrymae. Mr. Ryerson is, therefore, of opinion that the manner of choosing and excluding books is fraught with very serious consequences.

Of the abolition of the visitorial system also he complains. Mr. Ryerson has selected this as a point on which to get up a little feeling, to excite a little prejudice, and to inflame the ambition of ministers of the various denominations. These gentlemen have now as much right in the schools as any other class, and cannot justly complain that they are not elevated at the expense of others.—What the priests do in Lower Canada is not to the point. If the system there be bad, it is but an ill recommendation for us to become its copyists.—We never wish to see sectarianism in any shape, exercising its unhealthy influence in our national schools; and we are confident that the general desire is opposed to clerical interference. Let the ministers visit the schools, by all means, if they desire, but give them no power over the Teachers. . . .

Mr. Ryerson's idea of a school bill may be expressed in one word—compulsion! An Act that places power in the hands of the people, is of all things in the world most hateful to him. Hence his assaults on the new School Act. His objections when approached and closely scrutinized, vanish into air. They are mere figments of the imagination, or the production of an inventive genius. The Act may not be faultless: no human production is; but amongst the objectionable ministerial acts of last session we certainly do not rank the School Bill. Yet it is to be tomahawked at the dictation of Mr. Ryerson, with whose services the ministry could not dispense when he tendered his resignation.

Huron Signal, 24 January 1850.
DR. RYERSON AND THE NEW SCHOOL ACT
"The new Act contains provision relating to the ground and manner of admitting into and excluding books from the schools which appear to me fraught with the most injurious and painful consequences, and to which I DO NOT WISH TO MAKE FURTHER REFERENCE in this place." This is Dr. RYERSON'S sixth POSITIVE error of the New School Act, and we appeal to any man of ordinary intelligence, to say, if it is entitled to any further consideration than that generally given to an anonymous libel. . . .

Cant and Quackery are two words which are not exclusively confined to the vending of spurious medicine, and we only wish they were less applicable to this objection of Dr. RYERSON. In order, however, that our readers may be able to judge for themselves, we give the words of the Act as follows:

"Thirdly. To select and recommend proper books for the use of the Public Schools of their County, and to cause a list of such books as they shall select to be sent to each Township, Town and City Superintendent of Schools in their County, for his guidance and direction: Provided always, that no person attending any public School shall be required to read or study any book containing controverted theological dogmas or doctrines."

Here, then, is all that the Act says about admitting or excluding books, and we ask any reasonable man what "injurious and painful consequences" could possibly result from the authority here given to the County Boards of Education? Are we to be insulted by being told that there are not seven men in the County of Huron, just as capable of making a judicious selection of books for the schools of their own County as any seven men in Toronto? Or, if the present school books are so very superior to all others (and we believe they are unexceptionable), can it be supposed that the County Boards would be so wretchedly stupid as to supercede the use of them, by introducing an inferior class? This, we are certain, is not one of the "painful consequences" to which Dr. RYERSON alludes. There is something in the decline of power—something in the breaking of a circle of which one forms the center, that is far more painful than the mere changing of school books. . . .

We have now gone over the whole of the Rev. Chief Superintendent's objections to the New School Act. . . . And we are truly gratified to learn that notwithstanding Dr. RYERSON'S "Circular," the New Act has gone into operation in every Township, and we believe in every school section in the United Counties of Huron, Perth and Bruce. So far as we have been able to learn, the "Circular" and the Act as it stands, were presented to the various School Meetings held throughout the Counties on the eighth instant, and without a single exception the decision was given in favor of "the Law of the Land." The people of Upper Canada cherish too much respect for responsible Government, and for those who administer it, and are too intimately acquainted with the principles and sentiments of Dr. RYERSON, to pay the slightest deference to any mandate which he may put forth. We understand that a circular has issued from the Inspector General's Office to the several District Superintendents throughout the Province, requesting information in reference to several provisions of the new Act, and more especially as regards the duties of the contemplated County Boards. We are not opposed to a reconsideration of the new School Act, and we think there is wisdom in the act of the Government in endeavoring to obtain the fullest information on the subject. But we doubt if the District Superintendents are the purest source from which such information can be obtained. They are a part of Mr. RYERSON's favorite machinery, and we believe that many of them are under his immediate control, and consequently opposed to the men and measures of the present Administration. We fear it is, to a considerable extent a literal consulting of the enemy. And, as a feeble, but a faithful, friend of the Administration, we take the liberty of stating our honest conviction, that if the powers conferred by the new Act, on the County Boards are diminished, or any other popular provision of the Act interfered with at the suggestion of EGERTON RYERSON or his party, the real supporters of the Government will not feel complimented thereby.

PROBLEMS ON THE LOCAL SCENE

Aaron Zelner and Abraham O. Clemens to Egerton Ryerson, July 20, 1859. *Education Papers*, RG 2 C-6-C, Public Archives of Ontario.

Waterloo July the 20th 1859

By this pressent opertunity I will drop a few lines about our school afairs by the way the case stands we are in a way to loose our portion of this fund Due now as they will make us belive so but I think we are intitled of it if we are if we get our just due we had intended to keep the School open all the year and had hired Aaron Ely and he was a qualified Teacher The Latter end of April he took a notion to travel through som parts of the States and Left our school then we did not know where to get at that time so som peopel introduced Mrs Mary Bowman and that they thought that she had qualification to keep any School which I find is positively so she has a good and moral carachter for she was raised in this place about 3 years ago She went to Western Ville Ohio to the school and had returned this spring but to take for the examination She went to the local superintindent to get examined But he did not examine her and told her that she might keep the school so untill the Board met again then she went to the examination and undertook to get the second Class but did not succeed She say that they would not Grant any Certificate to any and only to those that got their education in Canada but the Act Dont provide for that So we have no one to sign his name to the Return We had a large School this summer for the last six months an average atendence of 42 one fraction less but if this is the way it will ruin our school but I hope you will humbly deal with us for I think it is a just portion that is due to us We have the honor to be, Sir

Your most obiedient Servant,

The Honorable
E. Ryerson

Aaron Zelner) Trustees
Abraham O Clemens)

N. B. Plies send au
letter as soon as
this comes to your
hand to
Preston Poste office
Aaron Zelner
Waterloo C.W.
To be referred to the Local Supt. [In another handwriting—obviously added by Ryerson.]

THE 'PRUSSIAN SYSTEM' UPHELD

I. D. Hageman to Egerton Ryerson, 11 February 1865. *Education Papers*, RG 2 C-6-C, no. 1403-65, Public Archives of Ontario.

Caledon Febr 11th, 1865

Rev. E Ryerson, Chief Supt Canada Schools
Toronto
Dear Sir!

Some few years ago I mentioned to you divers defects existing in the U.C. School Law & System viz 1) The arbitrary school district Lines. 2) the unjust distribution of the two school grants; Municipal and Legislative where the populus Districts are getting the Lyon share of the Grants because as chance would happen in their favor that they could send more Children to School than those sections where the population is sparse or where the Children are debarred from attending School by the brokenness of the Country, Swamps, Rivers, etc. 3) That Children so situated attending an adjoining or more convenient section are only admitted there by the grace of the Trustees and then provided the School House is not overcrowded by the Children of their own section in fact they can if they choose reject all outsiders not belonging to the section.

Now I have been Trustee of Caledon S.S. No. 4 for 9 years but on account of the great distance from our School House the Trustees have admitted my children to attend Chinguacousy S.S. No. 8) theirs. Ours and theirs are free Schools, but not for me. I have to pay $3.—a year for every child I send there this is the case with two more Familys in our section. You see the Tyranical and arbitrary working of the School District Lines.

Our School section is very unfortunate situated having swamps & the River Cridit and that not bridged on the whole of the N.W. side of the section which debarrs a large number of poor Families of sending their children to the school it greives me always when I have to call upon them for their School tax and as it happens all the well to do Farmers live within easy distance from the School House and the poor ones not; some other rough and sparsely settled School sections hire a cheap and unqualified female Teacher who boards round It appears (on reading the Journal of Education of July 1864) that the schools in the U. States were cursed also with these district School lines restrictions, but begin to do away with them please read Mr. W. C. Larrabee's Indiana School report page 99, but I *dont* understand Mr. Hodgins speach made at the Teachers association Meeting August 2 3 & 4th at Toronto, where he said that he travells a good deal in the U. States examined and inquired into their School systems and that he considered it inferior to our own that our System was the *best in the world* (I suppose he included the Prussion system too.) but it wanted one Improvement viz to do away with the multiplication of Schools in the Townships. and *no* smaller School limits made than those of a *full* Township now Mr. Hodgins says he travelled much in the U.S. but does not say that he travelled any in Canada there fore I take it for granted he is ignorant of the sizes of the Townships as most of the Townships are 12 miles along & 9 miles wide suppose there was but one central School in Chinguacousy at Edmonton and 2000 children of School age in the Township only from 75 to 100 would get any benefit from such an arangement the other 1900 would have to travell 6 to 11½ miles or 12 to 23 going & coming to do all Children justice and that no Child should travell more than 6 miles going & coming the people had to establish 26 School Sections. There seemed to be also at the Teachers association Meeting an Antipathy against Township Superintendents, Trustees, female Teachers and young men Teachers, which I dont wonder at because they do not like to be bossed by the Supt and Trustees dont pay them Money enough female Teachers and other young beginners Spoil their Monopoly and their high exalting Idea that they are superior to Teachers.

I read so much in the Journal of Education abt Free Schools why not go about it, me as a German I prefer the Prussian System where the Government takes it in hand furnishes for every child schooling (the most convenient the Child may attend) hires the Teachers no quarreling and squabling abt Rate bill School sites Trustees Election—good or bad Teacher, male or female etc. Hoping to see this get realised. I remain your most obt. Servant

I. D. Hageman
Trustee Caledon S.S. No 4
Address Cheltemham Post Office

THE NOVA SCOTIA FREE-SCHOOL DEBATE ACCORDING TO ALEXANDER FORRESTER, C. 1860

Alexander Forrester, *Address to the People of Nova Scotia, on the Support of Common Schools* (n.p. n.d.), pp. 1-22.

. . . The longer I continue in office, I am the more thoroughly impressed with the conviction that until something substantial is done with the Common Schools of the Province, we can neither keep pace with the general intelligence and progressive advancement of the age, nor furnish anything like an adequate supply of duly qualified students for the higher academic or collegiate institutions of the land. . . . To me, it appears plain and palpable that, whilst many things may and ought to be done for the removing of clamant [sic] defects and putting us on a career of high and ennobling progression, there is one thing lying at the bottom of the whole, without which all other remedial measures will prove of comparatively little avail,—I refer to the method of supporting these schools by compulsory assessment, giving effect to the principle '*that the property of all should be taxed for the education of all.*' . . .

REASON 1st.—*Direct taxation is the most effectual way of awaking in the minds of all an interest in the cause of education.*

We know not a greater impediment to the progress of education in this or any country than the general indifference that obtains, the all but universal prevalence of the notion that nobody in the District has anything to do with its educational affairs, save the individual who happens to have children to be educated. The Bachelor, the parent whose children are already educated, and a host of similar characters, seem to imagine that they are altogether free from any obligation to give of their substance for the support of the education of the District. They may as an act of charity, or of liberality, or for the accomplishment of some selfish end, dole out a paltry sum for the erection of the new District school house, but this they do with the significant intimation that not the slightest claim can be made upon them for any such contribution. And what does such a notion necessarily lead to? It leads plainly to the reducing of the whole support of the education of the District to some twelve or fifteen families out of the twenty-five or thirty, and these oftentimes the least able in the district to support schools. . . . And what is to be done to remedy this state of things, to rouse these parties to take any interest in the matter? Will appeals to their benevolence, their patriotism or their christian philanthropy prove of any avail? Or, failing in these, will the most palpable demonstrations of the innumerable indirect benefits which they and their property will derive from the sound and thorough education of the children in their midst, be productive of a more salutary influence? Alas! we fear, that these and similar pleadings will be allowed to pass away, like the idle wind, unheeded and unfelt; and that nought will produce the desired result but a direct and immediate appeal to their selfishness—their pockets. Let such be compelled by the law of the land to contribute according to the value of their property towards this object, and we guarantee an immediate revolution in all their views and feelings regarding the education of the young around them. Then will the rich old Bachelors and the venerable grey-headed Patriarchs manifest the deepest concern in education as regards both its quantity and quality—and this concern instead of decaying or dying will be but deepened and extended by every subsequent annual visit of the collector, and all this simply because they have so much involved, so much at stake. . . .

REASON 2nd.—*Direct taxation for the support of our common schools will aid largely in securing the adequate amount of education; in other words, it will vastly increase the quantity.*

That every child born in a professedly Christian country possesses an indefeasible right to a common school education and that it is the bounden duty of every such country to make provision therefor; and not only so, but to see that every schoolable child, that is every child between five and sixteen years is actually receiving it are propositions which however imperfectly carried out are all but universally admitted in theory. To attain this state of things, a fifth part of the population would require to be at school, and that not for five or six or seven but for ten months in the year. In these respects Nova Scotia is sadly deficient. From the utter want of machinery to obtain anything like a reliable body of statistics, we cannot pronounce with absolute certainty in the case; but we fear that there are not more than an eighth of our population at school, and that the average period of attendance of each scholar does not exceed six or seven months in the year. . . . Now it is our decided conviction, that direct taxation would operate very beneficially in obviating this state of things. It could not fail to add largely to the number of children attending school—in all probability, a third more in the course of two or three years. . . . But we believe that such a measure would operate still more extensively upon the length of time and regularity of attendance at school. Is it at all likely that people after paying for a boon will not avail themselves of its full benefit, and avail themselves to an extent exactly proportional to its cost? Not to do so would be to act in diametric opposition to their usual procedure in other undertakings and pursuits. The interest awakened by the application of the money principle would also naturally direct attention to the advantages of a thorough education and call forth a determined effort to obtain it.

REASON 3rd.—*This method of supporting schools will also enhance their quality.*

If the quantity of education given is sadly defective, much more is its quality. This is owing to a great variety of causes:—such as, the smallness of some school districts, and the mal-assortment of others, the number of schools in the District in direct opposition to the present school Bill—necessarily reducing the number of children in attendance to a mere handful and frittering down to a very trifle all the available resources of school support,—the utter inadequacy of the teacher's salary and his consequent lack of literary and professional qualifications, as well as his frequent changes from place to place;—the supineness and careless indifference of too many parents with the irregularity of the attendance of the children; and the months if not sometimes the years intervening between the leaving off of one teacher and the commencing of the operations of his successor—these and similar causes combine in rendering the quality of the education of two thirds of the schools as low as can well be imagined. And in addition to all these, and as one of the direct results of the above mentioned causes, many of the most enlightened, the best educated and the most influential of the parents withdraw their children altogether from the common school of the district and send them to schools where they will receive a higher style of education, transferring thereto all their educational interest, and leaving the whole local affairs to the management of a few individuals, devoid alike of the means and ability of doing so with any measure of success.

The compulsory assessment would alter, in this respect, the whole face of things. All being obliged to contribute, according to their means, the rich as well as the poor, the educated as well as the uneducated, they would feel the necessity of exerting themselves to the uttermost and uniting their energies to obtain an efficient school in the district—such a school, in fact, as would lay the foundation of intellectual and moral culture for any sphere of life, for any business or profession. The plan we have already briefly indicated would soon provide every District with a commodious schoolhouse, the necessary furniture and apparatus. The next step would be to procure a qualified and suitable schoolmaster for the situation, and here comparatively little difficulty would be experienced. The Trustees would now be prepared not only to hold out a competent remuneration, but without the least fear or apprehension that their doing so would involve them in any personal risk or liability. With such an equipment, a higher appreciation of a more elevated education would grow apace and would speedily pervade all ranks and degrees. The attendance of the children would gradually increase, and the very idea of having the schoolhouse door shut except during the usual vacation period, would soon be considered as savouring of semi-barbarism. In consequence of the number of scholars and the regular and sufficient supply of the necessary means and the growing appreciation of a still higher standard of education, the proper steps would speedily be taken for graded schools,—Primary, Intermediate and High;—male and female teachers would straightway be engaged; a thorough classification of the scholars effected; and the whole establishment put into working order. Who can fail to perceive the high toned style of such an education, or over-estimate the benefits flowing from the division of labour among the teachers, the entire devotement of their time and energies to two or three classes instead of ten or a dozen,—the real development of the mental powers of the scholars by the communication of wholesome instruction,—the feeding of the higher departments of the school by the lower, in consequence of the same system being pursued in all? &c. &c. Thus the lower and middle classes would obtain the best possible education for their children; the higher classes would get in their own immediate neighbourhood as good an education as they could find anywhere abroad, at one fourth the expense, and with the immense advantage of their children being all the while under the parental roof, for which the finest Boarding establishment however well or domestically arranged, could never compensate.

REASON 4th.—*Again, this method of supporting the common schools of the land, is the cheapest as well as the most efficient.*

We are aware that the very mention of the word cheapness in educational matters, falls like music on the ears of not a few. Ignorant of what education really is, and, therefore, incapable of realizing its results, either in reference to man personally or collectively; and yet feeling a desire to be like their neighbours and to give their children such an amount of education as that they shall be able to shift for themselves, their grand aim seems to be to get it as cheap as they can. Accordingly, when the teacher presents himself, they enquire, not so much after his credentials as his price, and the fact of his professing to teach at a lower rate than those around forms the highest possible recommendation. Never, we believe, was there a more egregious perversion of the term. As in everything else, as in every other marketable commodity, the best, whatever the cost, is always in the long run, the cheapest, it is pre-eminently so in the matter of education. . . . And here we have another argument in favor of compulsory assessment for the support of education. All the accompaniments of carrying into effect such a scheme, such as the enlargement of school Districts, the classification and grading of schools, the higher appreciation of education generally, &c. will have the tendency of diminishing the number of teachers, and yet increasing by one-third, if not by one-half the number of children receiving instruction. And who does not see that this must cheapen and cheapen largely the general cost, and that in perfect consistency with, in the full working out of, a more efficient system of education. . . .

REASON 5th.—*The principle for which we are contending will also operate beneficially in the matter of local supervision.* . . .

. . . There would then be no such difficulty, as there is now, to get the most eligible parties to act as Trustees, or to carry out the full terms of their instructions. They would be under no risk or liability to make up the defalcations of others; for all would be compelled to pay according to their means. The growing interest taken in the education of the District, would not only render their duties light and easy, but the office would become one of honour and respectability. They would labour, and labour zealously and perseveringly in the discharge of their duties, feeling satisfied that their labours would be duly appreciated, that they would not only have the approval of their own conscience but the gratitude of the wise and good around them . . .

REASON 6th.—*The Teachers too would share largely in the benefits accruing from the adoption of this principle.*

The saying 'The Teacher makes the school' is not less trite than true, and cannot be too oft repeated. Let the internal and external systems of education be what they may, no justice can be done to the one or the other without a staff of thoroughly qualified teachers,—teachers imbued with the spirit of their office and who have sat at the feet of the Great Teacher of Nazareth. To secure, retain and extend such a class of teachers, two things are indispensably necessary. 1st. They must have an adequate remuneration for their services; and 2nd, they must have every encouragement in the way of stimulating to higher attainment in their calling . . .

Now the principle of assessment will most materially affect . . . these points. It will equalize the endowment all over the Province and above all, it will secure the full payment of the sum promised. It will also indirectly affect the latter. It will involve a thorough grading or classification of the teachers, and this will demand competitive trials both in scholarship and in teaching powers; and thus elicit real merit in every department.

REASON 7th.—*This mode of supporting education will tend to diffuse a spirit of unity and mutual affection among the inhabitants of the District.*

It is lamentable to observe the heartburnings, disputes, and divisions that but too frequently take place in settlements in connection with our present educational system. Sometimes the higher classes are seen contending with the lower; at other times, the inhabitants of one extremity of the District, with those of the other,—it may be about the school-site, or the teacher; and, at other times, politics and denominationalism creep in with all their train of evils and leaven not a few with their baneful influence. Thus too often is the District torn in pieces, and the cause of education, and the interests of the young sacrificed. . . .

. . . In many Districts there are comparatively few who take any interest in the cause of education at all; and even those who do, frequently manifest nought but a spirit of selfish isolation, of wordly aggrandizement. They profess to take a lively interest in the cause of education, but this is but too evidently confined within the precincts of their own domestic circle. They cheerfully aid in the erection of a new schoolhouse and liberally contribute towards the support of a duly qualified teacher, but all because they have two or three children to be educated; and it would neither suit their wordly plans nor their family pride, to send them abroad without such an amount of scholarship as would enable them to earn a decent livelihood or, perchance, raise themselves to temporal affluence and respectability. Such is the nature of their educational zeal, demonstrating but too plainly, that it is selfish, isolated, grovelling and degrading to the very core; which, instead of strengthening the social bond, but loosens and rends it asunder.

Let, however, the compulsory system of supporting schools be introduced, let all be bound to pay in proportion to the value of their property; and, we are persuaded, that some at least of these evils would be removed. The fact of each contributing according to his means and not according to the number of children he has to educate, would naturally beget an interest in the general cause of education; and thereby generate and diffuse a fine spirit of mutual affection and of fraternal harmony among all ranks and degrees and parties. With the same objects, aims and interests, the social bond of the District would be strengthened, and those strifes and divisions, so injurious to society and so disastrous to the cause of education, be, to a great extent, averted.

REASON 8th.— *This principle is in consonance with the purest equity, and the strictest justice . . .*

. . . The veriest tyro in political economy knows that the real advancement of any country, depends on the intelligence, the skill, the industrial and moral habits of its inhabitants. It matters comparatively little as to the nature or extent of that country's territory. Let it present the poorest and most unpromising appearance—the barren heath or the craggy rock—if the inhabitants are signalized by the qualities above specified, they will in course of time convert the wilderness into a garden, the rock into a mine of gold. . . . Or, to speak without a figure, pauperism, and vice, and crime will, to the extent to which these qualities are diffused, be comparatively unknown, and taxation, for their support or punishment, be but slightly felt. All will be lasting, substantial gain. And the result of all this state of things will be the increased and the ever increasing value of property. It signifies little as to the nature of that property, whether it be the house or the field, the loom or the cloth, the ship or the freight, the personal or the real,—or as to its extent, for all will be benefited,—the labourer, the tradesman, the farmer, the manufacturer, the merchant, the rich and the poor, the learned and the unlearned. And what is the instrumentality or agency by which a population possessed of these qualities shall be reared and perpetuated and extended? It is education, and education alone,—education universal and efficient, such an education as will embrace all the component parts of our nature,—as will consist not merely in the imparting of knowledge, but in the training up of the young in the way they should go. The connection between a sound and thorough system of popular education and national prosperity in the highest sense of that term, requires no argumentation of ours; it is written as with a sunbeam on the page of past history; it is palpable in the present condition of the civilized world. . . . "That as the property of all is benefited by the education of all, so is it right and proper that, for the securing of this end, the property of all be taxed."

REASON 9th.—*But we proceed a step further, and maintain that this method of supporting schools is not only consonant with the law of equity but with the true principles and ends of civil government.*

Are any natural rights more fundamental and sacred than those of children to such an education as will fit them for their duties as citizens? If a parent is amenable to the law who takes away a child's life by violence, or wilfully exposes it to starvation, does he less violate the inherent rights of the child in exposing it to moral and intellectual starvation? It is noble to recognize this inalienable right of infancy and youth, by providing for them the means of the education to which they are entitled, not as children of particular families, but as children of our race and country. And how perfectly does it harmonize with the true principles of civil government for every man to support the laws and all institutions designed for the common good, according to this ability. This is an acknowledged principle of all just taxation. And it is the true principle of universal education. It links every man to his fellow men in the obligation of the common interests; it wars with that greatest, meanest foe of all social advancement—the isolation of selfish individuality; and implants and nourishes the spirit of true patriotism, by making each man feel that the welfare of the whole society is his welfare—that collective interests are first in order of importance and duty, and that separate interests are second. . . . Although we have already extended these remarks far beyond our original designed limits we must still notice a few of the more prominent objections urged against the scheme we have been advocating.

OBJECTION 1st.—*Some object to it because they do not see how teachers are entitled to any other guarantee for the payment of their salary or wages than any other labourer, or mechanic, or man of business.* The ground they take is this:—The teacher engages with the parents or guardians of his pupils to educate them for the time being at a certain rate per annum, the parents, if the teacher performs his engagement, are obliged to pay the sum promised, and, if they do not, he may sue them in a court of law. The whole of this objection evidently proceeds upon the idea that education is to be conducted on the voluntary and not on the national system, and by consequence that the teachers are to be regarded in the light of private adventurers and not as public officers. With such a view of education we have no sympathy. On the contrary, we raise against it our most unequivocal and decided protest. We hold it to be far more the duty and interest of the State, as such, to countenance and make provision for a national system of education than it is to support a police or constabulary establishment. No nation can subsist without education, and no other means can supply the adequate amount. . . .

OBJECTION 2nd.—*Many maintain that whilst such a method of supporting education may be very suitable for the States of Canada, it is altogether unsuitable for Nova Scotia.* Of course these individuals are bound to show precisely in what the dissimilarity between the countries referred to, consists, so as to substantiate the position that what is suitable in the one case, is unsuitable in the other. This, however, they cautiously avoid, contenting themselves with mere general statements or vague assertions. We maintain that in all essential points, affecting the matter of taxation, these countries are, as near as may be, in the same situation. When Massachusetts passed in 1647, the direct taxation principle, it was a British colony; so was Upper Canada when it did the same, and so is Nova Scotia. The inhabitants of these colonies are, in the main, sprung from the same stock, from men signalized for their high-toned patriotism, for their exalted views of civil liberty, founded as these views were on the only infallible standard of faith and morals. There exists, too, in these countries the same variety of religious denominations, and of political parties. If there is any difference between these countries and Nova Scotia, it argues far greater capabilities and facilities on the part of the latter to carry out our principle.

OBJECTION 3rd.—*Another objection, urged principally by the higher classes, is, that the Common Schools are of such a low and inefficient character, that they—the higher classes—cannot send their children to them and therefore it is unreasonable that they should be taxed for their support.*

Granting, for the sake of argument, that the common schools are really of this description, what, it may be asked has mainly contributed to render them so—what but the conduct of these objectors themselves? Instead of encouraging, in every possible way, the common schools of the District, they have sent their children elsewhere, to what they considered select schools, and thus left the support of these schools to a few families and these not the most competent, whether in respect to means or influence or educational qualifications, to do so. Let all and sundry in the District come forward and give their cordial support to these schools, according to their capabilities, and, so far as the elementary branches of education are concerned, they will soon rise to the highest excellence. . . .

OBJECTION 4th.—*Others object to our principle and maintain that it is unfair to be obliged to contribute towards the maintenance of schools from which they derive no immediate benefit.*

. . . On the same ground, might one and another come forward and plead exemption from paying for the support of the administration of justice, for they do not patronize either the civil or the criminal courts; another, for the erection of a jail, because he derives no direct benefit therefrom; and another, for the upholding of a Lunatic Asylum, because neither he nor his relatives stand in want of any such place of protection. In all good governments, the interests of the majority are the rule of procedure; and in all free governments the voice of the majority determines what shall be done by the whole population for the common interests, without reference to isolated individual cases of advantage or disadvantage, of inclination or disinclination. Surely the common schools involve the common interests of the nation far more than Jails, or Bridewells or Penitentiaries, and, therefore, it is perfectly justifiable for the state to impose a tax upon all for their support.

But the objection is groundless because it proceeds on an assumption in direct antagonism to the truth. It assumes that none are benefited by common schools save those who patronise them, by sending children to them. This is the lowest, narrowest, and most selfish view of the subject, and indicates a mind contracted and grovelling in the extreme. It is quite true that Bachelors, Parents whose children are already educated, and such like, do not derive any immediate benefit from the common schools of the District; but to argue from this that they do not derive any benefit, is just as absurd as to suppose, that none derive any benefit from the administration of Jurisprudence but those directly engaged therein, such as Judges, Lawyers, Jailors, Police, &c.; or that none get any advantage from a Railroad passing through a country, but the Car Manufacturers, Engine Drivers, Station Masters, and other officials of the establishment. We reiterate the sentiment which we have elaborated at length in the body of this address, that there is not an individual in the settlement who is not benefited, less or more, by the common school, and that in exact proportion to the stake involved. . . .

OBJECTION 5th.—*But others object to the scheme we have propounded because it does not go far enough. "Let the whole sum," say they, "requisite for the support of the common schools be raised by direct taxation, and we are prepared to give you our cordial support."*

So say we. Nay, we are ready to maintain that such a taxation would prove in every way advantageous to the cause of education, and that the contributors to this fund would not, at the end of the year, be one whit the poorer but all the richer. Still there may be some, there may be a majority of the friends of educational taxation unprepared to go this length, and, therefore, it would be inexpedient at the outset to attempt such a measure. We are persuaded, however, that such will be the felt advantages of the introduction of the assessment wedge to the extent we have indicated, that in the course of five years there will be not only a disposedness, but a demand on the part of the rateable population themselves to go the full length. In the mean time, let the friends of education and advancement be united, and insist on the immediate payment of a first installment. Let the Legislature grant, as usual, a third part out of the public Treasury, and enact that another third be raised by County compulsory assessment, and let the other third in its mode of exaction, be left to the option of the people; and we have no fear of the result. . . .

ALEXANDER FORRESTER

THE FREE-SCHOOL DEBATE IN TORONTO

Copies of Documents relating to the Common Schools of the City, Forwarded by the Board of School Trustees to the City Council and Ordered to be Printed (Toronto, 1858), passim.

Extract of such portions of Report No. 10, of the 6th May, 1856, by the Local Superintendent G. A. Barber, as bear upon the City School question. . . .

"I do not pretend to say that our School System is without defects; but I do say those defects are susceptible of improvement, and by degrees, with time and patience, may be either altogether removed, or so remedied as to be no hindrance to the working of the system. I do not, however, refer in this instance to the question of Free Schools, concerning which I am not at present called upon to express any decided opinion. But as regards the general character of our schools, I am bound to state, as my opinion, that they are not deserving, but on the contrary, are well worthy of public confidence; indeed I may with propriety go further and assert that our Schools, as a whole, have more and better grounds of complaint against the public, than the public have reason to complain of the Schools."

"None can be more impressed with the fact, that our City Schools have not, as yet, realized what was reasonably expected of them than I am; but the cause of this disappointment must be looked for elsewhere than in defects in the Schools; and I submit the following, among others, as prominent causes why the Schools of the City have not made better progress, in proportion to the cost and trouble expended in establishing and maintaining them, namely:—

1st—The total absence of all interest in the Schools by the affluent and influential portion of the community.

2nd—The neglect on the part of Ministers of Religion, to visit the Schools, and use their influence with their congregations in favor of popular education; for, while Clergymen of the various denominations in the City, except on some special public occasion, have kept aloof from our Schools, the Clergy of the Church of England have sought to create a prejudice against them, by misrepresenting them, as altogether devoid of religious instruction.

3rd—The chilling indifference shown even by the parents of the children attending the Schools, as proved by the great want of regularity and punctuality on the part of the scholars, their children—for a large proportion of them really seem to come to, or stay away from school, just as they please—and the most trifling matters of domestic life are considered to be sufficient excuse for being late or absent; as proved also by the fact, that out of a registered attendance of some 2,300, six or seven hundred are every day absent, some one day some another, thus exhibiting an extent of irregularity which, if not reformed, must sooner or later imperil the whole system; and as further proved by the necessity which exists for continually stirring up parents to avail of the great advantages provided for their offspring by the City Schools; and by the discouragingly small number of parents who have visited the Schools, or been present at the Examinations, or attended the School Lectures.

4th—The prejudices which many have given way to against the Schools, of which the following may be quoted in evidence viz:—Some parents confound "Free Schools," supported by an assessment upon every man according to his means, with mere "Charity Schools," and therefore, from a feeling of pride, will not send their children to the City Schools. Others consider the term "Common School," to convey a low, vulgar meaning, and in consequence object to sending their children to our Public Schools; and many insist that a teacher receiving a salary, does not bring forward his pupils as well as one who is more dependent on public opinion (too often in school matters public caprice) for his daily bread.

5th—The mischievous interference of Parents with the Teacher, and the discipline of the School; for, too many parents, instead of bringing the influence of domestic education to aid and assist the Teacher, and encourage the Schools, openly disparage what they cannot be supposed to understand; and expect that a general system arranged for the good of all, ought to, and must, be set aside, to gratify individual whims, too often unreasonable demands; and if the whim or demand be not at once yielded to, no matter how the concession may affect others, either the Teacher is vilified, or a grievance is nursed into active hostility, and then the School is complained against, and the child kept away.

6th—A serious drawback to the progress of the Schools is to be found in the fact, that parents cannot be prevailed upon, as a general rule, to supply their children with the books they require; while as regards needle work, so necessary for girls, the Teacher cannot, without difficulty, induce mother to provide the requisite materials.

7th—In numerous cases, the restraints and discipline, absolutely necessary in any system of School education, are felt to be so irksome even to parents as well as children, as to cause absenteeism to a great extent; and this impatience of control manifests itself in a disposition to find fault with almost everything relating to the Schools.

8th—But not the least fatal difficulty which has operated adversely to our Schools, is the feeling, that what is obtained so easily, and at so little cost, as the education afforded by the City Free Schools, is therefore of but little value, and is neglected accordingly."

Every Teacher in the City Schools will, I am sure, attest, that in what I have thus stated, I have advanced no more than what is strictly true.

"As already stated, I feel reluctant to advance any opinions with regard to the question of Free Education, as affecting or influencing the results, or the discouragement, of our Common School System; but, at the same time, I cannot shut my eyes to the fact, that during those periods when the Rate Bill System prevailed, and when the opportunities then afforded could not for a moment be compared with those now provided in our Free Schools, the attendance was greater in proportion than it is now; that the attendance was more regular and more punctual; and that the parents appreciated and took more interest in, and were better satisfied with, the then City Schools, than they are with the Schools now in operation."

"In my opinion one of the remedies called for is that some stricter rules, both as regards regularity and punctuality of attendance, ought to be at once enforced. No private School could be conducted with credit to the Teacher where these irregular and unpunctual habits prevailed; and why such ruinous habits should be tolerated in our City Free Schools, altogether passes my comprehension, unless indeed the elective principle, or the pressure from without neutralized vigorous legislation by the Board. . . . "

Copy of Report No. 25, By the Local Superintendent, G. A. Barber,

(1st December, 1857.)

To the Chairman and Members of the Board of School Trustees:

Gentlemen,—

According to the provisions of the School Act of 1850 (section 31), it is required of the Local Superintendent that he should "do all in his power to persuade and animate Parents, Guardians, Trustees, and Teachers, to improve the character and efficiency of the Common Schools; and to secure the universal and sound education of the young."

Acting under this requirement, I feel it to be my reluctant, but nevertheless my conscientious duty, to ask the Board to reconsider the whole question of the Free School System . . .

If I understand aright the principle upon which Free Schools, maintained by general assessment on property, have been established, and are justified, it means that the rich ought to educate the poor, not as a charity, but because in a social as well as a moral point of view, it is as a mere matter of economy, better to educate than to punish at the public expense; and because Schoolhouses are better public investments than Penitentiaries or Jails. Tested by this principle, the result of our experiment, as regards even those children who have attended, though irregularly, our Free Schools has been anything but encouraging or satisfactory (as shown by the Reports on the subject which from time to time I have submitted), while as regards the education, moral and social, of those children, large in number, for whose training and reformation the Free School principle is justified, we have failed altogether to bring that particular class of children, in any way at all, within the restraining influences of our Schools.

The Free School Theory presupposes that parents desire to have their children educated and trained up in habits of social and moral propriety, and that they are to be so educated accordingly; but I cannot bring myself to believe that the principle of the Free School system was ever intended to tempt any man's sturdy independence into taking from others, or rather, I might say, requiring, if not compelling others, to provide what he had the means and the ability to obtain for himself—thus weakening that great moral and natural obligation which requires every parent to provide, so far as possible, at his own expense, for the decent education as well as the maintenance of his off-spring. But at present the whole community is compulsorily taxed to provide free education for children, whose parents, to the extent of probably four-fifths, certainly three-fourths, are not only well able to educate their own offspring, but are further able to bear their share, in proportion to their means, of educating the unfortunate child of neglect, or of poverty, or of vice, for whom alone Free Schools ought to be maintained at the public expense. We set out, full of hope, to accomplish a certain purpose, namely, the "universal education of the young," as a means of social and moral improvement among that class of people who knowing little or nothing of the advantages of education, or who cared nothing for such advantages; or who, if they did know the value of, or did care for the education of their unfortunate offspring, were nevertheless, quite unable to pay for it—but thus far, after years of experience, and the expenditure of increasing annual thousands of the public money, we have accomplished little more than a partial, and by no means a cheerful recognition of the value of our Schools, even from those whose children, to a limited extent, do attend our Free Schools—while the more numerous, and at the same time more necessitous class of children, continue to frequent our streets, our lanes, and our wharves in idle swarms, growing up daily in ignorance and crime, the future abundant material for our Police Courts and Prisons.

II. Independent, moreover, of these main considerations, it becomes us to reflect upon the significant fact, that, notwithstanding, all we have done, and the expense we have gone to, by means of a compulsory assessment, and the inducements our Schools certainly offer, Parochial Schools, built and maintained on the voluntary principle, have made rapid advances during the last three or four years—and that in the close neighbourhood of our Free Schools, several private Schools, where fees are paid, actually attract a remunerating attendance from among a class of persons in circumstances precisely like those who are attending our Schools!

III. It becomes us also to reflect whether the present system, as a system, is appreciated by, whether, indeed, it be not actually distasteful to those even who do, to some extent, partially participate in its benefits (See my Report, No. 10, of May, 1856), and it may, I think, be properly asked whether the prejudices which exist, and that want of appreciation so discouragingly manifested, are to be any longer conciliated? How much further are we to go on exhorting and entreating parents to send their children to our Free Schools? Are we to go on continually seeking, almost as a favour, what ought to be hailed as a privilege? Are we to be always begging the question? and are we to go on year after year expending thousands upon thousands of a compulsory assessment, in the delusive endeavour to educate those who are comparatively indifferent about the matter? or those, the more numerous class, who never come near our Schools?

The time has arrived, I think, for a calm, dispassionate, but practical reconsideration of the whole question.

It will, or ought to be at once admitted, that all obligations are more or less reciprocal; if, therefore, it be right and proper to impose a compulsory tax to maintain Free Schools for the people at large, then, as a matter of equal justice, the reciprocal obligation should be imposed upon the people to avail of, and be benefited by, the opportunities so provided for the education of their children. A compulsory School Assessment and a voluntary School attendance are manifestly inconsistent with each other. But applying these considerations to the condition of our City Schools, and so far as my opinions, founded upon a long experience and an anxious consideration of the question, are of any value, I am compelled by a sense of duty to state, as my sincere conviction that, if the Free School system, as at present carried on, is to be continued, a more punctual and regular attendance must be enforced, and a compulsory law to secure a general attendance will have to be enacted. . . .

As the only other alternative, a return, either partially or wholly, to the Rate-bill system seems to me all that is left to be considered. I am fully aware that this phase of the subject is surrounded with almost as many difficulties as that of a compulsory attendance; and I cannot but feel that to retrace our steps and adopt a Rate-bill on parents, will bear the appearance of acknowledging that the Free School movement of 1851 was a serious mistake, and a step in the wrong direction.

Which of the two alternatives it would be better to adopt, I am not prepared to say. Some positive change is, however, unavoidable—and I incline more to a compulsory School Law, which would secure the moral and social improvement of those, the men, who, according to my views of the Free School principle, ought to be thus educated and trained up in good habits at the public expense. The Rate bill system would merely relieve the Tax-payers, but the compulsory system would better realize what the interests of society most require, and what the Free School principle was meant to insure, namely, a larger amount of universal education. But, notwithstanding the difficulties which confessedly surround the whole question, I have felt it to be my duty, as an officer of the School Law, to state to you my conscientious convictions that the results thus far of our Free School experiment, no longer justify the compulsory assessment of a whole community to accomplish at best a partial purpose; and that if the present system is to be maintained a material change in its working will have to be made. And having now discharged that duty, I leave to your wisdom the further determination of the question.

Respectfully submitted,
G. A. Barber,
Local Superintendent

Report No. VII

To the Board of School Trustees of the City of Toronto:

The Standing Committee on School Management beg to present their Seventh Report.

That, in pursuance with the resolution of the Board, adopted the 17th May last, your Committee have had under consideration the Report No. 25, of the Local Superintendent, dated October 1st, 1857. . . .

In that Report the Local Superintendent calls upon the late Board to reconsider the whole question of the Free School System, upon the ground that, as at present carried on, its results are altogether incommensurate with the cost of maintaining it. . . .

In considering the . . . [Report], it may be convenient to note the distinction to be made between questions of Administration and Discipline, common to all systems, and the discussions of systems on abstract principles of economy. Thus while your Committee lament that the number attending the City Schools is smaller than it should be, and whilst they have not failed to discover that irregularity and unpunctuality of attendance, which would seem to vindicate the necessity of a sterner discipline, and a bolder administration, they are unwilling to charge upon the Free School system, as such, the responsibility for evils which but distantly, if at all, result from it, and which may probably be capable of correction without resorting to fundamental changes.

It is worthy of observation that Common School Education in this City, as a system, has never yet been permitted to enjoy that stability and permanence of operation which is generally acknowledged as essential to success. Thus, until 1847, the City was sub-divided into School Sections, each having its own Trustees acting independently, and all on the Rate Bill System. In 1848 and 1849 the Schools were governed by a Board, nominated by the Corporation, and during those years the Rate Bill system was abandoned, and the Schools were free. In 1850 the Rate Bill was again in force—to be again abandoned in 1851, when the Schools were once more free—and during which year the Elective principle was applied to the Board of Trustees. In 1852, separate Roman Catholic Schools were established, by special enactment of the Legislature, and it was not until the Spring of 1855, that the School Buildings being completed, that the system now in operation was fairly organized.

It is vain to expect mature vigor and full fruit, from a system subjected to such frequent and fundamental changes; and although during the trial of the last three years, it may, in some particulars, have failed to justify the sanguine expectations formed of it, your Committee are inclined to regard as premature any such unmeasured condemnation as would result in its disturbance, until every effort shall have been fairly exhausted to secure that efficiency and value which it has achieved in other places. . . .

Your Committee having discovered that no code of Rules for the instruction and guidance of Teachers and Pupils had yet been issued, have prepared, and will immediately issue, Regulations in regard to the duties and powers of Teachers, to the admission and expulsion of pupils, to regularity and punctuality of attendance, and other details of discipline; and they trust thereby to arrest many of the evils which, although resulting from administration, are now regarded as evidence of failure of the system.

The Board has already, by resolution, determined to maintain the Free School System, as they found it in operation when they were elected; using every means at their disposal, further to improve and strengthen it, if possible, to full efficiency. It is therefore, unnecessary for your Committee to enter upon any discussion of the relative values of the Free, Rate Bill and Compulsory System—a discussion which belongs to, and must find its issue with, the Rate Payers.

Your Committee, within the limits of the duties entrusted to them, accept the responsibility of administering the system, which, as Trustees they were elected to administer; and they are not prepared to recommend that the powers committed to the Board by the Rate Payers should be used to initiate the fundamental changes suggested by the Local Superintendent; and in regard to which, the Electors, as yet, have had no opportunity of expressing an opinion.

All respectfully submitted.

(Signed,) F. W. Cumberland
Chairman of Committee.

Adopted by the Board, June 16th, 1858.

(Signed,) J. G. Beard,
Chairman, B. S. T.

Certified,
G. A. Barber,
Secretary, B. S. T.
Toronto, 16th June, 1858.

THE FREE-SCHOOL ARGUMENT IN BRITISH COLUMBIA

'The Opening of the Free Schools', *The British Colonist*, 2 Aug., 1865, p. 2.

For the first time since the colony of Vancouver Island came into existence the blessing of education has been presented to the poorest as well as to the richest child. No more shall the juvenile mind be "an unweeded garden that grows to seed." Poverty has at length ceased to be an excuse for idle and ignorant childhood. The opening of the Central School yesterday—the inauguration of the temple of free education—has removed the fearful incubus which has lain so heavily and so long on every parent's heart. Let us hope that what has been commenced so auspiciously, even though it has come at the eleventh hour, will be carried out with success—that sectional jarring will not interfere with the practical usefulness of the institution, but that every person who has a voice in the management of our public education will feel the almost sacred responsibility that devolves upon him. In a young community like ours the education of youth is a subject of even more tender solicitude than it is in older countries. We are forming the minds of those who are not only to become responsible for the material progress of the country, but who are to build up, if not indeed lay the foundation of the social as well as political fabric of British rule on this side of the continent. There is a power in the public system of education of creating a national sentiment and inculcating an earnest patriotism almost unknown in the private schools of instruction. With this power, however, comes occasionally a serious injury. In the United States children are taught from the first moment they lisp the alphabet that that portion of the world which lies between Mexico and the British North American Possessions is something like the centre of the solar system, and that round it revolve all the other nationalities as the planets describe their course round the sun. Looking so intently on so brilliant a luminary, it is only natural that the visual organs should be dazed and that all outside the centre should appear a blank: and so beyond the history and geography of the United States the American child however conversant with the more practical parts of education really learns little of the general condition of the world. America is the Alpha and Omega of its educational course. Its books would seem to be devoted more to instilling into the mind the greatness and glory of the native country, than to the general diffusion of knowledge. An American atlas means a map for every State in the Union, and the rest of the world dealt with summarily. By this system patriotism gains, but general instruction loses. Much, however, of the intense national feeling cultivated at the public schools in the United States, is due to the necessity which made itself felt after the Revolution of fostering a genuine American sentiment, and instilling into the rising generation a feeling of reverence for that which had cost their fathers so much to obtain. In carrying out a system of public instruction in Vancouver Island, let us copy the admirable groundwork of our American neighbors, but let us eschew carefully anything that will tend to give our youth a false estimate of themselves and the country. It is, of course, so long as nationalities exist, a necessity to cultivate a national feeling, and we think the school books which have been heretofore used by many of our schools have been wanting in this respect, some of them having been, indeed, the very essence of American teaching—but it is not desirable, in a community like our own, to indulge in a system of instruction, whether imparted by the tone of the teacher or the principles of the text-book, that will tend to mark out rigidly and immutably the lines of nationality, and create or maintain those feelings or prejudice, which, whether in religion, race or country, are sure to mar the best efforts to cultivate the human mind. We are here on the extreme verge of civilization, with all of nature's obstacles before us. The people who are to carry on the work of building up a prosperous and probably an influential country, must not be encumbered with the clogs of sectional feeling of any kind. They must be taught, also, the great practical principles of life, and especially of new country life. It too often happens that education, like many other things, is not appropriate, and that while a child's head is filled with a heap of rubbish never to be used throughout its career, the most necessary requirements for the country in which it resides and which is to be its future stage, are altogether neglected. Again, we have old country ideas about the various grades of life—the servility of one class to another—sickening enough at all times in the countries from which they draw their sustenance, but, transplanted in the repugnant soil of a new land, actually unbearable—we have these ideas sown deeply in the juvenile mind. We want a very different tone imparted to our youth. We want to see them not only fit to cope with the obstacles which nature has placed in their way, but imbued with a feeling of manliness that will carry them in after life straightforward and dignified in their intercourse with their fellows.

In conclusion, and while we are alluding to principles which should form the groundwork of a free education system in this colony, we hope that rumor is falsifying when she adverts that the education appropriation will have to be reduced 32,000, on account of the deficiency expected in the Treasury. If such a rumor is really correct, the injury which will be done to the cause of public instruction can scarcely be overrated; for the thronged condition of the Central School necessitates already some outlay for assistance, which if not obtained, will deter many a child from the privileges offered by the school Act.

SCHOOL ADMINISTRATORS IN ACTION

THE BRANTFORD 'SCHOOL DIFFICULTY'

Excerpts from Letters and Clippings filed under Peter Muir to Egerton Ryerson, 26 August 1859, *Education Papers*, RG 2 C-6-C, Public Archives of Ontario.

To the Reverend Doctor E. Ryerson,

My friend Mr. Ormiston advises me to apply to you for direction how to proceed in the somewhat difficult position in which I find myself. I gladly do so and feel it no small satisfaction (in common I doubt not with many of my fellow Teachers) that we have one to refer to will support us if right and courtesly [sic] counsel us if wrong. . . . It is not on my own behalf that I purpose (unless you advise otherwise) to bring the matter before you for adjudication, but in behalf of the interests of Education in this neighbourhood. . . .

I shall feel exceedingly obliged if you will take the trouble to advise me whether it will serve any end to bring the matter before you and if so what would be the proper course to follow so as to give no room for cavil . . .

Peter D. Muir, A.B.

Brantford, 26 August, 1859

Board of School Trustees

THE PRINCIPAL OF THE CENTRAL SCHOOL AND THE BOARD AT OPEN WAR!

A Meeting of the Board of School Trustees was held in the Town Hall, on Tuesday last, to take into consideration a charge made by Mr. E. A. Judson against Mr. P. D. Muir, the Principal of the School of unjustly suspending his son Henry from School.

There were present, Allen Cleghorn, Esq., Chairman of the Board; Messrs. D. McKay, T. Cowherd, Jas. Woodyatt, F. O. Dee, T. James, R. Sproule, W. B. Hurst, J. Taylor, G. Watt, H. A. Hardy; Rev. J. Alexander, Local Superintendent was also present.

The Chairman stated that the whole case had been referred to the Local Superintendent, who had given much thought to the subject, and he had prepared a Report, which he would suggest should be read to the Board.

Mr. Woodyatt wanted to hear the evidence before the Report was read.

Mr. Dee moved a resolution, seconded by Mr. Hurst, that the Principal be sent for forthwith, to hear the charges that may be made against him.

Mr. Sproule thought it unnecessary to make Mr. Muir leave the School.

The resolution was then withdrawn.

The following letters were then read by the Chairman, a perusal of which will enable our readers to form a pretty correct idea of the nature of the difficulty:

Mr. Judson's letter to Mr. Cleghorn

Brantford, August 17, 1859.

Allan Cleghorn, Esq., Chairman of Board School Trustees, Brantford,—Dear Sir,—I wish to call your attention to the following charge I make against Mr. Muir, Principal of the Central School, viz: of suspending my son without sufficient reason. This morning he was late at school, (not from his own fault) but omitted getting an excuse. On his arrival at school, Mr. Thomas Muir marked him late, and on taking his seat he (Henry) remarked to one of the boys, "Why did not he (Muir) mark Squires," another scholar who was late a couple of days previous. For this Mr. Muir suspended him from school, and on my calling on Mr. Muir for an explanation, he gave as a reason for sending him home, that the remark had been addressed to the Teacher, which he considered an insult. The matter was investigated, and the boy to whom the remark was made stated distinctly in the presence of the Messrs. Muir, that Henry did not address Mr. Muir but himself (the boy). I did not consider the charge made out by Mr. Muir, and therefore asked Mr. Muir if Henry might return to School, but he positively refused, until he made an apology . . . I beg that you will call a meeting of the Board of Trustees at an early day, when I can have an opportunity of more fully explaining to the Board this matter of grievance, . . .

I am, respectfully,
Yours, &c.
E. A. Judson.

Mr. Muir's statement of the case

Central School,
18th August, 1859.

Allen Cleghorn, Esq.

My Dear Sir:- I wish to state for your guidance, the facts of a somewhat painful occurrence, I have been obliged to suspend H. Judson until he shall apologise for what I deem an insult to his teacher, as well as a breach of the known regulations of the school. There is a difference between his statement of what occurred, and his teacher's impression of it, and though not quite satisfied, the teacher is prepared to suppose that he may have been mistaken wherein they differ, but the main facts are not disputed. It seems that in the morning Judson was late, and his teacher was observed by him taking note of the fact. On which he called out, "Why did he not put down Squire's name yesterday." This I deem insulting to the teacher, and demand that an apology be made before he can take his place in the class. To this the parent demurs, and demands that the boy be replaced without apology, which I have decidedly refused.

I think that a teacher may fairly exercise his discretion as to what case of delinquency he shall bring under special notice, without being subjected to the necessity of enduring charges of partiality, especially preferred in that insubordinate way.... The discipline of the school, which is now excellent, must not be imperilled to gratify any one's feelings.

Sincerely yours,
Peter D. Muir.

Mr. Judson then addressed the Board, relating the whole matter in dispute, according to his view. He said, that on Thursday morning when he went home, about 11 o'clock, he found his son Henry at home; on enquiry he found he had been sent home from school by Mr. Muir; he also found a note from Mr. Muir, stating that Henry had been suspended from school until he should make an apology for insulting his teacher. Upon enquiry, and believing that his boy had not insulted his teacher, but had addressed the remark he was charged with making to a schoolmate, he did not deem an apology requisite. Mrs. Judson then, with his consent, sent Henry back to school, with a note, stating that as the boy had not done anything demanding an apology, she expected him to be received in school. Mr. Muir, on reading Mrs. Judson's note had refused to receive the boy, and sent him away again, returning, also, Mrs. Judson's note. He (Mr. Judson) then, in company with Mr. Sullivan and his son, proceeded to the school, for the purpose of having an explanation. On reaching the school he was met by Mr. Muir, who said that, until the boy apologized for the insulting remark he had addressed to his teacher, he could not receive him into his class. Henry denied making the remark he was charged with, having said "Why did not he put down Squires," and not "Why did not you," &c. This he (Mr. Judson) thought made a material difference, and he would sooner believe his son than he would him (Mr. Muir). The boy, Foster, to whom the remark was said to have been addressed, was then produced, who confirmed Henry Judson's statement, that the remark had been addressed to him, and that the words were "Why did not he," &c. On this, said Mr. Judson, Mr. T. Muir expressed himself satisfied that he was mistaken, and that he was sorry for what he had done. Mr. Sullivan then said "I suppose it's all settled now, and Henry can go back to school." To this Mr. P. D. Muir said, "Decidedly not, until he apologizes." He (Mr. Judson) then said he would appeal to the School Board, and left. He at once addressed the letter to Mr. Cleghorn, which is given above. . . .

The Board, after hearing the above, and still declining to have the report of Mr. Alexander read, decided on calling the Messrs. Muir before them. . . .

Mr. T. Muir, teacher of the class in which young Judson is a pupil, said, the circumstances of the case were very plain. Judson, entering school on Thursday morning late observed him (Muir) recording his name in a book kept for the purpose. Judson immediately called out "Why did not you put down Squires yesterday?" On which he had desired him to withdraw into one of the side rooms. In a few minutes he went into the room, and asked Judson "Why he had called out from his seat?" Judson replied, "I was not addressing you." He (Mr. Muir) then explained to young Judson that the offence was the same, taking his own admission of the words used, and required an apology. Judson refused to make an apology, and he had at once made his brother, the Principal, acquainted with the circumstances, who then took the matter into his own hands. . . .

Three of the boys were then examined, but two of them did not hear the remark, a third heard words spoken by Judson, in an offensive, angry tone, but could not say what they were.

There being no further evidence. Mr. Hurst thought Mr. Alexander's report might now be read.

Mr. Dee and others objected. Mr. Woodyatt said the chairman had overstepped his duty in referring the case to Mr. Alexander, and that gentleman had no right to interfere in the case at all. It was no part of his duty as Local Superintendent to interfere in a dispute between the teacher, and the pupils.

A vote was then taken, and it was decided that the report should not be read.

Mr. Hardy then addressed the Board, arguing that as it appeared Mr. Muir had sought to punish the boy for an offence he had never committed, namely insulting his teacher, the remark of the boy having been addressed to a schoolmate, Mr. Muir was highly censurable.

Mr. Hurst moved, seconded by Mr. Woodyatt, that the Board strongly censure the conduct of Mr. Muir, in suspending Henry Judson, and they request him to receive said Judson into the school at once.

Mr. Woodyatt then spoke strongly censuring Mr. Muir's conduct, and alleged that he is utterly unfit for the position he holds in the school.

(We may state here that Mr. Woodyatt's manner throughout the whole proceedings, was uncourteous, overbearing, and boorish, and such as we were under the impression he was totally incapable of.)

Mr. Cowherd, Mr. Hurst, and Mr. Dee, also spoke in condemnation of Mr. Muir, and urged that a strong vote of censure should be passed upon him.

Mr. Sproule counselled moderation in whatever should be done. He thought there was fault on both sides, and he hoped both parties would give and take a little. He believed that if the Board passed the resolution it would have the effect of ruining the school, which he believed to be one of the finest in the province. By the course they proposed taking, they would encourage insubordination, and no teacher would ever be able to maintain discipline.

Mr. Alexander then, with the permission of the Board, spoke on the subject. He said he deeply regretted the circumstance which they had been considering, and while he was not disposed to exonerate Mr. Muir from all blame in the matter, believing him to have exhibited some temper, yet he thought the Board ought to look with some degree of sympathy upon him, considering the onerous and harrassing duties he has to perform. He had no hesitation in saying that if the resolution passed, Mr. Muir would resign his situation, and it might be a long time before another teacher could be found to fill his place. He looked upon the fact as being clearly proved that the boy Judson had insulted his teacher, by uttering the words imputed to him; and moreover he had heard that the boy himself had stated that the remark was intended for the ear of his teacher. The teacher had done right in demanding an apology for the insult, for the purpose of maintaining proper discipline in the school. The action of the Board to-day, said Mr. Alexander, may ruin the school forever.

Mr. Taylor proposed the following amendment to Mr. Hurst's resolution.

Moved by Mr. Taylor and seconded by Mr. Hardy,—"that from all the facts of the case now submitted to this Board, and after mature deliberation, they cannot but condemn the haste and indiscretion used on the part of Mr. Muir towards Mr. Judson in refusing to take back his son after explanations being made by Mr. Thomas Muir, which this board considers quite satisfactory, and that the Secretary be requested to instruct the Principal to take back Mr. Judson's son unconditionally; but while affirming the above, they believe that the discipline of the school may be seriously impaired if this Board does not express in unqualified terms their disapprobation of the course pursued by the said Henry Judson in speaking in a manner disallowed by the Teacher and against the rules of the school."—Carried.

Immediately upon the above being read, Mr. Hurst withdrew his resolution, Mr. Taylor's suiting him much better.

The resolution was then put and carried with only one or two dissentients, after which the Board adjourned.

Mr. Muir's reply to the Resolution of
the School Trustees
(copy)

Central School, 24 August 1859

Allen Cleghorn, Esq., Chairman of the Board of School Trustees:-

My Dear Sir,—I have to acknowledge the receipt of a copy of minute of the Board's action in the case of Mr. Judson's complaint. I have grave doubts as to whether in this action the Board have not exceeded their legal powers, as I am certain they have acted in a way far from conducive to the best interests of the school. In these circumstances while in deference to the Board, I have admitted Henry Judson to his place in the class. I have done so under protest, reserving to myself the right to bring the matter for adjudication before the Chief Superintendent, to whom the law makes both the Trustees and myself ultimately amenable.

I am

With much respect

Yours

Peter D. Muir

Principal of Central School

Brantford *Courier*, and Brant County *General Advertiser*
Saturday Morning, August 27.

A Stab at the Discipline of Our Schools

Elsewhere we publish the proceedings of the Board of School Trustees, who met on Tuesday last to investigate a charge preferred against the Rev. P. D. Muir, Principal of the Central School, by Mr. E. A. Judson, . . . An appeal was made by Mr. Judson to the Trustees, who pass the most absurd and ill-advised resolutions ever heard of, and which, if allowed to go by unchecked will destroy all discipline in our schools. As we have said the Trustees have taken an unwise step—one that will be productive of most evil results. A blow —a serious blow has been made against the best interests of our school, and from henceforth we may expect that the scholars will conduct themselves as suits their own peculiar views. A triumph has been gained by them over their teachers, and no opportunity will be lost by them to shew it in unmistakeable terms. The triumph is already appreciated and made manifest by the scholars, who, it is said, on young Judson returning to school cheered him lustily . . .

Brantford, 8th Sept. 1859

Revd & Dear Sir,

I am just favoured with yours of 6th No. 3317B for which receive my warmest thanks. I need not say how much the very spontaneity of your expression of opinion enhances its value in my eyes, as showing how truly you sympathize with all sincere efforts to make our schools what they ought to be.

I write now to solicit your permission to publish your letter in our local papers, as calculated in my opinion to be of unspeakable use in this town. . . .

Tomorrow I expect to be able to send you a paper containing an address which has been presented to me and my wife, which will shew you that this town generally is of your own opinion in the matter. This is encouraging, but still I am of opinion that the best thing I can do will be to resign. It will be the only thing I think to rouse the town to take steps to prevent such risks again thro exposing their schools to the mercy of incompetent parties.

Might I take the liberty of craving an immediate reply as the trustees meet again early in the ensuing week.

With sincere respect
Yours

Rev. Egerton Ryerson   Peter D. Muir

THE SCHOOL DIFFICULTY
Letter from the Chief Superintendent of Education
   We have much pleasure in publishing the following letter from the Rev. E. Ryerson, Chief Superintendent of Education for Upper Canada. It is an able document and will be read with much interest.

Education Office
Toronto, 6th Sep., 1859

Sir,—I have the honor to state, in reply to your letter of the 26th ult., that I have no positive authority in cases such as you have submitted. By the 5th clause of the 35th section of the School Act of 1850, I have authority to decide in questions affecting the expenditure of the school fund; and by the 7th clause of the 31st section of the same Act, I am authorized to decide upon questions referred to me by local Superintendents, also on appeals from dissatisfied parties; but there is no provision to enforce my decisions in regard to such appeals. The law, therefore, seems to have intended that I should express my opinion or offer advice, when applied to; but leaving it optional with parties to acquiesce in my opinion or advice or not, except in questions relating to the expenditure of school monies apportioned by me.

   In the case which you submit, I might decline expressing any opinion, as it relates to matters in which I have no legal authority, and which both parties have not agreed to refer to me. But I do not think I ought to refuse expressing an opinion in order to avoid the responsibility attached to it.

   I have read the account of the affair, and the proceedings of the Board of Trustees as reported in the two Brantford newspapers, and the correspondence laid before the Board. I may therefore be supposed to have heard both sides.

   The question seems to be in substance, that a pupil some 15 or 16 years of age spoke in the school, and spoke so as to be heard by his teacher, and in words and manner disrespectful to the teacher—involving an imputation upon the teacher's impartiality. Whether the pupil addressed the teacher or not, is not clear; but all admit that he spoke—that he spoke in reference to the conduct of the teacher—that his asking why the teacher had not marked another boy for doing what the teacher was marking him for, implied not only disrespect to the teacher, but an imputation upon him, calculated to excite suspicion against the justice of his conduct, and to weaken his authority. The boy's addressing a fellow pupil appears to me more objectionable than if he had addressed the teacher, as by doing so he added the school offence of whispering, or rather talking, to that of impugning the teacher.

In a small boy this would have been an offence requiring the exercise of school discipline; in a large boy it was certainly a serious offence. I have had my own son, my only son, when ten years of age, not admitted, but sent home for half a day, for being three minutes too late at the Model School, and sent home for whispering in his class. I thought it very strict, but I honored the teacher for his decision and fidelity, and I reproved my boy for failing in the least to observe the rules of the school. Masters responsible to me have employed language and shown feeling in cases of discipline that I regretted; but the evident tendency and object of the proceeding being to maintain order and submission in the school, I have felt it my duty to sustain them against complaints, when I have afterwards conversed with them on the propriety and advantage of exercising discipline in a somewhat different manner. The official school regulations state that a teacher should "practise such discipline in his school as would be exercised by a judicious parent in his family." If a father heard one of his sons say to another that his father punished him for what his brother did without being punished, such a father would probably employ the rod of correction to such a son rather than require an apology from him. A teacher, like a parent, must not only have large powers, but a large discretion, to maintain proper discipline in his large family; and in the one case, no more than in the other, should there be any interference, unless in acts of gross wrong or cruelty. A teacher, any more than a parent, might not always speak in such a tone of cool indifference as would correspond with the feelings of a chance visitor; but in all government the principles on which it is administered are what men should be judged by, and not the variable feelings to which afflicted humanity is subject, unless such feelings are suffered to outrage right and justice.

The example of the Toronto Board of School Trustees is, of course, of no authority elsewhere; but I think its practice worthy of imitation in cases like that under consideration. When difficulties have occurred in the Schools, the Local Superintendent has been directed to inquire into them and report the particulars to the Board of Trustees, who have first heard and considered his report, and then decided whether it should be adopted, or whether a committee should be appointed to inquire further into the matter. I never heard of their calling teachers and pupils from school before them, nor of its being objected to the Local Superintendent (the very officer for that purpose) inquiring into such matters, much less of an objection to his report being read. I should be sorry to be a Local Superintendent under such circumstances. I think it extremely objectionable for any parent to come to the school during school exercises, especially in the presence of the school, to demand explanations or enter into discussion with the teacher, in regard to matters of school discipline; and I would in all cases recommend a teacher to decline any such interview at such time or place. The teacher has to do, not with parents individually, but with the Trustees who employ him; and no parent ought to interrupt him during school hours; and if any parent wishes to see and converse with the teacher, he should do so out of school hours, and not before the pupils of the school, where the teacher must be supreme, and be acknowledged as such, until superseded, or unless when the school is visited by a superior school officer. But if every parent is to run to the school, and demand an account from the teacher, of any or every case of discipline in regard to the pupil child of such parent, there can be no order in the school, or respect for the teacher, much less comfort and independence on his part for the firm and impartial discharge of his, at all times, difficult and responsible duties.

It is always in the power of the Board of School Trustees to dispense with the services of a teacher on the expiration of his agreement with them; but while he retains his office, his authority should not be enfeebled and crippled by undue intermeddling, and, he, then, after having been degraded in the eyes of the pupils and their parents, dismissed for inefficiency. To maintain proper respect for the character and authority of the teacher is the best way to promote the highest interests of the pupils. In view of the whole affair, my belief is that the Board of School Trustees for the Town of Brantford would do honor to themselves and confer a great benefit upon the school interests and pupils of the town, if not elsewhere, by rescinding the resolution which the majority of them adopted, in respect for the very moderate reparation you required, for a serious breach of discipline (only resorting to suspension, though physical correction would then have been a justifiable remedy for avowed disobedience) and allow the whole matter to drop in silence. But with such a resolution under such circumstances recorded and remaining unrepealed, I should be sorry to undertake the management of your Central School a week, or to see any teacher trained in the Normal School engaged in it, as I do not believe he could either be happy or successful in his work.

I have the honor to be,
Sir
Your obedient servant,
E. Ryerson

The Reverend
    Peter D. Muir, A.B.,
        Principal of Central School
        Brantford.

A LOCAL SUPERINTENDENT ADVISES

Address to the School Trustees, Parents, and Common School Teachers, of the County of Durham, C. W., by the Rev. George Blair, M.A., County Superintendent (Bowmanville, 1866), pp. 1-7.

LADIES AND GENTLEMEN:
Although it is one of my duties as County superintendent to lecture, if circumstances permit, once a year in every school section, I have found it impossible

in some cases to give an evening lecture in consequence of the difficulty of getting an audience together. I therefore take this method of addressing the friends of education throughout the county. The points to which I wish to direct attention are the following:—

VISITING AND EXAMINING.—It is one of the duties of the superintendent to visit each Common School within his jurisdiction twice a year . . .

The object of the superintendent in his school examinations, is not necessarily to go over all the classes, which would be often impossible—often a mere waste of time; but simply to satisfy himself that the school is efficiently conducted, or to enable him to point out to the teacher in what respects his tuition may be defective as compared with other schools, or with the requirements of the law. It is evident that much of this can be better done in the absence of the public than when a crowd is present; and accordingly the School Law Manual recommends that the inspector's official visits be private, or "without previous notice to the parties concerned." . . .

I take this opportunity of stating, also, that the inspector is authorized and required to examine the school himself; for which purpose it is the teacher's duty to call out such classes as he may desire; and while any one class is under examination, it is the duty of the teacher to take care that the whole school shall be at liberty to give its undivided attention; for by this means the superintendent, while nominally engaged in examining a single class, on any subject, is really examining and instructing the whole school. . . .

My plan of examining is to call up the different reading classes in succession, beginning with the youngest—to see that they are all provided with books and other requisites—and to test the proficiency of the members of each class in the various subjects with which they ought to be acquainted at that particular stage of their school progress which is indicated by the book they are reading in. By this means I am enabled to see whether any child is passing through the school without receiving the amount of instruction, in all the branches, to which it is legally entitled. . . .

EMPLOYING TEACHERS NOT LEGALLY QUALIFIED.—It is one important duty of the superintendent to see that the schools are conducted by legally qualified teachers. In some cases I find that trustees have been employing teachers who had neither a certificate from any of the Boards in this county, nor a provincial certificate, nor a permit or licence from the superintendent.— This is grossly unjust to the holders of the legal qualification, many of whom are at present unemployed. I therefore give notice, that in the course of my next visit to any school, after this date, I shall expect every teacher to be ready to produce his or her voucher, whether a certificate or a licence; and that no irregularities of this kind will be permitted after the next meeting of the Examining Boards, when an opportunity will be given to all who possess the necessary qualification to obtain the legal title. . . .

QUALIFICATIONS REQUIRED IN THIS COUNTY.—Trustees are further requested to observe that, as the law now stands, certificates granted in one county are not valid in another, and that cases have lately occurred in which teachers who held second-class certificates from other counties were unable to obtain a third class in Durham. In this county the Examiners attach high importance to excellence in the elementary branches—especially reading, spelling, arithmetic and grammar—and no one who is deficient in these fundamental subjects can obtain a high class certificate in Durham, whatever may be his other qualifications. The attention of teachers cannot be too earnestly directed to this point. I am convinced that, in times past, our Examining Boards have too much overlooked the vital importance of excellence in the elementary branches, and have been too much disposed to estimate the qualifications of a Common School teacher by his knowledge of Grammar School subjects, without sufficient regard to his proficiency in the subjects that are of paramount importance in our Common Schools. I am convinced, also, that much injury has been done by granting first-class certificates to candidates who have had little or no experience in teaching, and who, in virtue of such certificates have been placed in positions of responsibility for which they lacked the highest qualification of all. I believe I am authorized to state, that the Examining Boards of this county have now resolved to attach the greatest importance to excellence in the common branches, and to successful experience in teaching.

TRUSTEES' REPORTS.—With reference to the Trustees' Reports for the half year ending June 30th, I have to complain that many of them were made out in a very unsatisfactory manner. Some of them were sent in without even the name of the teacher; others without the corporate seal, and some without the number of the school section. In all cases the columns ought to be added twice —first vertically, then horizontally—and the totals written down in both cases, as the manner in which the paper is ruled clearly indicates. The vertical and horizontal columns of totals will then serve as a check upon each other in verifying the correctness of the return. The horizontal line of totals ought, as a matter of course, to be carried over to the top of the next page; yet this was in many cases neglected. To do all this, or see it done, is expressly stated to be the duty of the teacher; and he has really no excuse for neglecting it or performing it in a slovenly manner, since the work can be given, as a practical exercise in addition, to some of the more reliable pupils. In many cases, too, the reports were very late in being returned to me, thereby delaying the distribution of the money to every school in the township; for the absence of even one report renders it impossible to proceed. . . .

PRACTICABILITY OF THE PRESCRIBED COURSE OF INSTRUCTION.—Another subject which I wish to bring under discussion, and which is perhaps of still more immediate urgency, is the practicability of teaching up to the standard prescribed by the Council of Public Instruction, and printed on the cover of the Registers. In the address which I delivered at our County Convention in May last, I expressed an opinion that the too general deficiency in our reading and spelling, as compared with the schools in the old country, may be attributed in no small measure to the fact, that in our prescribed course of instruction we attempted too much, or, rather, too many things at once; and I added as my opinion that "it would be well if our system were so modified that the pupil's attention should be drawn to almost nothing else before he could read and spell any ordinary word in the English language with perfect ease and fluency." I must state, however, that in several schools in which I have found the children in the third or lowest division tolerably conversant with most of the subjects prescribed in our authorized course, I found that they were even more expert at reading and spelling than in schools where nothing but reading and spelling had been attempted; and where, consequently, the children were much less intelligent. My conviction now is, that our failure in most cases to teach reading and spelling quickly and successfully, arises partly from the great irregularity of attendance in this country, and partly from our lax system of discipline, in consequence of which the eye of the child is allowed to wander at will during school hours—even during recitations—and is therefore too little accustomed to the printed page. In one hour, or even in one half-hour, of strictly enforced attention, with the eye constantly on the page, the child would learn more than in a day of our lax school system; and too often the child's school week consists of two or three days. We must, therefore, beware of adopting the methods and standard of the old country unless we adopt the old country discipline also, by insisting that the children, when in school, shall be constantly occupied with their lessons.

But how is it possible to keep the very young children always occupied? I answer that if they are allowed to talk or whisper, they will never be occupied with anything else but talking and whispering, or watching the opportunity to do so; and therefore the secret of keeping them very much occupied with their lessons is to insist positively that while in school they shall occupy themselves with nothing else. If strict silence is literally enforced, the child will find its lesson a relief; if whispering and talking are allowed, it will find its lesson a burden; and while doing no good to itself, it will distract the attention of the teacher, keep him or her in constant irritation, and annoy and hinder the whole school. The rule must therefore be, *perfect silence in school.* If a child is too young to be taught silence, the child is too young to be in school. If a young man or young woman is too old to be taught silence, the young man or young woman is too old to be at school, and should stay at home. If to some it may appear that the enforcement of this rule is impracticable, and would be too hard on the little ones, I have merely to state that in our best schools the rule is actually enforced at this moment; and that a teacher is forgetful of the most important part of his duty who does not bear in mind the fact, that *patient silence and respectful attention are perhaps the most valuable lessons which a child can learn in school.*

At the same time I do not deny, that so far as may consist with the enforcement of this rule of silence and perfect order, it is desirable to alleviate as much as possible to the little ones the burden of education—though not to the extent of making it mere sport and pleasure, as some superficial people imagine. The great mistake, I fear, on this continent, is the idea that education may be had without discipline—forgetting that this discipline itself is the most important part of education. The only legitimate means of alleviating the task to the learner are—first, constant cheerfulness and kindness, as far as is consistent with strict discipline, on the part of the teacher; and secondly, rendering the tasks themselves as attractive and interesting as possible. It is in connection with this latter consideration, that we are compelled to recognize the importance of varying the subjects of study even in the lowest division; and although I am still of opinion that the chief efforts of the teacher ought, at this early stage, to be directed to those branches of instruction—such as reading and spelling—which exercise only the memory and imitative faculties of the child, still I am now convinced by a pretty extended experience, that a child who is taught only to read and spell—and not to reason or reflect—remains in a state of mental stupor, and is no match, even in reading and spelling, for a child whose reasoning and reflective faculties have been cultivated into early development by a skilful teacher.

JOHN JESSUP REPORTS TO THE LEGISLATURE OF BRITISH COLUMBIA

Second Annual Report of the Public Schools of the Province of British Columbia for the Year Ending July 31st, 1873, by the Superintendent of Education (Victoria, 1873).

To His Excellency the Honorable JOSEPH W. TRUTCH, Lieutenant-Governor of the Province of British Columbia.

MAY IT PLEASE YOUR EXCELLENCY:—

As required by Section 8, sub-section 7, of the "Public School Act, 1872," I have the honor to submit, for Your Excellency's information, my Second Annual Report on the state of the Public Schools in the Province of British Columbia. . . .

Schools, Attendance, Books, &c.

TABLE A.—The returns under this head have come in far more complete and accurate this year than last. What was then but an approximation, is now pretty correctly carried out by figures. Number of children returned as attending school last year, 534; this year, 1,028—nearly double. The number of school-going children in the several School Districts is 1,706. To these may be added fully 300, who are not yet within reach of educational facilities—chiefly in the interior—making a total, in round numbers of 2,000. It will be seen that more than one-half of these are in the public schools; while about 400 more are attending the different denominational and private schools, leaving nearly 600 not yet gathered into the schools, either public or private. In the different school districts, 291 (the number in some of the districts is approximate) are returned as not attending school anywhere. Of the 1,028 in the public schools, 573 are boys, and 455 girls. Irregular attendance amounts to over 37 per cent.

This is much more than it ought to be, and detracts very materially from scholastic improvement. The district reports show that 272 children are in first or lowest reader, 223 in second, 182 in third, 164 in fourth, and 125 in fifth; in Arithmetic, 785; Grammar, 428; Geography, 478; History, 162; Book-keeping, 40; Mensuration, 20; Algebra, 37; Euclid 24; Natural Philosophy, 32; Vocal Music, 401; Linear Drawing, 104; Animal and Vegetable Physiology, 20; Writing, 847; Dictation, 478; Other Studies, 84. . . .

TABLE C.—At the date of my last Report we had only eight school houses returned as public property, now there are twenty-two—an increase of fourteen; of these, twelve are new buildings; two were not enumerated last year, namely, one in Victoria—school not then established; and one in Metchosin, from which there were no returns. The total amount expended for new buildings was $8,522 87; the buildings therefore cost on an average over $700 each; the most expensive one being at Nanaimo, which cost $2,250 without furniture; and the lowest, South Cowichan, built of squared logs, $170 50. Many of the building items, however, include furnishing also. . . .

TABLE D. exhibits a decided improvement over last year. Then, in a majority of the schools, a great variety of text books were used; now, with a few slight exceptions, the authorized books have entirely superseded all others. Sixteen Maps of the World were purchased last November, and distributed among those schools absolutely without any. There is much need of an uniform series of maps being obtained for the use of the schools; the few that are used being too old for service, except perhaps in Physical Geography. The number of black boards in the schools has more than doubled during the year. . . .

TABLE F. is appended for the purpose of shewing the cost of children, for the year, attending school in each of the Districts. It will be observed that in the small schools the average is very high, especially where new school houses have been erected, or the old ones extensively repaired. The lowest average on the current expenditure is Nanaimo, $12 49; and the highest, Sooke, $62 07 per annum; the average for the Province being $34 66 per annum for each pupil in attendance at the public schools. Although this table exhibits a heavy cost per pupil, yet it must be borne in mind that as the school-going population increases this average will decrease; because, were the attendance in many of the schools doubled, or even quadrupled, the annual expense would be nothing more than at present. . . .

VOCAL MUSIC IN SCHOOLS

This branch of instruction is not so generally taught in our schools as it ought to be. It should be considered an essential, instead of an unimportant non-essential. I would scarcely go so far as to assert that a knowledge of vocal music "is of more practical value than mathematics," yet there is no gainsaying the fact that probably nine out of ten persons of both sexes will find far more use for, and derive greater benefit from, a fair knowledge of this subject than from mathematics beyond the simple rules of arithmetic. But its practical value in after life is but one argument, among many, why it should be carefully and generally taught. Its utility in the school room in maintaining order, in the enforcement of discipline, and as an incentive to study, cannot be over estimated. It comes in here as a powerful auxiliary in aiding and assisting the teacher; and while occupying a place side by side with arithmetic, grammar, and geography, it becomes what the studies never are, namely, a healthful and soul-enlivening recreation. "Singing is as natural to children as speaking, and for any reason that appears to the contrary, it should be as universal." "If music is thus an instinct of our being," says the late Dr. Forrester of Nova Scotia, "If an endowment bestowed less or more upon all by the beneficent Creator, it must have been intended to be cultivated and developed, and how could that be more effectually done than by making it a branch of education in our Public Schools?" But it might be argued that all teachers have not a taste for vocal music, probably not, neither have all teachers a particular bias for English grammar or algebra, yet all are obliged to teach the former at least. With the requisite amount of application, the theory of vocal music can be acquired and taught by all; and in nineteen cases out of twenty the practical portion of it may be mastered even after the attainment of mature age. . . .

INSPECTION OF SCHOOLS

During the school year ending 31st July, I made sixty-four school visits, entailing 2,580 miles of travel, or an average distance of more than 40 miles for each visit; to this may be added 450 miles of travel in visiting Nicola Valley and Kamloops in September last; and Big Bar, Canoe, and Dog Creeks, and Alkali Lake, in June of this year; making a total of 2,930 miles. The great amount of travel necessary, in order to reach all the schools of British Columbia, will be readily understood, when I state that the schools on the Mainland, numbering twelve, are, on an average more than 40 miles apart; while those on Vancouver Island and dependencies, fifteen in all, have an average distance from each other of over ten miles. The labour and cost of inspection would, therefore, be but little more were the number of schools quadrupled from Sooke to Comox, and from Burrard Inlet to Barkerville. . . .

CONCLUSION

In closing my Report, I am thankful to say that we have much to animate our hopes for the future, and encourage our exertions. Although one-eighth of our school population is not yet deriving any benefit from free public school education, for the simple reason that schools are not within reach; yet the tangible improvement brought about during the past year leads us confidently to hope that, with the aid of an enlightened Legislature and a liberal Government, educational facilities will soon be brought within a reasonable distance of every household in the Province. A little judicious pressure brought to bear upon negligent parents in our school districts, by Trustees, will soon make chronic non-attendance almost a thing of the past. In several parts, public schools are entirely a new feature; and parents themselves, in some instances, require to be educated, in order properly to realize the fact that instruction is requisite for their offspring. In my visiting and lecturing tour this autumn, I shall endeavour to awaken a more lively interest in the education of the young; to show parents and guardians that everything possible is being done for them, and that it is their bounden duty to avail themselves of the very great educational privileges already provided for the benefit and advancement of those committed to their charge. The steady progress made so far, is but an earnest of what may yet be done by promoting the spread of sound and useful knowledge among the youth of our land; who, in a few years, will take the place of those who are now actively engaged in the bustle and business of life. A beginning has been made, and we believe a good one. From year to year, amendments and improvements will be found necessary in our school system; yet the foundation has been well and broadly laid, upon which we hope to erect an educational structure worthy of this Pacific Province of the Great Dominion.

I have the honor to be,

Your Excellency's most obedient, humble servant,

JOHN JESSOP.

Education Office,
Victoria, September, 1873.

AN INSPECTOR INVESTIGATES LOCAL CONFLICT

'The Nelson Public School Investigation', pp. 173-94. Public Archives of British Columbia.

(Memos from the Principal, Mr. Thompson, to Miss Olding)

November 8th, 1912.

Miss Olding, Division 14,

Please observe the following:

1. Secure order in your room, then maintain it.
   Talking aloud must cease.
2. Get the Phonetic sound of letters correctly.
   Better give the name of letter than wrong sound.
3. Continue dictation on the board, but see that the pupils' writing is improved rather than impared [sic].
4. Music, (Rote Singing), should occupy 7 to 10 minutes daily.
5. More attention should be given to Languages, Training through Object lessons, pictures, stories, etc.
6. Endeavor to get more spontaneity and responsiveness in your class.
7. Wait for the bell before any move is made for dismissal, 5 minutes will be given to get ready.

R. T.

At 3, we will dismiss by front entrance.

Supplementary Phonic Primers, for this term at least to be used then returned to Stock room for the use of other teachers.

The time to be amicably arranged with Miss Rath, and Miss M. McVicar who are using them.

We have 106 Phonic Primers, and 101 1st Primers.

Other paper:-   (n.d.)

Miss Olding,

Have pupils hand to you 1st Primers also Phonic Primers, pile them on the desk and I will count them to-morrow.

R. T.

The *Daily News*, Nelson, Friday, November 15.

THE SCHOOL BOARD SITUATION.

There will be general regret and a very considerable measure of disappointment throughout the city at the finding of the school board as a result of its investigation of the trouble between Mr. R. Thompson, as principal of the public school, and his staff. In summarily dismissing Mr. Thompson, as it did, the board dealt to say the least, harshly, and there are many who have read the evidence who will say unjustly.

The charges against Mr. Thompson, as presented by the teachers opposed to him, when presented to the public could not but strike the ordinary mind as trivial in the extreme. It is true that Mr. Thompson may have exhibited some hastiness but perhaps there were circumstances which would have provoked any ordinary man placed in a similar position and he may have lacked in the tact necessary to the successful holding of the principalship of the Nelson public school under existing conditions. But even at that Mr. Thompson leaves the school by no means a disgraced man, but with the confidence and support of a very considerable proportion of the people of Nelson, a good majority it would probably be safe to say.

In the trouble which has arisen Mr. Thompson was placed in a most unpleasant position. He was a stranger to the vast majority of the people of Nelson, without the large circle of friends and relatives possessed by the teachers who opposed him. Any sympathy or support which he may receive, and there have been many expressions of both during the last few days, and particularly last night following the decision of the board, is therefore based, not on personal friendships or acquaintanceships, but on the merits of the case as the public views it.

But apart from the personal side of the question, the position in which the whole affair has placed school affairs in Nelson is much more than unfortunate. Nelson has one of the best school buildings in the province and the people of the city contribute ungrudgingly to its support. These efforts to advance the interests of education in the city have been, to say the least, adversely affected by the contretemps which have arisen.

The open breach, which resulted in last night's action of the school board, The Daily News is forced to conclude, would not have occurred had there been a proper spirit among the teachers as a whole. If any of the teachers at any time thought he or she had any reason to complain they should have laid their complaint before the board and asked for action thereon. The result undoubtedly would have been the reaching of a proper understanding and the board would have been forced to a declaration as to whether its members were prepared to back the principal in the establishment of reasonable discipline among his staff. If they were not prepared to do this it would have been a good thing for the principal and the public to have known. Instead of this, petty complaints kept trickling out among the public, and possibly to some members of the school board, and the matters complained of not having been dealt with, members of the staff finally worked themselves up into a feeling that they had a number of very large grievances and presented their resignations in a body.

Apart from the diarrangement [sic] of school affairs, which has followed, the trustees are now face to face with the problem of how they are to re-establish discipline among the staff. As matters stand the resignations of nine members of the staff are before the board and the principalship is vacant.

What is to be done with these resignations and what is to be done to fill the principalship and how, in dealing with these problems, discipline is to be re-established, once and for all time, is the problem now before the school board. Strong action is necessary if this problem is to be satisfactorily solved. Is the school board strong enough to solve it?

Victoria, B.C.
December 18th, 1912.

Alexander Robinson, Esq., LL.D.,
   Superintendent of Education,
      Victoria, B.C.
Sir:

Upon the investigation into the cause of the summary dismissal of Mr. Robert Thompson as Principal of Nelson Public School, I beg to report as follows:

The investigation was held in the "Board Room", Nelson Public School building on November 28th, 29th and 30th, 1912, when all members of the staff were called upon to give evidence, with Mr. Thompson present, that he might be the better able to reply to any and all charges preferred by members of the staff.

Mr. Thompson was summarily dismissed, with salary to December 31st, 1912, on November 14th, 1912, after an investigation had been held by the full Board, into the cause leading to the tendering of a joint resignation signed by nine of the ten members of the permanent staff.

At the investigation held on November 28th, 29th and 30th, (the evidence taken thereat, together with other papers herewith accompanying) the Misses Scanlan, McKenzie, McVicar, Olding, Pettit, Mrs. Cryderman, and Mr. Cullen preferred charges of misconduct towards them individually by Mr. Thompson, and all, with the exception of the Misses Rath and Wade complained of his general attitude towards the members of the staff.

Miss McKenzie complained of harsh criticism before the class, that he 'stormed' at her before the class, (p. 44), of refusing to listen to explanation, and of using threatening language when informed that complaint would be made to the Board.

Miss Scanlan charged that Mr. Thompson became angry at a Teachers' meeting and used a coarse expression towards her which was confirmed by every member of the staff.

Miss Mabel McVicar complained, that Mr. Thompson treated her in a harsh manner; that he accused her, unjustly, of taking from the stockroom and retaining possession of a greater number of Supplementary Primers than was required by her class; in order that another teacher, who required the same book, might be inconvenienced through an insufficient number being available for her; and that he accused her of defying his orders with bravado. She also accused him of scolding her and of losing control of his temper while in her presence and of wrothfully [sic] striking the desk with his fist.

Miss Olding charged Mr. Thompson with accusing her of trickery, of being spitefully inclined towards another member of the staff, of 'storming' at her.

Miss Pettit complained that Mr. Thompson excused pupils from her Household Science classes without consulting her and of his withdrawing pupils from her room without explanation.

Mrs. Cryderman accused Mr. Thompson of using coarse language towards her and of using a threatening attitude towards her.

Mr. Cullen charged Mr. Thompson with becoming enraged at him, with addressing him coarsely; with criticizing his methods harshly before the school. Furthermore, that he was unjustly accused by Mr. Thompson of endeavoring to introduce militarism into the school, because he formed the pupils into forms, and marched the pupils into school to the beat of the drum.

In replying to these charges, Mr. Thompson passed over the complaint of Miss McKenzie as being of no importance; yet Miss McKenzie considered it of such importance that she tendered her resignation soon after it occurred, withdrawing it only upon the advice and persuasion of the Inspector for the District, who had, in turn, been prevailed upon by the Chairman of the Board, that the Principal might be given an opportunity 'to find himself'.

Mr. Thompson acknowledges losing his temper at the October teachers' meeting, and of exclaiming to Miss Scanlan, "My God, woman, sit down," but he attempted to make light of it by remarking that, "She was as angry as I was". There is no justification or excuse for the Principal of a school to become angry towards the members of his staff, no matter how great the provocation might be; his position is altogether different from that of the teacher, for he occupies the position of greater authority and should exercise that authority with becoming dignity. When this is not done, when the principal so far forgets his position as to wrangle over matters over which he has complete jurisdiction, he naturally loses prestige with every member of his staff.

The charges of Miss McVicar and Miss Olding are substantially the same. Mr. Thompson does not deny that he was angry upon this occasion; he does deny, however, some of the other charges made, others he cannot recollect. There appears here less justification than at any other time for anger on the part of the principal. When asked, they informed him of the number of books they had, that these were insufficient in number, and that they were in use every day. Yet, without reason, he accused both teachers of spite towards Miss Rath, and of keeping books from her. These teachers denied any feeling of the kind on their part; but Miss Rath says of Miss Olding, "I disliked her as soon as I saw her", and again, "I did not like her at all, did not like her way." On the barest suspicion Mr. Thompson becomes enraged and accuses the teachers of wrong doing.

In reply to Mr. Cullen's complaint that Mr. Thompson accused him of introducing militarism into the school, Mr. Thompson, alluding to a Cadet Corps which had been formed in the town under Mr. Cullen, says. . . . "No doubt these boys know that I had been approached on the matter, and they felt that I probably had opposed them, and the very fact of them lining up with Mr. Cullen in the matter set up a little opposition against me. He at sundry times had them in a little group, talking and conversing with them." These are suspicions unworthy of a Principal of a large school and could not be entertained by a man of moral strength. If Mr. Cullen's method of conducting the Physical Exercises was not satisfactory to Mr. Thompson, it was the latter's place to inform him in a proper and dignified manner; if Mr. Cullen refused to acknowledge Mr. Thompson's authority in the matter, Mr. Cullen should have been reported to the Board for insubordination. Instead of following the more dignified course, Mr. Thompson undertakes to argue the matter with his assistant, loses his temper, and makes criticisms which should have been made before, and in a different temper.

Mr. Thompson attempts to justify his conduct towards members of the staff by stating that when he took charge of the school it lacked organization, discipline, a full permanent staff; also that the members of the Board were not working in harmony.

Even presuming that these charges could be proved there could be no justification for disrespectful treatment of the members of the staff, nor could better organization nor better discipline be accomplished by antagonizing the teachers. If Mr. Thompson considered certain of these teachers weak; his proper course would have been to have notified the Board, with request for a change; this, however, he failed to do, and the members of the Board could not but presume that the teachers were satisfactory to the principal.

The Board was unanimous in the appointment of Mr. Thompson to the Principalship in July, 1912. There is nothing to show that he was not receiving the support of all the members up to the time that the Board's investigation was in progress. When Mr. Cullen, on October 22nd, charged Mr. Thompson with misconduct towards himself (Cullen) and requested an investigation by the Board, Mr. Thompson, in a letter dated October 25th refused to attend a meeting of the Board to be called for such investigation, and denied the right of the Board to investigate his conduct. Here was insubordination, but the majority of the Board must have been even at that late date, favourably disposed towards the principal for, apparently, the matter was not followed up. An investigation, however, was forced upon the Board on November 8th; for, when about that date Miss Olding and Miss McVicar were insulted by the conduct of Mr. Thompson, the majority of the staff resigned, feeling, apparently, that in no other way was it possible to force their grievance upon the attention of the Board.

The charge of each teacher complaining of personal wrongs is the same, viz: —loss of temper and abuse of Mr. Thompson. Principals are but human, and for that reason loss of temper may be excusable where considerable aggravation can be shown; such should occur but seldom, however. Between August 26th, and November 8th, Mr. Thompson exhibited a loss of temper on no fewer than five occasions, and, with the exception of Miss Scanlan's case, the loss of temper and abuse of the teacher was due to suspicion,—suspicion for which there was absolutely no ground. Miss McKenzie was suspected of promoting pupils who had no right to promotion; Mr. Cullen of undermining the principal's authority, and of introducing militarism into the school because the drum was beat and forms were formed; Miss McVicar of concealing books and Miss Olding of a like offence.

An occasional loss of temper might be overlooked, occurring so often though, and grounded on nothing but suspicion, it cannot be considered other than gross misconduct.

I have the honour to be,

Sir,

Your obedient servant,

(Signed) W. H. M. MAY,

Inspector of Schools.

3 A Question of Responsibility: Families, Churches, Schools, and Public Education

Characteristically, the initial establishment of provincial school systems and centralized administration intensified the debate on who had the responsibility for education. The informality of growing up in an earlier time, with its muddle of schooling, apprenticeship, and parental training, had apparently managed to encompass the varied interests of church, family, and community in the socialization of youth. However the structure of public responsibility, both administrative and financial, once articulated, placed the advocates of local, denominational, and parental autonomy on the defensive. What had for so long been regarded as praiseworthy, if not entirely satisfactory, had now to be promoted as a *right*.

Those opposed to the comprehensive and apparently homogenizing tendencies of public schooling made strange allies. One might well question what ground existed on which not only Anglicans and Roman Catholics, but Liberal voluntaryists as well, might agree. The Catholics, certainly, seemed to be a special case, for demographic as well as ideological reasons. While the issue of Catholic schooling was coloured by the politics of English-French relations in the united province of Canada, the major arguments advanced for Catholic school privileges echoed and re-echoed from Newfoundland to British Columbia. As school promoters knew all too well, the common school represented a critical compromise. Religious instruction was central to Victorian concern for moral training and preparation for civic and Christian responsibility. What would be left to Christianity if it were stripped of its sectarian identity? Nonsectarian religious training in an increasingly secular society might prove a fragile defence against the erosion of traditional spiritual and social values.

The documents relating to Roman Catholic separate schooling reveal the eclecticism of the Catholic argument: the appeal to traditional family and parental roles; to a simpler piety; and to seemingly obvious and unambiguous concepts of social authority and responsibility. Obviously, by the middle of the century, an unhyphenated Christianity, lacking denominational or sectarian conviction, seemed a fragile defence against the inroads of secularism. It was thought that a proper Catholic upbringing would entail Catholic schooling aimed at instilling obedience to religious and civil authority. Moreover Catholic schools had a special role to play in the lives of those Irish immigrants who, outside of Quebec, provided the bulk of the Church's adherents. Thus the classic conflict of Catholic rights in a Protestant community was compounded, in the pre-Confederation era, by the larger questions of Irish cultural survival and social mobility. To what extent, one must ask, might advocates of Church of England denominational schools share the philosophy of their Catholic counterparts? And how far is it possible to disentangle their divergent social and denominational interests? Between the legislature and the courts, on the one hand, and public opinion on the other lay a considerable margin of discretion for departments of education. How does one assess the practical impact of central bureaucracy in mediating between legislation and community attitudes and prejudices? What does local controversy over denominational schooling suggest about the effective means of exercising power and carrying out policy?

The variety of schooling that flourished during the early and middle decades of the nineteenth century has, until recently, been obscured by educational historians' preoccupation with the triumph of universal, tax-supported public schooling. Flexibility and diversity of educational opportunity were not restricted to an era of pioneer self-sufficiency. Nevertheless the mid-century years did mark a critical transition in the concept of responsibility for education: a shift from the traditional social institutions of family and church and community to a concept of 'public' institutions free and distinct from special social or denominational interests.

The provincial school system, with its ambition for comprehensiveness, promised to be efficient and economic and those claims proved difficult to counter. The experience of both England and the United States attested to the benefits and pitfalls of economic and social development. The twin pillars of improvement—economy and efficiency—would, hopefully, maximize the benefits and minimize the pitfalls. At every turn the transformation of Canadian society in the mid years of the century seemed to invest the school's mission with a greater urgency. Not only did the division of public resources among a variety of institutions seem profligate, but the casualness with which youngsters and their families had once regarded schooling appeared increasingly intolerable. *Regular* attendance at school for a definable period of years provided a measure against which the seasonal rhythm of rural life and the unpredictable mobility of urban working-class experience were judged and found wanting. What elements were involved in abetting the 'tyranny' of the common school? As 'being in school' quickly achieved the status of a social norm, what were the consequences of not being there? And finally, one should ask, how common was the urban common school likely to become? And what alternatives were available to those for whom the 'public' school might seem inappropriate?

The early Victorian educational crusade focused on the common school, but did not stop there. Education for all sorts and sizes of young people was promoted and debated as educators, politicians, and parents wrestled with the implications of universal schooling. As education became institutionalized, the influence of caste and character became even more explicit. It seemed that different school environments were needed to complement markedly different family experiences. The problems—and urgency—of female education were in many ways unique; however, parallel concerns underlay designs for the appropriate training of young men for the professions and positions of power. Why was discipline so emphasized in the calendars and prospectuses of private schools and colleges? How significant were geographical, denominational, class, and cultural differences in casting the education of adolescents in Victorian Canada?

THE STATE VERSUS DENOMINATIONAL PRIVILEGE

DENOMINATIONAL, RACIAL, AND CLASS VARIETY IN NOVA SCOTIAN SCHOOLING

Report of the Committee of the Legislature of Nova Scotia appointed to examine the various petitions regarding schools (1836), RG 5, series R, v. 22, Public Archives of Nova Scotia.

Your Committee by four of their number visited several Schools in the Town of Halifax without previous notice that they might inspect their condition and management and judge how far the Public money was properly applied. The Catholic School was very well attended both in its male and female departments, and the number of scholars fully justified the statement contained in the petition, and which is as follows:

	Male School	tuition money	Female School
children in 1833.	171	£21. 12. 3	167
1834.	180	19. 2. 4	199
1835.	278	30. 3. 8	213

The National School appeared also in a very creditable state being attended by many children which from their appearance did not belong to the higher classes, and these kept in distinct apartments, and the Master is reported as eminently qualified for the duties of his Station. Besides the usual grants of £100 for this Institution the petition solicits from this Hon. House a further sum for the repair of the Building as it needs a new roof which will cost not less than £60. Formerly this establishment derived annually from a charitable Society in England £150 for the Master and £75 for the Mistress both of which sums have been withdrawn so that without additional aid its friends assert that the School cannot be kept up in its usually efficient state and that the building this summer must suffer serious injury. The Acadian was also visited and the Committee regret to say that they cannot report favorably of its present condition. The boys and girls were all collected into one apartment and these few in number, the central range of forms being almost entirely empty. The Master explained that the attendance had much fallen off in bad weather and that the school appeared to greater disadvantage than usual at the present time. The Institution however has been for so many years beneficial to the Poor that the Committee recommends the continuance of the ordinary Grant and trust that the Committee of Management will endeavor to restore its former vigor and efficiency.

A new school founded at the commencement of the present year for the instruction solely of colored children, who hitherto have been rather over-looked by the benevolent was another object which drew the attention of the visiting committee. It contains already 53 daily Scholars and 99 Sunday Schol-ars and is placed under the charge of a Master and Mistress who are every way according to the Petition qualified for their pious labors. The progress of these children in their exercises for so short a time was most satisfactory and reflects great honor on the diligence and experience with which it has been conducted. A very commodious house has been built from funds drawn from England & contributions made in Halifax which have paid the expense of the building with the exception of a debt of £80. There is an annuity from England attached to this School amounting to £40 and if this Legislature would grant £60 more it would be placed on a level with the other Institutions of the kind. Your Committee are aware that room could be found in the other three Schools for the admission of these children were they not of African extrac-tion. But the known repugnance of the Whites to mix with them shuts them out from the benefit of the other Institutions, and if they are to be taught at all, they must receive their rudiments of knowledge in a separate and distinct establishment.

To the Petition from New Caledonia in Granville, which asked the aid of the Legislature for building a house of different apartments for a Male and Female School. The Committee were inclined to reply that the large sum required for Common Schools absorbs all that the Provincial liberality can afford and that the Act requires the erection of a building as the first requisite for claiming any public support.

Three Petitions were also taken under consideration presented by School-masters who complain of their being deprived of a participation in the Public Money in the last division made by the Board of Commissioners. Two of them came from the County of Halifax, the third from Cornwallis and all of them would have been entitled to their just proportions had their returns been forwarded to the respective Clerks of the Board in proper time. Instead of providing for them by distinct Grants, Messrs Wheeler, Donochy & Morton are favorably recommended to the Commissioners in their next division of the public money.

On a Memorial from the Colored People in the Town plot of Dartmouth it was determined that when any future application of this kind shall be made to the Commissioners they will apply part of the money at their disposal to assist the colored population to give the means of education to their children altho a school has already been entered on their books for that particular District and also that if a French or Highland Settlement desire a School to be established for teaching their children in their respective Mother tongues, the Board in the several Counties will give effect to their wishes.

Lastly, the Committee have agreed to subjoin to this Report the actual amount of the Provincial money expended in 1835 for the support of education in the Province which comes to £6830. 16s. as per abstract and to recommend that all the Academies now existing and other Seminaries of learning pass under review when the documents and papers in reference to the union of the Windsor and Dalhousie Colleges shall be furnished to the House in order that this vast sum drawn from the Treasury may be so subdivided and appropriated as to afford to the whole population of all sects and denominations a vigorous and efficient system of General Education.

Abstract—Education for 1835.

Common and Grammar Schools	£4711. 7. 4.
Academies—Windsor, £444.8.8—Halifax	594. 8. 8.
Grammar School, £150—Pictou, £400	900. 0. 0.
Horton, £300—Annapolis, £100—Yarmouth,	200. 0. 0.
£100—Liverpool, £50—Lunenburgh, £50.—Mr.	75. 0. 0.
Uniackes, £100.—Poor House, £25.—Indians	350. 0. 0.
Cape Breton, £50—Infant School, £50.	
National, Catholic & Acadian Schools, £300	
	£6830. 16. 0

THE CHURCH OF ENGLAND'S CASE: THE DIOCESE OF TORONTO

Adam Townley, *Seven Letters on the Non-Religious School System of Canada and the United States* (Toronto, Henry Rowsell, 1853), pp. 15-23, 26-9, 31-2, 34-7, 43.

Dear Sir:

I proceed to notice the Chief Superintendent's most certainly reckless assertion that Denominational Schools would "not only cost the people fivefold (!) what they have now to pay for School purposes, but would leave the youth of minor religious persuasions, and large portions of the poorer youth of the country, without any means of education upon terms within the pecuniary resources of their parents, unless as paupers, or at the expense of their religious faith." . . .

The gross impropriety of the statements under consideration I intend to prove in this letter . . .

I will proceed then, first, to state a plan for combining the religious and secular education of our youth by the establishment of Denominational

Schools—a plan which will, if it be ever fairly carried out, I am convinced, vindicate the accuracy of these statements. I propose then, that a Provincial School-law shall be enacted in substance as follows:

1st. That any religious denomination, or separate congregation, which desires to establish a Common School of its own in any particular locality, shall have the legal right to claim for that purpose the school assessment of its own members, and their corresponding share of the Provincial or local educational grant.

2d. That the appointment of the Teacher, with all other internal regulations of such school, shall be in the Minister and lay officials, "as church-wardens, elders, or class leaders," &c., of said denomination in such locality.

3d. That such Denominational School shall not interfere with the right of the school-section in which it is situated to establish other denominational, or non-religious schools.

4th. That where in any school-section there are only Denominational Schools, then, the parents or guardians not belonging to the denomination or denominations unto which such school or schools belong, shall have a legal right to send their children to such denominational schools, provided there be no other within—distance: Provided always, that in such a case the school assessment of parents so sending their children, and their corresponding share of the Provincial grant, shall then be paid to the denominational school to which they send their children; such parents also paying their equal share of such further tax as the managers of the school may find it necessary to impose.

5th. That parents or guardians not belonging to the Denomination to whose school they send their children shall have a legal right to require that they learn no catechism, or other religious formulary, the Bible only excepted, but such as they, the parents, approve.

6th. That the poor shall, without payment, have the same legal right with those who pay to send their children to any school, upon their solemn declaration of their inability to pay: the authorities of such school having a claim upon a public fund, to be established for that purpose for a certain rate of payment for all such scholars. In case of supposed imposition, an appeal laying to the council of the township in which such school is situated.

7th. That where there is but one school in a section, whether it be denominational or otherwise, it shall have the right to the use of the schoolhouse for the time being; but that, where there shall be more than one school, and only one schoolhouse, it shall rest with the majority of the inhabitants of such section to say, from year to year, which school shall have the use of it.

8th. That parents or guardians, not belonging to any denomination which shall have established a school of its own under the sanction of this Provincial law, shall *not* have a legal right to send their children, under the exemptions aforesaid, to said school, if there be a school of their own denomination, or one non-religious, either in their own or a neighboring school-section, within—distance. Nevertheless, be it enacted that, if such parents shall be content to subject their children to all the regulations and teachings, religious or otherwise, of such school, then they *shall* have a legal right to send their children to said denominational school, even though they, the parents, do not belong to that particular denomination—subject always to payments hereinbefore provided in such cases.

9th. That where no denominational school is established, then the majority of the inhabitants shall have a legal right, as now, to establish a school on such basis as they see fit, and to assess *all* the inhabitants for its support, excepting only such persons as may be sending their children to some neighboring denominational school, under the conditions hereinbefore provided.

10th. That all Common Schools, denominational or otherwise, shall publish annually, in the nearest newspaper, a statement of their entire receipts and expenditure.

11th. That it shall be competent for the Government to appoint inspectors of *all* schools receiving public money, denominational as well as others, whose duty it will be to see that the teachers are of competent ability, that the schools are properly conducted, and that the advance of the pupils in secular knowledge is satisfactory....

First, as to the expense. The plan I have proposed, instead of "costing the people five-fold more than the present system" does not ask one farthing more than *their own just proportion* of the public funds. Again; where there are not children enough to form two schools, and yet a denominational school is established, I provide that such school shall be bound to receive the rest of the children in such school-section; consequently there is no plea for increased expenditure; the only difference in such case, between the present system and the one I propose, being that the school is under especial religious direction, instead of being entirely secular. While in towns or villages no increased expenditure will be needed, because there will be a sufficient number of children of different denominations to form schools abundantly large, especially including the children of the minor sects, and those of no denomination, who would from choice attend the denominational schools.

But it seems probable, taking into consideration the vastly increased efficiency which would be given to our Common Schools by the religious supervision I am advocating, that their cost would be *absolutely less*, perhaps very much less, than under the present system; and for these reasons; first because the ministers and lay officials, taking a much deeper, because religious interest in the schools, than is done by the present township superintendents, trustees, &c. &c., the Schools would be much more efficiently and economically managed; and secondly, because from the personal efforts of the various Ministers and their friends, excited to exertion by the *religious* as well as intellectual advantages which they would hope the children would derive from their schools, *a much larger average of attendance would be secured throughout the Province than is now the fact*; and thus the average expenditure would be *lessened*, instead of increased five-fold, while the benefits of a sound education would be much *more generally* diffused than at present.

The fact is, that our present Provincial system of Common School Education is most expensive, and is causing great dissatisfaction throughout the Province.—From the manner in which the Report of Common Schools is published, it is perhaps quite impossible for the people in general to arrive at a knowledge of what is the real cost to the Province of education in proportion to the instruction given.

For instance, from the uncertain manner in which the returns are made, the real attendance of children cannot be discovered;...

In 1849 the Chief Superintendent of Education gave the average of attendance of the schools throughout the Province at 8½ to 10, and the average cost of education for each child as 15s. 1¾d. per annum. Now a friend of mine, a staunch Reformer, deep in the mysteries of local legislation during the short-lived days of District Municipal Councils, was startled at these returns, believing them, from his previous knowledge, to be totally incorrect; he therefore probed the matter thoroughly as respects the Niagara District; and found the results, from the public returns of the "Niagara District School Report," to be as follows:—

Average of attendance as 4 to 10, and the average expenditure per child to be £1 10s. 7½d. per annum. And this is exclusive of the cost of fuel, school-houses, and superintendence, local and general.

The gentleman who kindly gives me these statistics, declares that 40 per cent ought to be added for extras, the average expense given above being merely calculated from the teachers' salaries. These statements he has published in numerous letters, and defying contradiction, has not received it, as to any of his staple facts....

I think I have also fairly shown that Dr. RYERSON's second assertion—that if Denominational Schools were established "the youth of minor religious persuasions would be left without any means of education save at the expense of their religious faith"—is totally without foundation; since they would be admitted into the schools of the larger denominations without the slightest interference with their own religious principles. Indeed, on the contrary, I have proved, as I stated I would, that such youth would be in a far more desirable condition, as respects their education, than at present: for that they would be members of a school, the intellectual status of which would be more efficiently looked after than under the present system, while its moral securities would be incomparably greater than is possible on the non-religious plan: and that even the religious training of the child would be cared for, so far as non-interference with the particular religious views of its parents would admit.

The last of the three assertions of the Chief Superintendent which I undertook to answer was, that denominational schools "would leave a large portion of the country without any means of education save as paupers;" this, I think, I have successfully met by showing how they would be admitted, without payment, into religious schools. But there is a *cunning* in this objection unpleasant to a disingenious mind. For, while it is calculated to flatter the pride of the unholy poor, it is not honestly a denominational, but a free-school objection; as in non-religious schools, if not free, the poor must be educated by a charitable rate, just as much as in denominational schools. Hence, the respectable Superintendent would meet this difficulty, by educating the whole province as paupers.

In fact, Denominational Schools are the peculiar RIGHT of the poor; because in the church of God the faithful poor are not regarded as paupers, but as fellow members with their wealthier brethren of CHRIST; hence they and their children are cared for as brethren! Yes, give us religious schools, and we will answer for it, that the children of the poorest would not only have an education they now too often do not know how to value, offered them; but they would be sought out by the ministers of the different denominations, if sometimes with a mixture of sectarian zeal, yet still oftener, I trust, with the holy and patient earnestness of faithful and loving shepherds. In either case the poor would profit, being by the persuasion of love brought under secular tuition combined with religious training. Oh, non-religious schools, whether Free or otherwise, are a heartless fraud upon the rights and the happiness of the poor!. . .

How significant is the fact that the almost sneering critic should be equally ready with the Revd. Doctor to sanction religious training, if only he be permitted to secure his non-religious teaching first! Yet how sad is such a fact; for does it not prove that the sceptic feels that he need not fear what must be the feeble efforts of Christian training when thus separated. Yes, unquestionably the sceptic is wise in his generation; for most certainly the natural tendency of the separate secular education scheme is to ignore Christianity, and to make the Bible despised. How bitterly are the men of this generation proving themselves children, "after their own likeness and image" of those, who, preferring *intellect* to *love*, eat of the forbidden fruit of the tree of knowledge of good and evil.

The above observations have been suggested by the third "remark" of the Chief Superintendent, in the extract from his report which has called forth these Letters. It is to this effect—"but the establishment of denominational schools is altogether unnecessary, because common schools are not boarding but day schools." Hence he argues that time sufficient will be left for religious instruction to be given by parents and pastors in the morning, or after schools are dismissed, and upon Sundays. What does the Chief Superintendent understand by religious training? Surely *he* does not suppose. . . that it merely consists in teaching the creed and catechism, albeit these may be important portions of its foundation.—Religious training pre-eminently requires to be given in the manner intimated by Divine wisdom, in the passage placed at the head of this letter—"precept upon precept, line upon line, here a a little and there a little," and this training is to begin, be it remembered, as Jehovah there commands, with the youngest, "those weaned from the milk and drawn from the breast."

Of religious instruction that which is *incidently* given is, perhaps, the most effective; and for this, the hours spent at school afford the fairest opportunity. Thus the routine reading of Holy Scripture must afford frequent opportunities of plainly enforcing, on the young mind, its practical teaching; such as their own connection with the privileges it declares, the duties it enjoins, and the hopes it reveals. Of course I am not supposing or wishing any course of polemical instruction to be given by our school masters, but it cannot be safe to our children's feelings of veneration, nor reverential to Almighty God, to permit His Word to be read by a pupil to his tutor, and that tutor, to be either unable or unwilling to use it, as opportunity serves, for his pupils' religious benefit. . . .

Nor, let it be answered that I am extravagant in expecting such teaching from denominational school teachers. . . . In short, in Church Schools, I should hope to see Christian teachers, who, like Christian parents, would seize every suitable opportunity of making Christian impressions upon the minds of the children entrusted to them. . . .

But the Reverend Superintendent dwells much upon the importance and sufficiency of Parental and Pastoral instruction. It is well! most important are they, and it is precisely for interfering with these that we denounce our present Common School system. Our Chief Superintendent, in effect, says to the parent—You may train your child in religion as you like on the Sabbath and during the mornings and evenings of other days; but on the chief part of each week day I will have him taught as I see fit! So to the Clergyman, he says,—It is your duty to teach the child religion, but I will only allow you to do so, as best you may, on the Sabbath; all the rest of the week I will appoint such teachers for him as I choose! If this be not the bitterness of tyranny—a tyranny most recklessly interfering with the closest relations of life—I know not what is. . . .

Equally hollow and hypocritical is the semi-infidel plea that Sunday-School tuition will meet the religious wants of our children. I say semi-infidel, because, if there were any force in the argument, it would go far to show that, with adults Sunday religion is sufficient to serve for the whole week! Nay, but, as regards our poor children, it is even more cruelly inapplicable than to adults; for, from their young minds, impressions, especially of a serious nature, are but too certain to pass away as the "morning cloud and early dew," unless they are hourly renewed, and they themselves almost momentarily watched over, to guard them from the snares, and to snatch them from the power, of temptation. . . .

—But the Chief Superintendent's error lies deeper. He does not seem to know that the education of the human mind is in every department, and at each progressive step, a distinctively religious work; . . . Consequently, *where a government ceases to be distinctively religious, it loses every right*—save that of oppression—*to interfere with the details of the people's education*; hence that must, in common consistency, be left to those to whom such government has abandoned the moral and religious care of the people. It follows them, that in such a case, and it is that of this Province, the only office of the rules in the matter of education, is to assist the various religious denominations from public funds in establishing schools, and to see that the aid so granted is honestly and efficiently used, so far as the secular instruction given in such schools is concerned. The only exception to this principle would be, where the Clergy and their people so neglected their duty as not to establish schools when they had the ability to do so, then perhaps it might be permissible for a government, through its own officials, to establish a more secular school; if indeed, even then, such a non-religious school would not be more of a curse than a blessing; for we repeat that "knowledge is power," for evil as well as for good; and that naturally "the imagination of man's heart is evil from his youth."

It may, however, be objected that if a government is not to direct the education of its youth, it ought not to be expected to assist such education from the public revenue. But this objection is based on an entire misconception. Our argument is not, that the education of the people can be a matter of indifference to any rational government, but that when a government is itself grounded on no positive distinct Christian principle, and presides over a religiously divided people, it is, both in its own nature, and circumstantially, unable to conduct such education . . .

Again: It is the grossest folly in any Government *to make public works of those matters which would be more efficiently accomplished, and at less eventual cost, by private energy and skill.* Now this is precisely what the government of the Province has done in regard to Common Schools. It has sanctioned a very expensive central establishment, it pays Local School Superintendents all over the country; it puts power to expend the public money into hands of illiterate men as school trustees. The consequence is, that schoolhouses are built in unsuitable situations and at unnecessary cost, and other useless expenses are incurred from want of due knowledge; by the patronage also, which Government has given to Free-Schools, a premium is offered to the drunken and idle, at the expense of the hardworking man, especially of the farmer. No wonder therefore that the people are miserably dissatisfied; and more especially as the *real* average attendance is after all, as I have shown, most unsatisfactory. All this extravagance is the result of having the schools in the hands of those who have no high principled interests in their welfare. Did the Government really understand the true educational interests of the country, and care to save the Provincial revenues rather than to increase its own patronage by the multiplication of unnecessary offices, a very large proportion of this official educational expenditure might be saved by having the Common Schools, as far as possible, in the hands of the different religious denominations; at the same time, the interests of the schools would be a vast deal better attended to than at present. Thank God, with all our evils we are not yet a sceptical people; whatever may be the amount of the genuine piety of the land, certain it is, that the religious feelings of our people are the strongest which they possess; hence when our common Schools shall be connected with those feelings, or may we not say principles, they will take an incomparably deeper interest in them than at present. But especially, will the minister and official members of the different sects feel both their religious affections and personal honor concerned in the success of their various schools. Thus, by establishing denominational schools, instead of our present inefficient and most expensive system, the Government would secure a numerous body of the most respectable and earnest-minded men of the province as the *unpaid* officials and guardians of the common schools, with the certainty of their expending upon them an amount of earnest zeal and personal care which no mere money could ensure. . . .

A minor, though still very serious objection to the present Common School laws of this province, is, that they almost necessarily throw the management of the Schools into the hands of illiterate people. They do this because not only the most uneducated, but also the idle and the dissolute, vote on all school matters, and hence, as like loves its like, they delight to exalt one another into office; or at least to appoint those who will do their bidding; thus, as is notorious, the more educated portions of our community are not generally connected with our Schools, and this evil is deeply felt amongst the better disposed, because, in small localities, many persons fit to fill school offices, are not to be found: were, on the contrary, the management in the ministers and official members of the nearest prevailing denominations, such ignorant, injurious management would be greatly avoided.

CATHOLIC VIGILANCE IN A PROTESTANT COMMUNITY

Dr Ryerson's Letters in Reply to the Attacks of Foreign Ecclesiastics against the Schools and Municipalities of Upper Canada, including the Letters of Bishop Charbonnel, Mr. Bruyère and Bishop Pinsoneault . . . (Toronto, Lovell & Gibson, 1857), pp. 35-41, 56-7, 84-5.

GENTLEMEN,—I have before me a "Circular" addressed by Dr. Ryerson Chief Superintendent of Schools in Upper Canada, to the heads of City Town, Township, and Village Municipalities, in this section of the Province, on the appropriation of the Clergy Reserve Funds. In this letter the distinguished head of the Educational Department, takes upon himself to deliver a lecture to the Municipalities of the upper section of the Province, on the expenditure of the money accruing from the secularized Clergy Reserves. The Rev. gentleman *submits to the favorable consideration of the Municipalities, whether their highest interests will not be best consulted by the application of the whole or at least a part of the sum, for procuring maps charts, globes, etc., etc., for their schools, and books of useful, entertaining reading for all classes and ages in their Municipality. . . .*

. . . Whether the Act of the Provincial Parliament should be looked upon as a measure of distributive justice or an act of high-handed robbery I am not prepared to express an opinion. Bearing this in mind, I may be permitted to ask, whether it is right and proper now to appropriate to one portion of our people funds which the Legislature intended for the general use and benefit of all citizens, without distinction of creed or nationality.

I beg leave, in turn, to submit to the favorable consideration of the public, whether the end of the Legislature will be obtained by the application of the proceeds of the sale of the Clergy Reserves to the purposes mentioned by Dr. Ryerson, viz., to the furnishing Common Schools with maps, globes, and other school apparatus—public libraries? Pray what are these educational institutions which Dr. Ryerson proposes to endow with the proceeds of the Clergy Reserve fund? We look around, and behold huge and palace-like fabrics, stigmatized by public opinion as godless schools. What are these stately edifices, rearing up their proud turrets over the breadth and length of the land? What are these gigantic mansions which first meet the eye of the traveller on entering our city? Let the truth be proclaimed again for the hundredth time. They are Common Schools, built with Catholic as well as Protestant money. They are houses of education from which religion is banished, where the elements of Christianity cannot be inculcated to the rising youth, where the child of Christian parents must be taught practically that all religious systems are equally pleasing, or rather equally indifferent in the sight of God, be he a believer in the immutable decrees of eternal reprobation or a follower of the impostor Joe Smith. These halls of learning already so richly supplied with the most elegant school apparatus, are shut up against one-third, or, at least, one-fourth of the population of Upper Canada. Yes, a Catholic parent, who values his faith above all worldly advantages, and who rightly considers religion as the basis of all education, and the life of man upon earth, would rather doom his child to the horrors of the most degrading ignorance, than permit him to drink in the common Schools the poison of infidelity or heresy along with the pure draught of useful knowledge. These convictions are likewise shared by a large portion of the members of the church of England. Talk not to us of your superior training, splendid school apparatus, and highly qualified teachers. If these advantages, great as they may be are to be purchased at the price of our faith, we value them not; we do not want them; we spurn them; and fling them back into your face.

Sad would be the alternative left to the Catholic population of the Province, were Dr. Ryerson to have his own way. To send our children to the Common Schools, we cannot, without risking their faith, which we esteem above the most brilliant education, tainted with infidelity. To withhold them is to deprive them of the immense advantages held out in these richly endowed halls of learning, which the acute Chief Superintendent so earnestly recommends to the liberal patronage of our Municipalities. . . . He will, if allowed to have his own way, crush and annihilate our poorly endowed, and poorly furnished Separate Schools, by the overwhelming superiority of his school apparatus, and by the already enormous resources placed under his control. . . .

If Dr. Ryerson was sincere in his anxiety for the diffusion of useful knowledge among the rising generation, without distinction of creed or nationality, why does he not submit to the favorable consideration of the Municipalities, the propriety of applying, at least, a small part of the Clergy Reserve Fund to the use of Catholic Separate Schools? They too, and more by far, than Common Schools, stand in the greatest need of maps, charts, globes and other school apparatus. . . .

I conclude with expressing a sincere hope that the good sense, honesty and liberality of our Municipalities in Upper Canada will defeat the snares of the enemy of peace and good feeling in this section of the Province, by applying the funds placed into their hands to general purposes and to the members of the same community, and have an equal right to its resources. Let these resources with which a kind Providence has blessed us be spent in improving our Cities, Towns and Villages, in draining and macadamizing our streets, digging sewers where wanted, in founding institutions of general beneficence, such as common baths for the use of poor people, in establishing general dispensaries, where the sick of the poor class may procure whatever medicine may be necessary, in securing in each Ward of our large cities the services of one or two Physicians who would attend the most urgent cases of destitution. Let a part of the Clergy Reserve Funds be employed in erecting shelters for the aged, the infirm, the widow, the orphan, and the immigrant. Many of our Houses of Industry are in a lamentable state. In several Towns, and even Cities, the destitute and poor are yet without shelter. When the famishing widow will appeal to your sympathy will you reach her a *Globe* to appease her hunger? When the half-naked orphan will stand before you will you give him a map to cover his shivering limbs? When the anxious immigrant will reach your shores will you receive him with a chart to rest his wearied body upon? When sickness and pestilence breaks out in your midst will you be able to relieve suffering humanity by scattering around you books of useful and entertaining reading, such as Dr. Ryerson suggests to purchase with the money placed under your control. . . .

In conclusion, I beg leave to state that I will consider it as a favour if the Press in Toronto and elsewhere do me the honour of inserting in their columns the above views, imperfect as they are. The subject is of the utmost importance and should be placed before the public. On the conductors of a wise press devolves the duty of enlightening public opinion. To the good sense and kind indulgence of the public I submit these considerations, and beg to subscribe myself

Their humble servant,
J. M. Bruyère

THE OFFICIAL POLICY: DR RYERSON'S REJOINDER TO THE REV. MR BRUYÈRE

Controversy between Dr Ryerson, Chief Superintendent of Education in Upper Canada and Rev. J. M. Bruyère, Rector of St Michael's Cathedral, Toronto, on the Appropriation of the Clergy Reserves Funds; Free Schools vs State Schools, Public Libraries and Common Schools, Attacked and Defended (Toronto, Leader and Patriat Steam Press, 1857), pp. 23-5, 27, 29-32.

When I first read in *The Leader* of the 10th inst., the letter of the Rev. J. M. Bruyère (Roman Catholic Priest in this city) addressed to the "conductors of the Press in Canada," criticising a circular which I recently addressed to Heads of Municipalities on the application of the Clergy Reserve Fund, and assailing our Common School system generally, I thought his statements were too improbable and his objections too often refuted to require any notice from me. But I find by remarks in *The Leader* and other papers, as well as by observations in private circles, that I am expected to reply to this anti-public school champion; and I am induced to comply with wishes thus entertained chiefly by the considerations that Mr. Bruyère appears as the representative and organ of a party, and that the statements of his letter afford me another opportunity of exhibiting the fair and generous principles of our public school system, and of exposing the unfairness and baselessness of the objections urged against it by the party of Mr. Bruyère. . . .

Mr. Bruyère represents me as the most inveterate enemy of Romanism in the country, and employing every means in my power to oppose and destroy it. What may be my views as to the peculiar doctrines of Romanism and Protestantism, and of the comparative influence of each system upon religion, morals, intellect, social order, liberty, civilization, and man's well-being here and hereafter, is a matter which appertains to myself. I am responsible for my *official* acts; and to them I appeal for a refutation of Mr. Bruyère's imputations. . . .

I am quite aware of the object of thus wishing to banish all recognition of religion from our Common Schools, as well as Mr. Bruyère's object in asserting that such is now the fact. The same course was pursued by Bishop Hughes and his partizans in the city of New York some years since. Under the pretence of not permitting anything denominational in the schools, the Bible was taken out of the hands of the Protestant pupils, and every paragraph and sentence, and every word, in which any reference to religion, or even the Divine Being was made in the school books was crossed or blotted out. . . . I have endeavored to guard our school system and schools from a similar danger by equally protecting the rights and interest of both Protestant and Romanist; and this is the real ground of the alarm and denunciations of Mr. Bruyère and his country, who class all as infidels that are not of their party, and all teaching infidelity which is not given under their direction. I will not consent to Mr. Bruyère's wresting from the hands of a Protestant child his Bible—the best charter of his civil liberty, as well as his best directory to heaven—any more than I will force it into the hands of the Roman Catholic child, or wrest from him his Catechism. . . . Ten *Globes* and their contributors could not do as much to impair the influence of the Roman Catholic Church, and blight the hopes of its members in regard to such distinctions and advantages as depend on the popular elective voice, as have the Charbonnels and Bruyères of that Church during the last five years. Though one may not regret this as a Protestant, yet every benevolent and patriotic mind must lament that there is any class of children or citizens in the country so isolated as to deprive them of the mental development and culture enjoyed by others, and cut off from the prospects of all public offices and distinctions depending upon the elective voice of the people to which intelligence, talent, industry and worth are justly entitled, irrespective of religious sect or creed. It is to the Charbonnels and Bruyères— the infusion of a new foreign element into our country since the days of Bishops McDonell and Power—that our Roman Catholic fellow citizens owe the cloudy civil and social prospects that are darkening the future of themselves and their children. The palace-like schoolhouses, richly furnished with appropriate maps, charts, and other apparatus, which inflict such pangs in the heart of Mr. Bruyère, are so many voluntary creations of the people themselves; so many bright illustrations of a glorious progress, in which Roman Catholics, in common with all other classes, should, and may equally participate. I should falsify the whole of my past life, and despise myself, were I not scrupulous to protect the rights and feelings of Roman Catholics equally with those of any, or all other classes of the community. It is certain of their own ecclesiastics who have inflicted upon them burdens and disadvantages which their fathers had not to bear in the days of Bishops McDonell and Power; . . . the authors of such an enslavement and extinction of all that is expansive and dignified and noble in man, are alone responsible, if the Roman Catholics and their descendents in Upper Canada become "Hewers of wood and drawers of water" to other classes of their fellow citizens, instead of standing upon equal footing with them and rivalling them in intelligence, mental power, enterprize, wealth, individual influence and public position. . . .

My last remark is, that the same spirit which assails, misrepresents and calumniates our public school system, is equally hostile and calumnious against everything British, from the throne down to the school municipality. You cannot open the journals in which the letters of Bishop Charbonnel and Mr. Bruyère find an echo without seeing them largely devoted to selections and articles assailing the British Government as the most unjust and execrable in existence, both in its foreign diplomacy and domestic administration, and the British nation as the most heartless and unprincipled on the face of the globe. Were I to insert only those passages of this kind that I have marked, the reader would be surprised and shocked at the concentration of enmity which is cherished and inculcated by these journals against the Government, character, institutions, and prosperity of the mother country. Their hostility to our system of public instruction is only one aspect or phase of a crusade against everything that places Great Britain at the head of modern civilization, and makes her the asylum and guardian of liberty for the oppressed of all nations, and develops her national mind and resources beyond those of any other country in Europe. . . .

E. RYERSON

Education Office,
Toronto, Dec. 22nd, 1856.

THE WORKINGS OF AN EDUCATIONAL BUREAUCRACY: THE CASE OF THE TOWNSHIP OF WILLIAMS

Copies of Correspondence between the Chief Superintendent of Schools for Upper Canada and Other Persons, on the Subject of Separate Schools (Toronto, Lovell & Gibson, 1855), pp. 209-26.

London, C.W., *16th October*, 1852

SIR,

Being informed that it is in your power to appropriate a certain amount of aid annually, from the legislative school grant, towards the support of poor schools in parts of the country partially unsettled, I hereby take the opportunity of soliciting a portion of the funds at your disposal, for the above purpose, in order that a certain portion of the inhabitants of the township of Williams, in the county of Middlesex, may be enabled to support a school which is at present in operation, and has a daily attendance of about fifty pupils.

The locality is newly settled by Scotch emigrants, who arrived from the Highlands within the last two years, in a very destitute condition, and number between eighty and one hundred families. It has been represented to me by the teacher and the trustees of the school, that they have applied to the school superintendent for aid from the common school fund appropriated to the township, and that he refused any aid, on the grounds that he had received no notification from the township clerk of the legal erection of a school section in that locality.

I am further informed that the township councillors encouraged the inhabitants of the aforesaid locality to erect a school-house, and that they (the township councillors,) would do all in their power to enable them to support it. Not being conversant with the requirements of the school act, and relying on the promises of the councillors, they (the said inhabitants,) neglected to petition the council to have their locality erected into a distinct and separate school section. Under the foregoing circumstances I think it my duty to make this application, convinced as I am that a school amongst these people, who are under my spiritual care, and whose children are destitute of the rudiments of a common school education, is essentially necessary to fit them for the duties of society which may hereafter devolve on them.

Hoping that you will take the case into consideration, and make such allowance from the legislative grant as will enable these poor people to keep their school open during the ensuing season,

I have the honor, &c.
THT. KIRWAN,
Rural Dean.

Rev. EGERTON RYERSON,
Chief Superintendent Education, U.C.,
Toronto.

Education Office,
Toronto, <i>19th October</i>, 1852.</div>

SIR,

I have the honor to acknowledge the receipt of your letter of the 16th instant, and to state in reply that the power to which you refer of affording aid to poor school sections in new and scattered settlements, authorised by a former school law, has, by the present act (13 & 14 Victoria; chapter 48, section 27, clause I,) been transferred to the municipal council of each county.

I regret, therefore, that it is not in my power to comply with your request. All that I can do is to refer you to the municipal council of your county for assistance.

I have the honor, &c.

(Signed,) E. RYERSON.

London, C.W., 26th October, 1852.

SIR,

Your favor of the 19th instant was received by me on my arrival home after an absence of a few days.

I regret to learn that the pecuniary aid required for the support of the poor school in the township of Williams, to which I referred, cannot be directly granted by you. I have reason to do so the more as the daily attendance is rapidly increasing, for by the last report received from the teacher, I find that he has a daily average of sixty pupils.

When I applied to you I was under the impression that a certain amount of funds remained in your hands for such purposes as that stated in my letter, and that in all cases where a grievance exists in school matters it was my proper course to apply to you, as Chief Superintendent, to have it redressed or removed. . . . I considered that the terms of my letter of the 16th instant were sufficiently explicit to call your attention to the dereliction of duty on the part of the township council of Williams, and also of the local superintendent, but as it seems you have not considered their conduct of sufficient importance to even allude to it in your reply, I am now reluctantly compelled to give a more ample statement of the entire facts and circumstances as reported to me, that you will exercise the powers vested in you by the act referred to, in order that evenhanded justice may be meted out to the aggrieved.

The majority of the people who reside in the locality where the school is situated have paid the public school taxes for the last two years or more, although they had not the benefit of a school themselves, and now that they have one of their own, they are refused their proper and just proportion of the school funds to which they contribute themselves, and this in consequence of the township council having failed to perform the duty imposed on them by the third paragraph of the 18th section of the school act. You are aware, as stated in my last, that the township councillors encouraged the erection of a school-house, and promised to do all in their power to support the school when built. The reason they have not fulfilled their promises and performed their duty, is the manly stand the people had taken to prevent the introduction of proselytism into the school section, for there had been an attempt made to force an unqualified teacher on them, who inculcated during school hours, religious doctrines at variance with those of the people in general, and even announced that he would hold religious service on Sundays in their school-house. . . .

On the whole, I consider the matter requires a serious investigation, and I therefore respectfully demand it of you. A true copy of this communication will be furnished to the parties concerned.

I have the honor, &c.

(Signed,)   THT. KIRWAN,

Rural Dean, R.C. Pastor of

London & Williamstown.

P.S.—May I respectfully request that you will furnish me with a copy of my first letter sent you, as I have mislaid the one I had?

(Signed,)   THT. K., R. D., &c.

Education Office,

Toronto, *4th November*, 1852.

SIR,

I have the honor to acknowledge the receipt of your letter of the 26th ultimo, and to state in reply that from the tenor of the printed remarks contained in the fourth page of this letter, it would clearly have been improper for this department to have entertained the complaint implied (as you state,) in your previous letter of the 16th ultimo, until it was evident that the directions therein given had been followed.

Until I receive an explanation from the local superintendent to whom you refer, no opinion can be expressed upon the case you submit.

I herewith enclose a copy of your communication of the 16th ultimo, as you request.

I have the honor, &c.

(Signed,)   J. GEORGE HODGINS,

Deputy Superintendent.

London, C.W., *16th November*, 1852.

SIR,

I have the pleasure to acknowledge your reply dated the 4th of November together with a copy of my first letter to you, for which I beg to return you my thanks.

As it seems by your last favor of the 4th, that your department has entertained the complaint lodged by me against the conduct of the township councillors of Williams, and of the local superintendent, I feel it my duty to furnish you with some extracts of a letter written to me, bearing date the 22nd of September, 1852 by Mr. Charles McKinnon, the school teacher employed by the trustees, in order that you might understand that I have presented the case to you in its least aggravated shape, and that you may likewise be the better able to render impartial justice to the parties concerned:

"REV. FATHER,

"I have no doubt but you will be surprised to learn on receipt of this, that I have to my regret, given up teaching school here. As it is the duty of the municipal council to form new school sections, and to give instructions accordingly, I actually thought, when I commenced teaching here, that everything was legally arranged according to the requirements of the school act, until I went to see the Rev. Mr. McPherson, who is the local superintendent. He said that he was not furnished by the trustees of this school section with a legal notification describing the boundaries of said section. To this I replied, that the school trustees were not acquainted with the legal regulations of the school act, and therefore it was the duty of the township council to direct them in the proper course to be pursued; and especially as the council voluntarily imposed this duty on themselves by promising to do so. No arguments could prevail on the reverend Free Church gentleman. His quarrel with these poor Catholics was, that they were ungrateful and ignorant—because they did not accept of the teacher and preacher sent to them for the purpose of enlightening them in a knowledge of the Bible. To this I replied, that no law authorized him or any other person to force a teacher or preacher on any school section against the consent of the school trustees and of the people in general; further, that the Catholics held the Bible as sacred as he did, and that they have one great advantage over them; that is, the infallible voice of the church of Christ, to guide them in preaching and expanding the scriptures in the spirit of unity and truth, as they ought to be; they did not interpret the scriptures according to the private interpretation of every [one] who could scarcely read a passage in the Bible. This let me into a warm controversy, which detained me three hours. I went away fully convinced that his reverence met with one who knew more about the fruits of Protestantism than he did himself.

"Next day I called a meeting of the school trustees and householders, at which they unanimously declared that Mr. Gray, the councillor, requested them *to build the School house*, and that they (the council) would do all they could for them. This they certainly would have done, had the people accepted of the services of the inspired teacher, whom they had sent to them for no other purpose than to *convert* them! When the people opposed their erroneous presumption, they (the councillors) immediately resolved that whereas the people did not make a legal application to the council for the dividing and formation of their school section, as required by the school act, *no provision* could be made for them this year. Here I must appeal to reason, justice, humanity and the sacred laws of christianity, and ask, with confusion and astonishment, has there been manifested, since Cromwell's time, such injustice, hypocrisy, intolerance and ungodly ill will, in any one civilized country or place,—that these poor destitute and harmless Catholics should be compelled to pay school tax for the last three years, without having the benefit of a school for themselves, and now deprived of what they had to obtain, because they did not immediately comply with the requirements of a school act which they knew nothing about; and with which they could not, on account of the course pursued by the township councillors,—is, in my opinion, an injustice, the parallel of which cannot be found in any christian country or community. As the poor people had thus been deceived, they could not keep me any longer; but it was with difficulty I could get away; for many of them preferred to sell the only corn they had, to make up my salary. I am determined, please God, to return next year to Nova Scotia, my dear native land, where freedom, every spiritual blessing, and religious privileges abound, and where such intolerance over Catholics would not be attempted. 'Blessed are they who suffer persecution for justice sake, for theirs is the kingdom of heaven.'

I remain, reverend father,
Your obedient servant,

(Signed,)   CHARLES MCKINNON."

P.S.—I have stated in my last letter that the householders of this colony have paid school tax for the last two years and upwards. The reason I have done so is, though the majority of the ratepayers are residents for the last three years, some few have settled on the land within the last two years. The number of Catholics of which this colony is composed, is about seven hundred, they live in one continuous settlement in the north-west part of the township of Williams; I may safely say, that the nearest school to them, which is on the old settlement, and is decidedly sectarian, for the parents of the children who attend it, without exception, belong to the Presbyterian creed, is four miles distant from the majority of the inhabitants of the new Catholic colony.

I have the honor, &c.

(Signed,)   THT. KIRWAN,

Rural Dean, R. C. Pastor of
London & Williams.

London, C. W. *4th February*, 1853.

SIR,

In my first letter to you, dated 16th October, 1852, I called your attention to the conduct of the township councillors of Williams, and of the local superintendent, the Rev. Mr. McPherson, in the full expectation of obtaining immediate redress. In my subsequent letters I gave a fuller explanation of the subject of complaint, as represented to me by the teacher and the Catholic inhabitants in whose behalf I took the liberty of addressing you. I did expect that the matter would be fully investigated before this time, as it seemed to me that the true facts of the case might have been easily elicited and an impartial decision in accordance therewith given by you.

I would not be anxious to press for a final decision, but as it is a source of anxiety to the Catholic inhabitants, who are much interested in the education of their children, I feel that I would not be worthy of the trust reposed in me if I did not again solicit you to bring the matter to a final conclusion.

The Catholic inhabitants complain that the usual time for the distribution of the school funds is now passed, and as there has been no decision given as yet, that they are likely to be deprived of their just portion, to which they would have been entitled by law, were it not for the obstructive course pursued towards them by the township councillors and the local superintendent. What still more aggravates the disadvantages arising to the inhabitants from a delay in the decision, is the fact that they are unable to pay the school teacher the stipulated salary. So convinced was the school teacher (Mr. Charles McKinnon) of it, that as soon as he discovered the obstructive course pursued by the township councillors and the local superintendent, he wrote to me, stating that "as the poor inhabitants are unable to maintain the school for want of funds, he would be obliged, though with reluctance, to give up teaching." The school would have been discontinued had not I written to him, and taken upon myself the responsibility of maintaining it by promising him an adequate remuneration for his services. I did so with the hope that no quibble would deprive the school of its just proportion of the funds to which it was entitled by the spirit and purport of the school law, if justly and impartially administered. I further relied on a speedy and equitable decision from you, to whom, as the law directs, I referred the matter.

Up to the present time the school has been continued, principally at my expense, and I trust that the above reasons will be a sufficient excuse for me to urge you to give a final decision on this much vexed and agitated question.

Expecting the favor of a reply as soon as convenient,

I have the honor, &c.

(Signed,)   THT. KIRWAN,

Rural Dean.

Education Office,

Toronto, *15th February*, 1853.

SIR,

I have the honor to acknowledge the receipt of your letter of the 4th instant, and to state in reply that I have no assurance that copies of any of your letters of complaint against the council and local superintendent of the township of

Williams have been furnished to the parties concerned, as required by the regulations of this department and as intimated to you in the letter of the 4th November. Nor do your letters furnish me with any facts on which it is possible to found any official decision.

You do not say when the school section to which you refer was established, or how established. You do not furnish me with any copies of the proceedings of the township council of Williams, containing the promises which you say it made and violated; nor whether the returns required by law have been made to the local superintendent, on which alone he could act, were the section entitled to receive what you claim for it.

As far as I can gather from your letters, and from an extract in one of them some of the township councillors encouraged the building of a *public* school-house but not a *denominational* or separate one: nor has any council authority to levy any *assessment* for the erection of a separate school-house; such a house must be built by the denomination requiring it.

A separate school, whether Protestant or Roman Catholic, cannot be established before the 25th December of any one year, and on the written application of twelve heads of families, as required by the 19th section of the school act.

You complain that the township council did not instruct the Catholic inhabitants to whom you refer, how to proceed in their school affairs, so that they might fulfill the requirements of the law; but surely such a duty no more devolves upon a municipal council, than it devolves upon the government or parliament to teach all parties concerned how to obey the law in order to secure its advantages.

If, according to your representation, the whole or great majority of the inhabitants in the part of the township to which you refer, are Roman Catholics, they could elect trustees, employ a teacher, and erect a school-house, according to their own wishes, under the general provisions of the school act. But if, instead of doing so they have preferred to have their section and school organised and established as a separate one, they can only receive assistance according to the provisions of the 19th section of the school act.

I have the honor, &c.

(Signed,)   E. RYERSON.

London, C. W., 28*th February*, 1853.

SIR,

I have received your letter of the 15th instant, and am bound to acknowledge that its contents have not a little surprised me.

It was my impression since the receipt of your letter dated the 4th of November last, that you had taken steps to hold an investigation into the case as demanded in my letter of the 26th of October, and in which I stated that the parties concerned had been furnished with a true copy of the complaint preferred against them. Yet after a lapse of upwards of three months you reply that you "have no assurance that copies of my letters of complaint have been furnished to the parties concerned;" and, also, that my letters do not furnish you with any "*facts* on which it is possible to found any official decision."

Some men are in the habit of estimating the character and veracity of others by their own personal standard; and I am, therefore, not much astonished at the insinuation you seem willing to cast upon me. But, setting aside your implied allusions as a matter to be attributed to your peculiar mode of controversy, let me for a moment refer to the statements and reasoning contained in your letter now before me. It is apparent from the wording of your reply, dated the 4th November last, that you were then under the impression I had complied with the tenor of the printed remarks contained on its 4th page. You stated then that you could express no opinion upon the case I submitted, until you had received an explanation from the local superintendent, thereby implying that you awaited his explanation before you could proceed further in the matter. It seems now that you have not thought it worth your while to require the local superintendent to furnish you with any explanation, or that he has failed to do so. This is the only inference I can deduce from your remarks.

Referring to the second paragraph of your present reply, where you state I did not "say when the school section to which I referred was established," &c., I have to remark that you might readily have perceived from my letter of the 26th October, that I complained of the township council for not fulfilling the duties imposed upon it by the 3rd clause of the 18th section of the school act, where it is expressly enacted that it shall be the duty of the municipality of each township in Upper Canada, "to form portions of the township where no schools have been established into school sections." Had the municipal council performed its duty I would have been right in the legal acceptation of the term *school section*, but as the council had not fulfilled the requirements of the law, the term which I thought fit to use was only meant to describe the part of the township for which I was claiming fair play and justice. The local superintendent could have acted, and did act, when the people did not require his interference, but when he would not be permitted to tamper with the faith of the children, through the agency of the teacher whom he had introduced for proselytising purposes, then he could easily find a subterfuge in the technicalities and intricacies of your school law; and you, as Chief Superintendent, seem inclined to shield him with your evasive logic. The local superintendent might possibly, by a quibble of the law, try to justify himself in refusing aid to the school; but no law in the Canadian statute book could sustain him, as a public officer, in using the language which he employed towards the unfortunate people who had been the victims of his bigoted and persecuting policy.

You endeavor to explain away the charge which I preferred against the township councillors for not fulfilling their promises and duty, by saying, "nor has any council authority to levy any assessment for the erection of a *separate* school-house." A *separate* school, let me distinctly say, was not asked. The people wanted a school of their own, and claim the management of it without the unjust dictation or interference of the township council or local superintendent. And because they have not allowed such dictation and interference, you can *"gather* from my letters, and from an extract in one of them,"* that the school is a *denominational* or *separate* one. It is very unfair on your part to sustain your argument by hypothetical deductions which have no foundation in the *facts* stated for your consideration.

You go on to say,— "a separate school, whether Protestant or Roman Catholic, cannot be established before the 25th December of any one year;" although I look upon this statement as unnecessary under the circumstances of the case, I may observe that it seems to me a very strange provision in the law regulating the common school system of this section of the Province, but quite consistent with many other equally strange provisions of the same school act. According to the above quotation, there are only six days in the year set apart for establishing separate schools, and supposing Christmas day should fall on Monday, then only five can be used for that purpose. Well, I hope the legislature of the Province will see the necessity of extending the time to be used for this important purpose beyond the present illiberal bounds.

You say that I "complain that the township council did not instruct the Catholic inhabitants to whom I refer how to proceed in their school affairs, so that they might fulfil the requirements of the law." I am not aware that I have complained of any such thing; it is a supposition on your part, as far as my letters go. I said in my first letter that the inhabitants neglected to petition the council to have their locality erected into a distinct and separate school section; that is, separate and distinct from the portion of the township and the school section with which it is geographically connected, but from which it extends to such a distance as to render it utterly impossible for one school to answer the whole, on account of the great distance. But when I referred to the school act, which I had not then at hand, I found that the inhabitants were not required by law to present a petition. The council had their duty to perform without any petitioning about it.

I add another extract from your reply, which fully proves the justice of the claims I advanced, and which firmly established the illegality and impropriety of the conduct of those against whom I appealed to you. You remark, *"if,* according to your representation, the whole, or great majority, of the inhabitants in the part of the township to which I refer are Roman Catholics, they could elect trustees, employ a teacher, and erect a schoolhouse, according to their own wishes, under the general provision of the school act." This is exactly that for which they have been contending; but the bigotry and unchristian spirit of sectarianism adopted towards them, by those who have been entrusted with the local administration of the law, has prevented them from obtaining their just and constitutional rights. I appealed to you against a masked system of persecution; you try to evade the question by technicalities; I demanded an investigation; you have delayed for months, and at length attempt to impugn my veracity. I now consider that it would be unbecoming on my part to hold any further correspondence with you through your department; I will accordingly appeal to his Excellency the Governor General, to whom it seems by the 81st section of the school act, you are responsible for your official conduct. I forward herewith a copy of my letter of complaint against you, which I have forwarded to His Excellency in council; and, in the meantime, I wish to inform you that for the public information, I will have the correspondence inserted in the public press.

It is well the people should see some of the features of that boasted municipal system, which to an almost unlimited and intolerable extent controls the education of the children of the country, and which usurps parental duties and responsibilities, to an extent far beyond the limits which divine or natural law would seem to define.

I remain, &c.

(signed,)   THT. KIRWAN,

Rural Dean.

London, C. W., 28th February, 1853.

HON. SIR,

A case of great grievance occurred in the township of Williams, in the united counties of Middlesex and Elgin, during the past year, between the Roman Catholic inhabitants residing in the north-west part of said township, and the local school superintendent and township councillors of the same.

The part of the township to which I allude is peopled by Scotch emigrants who came from the Highlands within the last three years, and are under my spiritual jurisdiction. The settlement occupies six miles in extent and comprises, at least, between six and eight hundred inhabitants. They had no school till last summer, when by the encouragement of the township councillors, they erected a school house at their own expense. The then local superintendent, the Rev. Mr. McPherson, is a minister of the Presbyterian Free Church, and so were and are, I believe, all the township councillors. When the school was built, a young man, who represented himself as having been sent by the Free Church society of Toronto, to give gratuitous education to the children who might attend, presented himself as teacher. Certain of the inhabitants suspecting that a private conspiracy had been formed for proselytising purposes, consulted me on the propriety of allowing him to conduct the school, and although I knew that nothing good could come out of Nazareth, I advised them, in consideration of their poverty and want of school convenience, to send these children to him, provided he would not attempt to interfere with their religious beliefs. Scarcely had he occupied the school four days, when he commenced to introduce religious exercises at variance with the religious principles of the children and parents. The first Saturday, he announced to the pupils that he would hold religious services in the school, and at which he desired them and their parents to attend. The people at once discovering that he was a preacher withdrew their children, and employed Mr. Charles McKinnon, who is a legally qualified teacher, and conducts their school to the entire satisfaction of the people.

The township councillors, who had previously promised aid, refused to do their duty when the former teacher was discarded, and the local superintendent, of course in concert with the councillors, refused aid from the public school funds, alleging that they were "*ungrateful wretches who would not accept the teacher sent to enlighten them in the Bible.*"

On behalf of the people, I appealed for aid to the Chief Superintendent of Schools, the Rev. E. Ryerson, Toronto.

The application was unsuccessful, and I then appealed for an investigation into the matter, and had reason to believe, from the tenor of a letter dated 4th November last, that he would fully investigate the case. But to my astonishment, I find by letter of his dated the 15th instant, that he did not think proper to give even the satisfaction of a mock investigation, after a delay of more than three months. I am, therefore, reluctantly compelled to appeal to his Excellency the Governor General in council, against the extraordinary conduct of the Rev. Egerton Ryerson Chief Superintendent of Schools for this section of the province, and hope that his Excellency, in whose wisdom, spirit of justice and impartiality, I place the fullest confidence, will take the matter into consideration.

A copy of this complaint, I this day transmit to the Chief Superintendent aforesaid, and would most respectfully request you to call on him for a copy of the whole correspondence existing between him and me on this subject, for the better information of his Excellency, under whose notice I hope you will bring the matter at your earliest convenience.

I have the honor, &c.

(Signed,)   THT. KIRWAN,

Rural Dean.

Hon. A. N. MORIN,
Provincial Secretary,
Quebec.

Endorsed

Secretary's Office, 11*th March*, 1853.

Referred to the Chief Superintendent of Education for Upper Canada for report.

by command,

(signed,)   E. A. MEREDITH,

Assistant Secretary.

Education Office,

Toronto, 4*th May*, 1854.

SIR,

In reference to the letter of the Rev. Tht. Kirwan, Roman Catholic rural dean, at London, Upper Canada, addressed to you the 28th February, and transferred to me the 11th March, for my explanations as to the complaints and statements contained in that letter against me, I must apologize for the length of time which I have suffered to elapse before transmitting, for the information of his Excellency, the explanations or report required. The reasons of this delay are, that I did not return from my tour of the several counties of Upper Canada until about a month since, and there have been so many questions and duties requiring immediate attention, and which appeared to me to be more important than the vindication of myself from the imputations contained in Mr. Kirwan's letter, that I have allowed his charge to remain unanswered until I could attend to them without prejudice to the public interests and duties of this department.

Mr. Kirwan has not furnished you with copies of his correspondence with me. Had he done so, that correspondence would have contained sufficient proof of the groundlessness of his charges and the propriety of the course which I have pursued. I herewith enclose, for the information of his Excellency, copies of that correspondence.

Before remarking on this correspondence, I may observe, that up to the present moment I have not received any communication whatever from the only parties with whom I am officially required to correspond on the subject—namely, the trustees and teacher of the school in question—that whatever letters I have addressed to Mr. Kirwan, have been from courtesy and respect for his position, and not from any right which the law gives him to interfere in a matter of this kind, or any obligations on my part to correspond with others than local school authorities and parties personally interested. The only instance of non-residents of municipalities assuming functions which belong to local school authorities in correspondence with this department, are those which are furnished by this correspondence, and that which was laid before the legislature some months since on the subject of "separate schools." And these instances show to what inconveniences this department has been subjected, in yielding from motives of delicacy and courtesy to correspond on school matters with parties who are wholly irresponsible in such matters, who appear to be wholly uninformed as to the provisions of the school act, and when informed of their omissions and errors, as I informed Mr. Kirwan in my letter of the 15th February, immediately begin to assail me and attack the school law.

Now, had Mr. Kirwan acquainted himself with the school law, he would have known that I had no power to do a single thing that he had demanded—that the utmost I could do, in regard to his complaints, even were his allegations well founded, would be to offer friendly advice with a view of allaying differences and inducing useful co-operation. In my last letter to Mr. Kirwan, dated 15th February, 1853, I pointed out to him the kind of information necessary to enable me even to form an opinion on the subjects of his representations; but instead of supplying that information, he replies in a long, and in several respects, offensive letter, dated 28th February; and on the same day that he sends that letter to me, he sends a copy of it with copies of the preceding correspondence, to the "*Toronto Mirror*" newspaper, and another letter to you complaining of me, and at the same time assailing other parties.

A reference to Mr. Kirwan's complaint and statements will, I think, abundantly justify the foregoing remarks; he complains that I would not institute an investigation into his complaints against the municipal council of the township of Williams. In reply, I observe that the law nowhere provides me with means or gives me the least authority to institute the investigation demanded; that municipal councils are in no way responsible to me, and that the local superintendent (who is so unscrupulously assailed, as well as the religious denomination to which he belongs) could not act in respect to the parties referred to without the previous action of the township council. Mr. Kirwan says that in my letter to him, dated 4th November, 1852, (addressed to him by Mr. Hodgins during my absence at Quebec), I gave him to understand that I would institute an investigation into his complaint against the municipal council and local superintendent of the township of Williams; but it will be seen by referring to Mr. Hodgins' letter of that date, that nothing of the kind was intimated. All I had authority or could hope to do, was to offer suggestions and advice to each of the parties concerned, after having heard their respective statements.

Mr. Kirwan complains that "the Free Church Society of Toronto sent a teacher to give gratuitous education" to the children of the new settlers of whom he speaks; but surely I had no right to interfere with the operations of that society, nor even to express an opinion respecting them, however anxious Mr. Kirwan himself might be to stigmatize and repress them. It appears, according to Mr. Kirwan's own statements, that he "knew nothing good could come out of Nazareth," yet he "advised them (the settlers in question) in consideration of their poverty and want of school convenience to send their children" to the gratuitous school of the Free Church teacher. I certainly had no more right to inquire into the nature and grounds of the Free Church Society's proceedings among the newly arrived emigrants referred to, than into those of Mr. Kirwan's advice to these same emigrants. . . .

It will be seen by referring to Mr. Kirwan's letter of the 16th October, that he applied to me to grant aid to the settlement in question, having, as he states, "been informed that I had power to apply a certain amount of aid annually from the legislative school grant, towards the support of poor schools in parts of the country partially unsettled." Within three days, 19th October, 1852, I informed him that the power which he had supposed to be vested in me, had been transferred to the county councils—referred him to the clause of the statute bearing upon the subject—expressed my regret at not being able to comply with his request, and recommended him to apply to the municipal council of his county. In Mr. Kirwan's letter, to which this was a reply, he made no formal complaints against the township council or local superintendent of Williams. He states, indeed, that the inhabitants had not even applied to be formed into a legal school section, through, as he says, "not being conversant with the requirements of the school act," and relying on the promises of councillors to do all in their power to support the school in case of their erecting a school-house. Nor did Mr. Kirwan apply to me for aid to pay the teacher for last year's services, as he demanded in subsequent letters, but concluded his first letter in the following words: "Hoping that you will take the case into consideration, and make such allowance from the legislative grant as will enable these poor people to keep their *school open during the ensuing season.*" Mr. Kirwan, instead of acting upon my friendly suggestion, and applying to the only body who could aid "these poor people" under the circumstances, changes the whole aspect and issue of the question by proceeding to prefer formal charges against the township council and local superintendent for "dereliction of duty," and to the letter (26th October, 1852) containing these charges, Mr. Hodgins, during my absence at Quebec, addressed the note of the 4th November, and to which Mr. Kirwan makes such frequent reference. But finding nothing on which I could form an opinion or give advice in Mr. Kirwan's reply of the 16th November, and hearing nothing from any other party, left the matter without further notice until I could visit the counties to the west—which was in January or February; but no party applied to me on the subject, nor did I hear anything more respecting it, until, on my return from the western part of my tour, I received Mr. Kirwan's letter of the 4th February, to which I replied the 15th—pointing out his omissions and how impossible it was for me to form any opinion on the question under such circumstances, and that I had no authority, under any circumstances, to do what he demanded. To his insulting reply of the 28th February, which I first read in the Toronto newspapers, I have not thought proper to return any answer.

From a review of the whole correspondence, it will, therefore, be seen,

1. That Mr. Kirwan applied to me for assistance to the school, as a poor school—assistance which appertained to the county council, and not to me, to give.

2. That instead of applying to the county council for the assistance sought, Mr. Kirwan commences formal complaints against the municipal council and local superintendent of the township of Williams, demanding of me the exercise of power which the law does not confer upon me.

3. That Mr. Kirwan has made a variety of charges against the councillors and local superintendent of the township of Williams, and when informed that he must, in order to receive an opinion on the matter, adduce some official proceedings of the parties of whom he complains, he furnishes not the copy of a single act of council or councillors or local superintendent—not the application of a trustee, or even a rate-payer, to them, nor the statement of any one of them to me, but forthwith enters a complaint to His Excellency of my non-compliance with his demands.

I may remark, in conclusion, that if the school trustees or inhabitants of the settlement in question had represented their circumstances and wants to me, I should have felt it my duty to refer to their local superintendent, and council if necessary; but when, first, an application is made in their behalf as paupers, I had only to advert to the provisions of the law on that point, namely, that application must be made to the county council for assistance on that ground;

and when, secondly, a complaint is made to me against the councillors and local superintendent of a township—the latter a clergyman—by a clergyman who is *not a resident* in the township, I think it would be partial and insulting on *my* part to *call upon* one clergyman to answer to the charges of another clergyman made under such circumstances, or to refer to the councillors in regard to charges made against them in such a manner, or to adopt any other course than that which I explained to Mr. Kirwan in my letter of the 15th February, 1853.

I think Mr. Kirwan would have evinced a more charitable spirit and a more discreet and intelligent zeal in behalf of the poor people for whose interests he professes so much concern, had he gone among them and advised and aided them in applying to the council to be formed into a separate school section, and to have a tax imposed upon themselves for their needful school purposes, rather than to counsel them in a course which can secure them no benefit, but must be injurious to them, and which puts it out of my power to aid them, as I should be happy to do, by advice and recommendation for special assistance.

The Rev. Mr. McPherson is not the local superintendent of schools for the township of Williams for the current year. Whether he has received copies of the letters addressed to this department against him, I do not know from himself, as he has never written me a word on the subject. If he had received copies of those letters, I suppose he has thought himself only obliged to answer to representations of parties with whom he was officially connected in the township, but did not feel himself called upon to notice the gratuitous representations of a non-resident clergyman.

I have the honor, &c.

(Signed,)   E. RYERSON.

The Hon. A. N. MORIN, M.P.P.,
Secretary of the Province,
Quebec.

A HUMBLE PROTEST AGAINST PREJUDICE

James Feagan to Egerton Ryerson, March 5, 1859. *Education Papers*, RG 2 C-6-C, Public Archives of Ontario.

Tyendenaga March 5th 1859

My Lord
    Your Honour and athority whereas about 4 weeks ago came from the Orange lodge of school section No. 21, 18 men of hoom was some of the trustees the school master and some of the scholars and Haulted opsit my door with fife and drum gave 3 shouts and went of threatning pope and popery this past on till Monday last I was going by the school House the master came out of the school House and went a kicking some stove wood out of the snow the

master stood between me and the window Where the scollars was looking out the opened the door off a sudent raising their hands and shouts to frightened the Horse from under me and is [ ] myself by bodley strength and by threatning the law on the scllars and on the Master the Master said nothing to the schollars to prevent them from dooing so I went to 2 magistrates the told me to go to the local superintendent about it I went to him and told him my case he told me he could do nothing about it but write a letter to the Master how he should conduct the school he gave me a letter to that affect for the master I told him that I dear not send my children to that school as some of the trustees told me that my children would be deprived of privilyg which might be optained of education and if I did send them I would be glad to keep them at home he told me to send them to school section No. 18 as I have kept them from school this pas five years

there is one boy the Master kicked out of school for asking him to write for Him a head line one trustee gave it against the Master the other 2 gave it against the schollar the schollar is a catholic papist what about it

I pray that god may send better times than this

Your obedient
James Feagan

Tyendenaga
County of Hastings
Blessinton post office
to the care of Mr. James Meagher Esquire

THE CATHOLIC CASE IN BRITISH COLUMBIA

Secular Schools Versus Denominational Schools (St Mary's Mission, B.C., 1881), pp. 3-4, 24-8.

PETITION.

To the Legislative Assembly of the Province of British Columbia.
The humble petition of the Catholic Bishops of British Columbia, in the name of the Faithful under their spiritual jurisdiction,
SHOWETH:

First. That the Catholic population paying taxes for public school purposes do not receive any benefit therefrom, as they are in conscience compelled to keep up their own schools in order to procure to their offspring such education as their Church requires.

Second. That the School Law, as at present framed, is partizan, favouring only the sect of irreligionists; and in abolishing religious instruction in order to suit those who do not want it, such law oppresses those who do want religious instruction for their children.

Third. That the absence of religious instruction in school does generally bring forth immoral youths, and consequently is a source of evil. This is a fact acknowledged by Catholics and by non-Catholics.

Fourth. That the present system of public schools requires poor people to pay for the schooling of the rich man's children; whereas the rich should pay for the instruction of their own children, and the State assist in educating the children of the poor.

Fifth. That education is a duty belonging to the parents of the children, not to the State.

Sixth. That we beg of your honorable body to grant to the Catholic minority in this Province the same educational advantages which the Protestant minority enjoys in the Province of Quebec.

Your petitioners therefore humbly pray that your Honorable House favourably receive our request.

And your petitioners will ever pray.

John B. BRONDEL, Bishop of Vancouver Island.

L. J. D'HERBOMEZ, Vicar Apostolic of British Columbia.

P. Paul DURIEU, Aux. Bishop.

In following the discussion which has lately occupied the attention of the House of the Legislative Assembly of this Province on the all important question of education, we have with much pleasure observed that many of the Hon. Members appear to understand that *godless* and *purely secular* schools are, as experience proves, calculated to produce generally a class of *hoodlums* and other evils which tend to effect by slow but sure degrees the ruin of social order, and consequently that truly christian parents should not choose for their children.

We sincerely hope that the Hon. Members who have the prosperity and welfare of this Province at heart will not confine themselves to the mere introduction of some brief form of prayer into the public schools.

We cannot see any reason why they should not adhere to the wise maxims of eminent statesmen both protestant and catholic who perfectly agree that religion is essential in schools, in order to procure a good and advantageous education for their children.

Men of true wisdom and much experience acknowledge that to attempt to bring up the rising generation without religion or knowledge of their duties towards God, their neighbour and themselves, is in reality nothing less than setting them adrift on the tempestuous sea of this world, without compass, exposed to a sad and inevitable shipwreck and utter ruin; hence it is that the truly wise and enlightened rulers of nations have approved of religion as an essential element in schools for the better education of youth. We shall not enter into detail; we give but a few instances.

In England, the mother patria of this Province, for example, they have not adopted a purely and exclusively secular school system as a kind of monopoly for the citizens who do not want religion into the public schools.

The English Statesmen are too fond of justice in the matter of education not to acknowledge the rights of liberty and equality in such an important affair. The words *justice, liberty* and *equality* are not empty words in their estimation.

Thus it is that, while they support public schools which are neither purely nor exclusively secular, they do not refuse a liberal subvention to denominational schools where religion is taught, and parents are at liberty to send their children to the school of their choice.

We have another example in the Island of Ceylon, an English colony, where the schools are denominational, and where each school secures from the State a *pro rata* of the Educational fund.

In the Island of Maurice, another English colony, they have common schools supported by the Government, but the State gives a liberal subvention to the schools of each religious denomination and establishes schools only in such places where there were no others.

Nearer home, we see that in the Province of Ontario the Protestants, in their love of liberty and equality, have adopted the separate school system, thus giving entire satisfaction to the just and reasonable demands of the Catholic minority.

It is also well known that in the Province of Quebec the Protestant minority are enjoying the same educational advantages as the Catholic majority.

The State awards the same protection to each religious denomination; in fact it unites itself with the different creeds and in matters of education does not authorize any *atheistical* or *Godless* schools, but if it asks that the school be christian in order to entitle it to a subvention, it does not insist that it should belong to either one Church or the other; entire freedom is left to the respective creeds, consequently perfect harmony and good will reigns among the people.

The Statesmen of that Province know by experience that a sincere Christian is a good citizen, and combine their efforts with the Churches to obtain a true national educational system, which gives the surest guarantee of prosperity for the present and the future. Such system works satisfactorily not only with regard to the advantages of education, but also as regards the peace and harmony amongst the religious creeds.

It has recently been declared by Specialists of the Paris Exhibition who have been charged to examine the existing educational systems in vogue throughout the world that *the elementary system in the Province of Quebec is one of the most perfect in existence*, and have in consequence awarded to it four bronze medals and four diplomas.

The same system of education with some modifications has been adopted in the new Province of Manitoba.

It is far from our intention to presume to dictate to the Hon. Members of the Legislative Assembly the best educational system to adopt for this Province. We simply give a few precedents which we consider worthy of imitation, and respectfully submit the same to their wise and prudent consideration.

The systems above referred to are, no doubt, the result of deep thought and enquiry of conscientious men of State.

Every place where they have been carried out, they have given much satisfaction to the people who enjoy the benefit of its influence based as they are on the principles of justice, liberty and equality.

Should the Hon. Members of the Legislative Assembly adopt the same principles, we have every reason to believe that they would obtain the same satisfactory results.

FEDERALISM AND THE POLITICS OF DENOMINATIONALISM

Synoptic Report of the Proceedings of the Legislative Assembly of the Province of New Brunswick (Saint John, New Brunswick, 1874), pp. 126-8.

The Attorney General said an impression had gone abroad that the Government was unfairly seeking to make the matter of this Separate School agitation the question of the coming elections, but those who had endeavored thus to shift the responsibility on the Government seemed to realise but little of what was transpiring in the world outside of New Brunswick. The subjects of education and the Irish question had absorbed all the great interests in the late elections in Great Britain, and it was really the education question that was revolutionizing the domestic politics of England. Other countries of Europe and the United States were also sharing in the agitation, which, therefore, at the present time, commands attention of the minds of the ablest statesmen, and also stirs with its influence the masses. It is the subject that to-day is of the most vital importance, and in its settlement is involved the question, as to how we shall lay the foundation of our political future. It is a question in which the majorities and minorities each have their rights, but it is also one not exempt from the political rule by which the minority must bow to the will of the majority, and not the majority to the minority. It is a question in which those who are in the majority should not abuse the power they possess, while, at the same time, they should not allow any false notions of chivalry to lead them to wrong themselves....

Those who blame the Government for precipitating the question seem not to know what is going on in Europe and the United States. It is the question in Prussia, in Austria, in Switzerland, in England and in the United States; in fact the Catholic Church is making a stand everywhere for new privileges and powers, and it is being resisted everywhere. Referring to an article in the Montreal *Gazette* on the subject of the New Brunswick School Act, stating that it was oppressive to the Catholics who resisted it as galling tyranny and a matter of conscience, he asked when it was discovered that schools of this kind were not the same galling tyranny in every State in the

Union, in Nova Scotia and Prince Edward Island. New Brunswick is only following the general law of the continent; and because it does not follow the peddling, compromising policy of Ontario and Quebec, it is to be said that the Government is tyrannizing over the consciences of Catholics. From the Atlantic to the Pacific, in the United States, there is no relief for these burdened consciences, yet the New Brunswick Government is to be assailed and maligned because it has done what other enlightened countries have done before it. The Irish immigrant who comes over from the Green Isle settles down amongst the people of the United States, and shares with them for his children the advantages of the free non-sectarian schools of that country. He is grateful, and becomes a good and satisfied citizen, and the iron does not enter into his soul. The tyranny is not there and he feels that it is not. It is true that the Catholics are endeavoring, in the large cities of the United States, to get parochial schools, but no such attempt is being made general. The genius of the politics of Christian nations is not in favor of separate schools. In the new English Education Act the provisions of the future are non-denominational, and after two years new board schools must be non-sectarian. In Scotland the rights of denominations in the board schools have been swept away. And, yet, with these facts before us, we are told that we are to imitate the weak kneed policy of Ontario, and that we are not to set up such schools as the people desire under our constitutional rights.

Citing the portion of the Pastoral letter of the Bishops of the Maritime Provinces, in which it is stated that they will be satisfied with nothing less than Separate Schools for the whole country, he said this style of dictation, with the nauseous utterances of a portion of the press of the Upper Provinces on the subject, and the unsought, and impertinent meddling of the Parliament of Canada with our School Act, seemed to indicate that it is scarcely recognized that the Union is a federal one. They all seem to forget that in this matter we have the right to legislate for ourselves. If we are not to use the power thus placed in our hands then the giving it to us was a mockery and a sham. In view of the danger that threatens the province in this matter—this attempt to override our local Constitution, and fasten forever on the province, against the wishes of the people, a system of Separate Schools—it becomes the duty of the Government to expose the schemes of those who would drive it from its position as the guardian of its rights and liberties. Should the attempts now being made succeed, it would give one class of subjects a hold on the revenues of the provinces which could no more be shaken off than the coil of the anaconda. Talk of the railway bill and its absorbing clauses—with a State Church gnawing at our vitals, we would be glad to get our money out of its grasp to give to railways or anything else.

This attempt upon our constitutional rights is of a piece with the scheming of the same parties who thought they had, long ago succeeded in securing their ends by working in the dark and in secrecy. When the Quebec scheme was before the people it contained nothing but a general clause vesting the powers of legislating in regard to education in the several provinces, but when our delegates met at the Westminster they found, sitting side by side with them archbishops and clergy of the Catholic Church. The people of New Brunswick had sent to that conference representatives vested with large powers, and the British North America Act was passed through the British Parliament. The news came to this province, and with it the people learned that something had been put in the act curtailing their powers in the matter of education—that something had been placed in the act surreptitiously, so far as the people were concerned,—and it was thought at first, and by those who placed it there that it covered and perpetuated the liberties the Catholics were permitted to take with our Parish Schools Act. It was a conspiracy against the people. When the present school act was being passed through the Legislature it was asserted that a coach and six might be driven through it, but the late Mr. Palmer's amendment had met and fixed that point.

The theory of the school law is one of equality—symbolising the genius of the country, which says that all men are equal before the law, and that there shall be no State Church. The school law patronizes no creed and coquets with none. There are, no doubt, fathers and mothers belonging to all the churches of the land, who would have their children instructed in their peculiar religious faith in the public schools, were the matter one of choice, but they realize that it cannot be done for all, and they are agreed that it shall not be done for any. They say, "what we deny to ourselves we will not grant to any other."...

We cannot go back from the position we have taken in the matter of education and through repeal permit the establishment of Separate Schools, because they are opposed to the fundamental doctrines of the State, and of the Church—mere subsidized Sunday Schools; it would be the endowment of religious denominations and the means of rendering our school system thoroughly inefficient. Dr. Ryerson in his Report says of the 171 separate schools of Ontario; "Several of these are admirably managed and are doing good work for their localities." The natural inference is that while "several" out of 171 are well managed, the great remainder must be poorly managed. Even the Catholic organ, the *Canadian Freeman*, said, several years ago that the separate schools were less efficient than the free non-sectarian schools.

We cannot afford to give the Catholics what they ask by law for we cannot experiment in the matter. If they are once allowed by law to draw $40,000 or any other sum for their schools from the Provincial Treasury it cannot be taken away from them again, neither can we give them less without first going to Ottawa for leave to do so.

The Catholics may think we are hard with them in compelling them to pay the school tax when they are called upon as a matter of conscience to support their own schools also. It will seem strange, however, that Catholic conscience in New Brunswick is not the same as Catholic conscience in Ontario. There are 70,000 Roman Catholic children attending the public schools of that province. Their parents have the choice of sending them to the separate or the non-sectarian schools, and yet the statistics show that out of the 70,000 but 20,000 attend the separate schools. What shall be said of the parents of the other 50,000? Have they any conscience? This claim on the ground of conscience will not stand and is evidently fallacious. If separate schools are set up in many Catholic districts, the Protestants also might not care to attend them, and would be entirely shut out from school privileges, as such districts could not support two or three sets of schools.

ATTENDANCE AND THE QUESTION OF COMPULSORY SCHOOLING

THE BANE OF IRREGULAR ATTENDANCE

Reports of the Visitors for the Three Counties of Prince Edward Island for the years 1868-69 (Charlottetown, 1869), pp. 9-10.

Many parents seem to think that when the necessary school accommodation, furniture and apparatus are supplied, and the teacher engaged, nothing more is required. They allow trifling matters to prevent the regular attendance of their children at school. The poorer classes, having greater difficulties with which to contend, need encouragement. They require sympathy rather than censure, and in their struggle for subsistence, it is not at all surprising that they should avail themselves of all the assistance their children can render, and thus deprive them of the benefits of Education.

But many who have surmounted the hardships and difficulties of poverty, are too apt still to be guided by a modification of the motives which previously influenced them. If they do not now require the help of their children to earn a comfortable living, they do require it to enable them to "make money." If then, from the poverty, the cupidity, or the apathy of parents, the education of their children be neglected, it is surely the duty of the State to interpose its authority in their behalf, by means of a compulsory law. So keenly are the evils of irregular attendance felt by the Teachers, that many of them frequently express their conviction that nothing short of a compulsory enactment would suffice as a remedy. I have heard Trustees express the same opinion, and I have reason to believe it is gaining ground in the country.

Neither the building of School-houses, the furnishing of them, nor the payment of the taxes that go to make up the Teachers' Salaries is left to voluntary effort. Government enforces the payment of taxes. A majority of householders compels the minority to share the expense of building the School-house. Why then, it is asked, should the attendance of pupils at School,—that point at which the machinery of our Educational System ought most prominently be brought to bear—be left to the caprice or the negligence of parents.

It is stated on good authority, that "in nearly every civilized country except Great Britain, there is a law of some kind requiring parents to educate their children, as in Prussia and every state in Germany, except Hamburg and Frankfort; in most of the Cantons of Switzerland; in Denmark, Sweden and Norway; in Italy; and in many of the most advanced States of the neighboring Republic. In Holland there is no compulsory law, but relief is withdrawn from paupers where they do not send their children to school." And further, "that wherever coercion is applied, education is good and morality is high; but that wherever coercion is not applied education is deficient and morality comparatively low." There is, indeed, something very nearly approaching indirect coercion provided for by the 27th section of our school act. It provides that the Government allowance to the teachers in those districts which fail to keep up the average attendance required by law, shall be reduced in proportion to the deficiency in the said average, and that all parents of children within such districts shall be liable to make up and contribute towards such reduction in proportion to the number of their children. This is certainly a penalty for non-attendance, but it falls as heavily upon the parents who send regularly to school, as upon those who do not. The subject is worthy of favourable consideration. I believe it will yet be found advisable to pass a measure authorizing trustees having first obtained the sanction of a majority of householders, to enforce, during at least a part of the year, the attendance of all children between the ages of five and fifteen years, who were not being educated at home, or who were not prevented from attending by sickness or other sufficient cause.

A GLIMPSE OF REALITY, TORONTO, 1872

Excerpts from the diaries of W. C. Wilkinson, Truant Officer

Tuesday, May 14

Called at the office of the City Inspector at 9 a.m. and found four cards from Mr. Gill at Palace St. School. The first case was that of *John Smith* age 9 years residing on Cherry St. Saw his mother who stated that she kept him at home to bring chips as she was out of wood but would send him in the afternoon.

John Chandler. Ascertained that he had returned to school with an explanation for his absence.

Alfred Sears 61 Parliament. Saw the mother of this boy who stated that she had taken Alfred and the rest of the family attending school from it and was sending them to a private school.

Alfred Effer 439 King St. East. Saw the mother of this boy who stated that she had used every effort to make her boy go to school but with no avail. She promised to bring him to the school in the afternoon. I informed her of the consequence and said the clause referring to her or the father of the boy being liable to be prosecuted.

In walking down the Esplanade I came in contact with a pupil of George St. by the name of *Gilmore* whom I believed to be a truant. After ascertaining his name I enquired of Mr. Lewis and found my impression to be correct.

I also found a boy by the name of *Rennie* loitering his time away by the wharf. I found that he was a pupil in the Palace St. School. I waited on his parents and they told me they had detained him at home to bring water. I cautioned them in future to be careful as they were answerable to the law for his idleness. I found a number of boys playing about the Star Green and in that locality named Quinn, Boyle and McQuin and others who stated that they belonged to the Brothers School but had a holiday today. On Duke Street I found two boys named Aikens and Hogg. The first belonging to the George St. School and the other to the Park on Seaton St.

I found *Mr. Alwand* 72 Seaton of George St. School. His mother told me she kept him home to mind the smaller children but would send him in the afternoon.

Also *Albert Evans* 18 Sherbourne St. of George St. School who was detained for a similar purpose.

And in the case of the *Gilmore* boy I ascertained that they are contemplating moving to the country and was detained home on that account expecting every day to receive word from her husband to move the family and promised if they remain to send them to school.

Then went to the office of the inspector where I received three more cards from Mr. Lewis of George St. School.

Robert & William Howe of 144 Seaton St. When I next visited this residence I found the two boys digging in the garden who stated they were detained at home for that purpose, their parents being absent from home.

John Philips. I waited upon this boy's father who resides corner of Sherbourne & Duke Streets who stated that the boy was 14 years old but that he was desirous of him continuing school provided that he would be under a male teacher but informed me that he would not send him any longer to the George St. School under a female teacher.

Wednesday, 29th May

Called at the office of the City Inspector. Found no truant cards. Went from Church St. to Queen's Wharf on the Esplanade. Met and conversed with a number who were differently occupied fishing, gathering chips and sitting on the edge of the dock. Six of them I talked with said they were Roman Catholics. I took their names. Two gave their names as Powell & Martin who said they were 13 & 14 years of age respectively. At the foot of Brock Street there were five boys. I ascertained the names of two who said they were pupils in the Phoebe Street School, Mister Alexander Lee & Robinson the latter residing at the corner of Brock and Queen Streets. I proceded then to Bathurst Street and to the place where I noticed the number of boys referred to in Thursdays report. I saw the carpenter who promised if possible to ascertain the name or names of some of the boys. He had ascertained that one of the boys names was Mr. Barry residing on Denisen Avenue at no. 19. I then went to see the head master Mr. McCausland and ascertained from him that the boy had been to school one day last week and had not been this week as yet. Mr. McCausland sent a boy to see if he was home and his guardian, the grandmother of the boy and informed her of what I knew—that he and another 10 or 11 boys were in the habit of congregating in the locality referred to, during school hours. Mrs. Coady was very much astonished to hear of his absence as she was under the impression that he was attending regularly. I informed her that since the opening of the school 4½ weeks, he had been present 10½ days. She said he was ill for 8 days and the remainder of the time she thought he was at school. She promised me to detain him at home until 8:30 the next morning when I arranged to call with the view of ascertaining if possible the names of the remainder of the boys.

Friday, June 14th, 1872

Called at the office at 9 a.m. Proceeded to investigate the case of *Frederick Thornton* age 7 reported by Mr. McDonald of Louisa St. School. Saw the mother of the boy who resides at 49 Alice Street. This is the second time the boy has been reported. The mother told me as on a former occasion that she could not do any good with him. She had used threats and flogged him. She brought the boy out to the front room to me and I talked to the boy with reference to his conduct. Found the boy to be very hardened. Believe him to be fit subject for the Industrial Schools. His mother also talked and was very anxious for him to go to school. She promised to try him again and bring him to school in the afternoon. I reported the result of the investigation to Mr. McDonald when that gentleman stated that he would do what he could and call if necessary every morning and bring him to school.

Monday, June 17th, 1872

Robert Johnson age 10 years, Grosvenor Avenue. After going the length of this street and enquiring all the way along I ascertained from a lady living in the same house with Mrs. Johnson that the boy and his mother had been in the country for the past three weeks and did not know if he would be sent to the Bathurst St. School when he returned owing to the boys mother being a Catholic, this person being his stepmother and his father having died a few weeks ago.

Joseph Bell age 8 years, Monk Street. I found that this boy had been kept at home about four weeks owing to his having a sore throat and the past week for weeding the garden. I informed his mother of the law in the case—that he should attend school—and she promised to bring him in the morning.

Alexander Anderson age 10 years, residing at 58 Muter Street. Saw the boys mother who said that he had not clothes fit to send him to school in and had kept him home on that account but during the present week she fully intended that he would be properly clothed and promised to see that he was at school on Monday next.

William Brown age 14. I saw the boys mother who said that she could not get him to go to school. He had a bad lot of associates and his father had left her, being very much given to intemperance. She had used every effort but found that he was continually playing truant. So at present he had got himself a place at a wholesale drug store but thought he was tired of his job and in the event of his quitting that place she would make every effort to send him to school and notify me, so that I might assist her if possible to make him go to school since I could not hold her responsible for him as he did not come under the truant regulations.

Robert Johnson age 9, 151 Lumley St. This boy had been playing truant for nearly 3 weeks. I had met him on a vacant lot in the forenoon and had taken his name and found he had given me a wrong name and address. He was reported by card to me and I at once recognised him and informed his mother of the lies he had told me. She promised to report the case to his father in the evening and get him severely flogged. She said she had great difficulty in getting him to go to school at any time but undertook to fetch him to school in the morning and if possible make him attend in the future.

Friday, June 21st

Henry Harper age 12 years, residing at 441 King St. At the residence I saw the mother of the boy who said that he had not been home for a fortnight. She said they had no control over him. The father of the boy was anxious to send him to the reformatory as he could not be depended upon at all. He had stolen money from the father before leaving and had been in gaol for a week. He would be 13 years of age in a month. I afterwards ascertained that he had got a place and was working for an ice company for $1.25 per week. Told Mrs. Harper that I would report the case to the City Inspector.

Albert Effer age 9 years, residing below the railway crossing on the Kingston Road. This is the second time this boy has been reported. The first time from the Palace St. School and this time from the Parliament St. School card no. 2 (Harper was card no. 1) I went to his residence and saw his mother who told me she had done everything in her power to make him go to school. She had took him there and as soon as he got out he ran away. She also had told me that her husband had left her and she had six children to provide for and she could not go with him every day. Besides that her eyes were diseased and she could not see out in the sun. From the appearance of the boy, his clothes etc. I think him a fit subject for an Industrial School. The mother promised to bring him on Monday if possible.

Friday, September 6th

Robert Bundy age 11. Charge of continual absence, residence 35 Cherry St. Reported by Mr. Gill Palace St. School. Found the boy had been absent one week. I visited the parents and found them both at home. The father told me that the boy had been sent home as he required new books and that he, the father could not afford any at present. He said he would receive his months pay a week hence and then he would procure the books necessary. I reported the case to Mr. Gill. He stated he did not send the boy home. He said it would be necessary for the boy to procure the books and further said that if the parents would promise to have the books in another week that he would suffer him to attend for that time. The parents promised that the books would be supplied and the boy would be at school on Monday.

I went to the direction of the bay and up the Esplanade and conversed with the following boys and girls; Thomas Kingston age 12 years; Michael Innes and William Peach of South Park Street; Alice Beamish 11; Yvonne Campbell 11; and Maggie Welsh a Roman Catholic. Each of the above Protestants told me they were on the Palace St. School register. I also conversed with Jerry Cranyn and 8 other boys which I had reason to believe were Catholics all saying they attended the Brothers School and all had reasons such as gathering chips for their mothers and kept at home to get their clothes mended etc. I also met 2 little English boys sailing on some logs at the foot of the street. One gave his name as Edward Crease who had only been here a week who promised to tell his parents what I had told him of the rules with reference to boys playing about the wharves etc. and went right home when I told him to do so.

THE OFFICIAL VIEW OF TRUANCY

Annual Report of the Local Superintendent of the Public Schools, Toronto, 1863, pp. 46-7.

TO THE CHAIRMAN AND MEMBERS OF THE BOARD OF SCHOOL TRUSTEES

The Report of the Special Committee, to whom was referred the taking of a School Census, beg to report that the same has been completed; and your Committee herewith submit a full abstract of the Enumerators' returns for the several Districts . . .

From this summary it will be seen that the whole number of children of school age viz., from 5 to 16 both inclusive, is returned as 9508, namely, 7053 Protestants and 2455 Roman Catholics—that the whole school attendance up to June 30th 1863, is returned as 7876, namely, 5877 Protestants, and 1999 Roman Catholics;—and that the whole number who neither attended school nor were taught at home during the period of the 6 months ending June 30th 1863, was 1632, namely, 1165 Protestants, and 467 Roman Catholics; the cause of non-attendance being in almost all cases employment, want of clothes, considered too young, or too far from school. . . .

The following summary, furnished by the Secretary of the Board, accounts for the non-attendance at School of 1632 inhabitants of the City who are of school age, namely, from 5 to 16 years, inclusive:

	Protestant	Roman Catholic	Total
Employed	340	113	453
Wanted at Home	203	60	263
Sick	91	37	128
Too Young/Too Far	149	68	217
Want of Clothes	127	89	216
Lately Come to City	38	1	39
No Return	217	99	316
	1165	467	1632

Annual Report of the Local Superintendent of the Public Schools, Toronto, 1874, pp. 43-5.

TO THE CHAIRMAN AND MEMBERS OF THE PUBLIC SCHOOL BOARD OF THE CITY
OF TORONTO

GENTLEMEN—

I beg to report that for the year ending 31st of December, 1873, there were reported to me by card 528 cases of violation of the Truant Regulations, namely—

From Bathurst Street School .308 cases.
. . . John 41
. . . Park 38
. . . Phoebe 34
. . . Palace 30
. . . George 23
. . . Parliament 14
. . . York 9
. . . Elizabeth 8
. . . Louisa 7
. . . Victoria 8
. . . Givins 6
. . . Church 3
. 528

In each of the above cases the necessary attention has been given, by visiting the parents or guardians of those reported, and informing them of the law requiring the attendance of children between the ages of 7 and 12 years; the responsibilities resting upon the parents or guardians, and the penalties attached for non-compliance.

Of the aforesaid number a large majority were not, properly speaking, truants, but violators of the truant law which now exists, who were kept at home for reasons, many of them valid, such as poverty, sickness, sickness in the family, too great a distance from school, &c. While, on the other hand, in many instances children were kept at home for the most frivolous reasons by their parents, such as to run messages, assist in domestic duties, cut wood, and many such reasons, that I am compelled to accept, although reluctantly, as the law at present only requires the attendance four months in the year.

Since the appointment of a Truant Officer, *real truancy* (that is absence without the parent's knowledge) does not exist to any great extent in our schools, because those who would be guilty of that habit know that if they absent themselves three times without an explanation from their parents to the teacher, their parents will be made aware of it through the Truant Officer.

There exists in our schools one class that I experience considerable difficulty in dealing with: I refer to those whom their parents have lost parental control over, and who freely admit that such is the case; they willingly promise to do all they can to remedy the complaint, but without effect. Several instances have come under my notice where their parents have brought them to school; and, as soon as recess, they have left without permission. Those referred to generally are children of widowed mothers, or of drunken fathers, and in some cases the fathers are employed out of the city. The influence on pupils attending the schools of this class cannot but have a demoralizing effect.

My attention during the year, as Truant Officer, has been principally devoted to investigating cases reported by card, which have been numerous, especially from the Bathurst Street School. The reason, I believe, of the very irregular attendance at this school, is owing to the sparse population of that part of the city in which it is located, and the very great distance that many of the children have to go to school, the want of sidewalks, and in many cases, especially in the winter season, the impassable state of the roads.

On going from school to school, I have come in contact with many of the vagrant class that, according to the requirements of the law, should be attending school; but, unfortunately as yet, no provision has been made for them by establishing of Industrial School, or some kindred institution, where such children could be sent.

Most of the schools in the city being in an over-crowded state, and especially in the Junior Divisions, it has placed me to some extent in an inconsistent position when I have waited upon the parents of children that I have found loitering about; and have been informed that they have sought admission for their children, and have been told by the Teachers in charge, that no more could be admitted, as there was no accommodation.

My being engaged during the holidays in superintending and arranging for the repairs and improvements in the different school-houses, I have not had any opportunity of taking a school census of the city, as was originally intended when I was appointed to the position of Truant Officer; but from observation in the discharge of my daily duties through the city, I am satisfied that there are in the city sufficient Protestant children growing up uneducated to fill an Industrial School; and I am also impressed that if such an institution existed it would have the most wholesome effect on the irregular attendance now on our registers. I would, therefore, earnestly impress on the Members of the Board, if they desire to have the streets cleared of the boys of school age, who now infest the thoroughfares of the city, to use their influence in the establishment of an Industrial School, whereby the large numbers who are now growing up in ignorance might be made useful members of society.

By the instructions of the Chairman of the Board, during the illness of the Inspector and of the Secretary, I was also engaged in attending to such duties as those officers have desired of me.

Respectfully submitted,
W. C. WILKINSON,
Truant Officer.

Toronto, February, 1874.

AN EVERYDAY PRACTICAL QUESTION

Charles Merrill to Egerton Ryerson, October 24, 1859. *Education Papers*, RG 2 C-6-C, Public Archives of Ontario.

Waterford 24 October 1859

Rev. Egerton Ryerson
Superintendent of
Education
Dear Sir

Permit me to enquire of you, whether a Teacher, or the Trustees of a Common School have a right to lock the door of his School house against any Child, or Children for late attendance to School. As for instance a Child attending said School is living some three or four miles distant from the said School house, and it happens that he is ten or fifteen minutes too late, on his arrival at the School, he finds the door locked and no entrance, possibly it prove a wet disagreeable day, Where is that child to go for Shelter, or must he return home in the Inclemency of the Weather with his Books. Also, provided a Child living within the limits at a reasonable distance from the School, happens to be too late he cannot enter the School as the door is locked upon him. Considering that the Parent or Guardian of their Child has the time lost to pay for, under these Circumstances I am requested to make the enquiry from you, to know if such a Law is absolute—we may be wrong in our opinion. Still as it is not practised in any other School within the Province, to our knowledge It is deemed one of oppression and I hope and trust will not be tolerated by you.

I am—Dear Sir

Your Obedient Servant
Charles Merrill

A DISSENTING OPINION

Edward Blake, *Remarks on the School Bill* (Toronto, 1871), pp. 7-8.

With reference to compulsory education, my own opinion is, that, except perhaps in cities, this clause will not be found a living letter of the law. Even in cities to a large extent, and in counties almost entirely, the law will be a dead letter. I agree with the hon. member for Lincoln (Mr. Rykert) on the subject of perpetual imprisonment. This perpetual imprisonment clause is so outrageous, that I will assume it to be an error, and pass it by. It must be struck out, and other changes must be made. The right of home education must be recognized. My opinion is, that we can get as high a degree of education as is procurable under any compulsory system, by judicious management and a liberal expenditure of money in connection with our present Common School system. I do not believe that our population is indifferent to school education. I am proud to believe that, from year to year, the desire for education will increase, and that it will be regarded as a badge of shame that a parent does not send his children to school. The man who neglects to do so, is just the man you cannot force by saying, "you shall pay a fine or go to jail." I have made some investigations on this subject, and it is highly satisfactory to say that, as a general rule, in the lately settled districts, where the parents were at first poor, and unable either to provide for schools, or to deprive themselves of the little aid of their children, the attendance of the children at schools, notwithstanding various drawbacks, has largely increased. In the County, one of whose Ridings I have the honour to represent, the increase since the last census is quite disproportionate to the increase of the population—the attendance is nearly double the attendance of 1861. There are similar results in other counties— and counties which once stood, as regards school attendance, as one to five and one to six, now stand as nearly one to four. I believe it is a reasonable estimate, that about 25 per cent. of our population—men, women and children—in this Province of Ontario, are going to school. When this state of things exists, I do believe that you will get by judicious legislation, by liberal encouragement out of the public purse, and by preserving the elements of elasticity and local control, all the educational advantages that the people desire, and will avail themselves of. I do not believe the compulsory clause is one that will do much good. It will not be enforced. I dare say that in cities there is a class that ought to be compelled to go to school; but as regards the other parts of the country the working of a compulsory measure is practically impossible. And I need hardly add that a law which is not observed is a positive injury to the community. It encourages lawlessness.

Again, with regard to the Roman Catholics, they should not be forced, in spite of those conscientious scruples which have produced Separate Schools, to attend the public schools. That is not calculated to promote,—it is calculated to retard, what we all hope for—the general use, by the whole school population, of the public schools.

THE AMBITIONS OF THE TEACHING PROFESSION

Archibald Macallum, 'Compulsory Education', *Annual Report of the Ontario Teachers' Association, 1875* (Toronto, 1875), pp. 24-31.

MR. CHAIRMAN AND FELLOW-TEACHERS,—

The subject to be discussed this afternoon is Compulsory Education. Education is that preparation in early life which will enable a person to prosecute successfully the business of life in after years.

Compulsory Education secures to each individual "that his faculties and capabilities shall be educated, brought out so much that he may know what there is to be done and learned in this world, in which he must needs live, and what of that he himself must learn and do."

The first principle involved in Compulsory Education is that it must be national; the State must educate the whole people in everything except religion; the property of all must pay for the education of all, from the lowest primary or kindergarten school to the highest seat of learning—the university of the nation. England, until recently, had not a national system, and, by their own estimate, a few years ago there were in England and Wales eight million men and women who could neither read nor write.

The legislative provisions for the free and liberal education of every youth in Ontario are amply sufficient. The State, in mere self-defence, should insist on those rich provisions of the law being carefully carried into effect. Society has suffered so cruelly from ignorance, that its riddance is a matter of necessity, and by the universal diffusion of knowledge alone can ignorance and crime be banished from our midst; in no other way can the best interests of society be conserved and improved than by this one remedy—the compulsory enforcement of this great boon—the right of every Canadian child to receive that education that will make him a good, loyal subject, prepared to serve his country in the various social functions which he may be called on to fill during his life; and prepare him, through grace, for the life to come. This is the end of education.

Compulsory education is the necessary sequence of free public schools, and may be regarded as the crowning act in the great educational drama we have been permitted to witness during the past thirty years. It may be said the ballot has been placed in the hands of every man, and in no other way can this great right be exercised to the advantage of all concerned than by the universal diffusion of knowledge. Our form of government is the best in the world, but without intelligent voters it can neither be continued pure nor improved to meet the necessities of the coming time. Three great privileges we enjoy: a free State, a free Church, and a free School. We owe to posterity that the people should be sufficiently educated to hand down not only unimpaired but augmented, the blessings now secured to all by our excellent system of instruction, which embraces the Public Schools, the High Schools and Collegiate Institutes, and the National University. However important other institutions may be, the public schools alone affect the standing of the masses; and so beneficial are the influences of education on the masses, that "the material prosperity, intellectual and moral development, respect for law, and obedience to it in any state, may be relatively measured and calculated by the condition of the free public schools."

The importance of this great cause may be perceived from the great amount of property invested in its interests by the various Provinces constituting our Dominion, as well as in other educating countries. . . .

I. COMPULSORY EDUCATION PREVENTS PAUPERISM.

In the States of Pennsylvania, Ohio, and Illinois, statistics bearing on this point have for some time been kept, and it is found that, of illiterate persons, *one* in *ten* is a pauper, while of the rest of the population only one in *three hundred* is a beggar. Thus it appears that persons allowed to grow up in ignorance produce *thirty* times the number of paupers that an educated community would be troubled with. The statistics of England, Ireland, and Scotland, not less than other countries of Europe, show that *(ceteris paribus)* poverty and paupers are in the inverse ratio of the condition of education among the masses: as "education increases, pauperism decreases, and as education decreases, pauperism increases."

II. COMPULSORY EDUCATION DIMINISHES CRIME.

Of the prisoners committed to jail in Ontario during the year 1870, 1,722 or 27 per cent. could neither read nor write, and 427 of them were under sixteen years of age. The Commissioner of Education for New York avers that 85 per cent. of the crimes in that State is committed by the uneducated. Eighty per cent. of the crimes in New England in the same year was committed by parties whose education had been wholly neglected or nearly so. Only seven per cent. of New England's population over ten years of age can neither read nor write; yet 80 per cent. of the crime in these States was committed by this small minority; in other words, an uneducated person commits fifty-six times as many crimes as one with education. In the whole United States an ignorant person commits ten times the number of crimes an educated one does. Of 11,420 juvenile offenders committed to jail in one year in England, only 196, or less than *two* per cent. could read and write well. The statistics of our own Penitentiary but too surely corroborate these lamentable facts. . . .

In France, from 1867 to 1869, one-half the inhabitants could neither read nor write, and this one-half furnished 95 per cent. of the prisoners arrested for crime, and 87 per cent. of those convicted. In other words, an ignorant person, on an average, committed ten times the number of crimes that one not ignorant did. . . .

IV. COMPULSORY EDUCATION WOULD INCREASE THE BLESSINGS OF LIFE.

The tendency of education is to increase the happiness of mankind; if education were general and compulsory, the greatest good to the greatest number would be secured. Lord Brougham says that science or education would not only make our lives more agreeable, but better, and that these pursuits are found to be the sure paths of virtue as well as of happiness. . . . Dr. Potter states, in "School and Schoolmaster," "that education, if imparted to all the rising generation, will make the young provident, industrious, temperate, and frugal. Could the paupers of our own State be collected into one group, it would be found, without doubt, that five out of every six owe their present humiliating position to some defect or omission in their early training."

The Boston reformatory for young persons and prison for criminals are on Deer Island, a few miles from the city. In company with James Hughes, Esq., Inspector of Public Schools, Toronto, I had the pleasure of visiting these institutions in November last. I am quite prepared to believe the statement of the Superintendent, for everything was so nice, and every person seemed so happy, that the influences must have a very beneficial effect on the inmates. The children receive a good education, and the result is thus stated by the gentleman referred to: "In regard to the children, we have one fact to record, which is very encouraging. *It is very seldom that any of them return to this island.*" Such is the result of education. . . .

V. WHAT ARE IMPLIED IN OR BY COMPULSORY EDUCATION?

First, the universal diffusion of knowledge, especially among the young, and particularly that which prepares for better work in after life. . . . Second, improvement in school architecture, so that the surroundings of the pupil during the plastic period of school life shall improve the taste as well as gratify the longings for the beautiful. Every facility for imparting instruction, not of words merely, or names, but of things, every means for conveying these ideas, must be provided and put into requisition. Schools must be better graded; the number of pupils to one teacher must not be above *forty*, irregularity in attendance greatly improved, and special attention paid to the health, comfort, and normal development of the pupils.

Third, there is also implied a better supervision of schools. At present the great step taken in establishing county inspectorships is merely a beginning; no Inspector should have more than *forty* schools in his district; monthly instead of semi-annual visits by the Inspector should be made; the authority, as well as the pay of these officials in country parts, should be increased, and their term of office made, like that of our Judges, during good behaviour; and the incumbent should be removable by the Government only, to which alone he should be responsible. No person should be allowed to teach even a private school without proper preparation, and all schools should be inspected by the proper official. Township boards, by which more equitable school taxation will be secured, are also implied.

Fourth, but of little avail will every other improvement be unless the position of the teacher is made more secure, and his effective ability as well as his pay largely increased. Other things are important; this is absolutely necessary. It is the teacher that makes the school; the surroundings aid, but the instructor accomplishes; he moulds the heart and forms the character of the future occupant of every position in society. The true teacher will bear in mind that education is not a mechanical routine of duties, but a dynamical process; that it is effort that secures real improvement, and that he is responsible, not merely for what his pupils accomplish, but for all they could realize or should achieve. Much has been done for teachers, still much remains to be done. . . .

I am fully convinced that with proper facilities and good teachers, our pupils at ten years of age will be as far on in their studies—by which I mean the real work of education—as they now are when two years older; and two years at twelve are equal to five at twenty.

Moreover, the influences of education—for it simply means the formation of character, and character is the highest gift God has placed within our reach —are like our personal identity, of the most enduring nature. As it is so abiding, surely it should be of the purest and best possible type and kind. . . .
Hamilton, August, 1875.

INSEPARABLE ISSUES: SCHOOL ATTENDANCE AND JUVENILE DELINQUENCY

Ontario Department of Education, *Report on Compulsory Education in Canada, Great Britain, Germany and the United States* (Toronto, 1891).

MAYORS' REPORTS ON TRUANCY IN ONTARIO CITIES AND TOWNS, 1890

Town or City.	Number of children under 14 years of age arrested during 1890.	How many of these were known as habitual truants?	Would compulsory attendance at school in your opinion tend to the reduction of juvenile offences?
CITIES:—			
Belleville	15	7	Yes.
Brantford	55	19	Am quite certain that it would.
Guelph	10	7	It certainly would if it were strictly enforced.
Hamilton	91	A large majority.	Very much, most of the above do not attend school.
Kingston	14	None that I am aware of.	Yes, would keep children off streets, thus removing them from temptation and crime.
London	14	None.	Not in this city. All offences have been committed after school hours.
St. Catharines	9	9	Yes.
St. Thomas	9	None.	Yes.
Stratford	25	2	It certainly would.
Toronto	650 (under 15.)	Not known.	Yes, most decidedly.
TOWNS:—			
Almonte	None.		Yes, I believe it would be a good thing.
Aylmer	None		It would. I do not approve of arresting and locking children up.
Blenheim	1	None.	Would lessen juvenile offences; there is much truancy here.

Town			
Bothwell	None	None	It would do a great amount of good here.
Bowmanville	None		Truancy is rare in this town.
Brampton	1		It would most decidedly.
Brockville	23	1	Not the slightest doubt of it. School boards should appoint truant officers.
Chatham	11	Most of them.	Truants invariably get into trouble.
Clinton	None.		Do not know, have had no complaints from teachers.
Cobourg	3	None.	I think so. Parents should be compelled to send children to school.
Collingwood	14	14	Yes. Truancy should be punished by fine and imprisonment.
Deseronto	None.		Would favor it strongly, especially during winter months.
Dresden	None.		Yes.
Dundas	None.		I think it would.
Galt	None.		I think compulsory attendance should be strictly enforced.
Gravenhurst	None.	None	I believe it would reduce juvenile offences to a large extent.
Kincardine	None.	None.	Yes.
Lindsay	3	None.	Yes.
Listowel	3	3	Yes, in my opinion it would.
Meaford	5	5	It would reduce offences. Truant officers should have power to lock up for truancy.
Mitchell	None.	None.	Yes.

Milton	1	None.	Yes.
Napanee	5	2	Yes, would materially tend to lessen offences.
Newmarket	1	1	Possibly, but to a limited extent here.
Niagara	4	4	Yes.
Niagara Falls	2	None.	Yes.
Oakville	None.	None.	Yes, truancy exists to a large extent in this town. A truant officer would be a great advantage.
Orangeville	None.		I would answer this question in the negative.
Owen Sound	6	6	I think it would. A truant officer should be appointed.
Palmerston	None.	None.	Compulsory attendance would be good.
Parkhill	None.		I think it would.
Paris	1		There are several truants in town. It should be binding on parents to send to school.
Parry Sound	None.	None.	Attendance at school should be made compulsory.
Pembroke	4	4	Yes.
Peterboro	17	8	I think it would. The worst children we have do not attend school.
Port Hope	10	None attended regularly.	Am sure it would.
Prescott	Several.	Nearly all of them.	I believe it would.
Sandwich	2	2	Yes, materially.
Sarnia	7	None.	We have a truant master and but little truancy in consequence.
Seaforth	7	7	Yes.
Simcoe	6	4	Would undoubtedly have that effect.
Smith's Falls	5	1	I think so.

Strathroy	None.		Yes, very much.
Thornbury	3	3	It certainly would.
Tilsonburg	None.	None.	Yes, most certainly; have visited 63 families during the year with reference to this with good effect.
Trenton	23		Factory Act and present school law should be carried out, and truant officer appointed.
Walkerton	None.		Yes, truant officer should be appointed with power to compel attendance.
Waterloo	8	5	Yes.
Welland	None.		Decidedly so.
West Toronto	4	2	I am decidedly of opinion that it would.
North Toronto	None.		Yes.
Essex	None.	None.	Yes, we have several children who do not attend school.
Forest	None.	None.	Yes, it is much needed, many children do not attend school; fault of parents.
Gananoque	8	5	I think it would if followed up sharply.
Little Current	None.	None.	I would be in favor of compulsory attendance.
Midland	None.	None.	Yes.
Bracebridge	None.	None.	Undoubtedly.
Gore Bay	None.	None.	I think it would.

THE SCHOOLING OF ADOLESCENTS

IN THE CAUSE OF HIGHER EDUCATION

Annual Report of the Superintendent of Education for New Brunswick, 1855, pp. 26-38.

. . . It is sufficient for us to know that the state of education in this Province is a prosperous one *in spite* of existing difficulties, and that the representatives of the people are anxious to make it more so. The Commission appointed in 1854, and the Report laid before the House in the Session of 1855, plainly proves this; and it cannot be doubted that, acting upon the recommendation of the Commission, it will be possible to devise such a scheme of Collegiate and Common School Education as shall best conduce to the advancement and prosperity of the Province. I say Collegiate and Common School Education, because I feel that it is the duty of every true friend of Education to invoke Legislative protection and provision on behalf both of the College and of the Common School, each being to the fullest extent possible fitted for its peculiar and widely different duties.

It is true that men from whose position in society we might fairly anticipate wider and nobler views, have formally and repeatedly denounced the College as an Institution for the education of a very small number of young gentlemen at an annual cost per head, which naturally strikes their hearers as preposterously large; but the really zealous and sincere friends of education must be warned that the question is not fairly stated by giving a year's income of the College, and dividing that income by the number of students at the College during any one average or selected year. There are several other considerations to be taken into the account besides the number of pounds currency stated at the maximum, and divided by the number of students at the minimum. The extent and character of the Province, the duty and character of its Government, the rights of those of its inhabitants who both need and desire a Collegiate Education, the obvious propriety of increasing the *number of students*, and the evident impossibility of doing so, but by means of a sufficiently though moderately supported College,—all these points seem to me to be as important towards the real question at issue, as the precise number of students who in any selected year attend the Collegiate course.

If a very great number of comparatively or positively wealthy men are so unconscious of the advantages of a liberal education, that they will not send their sons to College, that is clearly the fault of the parents and the misfortune of the sons; the College is open to them. Let the parent do his duty as the Government has done the obvious governmental duty, and there will be small occasion to complain of the paucity of students. To provide a College is a duty of one part of the community; to send students thither is both the right and the duty of quite another part. Whether six or six hundred students be at College during any given term must depend upon the wealthy men of the Province; but if only six desire and require collegiate education, it is the duty of the Provincial Government to enable them to get it without leaving their native Province, to degrade it in the estimation of all to whom their reason for leaving it would undoubtedly appear to be disgraceful equally to the sense, the spirit, and the liberality of New Brunswick.

As the Common Schools become perfected, the youth there educated will become the fathers, the men of business, and in many cases the men of wealth and the legislators of the Province; and he had studied human nature to little purpose who does not know that a man who has received a tolerable education, and is blessed with even comparative worldly prosperity, almost invariably aspires to bestow upon his son a better education than he has himself received. Are we to suppose that New Brunswick is so completely an exception to all general rules that the rising generation will neither improve upon the fortunes of their fathers nor desire the intellectual and social advancement of their sons? Will the education we propose to give them in the Common Schools neither aid them in procuring wealth nor direct them in using it? Is their education to cause them to retrograde as men of business, and to utterly denaturalize them as parents? If otherwise, it is certain that a few years will greatly increase the number demanding collegiate education; equally certain that it is the duty of the Government to be provided with place and with Professors, with system and with apparatus, to afford that education to all who apply for it, without reference to the fact that it is from the sons, not of the illiterate of a passing generation, but from the sons of a living generation that such an increase is to be expected in the number of students as will render the College profitable or even barely remunerative.

Another consideration passed over by the opponents of the College, but by no means to be overlooked by its advocates, is the fact that, many or few, the graduates serve as just so many standards of language, morals, and manners, and as just so many patterns of and inciters to liberal studies. Each even unconsciously, benefits the circle in which, professionally or as an independent private gentleman, he moves after leaving College. However few in number for a few years, such men both by precept and example, will and necessarily must aid powerfully and continually in inspiring that sense of the value, and that desire for the distinction of a College education, which alone are required to render the College as numerically prosperous as it is in other respects honorable to the Government and to the Province.

Again, it may fairly be argued that the expense of the College is even to its opponents' own shewing, but a small matter to complain about. It will not do to say, as can be said in most similar cases, that it is not the *amount* but the *principle* that forms the real question at issue: here the direct converse is the truth. The College is an institution the existence of which is indispensable to the character of the Province, and clearly due to the rights and interests of those who now are or who hereafter may become wisely aware that they but half do their duty to their sons, whatever amount of wealth they may accumulate for them, if they deny them a superior education. The most unblushing apostle of ignorance that ever illustrated bad theory by worse practice, will not I presume venture to state openly that because he has secured wealth and social position *in spite* of his defective education, he would have the young intellect of the Province driven forth to Canada, to Europe, or to the States, for collegiate training,—he will not venture to state this directly; he concedes or at the very least passed over *sub silentio*, the principle that we ought to have a College, but he knows how sensitive a portion of social man is the purse, and he complains not of the College, but of what he most unjustifiably calls "its exorbitant charge per head for Education;" but here he must be sternly and plainly dealt with—fastened down to the principle that the College is a necessity as to the character of the Province, and the inalienable right of those, however few in number, who have the brains and the heart to desire a superior education for their sons, and that if the gross income—a really small one—of the College is divided by only so few students per annum, that is the fault neither of the College nor of the students who attend it, but of the great body of the people who do not send their sons. . . .

That the advantages of a good education are to some considerable extent appreciated in this Province, is evident from the fact that Academies and superior Schools are numerously attended, and that when fostered, supported and encouraged either by the Government or by a party, they are also supported and encouraged by private individuals. In the case of King's College, the converse of this has been the case. Public opinion has been constantly and strenuously directed against it, and the most certain evidence which can be adduced in favour of its real claims, and of its intrinsic merits, is to be found in the attendance of even those few students, in spite of all that has been urged against it, who avail themselves of the vast advantages it affords, and which cannot be afforded elsewhere in the Province. . . .

The early age at which youths leave School and enter College, imperatively requires such a system of discipline as shall satisfy parents that the morals of their sons are as carefully attended to as their intellects. The laxity which prevails in English Universities in this respect, must be exchanged for the strictness which governs the household of the private tutor; the decorous restraint imposed by the Professor in the College Halls, must be continued and enforced by the authority of a Master during the rest of the day; and I cannot but feel that as parents have a right to claim this, so they would be satisfied if they could obtain it, and that the number of students would at once, and very materially increase, were this security for their moral training provided.

I come to this conclusion, from the fact that the excellent Collegiate School in this City, which has for so many years been under the able management of Mr. George Roberts, has never been so well attended—has never reckoned among its pupils so large a number of boys from all parts of the Province as at the present time, and [especially] since the establishment of a Boarding School in connexion with it, which affords to parents every desirable guarantee for that domestic education, without which mere intellectual development but too often excites principles of insubordination hurtful to the boy, and dangerous to society. . . .

One fact is worthy of particular notice; the number of pupils who wish to receive a classical education is on the increase, and I heartily rejoice that it is so; for although a cry has been raised against the study of the classics—although it has been proclaimed to be a sheer waste of time, a frittering away of years in the acquisition of dead languages which are said to be perfectly useless when acquired—and it has been asserted that all the information to be obtained from Greek and Latin authors could much more readily be imparted by translations;—yet who are they who say this? of what value is their opinion in this matter? . . .

So long as society exists it must be composed of various grades, and I do not presume too much in adding that ripe as the world is, it cannot yet do without Divines, Physicians, Lawyers and other members of the various learned professions—doubtless a time may come when every man will be all sufficient unto himself, but as yet the time is not come—and the interests of that society require that men who aspire to protect either the souls, bodies, or estates of their fellow-men, should qualify themselves by special studies for the task, and those who have done so will always be preferred to any theological, medical, or legal pretender who may assert that he has *per saltem* acquired the requisite amount of instruction.

Fortunately society has so decided, and the well educated man will ever find its voice raised in his behalf. It recognizes the claims of those who have painstakingly passed through their collegiate course, and receives them with open arms as welcome additions to its ranks.

But while I thus maintain the necessity of an acquaintance with the works of the ancients, I would not be understood to undervalue other and equally important studies, or to assert for a single moment that classical literature is all sufficient, and that he who has learnt Latin and Greek need learn no more. To them their proper place—to mathematics and all the sciences, as indicative of truth discovered—error prevented—inquiry organised—judicious habits formed, and mental energy strengthened—all due honor, all due weight. To history—"the witness of ages, the light of truth, the life of memory, the school of life, the messenger of antiquity,"—its deserved need of respect and cultivation. To foreign languages, and especially to French, the universal tongue—the language of Courts—the medium of intercourse throughout the civilized world,—that weight which its importance deserves. To eloquence—the art of speaking well—of speaking to instruct—to prove—to refute—to move, and to persuade,—the time, the study needful to acquire it. . . .

And lastly to good breeding and to good manners, that special attention which is indispensable in the scholar who seeks moreover to be a gentleman, who has reflected on all the obligations which society imposes upon him, and who endeavours to discharge them gracefully, polite but not obtrusive, gallant but not importunate, an attentive observer of the rules of propriety, kind hearted and gentle, witty upon occasion, discreet, indulgent, generous and brave, the well bred man exercises a sort of moral authority over his fellows, and it is him and him alone whom they should endeavour to imitate.

A good education will not confer all the qualities which society requires us to possess, but it will better enable us to develope and to exert them. These a young man at his entrance into the world must endeavour to acquire, and this he will readily do if his judgment be correct, and if he select a good model for imitation, remembering that the highest mental and moral qualifications lose half their value when they are not combined with politeness, and that the best and most learned man may, if ignorant of the rules of society, render himself ridiculous.

J. M. D'AVRAY.

A FRENCH-CANADIAN UNIVERSITY

Annuaire de l'Université-Laval pour l'année académique, 1858-59 (Québec, 1858), pp. 28-36, 44-7. Translated by Janna Best.

INSTRUCTION

In all the Faculties, instruction is given, each year, in three terms. The first begins on the Wednesday following the eighth of September, and ends at Christmas; the second begins on the second day after Epiphany and ends at Easter; the third begins on the second Tuesday after Easter, and ends on the second Tuesday of July.

The classes are private in the Faculties of Theology, Law and Medicine. However, any ecclesiastic may be admitted to those of the Faculty of Theology without needing special permission for this. The same applies to men of the law, for the Faculty of Law, and to Doctors and Surgeons, for the Faculty of Medicine. In the Faculty of Arts, there are public classes and private lessons. The latter are for the students of the Faculty only. Students of the Faculty of Medicine are counted as Arts Faculty students for Chemistry and Botany lessons.

The classes are organized so that the same student receives no more than four lessons per day in his own Faculty, and so that he can follow, in the Arts Faculty, that part of the public instruction that is compulsory for him.

The lessons last no less than one hour and no more than an hour and a half. As much as possible, they constitute an explication of a work that all the students have in their hands. Where this is not the case, the professor, at the end of each lesson, gives to the students, orally or in written form, an analysis or summary of the next lesson, and indicates the works to be consulted. During the lessons, the students take notes, which serve, after draughting, as a report. The professor, through the examination of this report, and questions asked during the same lesson, can satisfy himself of the attention and work of the students.

In all the classes, after each period of five or six lessons, the professor devotes one, at least in part, to some exercise designed to examine the progress of his students, and to instil in them a praiseworthy emulation.

Immediately after each term, all the students are examined on everything that has been taught to them during the term. . . .

DISCIPLINE

. . . Every student must fulfill the duties of religion scrupulously. Catholics attend divine service in their parishes on Sundays and religious holidays. Frequent participation in the sacraments is recommended.

The Rector may provide lectures on religion to the Catholic students, when he finds it appropriate. All must attend them regularly. Attention to work, obedience to and respect for the Officers and Professors of the University, honest proceedings towards everyone, and, finally, the observation of all the rules of the University, constitute the duty of all students, the infraction of which is subject to reprimand and, if need arise, severe punishment.

Blasphemies, obscene words, actions or talk which might lead to a student being judged guilty of irreligion or immorality, or to the honour of the university being compromised, render students liable to even more severe penalties and even expulsion.

Frequenting theatres, gambling houses, and drinking establishments is rigorously forbidden, as is entry into houses of ill or dubious repute.

Since the books that the students need are available to them in the seminary library, they have no need to use any others. Nor are they allowed to frequent lecture halls in the city, where some might find the opportunity to waste time and neglect their studies.

They may not form associations, nor may they make collective demonstrations, without obtaining permission.

Unless they live with their father or their mother, or with someone who has taken the place of their parents for several years, they must board in a college or pension of the seminary, and observe all its rules.

They must return to their lodgings at half past nine in the evening, from the end of the vacation to the 30th of April, and at ten o'clock during the rest of the year.

They are required to attend classes punctually. The professors take note of absences, and turn in a list of all that have occurred during the week to the secretary of the Faculty every Saturday. He, after entering them in the Term Register, transmits the list to the Moderator.

Students may not miss lessons, nor may they leave town for one or several days, without the authorization of the Moderator, and, when they are confined to their lodgings because of illness, they must inform him as soon as possible.

When a student has been absent frequently or for a long period, he may have the reasons inserted in the Term Register, as long as he puts them concisely, in writing.

Penalties authorized by the University with respect to students are:-
1) Private reprimand
2) Reprimand in front of all the students of the Faculty
3) Suspension of the right to attend classes, or to attend one of them
4) Temporary suspension
5) Suspension for an indefinite period
6) Permanent expulsion.

Boarding Hall
M. Octave Audet, *Director*
RULES FOR STUDENTS RESIDING IN THE UNIVERSITY

Art. I. The purpose of the seminary, in opening a boarding hall for students of the University, was to sustain them in the practice of their religious duties, and to remove them from the dangers to which young men are ordinarily exposed in cities. In order to achieve this end, it is required of all boarders that they behave at all times and in all places in a Christian manner, and carefully avoid anything that might imperil their virtue or that of their colleagues.

Art. 2. As all students are obliged to obey the rules of the University, the boarders must observe them faithfully, and it is even desirable that their correctness in this respect should serve as an example to non-resident students.

Art. 3. Boarders will be allowed to go into town every day, during the noon recreation, and on Sundays and holidays, from eight A.M. to dinnertime, not counting the hours of religious services or lunch. The Director may allow students to go out during the day at any time, if there is sufficient reason. As for going out in the evening, he will permit this only rarely, for serious causes, and taking every necessary precaution to see that the privilege is not abused.

Art. 4. Students who must frequent the office of an employer will obtain a general permission, spelling out the conditions which they must observe, one of which will always be to go nowhere except on the orders of their employer. A similar permission will also be necessary for students frequenting hospitals.

Art. 5. The Professors of the University and members of the clergy are admitted to communal recreations whenever they wish; but the agreement of the Director is required to introduce any other person.

Art. 6. Students will ordinarily receive their visitors in the parlours. They may, however, occasionally admit their parents and men who are well known, or are respectable, whether by virtue of their age or conduct, into their rooms; In order to receive women in their rooms, they must obtain the permission of the Director, which will only be given for the student's mother, his older aunt, older sister, or for persons accompanying his parents.

Art. 7. When the students are in residence, they must ordinarily spend their hours of study in their rooms. They may use the reading room, however, provided they don't converse if they meet others there.

Art. 8. At the signal for a lesson, students who are to attend it must go quietly and quickly, and they must come back in the same manner as soon as it is over, unless they are prevented from doing so for some legitimate reason.

Art. 9. When a student is in his room, the door must never be locked, and the key must always be in the lock on the corridor side. No one will be permitted to fix bolts on the doors or any other mechanism designed to prevent them from being opened.

Art. 10. Students will not go into each other's rooms, even for an instant, without the express permission of the Director. Permission will only be granted between evening prayers and morning prayers, in the case of illness.

Art. 11. Recreation will be taken in common. If it happens however that a student prefers to spend the time allotted for this in his room, he may do it, provided that he remains alone there.

Art. 12. No intoxicating drinks, dangerous or even useless books and newspapers, pipes or tobacco will be permitted in students' rooms. Students may smoke in the house only in the room designated for that purpose, and only during the recreation periods.

Art. 13. Loud talking, singing, and the playing of musical instruments are not permitted, except during recreation periods. During study periods, students will avoid conversation; they will not even talk to visitors, unless politeness requires them to do so, and always in a manner calculated not to annoy their colleagues. From evening prayers until those in the morning, they will remain silent.

Art. 14. The daily routine will be as follows:

at six o'clock, rising;

at six-thirty, morning prayers;

after prayers, study (or mass for students wishing to attend);

at quarter past seven, breakfast;

after breakfast, recreation;

at eight o'clock, study;

at quarter to eleven, recreation;

at eleven o'clock, study;

at quarter past twelve, lunch;

after lunch, recreation;

at one-thirty, study;

at quarter past four, recreation;

at four-thirty, study;

at quarter to six, dinner;

after dinner, recreation;

at eight o'clock, study;

at nine o'clock, evening prayers;

after prayers, study;

at ten o'clock, bed.

On fast days, dinner is at noon, and the light meal at six-thirty P.M.

Art. 15. On Sundays and holidays, there is study only in the morning, after breakfast (for those who don't attend low mass) and in the evening, after prayers.

Catholic students will attend services at the Cathedral on those days, seated in spaces assigned to them.

Art. 16. During vacations, those who remain in the boarding hall will observe, with respect to study and going into town, the rules for Sundays and holidays.

Art. 17. Any damage done by a student to the house or furniture will be repaired at his expense.

REACHING DOWN

'The Education of our Young Mechanics', *Journal of the Board of Arts and Manufactures*, I (1865), 225-6.

Considering the very favourable opportunities afforded the youth of this country, engaged in industrial pursuits, for obtaining knowledge at the very lowest cost, and with but little sacrifice of time, it does seem strange that so few avail themselves of the facilities so freely provided.

In this city, for two or three years, the trustees of the public schools opened one of their best school-houses for the purposes of evening instruction, providing teachers, fuel and light, free of charge; but finally were constrained to discontinue their efforts, on account of insufficient attendance, and want of appreciation of the object sought to be attained.

The Mechanics' Institute, too, every season opens a series of classes, which are continued for terms of five months, at a very low rate of charge. Good teachers are furnished and rooms provided, and yet how few there are, compared with the number of youths that should be found in these classes, that avail themselves of them—only about 100 to 120 each season.

And here we would seriously enquire the cause of this want of interest in these educational efforts? It is not that our mechanic youths are so well instructed that they do not need any more, for a large proportion of them have only received the most rudimentary education, and many of them not even that. We remember entering a mechanic's shop on King-street, in this city, to pay an account, and it was with the greatest difficulty that the foreman, in the absence of his employer, could write his name to the receipt; and even those who have had the advantage of school education, before entering on business, very soon forget the most they may have there learned, and stand in need of occasional evening instruction.

We refer our youthful readers, and their employers and guardians also, to the practical and useful instruction given in Mechanics' Institute evening classes, as evidenced by notices in our pages for the past four years; and we call on them to ponder well the loss they are sustaining in letting these golden opportunities for mental improvement slip by.

It is a constant complaint amongst mechanics and artisans, that they are considered by the commercial and professional classes as belonging to a lower caste of society. Those who indulge in such complaints should be aware that education and manners alone constitute the difference—in our day—between these classes. We have not yet seen the mechanic who has received a fair education, and whose manners and deportment have shown that he respects himself, but what he has been respected by all classes of the community, and could take his position amongst them without any feeling of inferiority either on the part of himself or others.

If our young mechanics and artisans will lounge about the streets, or taverns, or places of improper resort, with their hands in breeches pockets, and pipes or cigars, or the chew of tobacco, in their mouths, and dress to match; and take every means within their power to demonstrate their independence of all legitimate restraints on impropriety of conduct, they must expect to suffer the inevitable consequences in the loss of respect from their more educated and better behaved fellow citizens; as well as the total absence of opportunities for advancement in life.

Young men who are accustomed to resort to the theatre and the bar-room, and to indulge in the grosser vices and passions that human nature is too apt to give way to, cannot expect to be placed in respectable and responsible positions—the fault is not in society but in themselves.

Young men! assert your manhood! not by a foolish independence of feeling in regard to the conventionalities and proprieties of respectable society, but by doing what is right; by shunning everything that in its practice tends to immorality or vulgarity; by improving your mental and educational acquirements, and determining that you will be a credit to society; and that your example shall not tend to debase those with whom you associate, but rather to elevate them in the social scale.

We have known one workshop in this city, in which for several years it was the object of a portion of the workmen therein to improve, by the influence of example and precept, the character of every fellow-workman that entered it; and it is encouraging to know that their efforts were remarkably successful. Let a similar object be the aim of every intelligent young mechanic, and the improvement that would take place in the morals of workshop society in one twelvemonth, would be truly astonishing.

Parents, guardians, employers! are you doing your duty in respect to the youth placed under your charge and control? Do you look after the moral and educational improvement of those youths, with the same zeal and anxiety that you watch their progress in the art or business in which they are engaged? Do you, employers, fully realise the importance to your interests, and to the safety and well-being of society resulting from a high moral and intellectual training of your apprentices and employees? If not, and we are confident that you do not, we entreat you to take the initiative at once.

If the youth in your employ attend no evening classes during the winter months, purchase tickets for them for the coming season, and induce them to enter for instruction, if possible. Some of them will no doubt feel it irksome at first, but after a while the associations of the class room will be more attractive to many of them than were their former associates.

Encourage the institutions that are organized for the education of the industrial classes. Why should the managers of these institutions work on alone for the benefit of the employed, while the employers—in whose interests their labour is also to a great extent given—stand aloof, both as to their presence, and material assistance? Consider of how much more value to you is the workman or apprentice whose intellect has been sharpened by education, and correct moral training, than is the one whose mind is a vacuum to all but the grosser passions and indulgences, and whose mouths are frequently filled with oaths, or the coarse ribald jest.

Our language is strong, but not too much so. We know whereof we write, for we have both seen and heard the evil for ourselves, through a long series of years, and are anxious to see our fellow-mechanics take that position in society to which they *should* be entitled, and to which they should ever aspire.

Journal of the Board of Arts and Manufactures of Upper Canada, I (1861), 184-5.

TO THE EDITOR OF THE JOURNAL OF THE BOARD OF ARTS
AND MANUFACTURES

SIR,—I have read with much interest the Reports of Mechanics' Institutes published in your Journal. They bear evidence of progress and effort in the right direction. The establishment of reading rooms and libraries within the reach of the laboring classes, forms an important step in adult education; and the delivery of popular lectures, however general and unsystematic in their order, must give a beneficial impulse to these efforts. The great purpose, however, of these Institutes still remains neglected—the establishment of classes for adult education. This is the most important, as it is no doubt the most difficult work to be accomplished. The news room and library are not used for educational purposes. The library is used for amusement, and works of solid information are very rarely demanded; whilst the patrons of the news room seek its resources for political or general information, or the pastime of a leisure hour. No doubt these branches of a Mechanics' Institute have an important influence on the character of its members; but no Mechanics' Institute is worthy of its name, or the patronage of the friends of progress, which does not offer the advantage of *class instruction* to the working classes. The countless opportunities for making discoveries, inventions and improvements, which lie around them in their daily avocations, are lost, because notwithstanding all our educational efforts, the great body of the people in every department of labour are ignorant of the principles of physical science. Were our farmers familiar with the elements of agricultural chemistry, our artizans with those of mechanical philosophy, our miners with those of geology, and were these educated to that degree of intelligence which would enable them to communicate to others the suggestions inspired by their avocations, it is impossible to over-estimate the advantages that would follow. Instead of inventions and discoveries being isolated and confined to the theorist and the philosopher, they would spring from their natural sources, the field of labour, and be as extensive as the number of experimenters.

Now, the Mechanics' Institute is the college of the people. What an efficient common school system commences, they would continue; and no national system of instruction is complete without this adult college of the people. The common school, under the best conditions, can only supply a general elementary education. The special instruction needed by adults in their different pursuits is acquired best as it is needed, and in the evening classes of a Mechanics' Institute that instruction could be best obtained. Much may be done in this regard by the members forming themselves into mutual instruction classes. But the best amateur teaching is limited and of little value. It is too often unmethodical, uncertain, spasmodical and defective. Thorough instruction must come from the qualified and professional teacher, and we have no right to expect such instruction unless we pay the just value for it. Hence it should be the chief object of the directors of these institutes to encourage and aid the formation of classes, under efficient teachers. The fees should be such as would enable the poorest member to become students; and as it is not probable that these fees would remunerate the teacher, a portion of the funds of the institute, and of all other available resources, whether of benevolent subscriptions or Government aids, should be devoted to this all-important object.

The Periodical Examination which the Board of Arts proposes to hold, and the certificates it offers to successful candidates, is of such importance that it ought to receive every encouragement, while the programme of examination at once suggests the proper subjects of study for the classes of a mechanics' institute. In the present depressed circumstances of these institutes, it would be impossible to take up all the subjects; and in making a selection, whilst the tendency would probably be to take up the most practical and necessary— such as arithmetic, mathematics, chemistry, mechanics, drawing and agriculture—the claims of those branches which have relation to the communication and the discipline of thought should not be neglected. The study of English, in all its forms of grammar, composition, and the examination of high-class literature, and the practice of discussion, under judicious management, have the highest claims in the education of the common people, where the common people hold such civic and political power as in this country.

But as the kind of instruction and the management of classes must form a subject of large consideration, I forbear to trepass any further on your columns for the present.

I am, Sir, respectfully yours,
R. L.

Toronto, June 19, 1861.

WHAT WAS AVAILABLE

Journal of the Board of Arts and Manufactures, IV (1864), 138-41.

TORONTO MECHANICS' INSTITUTE

The Annual Meeting of this Society was held in its Lecture Room, on the evening of Thursday the 9th instant. The President, Mr. Wm. Edwards, in the chair.

From the Report of the Directors, as read by the Secretary, we make the following extracts: —

The Membership

"Though there has been a slight decline in the entire numerical strength of the Institute during the past year, there has been an increase in the membership proper, as will be seen from the following statement:

The number of members at the date of the last Annual Report, was	698
Honorary Members	18
Life Members	81
Subscribers	264
Total	1061
From which deduct by deaths, removals and withdrawals	526
Leaving	535
New Members admitted during the year	197
New Subscribers	270
Leaving a total of	1002
Classified thus—	
Members	704
Subscribers	199
Life Members	81
Honorary Members	18
	1002

Reading Room

"The Reading Room has also been improved, several of the more important English and American Commercial Publications, besides various Periodicals and Magazines, have been ordered since last Report. The addition of the Commercial Publications has rendered the Reading Room still better adapted to the requirements of the Mercantile Community."

[Here follows a list of 68 British, American and Canadian Newspapers and Periodicals paid for by the Institute; and a list of 42 others furnished gratuitously by their respective publishers, and by private individuals, and which are thankfully acknowledged by the Directors.]

The Classes

"The Classes in connection with, and under the immediate control of the Institute, for tuition in the various branches of useful knowledge, which were established in the fall of 1862, were continued during the past season, and have succeeded as well as could possibly be expected. These Classes, though well adapted for all, were more especially designed for young artizans, clerks, and those whose avocations rendered study impossible during the earlier hours of the day. There were in all five of these classes in successful operation, namely:—An English Grammar and Composition Class, numbering 21 pupils, under the charge of Mr. Samuel McAlister; a Book-keeping and Penmanship Class, numbering 58, under the charge of Mr. W. R. Orr; an Ornamental, Architectural and Mechanical Drawing Class, numbering 20, under the charge of M. Berger; a Mathematical Class, numbering 6, under the charge of Mr. Huggard; and a French Class, numbering 10, under the charge of M. Pernet. The pupils composing these classes numbered in the aggregate 115; among them there were several who attended during the preceding season, who, it is hoped, will again present themselves. It is much to be regretted that the attendance was not greater—that so few comparatively of the working classes have taken advantage of the privileges thus afforded them, and this is the more surprising as the terms were so very moderate as to be within the reach of the whole community. In the course of a few seasons, young men might through the agency of these classes attain such a knowledge of the rudiments of the various branches of a thorough English education, as would eminently fit them for such a course of study as would ultimately render them thoroughly competent to discharge creditably such duties as may hereafter devolve upon them in almost any position in life. . . .

PRIVATE PRIVILEGE

Excerpts from *Calendar of Stanstead Wesleyen College*, Stanstead, P.Q., 1884-85 (Montreal, The Geo. Bishop Engraving and Printing Co., Ltd., 1885).

DESIGN

The aim of the Founders of this Institution was to provide for the youth of both sexes the means of a higher education under Christian influences. Accordingly, the range of departments in which instruction is given has been made extensive, adapting the College to the wants of the country. While the Methodist Church has assumed the responsibility of its maintenance and moral government, the leading Protestant Churches are represented upon its Board of Trustees, Executive Committee, and Faculty of Instruction. Parents may rest assured that their denominational preferences regarding their children will be scrupulously respected.

The Institute is located in the Village of Stanstead Plain, in the County of Stanstead, P.Q.

Situated upon an elevated plateau, Stanstead is noted for the salubrity of its atmosphere, the purity of its water, and freedom from all forms of malarious disease. Unquestionably, in a sanitary point of view, no better location for an Educational Institution could have been selected.

Stanstead is celebrated for beauty and variety of scenery, and the College occupies one of its finest sites. In the foreground the country slopes away to the far famed Lake Memphremagog; the picturesque Green Mountains and an amphitheatre of lofty hills skirt the horizon, and the intermediate country is beautifully undulating and diversified. These rare natural advantages are well supplemented by art and culture. Residences and churches indicate a degree of wealth and taste not often found outside of large cities.

The quietness of the village and surrounding country invites to studiousness, while the absence of many temptations peculiar to large towns and cities renders the place eminently safe for the residence of students removed from the watchful guardianship of home.

DESCRIPTION OF BUILDING

The building rests upon a granite foundation, is five stories in height, has a lofty central tower, and presents a fine architectural appearance. Its dimensions are 142 x 52 feet, with a wing 37 x 42 feet, and it is sufficiently capacious to accommodate a large number of students.

The health of students is considered of the first importance, and the arrangements of the College are made with this end in view. The halls, parlors, bedrooms, schoolrooms, dining-hall, and corridors are spacious and well lighted. An entirely new and improved system of heating has been determined upon, and will, it is expected, be completed before the College opens.

Improved sanitary arrangements are also in process of construction, and the building generally is being refitted and refurnished throughout.

Each bedroom contains a closet, and is furnished with bedstead, bedding, (except sheets and pillow-slips) wash-stand, stove, bureau, mirror, chairs and table.

Every effort will be made by the Trustees and Faculty to make the College comfortable and attractive as a *home* for students generally.

NOTES ON THE COURSES OF STUDY

The Revised Curriculum

Our curriculum has recently been very carefully revised and remodelled, bringing our work into greater harmony with the plans of the Protestant Board of Education, providing more perfectly for the scholastic needs of the youth of our country, and realizing, it is hoped, more fully the ideal of the projectors of this Institution, "a real People's College."

The Common English Course

First of all, and as the foundation of all, is provided a thorough course in the Common English branches, the importance of which cannot be too highly valued.

The Teacher's Preparatory Course

The higher standard of qualifications, and system of uniform written examinations, now required of candidates for diplomas of all grades in the Province, have rendered more apparent the necessity of providing improved facilities for and of giving greater prominence to the training and instruction of intending teachers. To such we offer the advantages of our Teacher's Preparatory Course. The first year prepares for the Elementary Diploma, the second year for the Model School Diploma, and the third year for the Academy Diploma.

The Commercial Course

Affords young men as thorough a preparation for business life as school or college can impart. No Commercial Course can take the place of that business tact and skill which long experience alone can impart, but a thorough Commercial Course can and does give a young man a great advantage at the outset of a business career.

The Collegiate Courses

Include substantially the work hitherto embraced in our "Ladies' Collegiate" and "College Preparatory" Courses, but extended in lines of study, abridged in others, adapted in all more perfectly to the educational standards of the day, and classified according to the nature of the subjects, viz.: English, Mathematics, Sciences, History, Latin, Greek, and French. The following options are offered:

I. The Ladies' Collegiate Course for M.L.A.

(A.) Imperative—English, Mathematics, Latin, History.

(B.) Optional—Any one of the following:—Science, Greek, French.

II. The Ladies' Collegiate Course for M.E.L.

(A.) Imperative—English, Mathematics, History.

(B.) Optional—Any one of the following:—Science, Latin, Greek, French.

III. The Junior College Preparatory Course, embracing the first and second year's work in the following: English, Mathematics, Latin, and Greek; also British History.

IV. The Senior College Preparatory Course, embracing, in addition to the subjects of the Junior Course, the third year's work in Mathematics, Latin, and Greek; also English Composition, Inorganic Chemistry, and French.

V. Special Collegiate Courses, for students who desire to make a speciality of a single Subject, as French, etc.

The Junior and Senior College Preparatory Courses include the work required respectively for Junior Matriculation (Freshman Standing), and Senior Matriculation (Sophomore Standing), in the Provincial Universities.

The first and second year's work in the Collegiate Courses includes the subjects prescribed for the title of Associate of Arts and with the third year's work embraces those subjects prescribed for the higher examination of women, by the Provincial Universities.

Penmanship

Too high a value cannot be set upon a clear, graceful handwriting. For several years past the beautiful penmanship of many of our students has won the admiration of visitors, and upon more than one occasion has elicited the especial commendation of the Provincial Inspector.

French, Music, Etc.

In these and kindred branches the instruction imparted here has attained a very high reputation.

Declamation and Composition

Declamations will be required from the gentlemen, and Compositions from all students once in three weeks. The exercises of advanced students only are required to be rendered in public.

Admission

Students will be admitted to desired classes or courses upon passing the requisite examinations, or on the certificate of their former teachers in any recognized school; their continuance in class and their advancement will be determined by term recitations and examinations. . . .

Examinations

Students will be examined in each subject twice in each term. Final Examinations will be required in each subject when completed, or at the close of the Academic year. Pass mark, 40 per cent; Second Class Standing, 60 per cent; First Class, 80 per cent; First Class with Honors, 90 per cent, and over.

Merit Roll

A record will be kept of conduct and daily recitations, and at the close of each term a report will be sent to parents and guardians, showing standing in *each study*, and deportment both in day school and domestic life.

Degrees, Diplomas, Certificates, and Medals

The degree of Mistress of English Literature, or Mistress of Liberal Arts, is conferred upon ladies who complete satisfactorily the Ladies' Collegiate Course.

Diplomas are granted to graduates in Vocal and Instrumental Music, or in the Commercial Course.

Students who complete other courses, or partial courses, may, upon application, obtain certificate of standing.

In no case, however, will degree, diploma, or certificate be given unless the student has undergone thorough and satisfactory examination in the subjects prescribed for the course, or partial course, for which such degree, diploma, or certificate is awarded.

GOVERNMENT

The design of the Trustees and Faculty is to conduct the Institution upon the principles of an earnest, evangelical, but unsectarian Christianity.

The government exercised will be as nearly as possible *parental*, characterized by kindness, firmness, and impartiality.

Religious Instruction is given in Sabbath Bible Classes and in the daily devotional exercises of the Institution. Students will be required to attend regularly the church selected by their parents or guardians.

Correspondence with the home circle will be allowed without supervision. Beyond this, each student must furnish the Governor with a list, signed by parents, of those with whom correspondence is permitted. A Post-box is kept in the building. Mail matter addressed in care of the Institution is promptly delivered on arrival.

Visiting and receiving visits will be subject to the following regulations:— All persons, except near relatives, wishing to visit young ladies, will be expected to present a letter from parents or guardians, or to be otherwise suitably introduced. Students will be allowed at proper times to visit such families as the parents or guardians may name to the Governor, but not to remain out over night or on the Sabbath, except with a near relative. Young ladies when visiting will always be in charge of some one fully responsible.

When young ladies are about returning home, particular arrangements for their departure should be made by their parents or guardians, that the Governor may know when and with whom they are to leave.

Constant attention is given to the health of students. Daily out-door exercise is required, except in inclement weather.

Various reasons render it desirable that money intended for use of students should be deposited with the Governor for safe keeping. The practice of supplying students freely with pocket-money is to be deprecated.

The rules regulating the deportment and privileges of students are *just and reasonable*, not arbitrary, but such as experience has proved to be wise and necessary. Observance of our rules and general conformity to the proprieties of good society are conditions of admission, and continued connection with the College. Intractable students, and those whose influence is found to be demoralizing, will be dismissed. . . .

TERMS OF PAYMENT, SPECIAL RATES, ETC.

. . . A discount of 15 per cent is made to sons and daughters of Ministers, and to young men preparing for the Christian Ministry. Special reduction is made when two or more students attend from the same family.

When the fees for board and tuition for the year are prepaid in full, a discount will be made equivalent to 10 per cent interest per annum, for the time the payment is made before it would be due by our term rates.

All injuries to furniture, lamps, or other property, will be at the expense of the students concerned.

Boarders are liable to an extra charge when meals are taken to their rooms, or served at other than the regular hours.

Boarders must provide their own sheets, pillow-slips, towels and table napkins, and every article should be plainly marked with the owner's name. Twelve articles are allowed weekly in the wash. Additional articles will be charged at the rate of 50 cents per dozen extra.

Removal of a student from College requires previous notice of five weeks to the Governor, and the payment of all College dues . . .

DOMESTIC ARRANGEMENTS, ETC. . . .

(For Young Ladies:)

Due attention will be given to the preservation of health, and the cultivation of refined taste and lady-like manners. With this object in view, familiar Conversational Lectures will be given by the Preceptress or by other teachers, on the Personal, Domestic and Social Proprieties of Life. These Lectures will embrace such topics as private personal habits,—as to exercise, exposure, eating, sleeping and sitting, walking, dress, and room; domestic manners; table manners; manners in public assemblies,—as in church, concert, parties and parlors; manners towards kindred and friends; manners in intercourse with other ladies; manners and intercourse with gentlemen. In short, no pains will be spared by these lectures, and by private hints and suggestions, as occasion shall require, so to regulate the daily deportment of each pupil as to make easy and habitual all the graces and proprieties of refined and accomplished womanhood . . .

SECONDARY EDUCATION IN ONTARIO IN RETROSPECT

W. J. Robertson, 'Secondary Education in Ontario, its Development, Present Condition, and its Needs', *Addresses and Proceedings of the Dominion Educational Association* (Halifax, 1898), pp. 88-107.

The theory on which our educational system is based is, that it is a continuous chain, or ladder, reaching from the lowest grade of the Public School to the Provincial University. A child beginning with the Kindergarten, may pass through all the stages of Public School education, to the High School or Collegiate Institute, and from thence, by a gradual transition, to the University. The state, aided by the municipality thus provides the means of a liberal education with little cost to the ambitious student. But this theory, while ever present before the mind of Dr. Ryerson, could not be realized in its completeness in his day,—it remained for his successors to work out and develop his ideas. . . .

The most noteworthy feature of the present administration is the successful effort to bring about a simplification of the courses of study in our Secondary Schools and a greater uniformity in the examinations for entrance to the professions and to the Universities. . . . By an agreement between the Education Department and the different Universities, a joint Examining Board has been appointed and we have secured the great boon of a uniform matriculation examination, which is accepted by the different professions of Law, Medicine, Dentistry, etc. A still more radical step was taken recently when the courses of study for teachers' certificates and matriculation into the Universities were practically unified. This was accomplished by raising the matriculation standard in some subjects, such as Mathematics, Physics and Chemistry, and by introducing into the course of study for the higher grades of certificates, Latin and the Modern Languages. One result of the change is that candidates for certificates can at the same time prepare for matriculation into the Universities. This has had the effect of greatly increasing the attendance at these institutions,—in fact, this change has completed the chain of our educational system. This unification of courses of study and the greater uniformity introduced into our examinations has aided our Secondary schools materially in carrying on their work. The time wasted formerly in preparing candidates for many different examinations, can now be utilized to good advantage in giving greater attention to branches of study formerly neglected. It is questionable, however, whether the results of the new regulations have been wholly good. The universities have undoubtedly gained by introducing Latin and the Modern Languages into the course of study for teachers' certificates, but it is, to many quite apparent, that this change is likely to prove highly detrimental to Public School education. The time now devoted by candidates for certificates to Latin, French and German, is largely wasted. A smattering of knowledge in these languages is obtained at a great expenditure of time, while the much more essential subjects of Mathematics, English and History are necessarily neglected. Our Public School teachers are going out from our Secondary schools inadequately equipped in the essentials for Public School work, while our classes are thronged with pupils endeavoring to master the elements of Latin, French and German.

Still another evil of no small importance has developed itself as the result of our recent legislation. Our Secondary schools—up to a certain point—undertake to provide a good English education to those preparing for the ordinary avocations of life. No child is compelled to take Latin, Greek, French or German in the lower forms of our High Schools—his whole attention may be given to English, Mathematics, Elementary Science and subjects having a direct bearing on commercial life. This is in accordance with our ideal of a High School, that it should prepare our youth for the duties of ordinary citizenship, as well for the teaching and other professions. But while the theory is unobjectionable, the practical working out cannot be said to be free from evil results. A boy enters one of our Secondary schools without any definite ideas of a future career. The Head-master realizes that unless Latin is begun immediately, the pupil will give a great deal of trouble later on in his course, should he decide upon entering the University or one of the learned professions. Should such a decision be reached, his lack of linguistic knowledge would render it necessary to organize special classes in Latin, or French, or German, as the case may be, to meet the special need of a few pupils. This the teacher avoids as far as in his power, by compelling or inducing as many as possible of the entrance candidates to begin the study of Latin, and later on of French and German. As by far the greater number of these pupils never go beyond the lower forms of our High Schools, the time given to Latin is so much time wasted. The few years, two or three at the most, which the pupil spends in the High School, should be devoted entirely to the acquisition of a good knowledge of English, History and Arithmetic, instead of being thrown away on the elements of Latin Grammar. In fact we are in some degree reproducing the evils so graphically described by Professor Young in his famous report of 1866. It would be, of course, very unjust to say that our High Schools are, to anything like the same extent, as inefficient as they were at that date; but it is true that we now are reproducing the evil of that time in practically forcing into Latin young boys and girls whose time should be spent in obtaining a more thorough knowledge of English and Mathematics. This defect in our system has given rise to various suggestions. One remedy proposed is to revert back to the old practice of making a clear distinction between the qualifications required in order to obtain a teacher's certificate and those required for matriculation into our Universities. It would not be a matter of much difficulty to raise the standard required for admission into our High Schools and thus raise the standard of English and Mathematics in the High Schools themselves. Our Public Schools, too, teachers and pupils alike, would benefit by having a higher standard of admission provided the qualifications of the Public School teachers in English and Mathematics were raised. Against this proposal, we find arrayed those interested in securing a large attendance at the Universities. Unless pupils begin the study of Languages at an early age, it is urged, there is little hope of their becoming good linguists. So it has been suggested that the division of our Secondary schools into two classes, Classical Schools and English Schools, should take place. The former —few in number—would be specially devoted to preparing candidates for entrance into the professions and for matriculation. The latter would give their attention to furnishing a good English education and to training candidates for teachers' certificates. This proposal has not as yet found many supporters. Local interests and jealousies are against it. Every man who wishes to give his child a professional or University career finds it convenient to have at his own door a High School, where Latin, Greek and French are taught. He prefers to support a small High School in his own locality, rather than send his son or daughter a few miles away from home to attend a Collegiate Institute. Besides, it is quite obvious that such a division as is proposed would destroy that unity and uniformity in courses of study and examinations which now exist. This, as I take it, is the chief difficulty we experience at the present time in the working of our system of secondary education.

Let me now in concluding call attention to some of the results of the wide extension of our Secondary School system. As stated before, the last twenty-five years have witnessed a marvellous development—not so much in the number of our Secondary Schools, as in the attendance, municipal aid given, class of teachers engaged, equipment, buildings and play grounds, and widening of course of study. What effects have been produced by this development? Have our Public Schools gained or lost ground during this period? Has there been a corresponding increase in the intelligence and civic morality of the community? To these questions different answers will be given by different people. To me it seems apparent that the Public Schools are not less efficient than they were a quarter of a century ago. While the desire to enter a High School does in some cases injure the efficiency of a Public School, the general effect, I believe, is to stimulate them to better, to more thorough work. It is still more obvious that the general intelligence of the community has been increased, although it is to be regretted that so few of the children in our schools ever get beyond the mere rudiments of an ordinary English education.

Another effect of this extension of the means of obtaining a higher education at small cost has been a deplorable over-crowding of the professions. Law and Medicine, for instance, in spite of the barriers erected by high fees and lengthened courses of study, are now full to overflowing. If this is the case in professions where artificial hindrances are created by legislation, what shall be said about the teaching profession? In spite of denials to the contrary, I have no hesitation in saying that the eager rush into this profession is so great as to demoralize teachers' salaries in the Public Schools of large sections of the Province. Teachers holding the highest grades of Public School certificates can now be engaged (or hired?) at wages little better than that given to corporation laborers. The profession is becoming degraded by the wholesale introduction into its ranks of young men and women prepared to teach for the most petty remuneration. This, of course, is the natural outcome of the economic law of supply and demand. An education procured at small cost cannot expect to bring large returns. It may here be noted that one result of this enormous influx into the ranks of the teaching profession has been the recent abolition of the lowest grade of certificate—the Primary. Whether the remedy will meet the evil, time will tell.

One other phase of our system of Secondary education must be noted before I close. Examinations, as already explained, have now reached a remarkable degree of uniformity. Every certificate is the result of an examination conducted by the Education Department. There the papers are prepared, and there the answers are read, the latter by a small army of examiners selected from the teachers themselves. Examinations are looked upon as one of the most important agencies in carrying out the educational programme of our High Schools. Examinations meet the candidate for entrance, for promotion, for different grades of certificates and for admission to the Universities. You may secure a certificate by taking the subjects required, in sections, and you may matriculate in the same fashion. *Nominally*, these examinations are uniform, for the same papers go to every part of the Province—*really*, they are not uniform. In the first place, the oscillations from being very easy to very difficult are notoriously frequent. One year we have an extremely difficult Algebra paper; an outcry follows, the regulation percentage on that paper is lessened, or the paper is cancelled. The next year the pendulum swings in the other direction and everybody complains how the standard is being lowered. And so the work goes on—now one subject, then another, furnishing the objectionable papers. The Education Department takes many precautions to prevent these constantly recurring mistakes, but examiners are fallible, and not being engaged in High School teaching, they lose touch with the schools and the work there carried on. In the second place, these examinations are not uniform because those who read the answers, the "Sub-Examiners," as they are called, are of all degrees of efficiency. Some are disposed to be lenient, some are naturally severe, while others are incompetent through lack of knowledge and experience. Hence the most startling results. Within a certain range, the chances of a badly prepared candidate are as good as those of one thoroughly well-informed. To teachers and pupils, the whole affair partakes a good deal of the nature of a lottery. Another feature of the examination system is so decidedly objectionable that a brief reference must be made to it. These examinations take place once a year, in the month of July; that is the hottest month of our year. For four or five weeks prior to the examinations, during the warm month of June, thousands of boys and girls ranging from 15 to 18 and 19 years of age are going through a process of hard reading and "Cram."

The teachers are anxious, for they know that praise or blame will follow the success or failure of their pupils, and they use every legitimate means to incite the candidates to effort and diligence. The candidates themselves are anxious as the time approaches, and every hour is felt to be of importance. Sleep and rest are denied themselves—in the hope that hard study may triumph over mental weakness or incapacity. What follows? The candidates enter the examination hall fatigued and worn out, physically and mentally, to undergo the tortures of a one or two weeks' struggle with conundrums evolved during the hours of leisure of the examiner. Is it any wonder that the examination leaves mental and physical wrecks behind it? wrecks, too, among the more sensitive and gifted of the pupils—wrecks, in particular among girls and young women, whose ambition to excel far exceeds their physical strength. Why such sacrifices should be annually offered up to this examination system is a wonder to any sane educator or parent. No good reason exists why these examinations could not be held earlier in the year, before the extreme heat of our Canadian summer begins. But the desire of many ignorant people, that teachers' holidays should be kept within the smallest limits, is sufficient justification for the continuance of the present cruel and senseless practice.

This paper has been devoted almost exclusively to a consideration of the growth and development of the Secondary schools . . . Everything, it is seen, is under rigid state control, except the engagement of teachers and the erection and maintenance of school buildings. We have seen how inefficiency has been replaced by efficiency, and how public apathy has been changed to public interest and generosity. The District School of the earlier years of this century has developed into the High School or Collegiate Institute—justly prized and appreciated by the community as no longer a school for the classes but the special friend of the masses.

Under such a rigid system of state control as exists in Ontario, voluntary schools . . . have a sphere of influence and usefulness which the state schools cannot reach. Most of the former are denominational in their character, and as such receive denominational sympathy and support. Others, however, have to depend entirely upon the fact that they supply an educational want to the community. Their efficiency from the purely intellectual and scholastic standpoint is perhaps not quite up to the standard of our best High Schools and Collegiate Institutes; but what they lack in that respect is frequently atoned for by the amount of attention given to physical, social, and artistic culture. One thing seems certain, and that is, that the advancement in our High Schools and Collegiate Institutes has had a stimulating effect upon the voluntary schools. To a very large extent the standard of the Collegiate Institutes is becoming their standard. Pupils from these institutions prepare for the same examinations, and their success is becoming more marked year by year.

4 Ethnicity, Race, Sex, and Social Class in Nineteenth-Century Schools

If creeping institutionalism is the most noticeable theme of educational change in the nineteenth century, an equally important one is the transformation of the family. Throughout the century the family remained a vital educational force in Canadian society, an object of frequent admiration but also of alarm. Little analysed to date, and clearly a subject as difficult as it is fascinating, the Victorian family in Canada deserves closer attention both for its intrinsic interest and its relationship to education. Although by the later years of the century Canadian children spent more of their time than ever before in institutions called schools, it is also true that for many children 'school' remained a brief and peripheral affair, one that was frequently delayed, and in the case of quite a few children an experience that may have been missed altogether.

Ironically, as brick buildings and public policy increasingly circumscribed and superceded traditional family responsibilities, the idealized family of popular culture only gained in strength. It is not surprising then that schooling for some youngsters was directed to compensating for some perceived inadequacy in their family life. Both the continuity and change in the experience of growing up and in the objects of educational policy are suggested in the documents that follow. Most obviously, perhaps, the experience of the relative isolation of pioneer settlement, repeated in Canada well into the twentieth century, maintained continuities with an older, more inclusive model of family life. Certainly the drama of settlement has traditionally provided an analogy to educational development: the provision of schooling to more and different Canadians is viewed as the triumphant accompaniment of the extension of population and prosperity to the farthest reaches of the country. To a point, of course, the analogy is sound enough; the more people, acres under cultivation, and industrial establishments, the more school sections and schoolhouses. However the extension of educational opportunity in the second half of the nineteenth century was neither as linear in its progress nor as free of ideology as a quantitative metaphor would suggest.

By the last quarter of the century public schooling in the established communities of eastern Canada had lost much of its missionary cast. Attending school had fairly quickly become the norm for the middle ranks of both urban and rural society. Once secured as school supporters, the working and middle classes were, perhaps, not an entirely appropriate audience for the school's civilizing message: earnest regularity of attendance was itself evidence of conversion. Where was the schoolmaster's new frontier?

Soon the deepening slums and urban disorder that accompanied rapid growth and industrialization made new demands on the school system. And inevitably the immigrants who invaded the cities as well as the prairies seemed obvious, if not always willing, objects of the school's concern. What exactly was schooling to accomplish?

Is it entirely justified to label public-school systems agents of English-Protestant imperialism in Canada? Moreover, what would the school offer to those who lived outside the mainstream of Canadian society, whatever the reason for their isolation? How did established social institutions, especially schools, define the problem of being poor or Indian or Black? Did it matter much where in Canada these groups lived? Were they perceived very differently? Various constraints—ideological, financial, and bureaucratic—narrowed and hardened the role that the educational system played in relation to cultural minorities and the economically disadvantaged. What alternatives were there?

It is no special indictment of Canadian social reformers and school promoters to suggest that the reality of the school environment belied the popular argument that the educational system would foster harmony between different social classes. Much the same story can be told of other places and other times. But if the nineteenth-century schoolroom was meant to be a civilizing, disciplining, Canadianizing force, under what circumstances might one not benefit? What other 'educational' experiences were available? As more young people stayed in school longer, what lack of opportunity did those without schooling experience? To what extent might it be argued that adolescence was a stage in life that only some Victorians could afford? And what were the consequences of the fact that economic change might reduce work opportunities for young people before other institutions had been devised to occupy the years between the end of childhood and marriage?

THE QUESTION OF SPECIAL SCHOOLING

A FORGOTTEN LINGUISTIC MINORITY

James Mahony to Egerton Ryerson. *Education Papers*, RG 2 C-6-C, Public Archives of Ontario.

Windsor Canada West
Township of Sandwich & of Essex
School Section No. 7. Feb 21st 1859

Doctor Ryerson
Sir

I have the Honour to represent that I have resided in the above school section since the establishment of Common Schools in Canada.

That I am the highest rate payer (but one) in the Section and that I have a large family consisting of four girls and three boys, the oldest of whom is fifteen and the youngest two years old.

That since the first day there has never been a school master in the section who even could speak a word of English except one, and he only could speak broken English of the poorest description.

Rev.d Sir You may suppose what an injury this is to me and my poor Children, not having the means of sending them to a boarding school.

My wife and myself manage to teach them, but they make but little Progress, as their time and ours is pretty well filled up in procuring the physical necessaries of life. For a long time I put off making this representation, hoping to be able to dispose of my Farm here and removing where I could have an English School, but now all hope of that has vanished. I have every reason to know that all the people in this School Sec. are desirous to have a Teacher who may be capable to teach in French and English, but they are overruled by other influences over which they have no Control.

In fact all the Catholick Clergy here are French men, and there is only one among them who can speak a little bad English, who officiates in the Irish Settlement. In the next school section there are several Old Country families, similarly situated with myself. Rev.d Sir May I hope you will take this case into your favourable consideration, and cause the Trustees and the Township Superintendent to employ a teacher who shall be able to teach English as well as French. by so doing Rev.d Sir you will confer a lasting benefit on your Obed.t

H[?] Servant
James Mahony

A PLEA FOR BILINGUALISM

Report of the Seventh Annual Convention, Provincial Association of Protestant Teachers of the Province of Quebec (Montreal, 1871), pp. 6-12.

Mr. Duval opened the discussion with the following paper.

ON THE STUDY OF THE FRENCH IN OUR
ENGLISH SCHOOLS

MR. PRESIDENT.

No country, perhaps, offers a better opportunity to its people, of acquiring two languages than does Canada, and especially the Province of Quebec to its inhabitants.

Having a population composed of the offspring of two nations, who have for several centuries stood in the van of civilization, progress and enterprise, and who have distinguished themselves by the number of remarkable and superior men they have produced in almost every branch of science and literature, this country ought to be proud of its origin; and its inhabitants should endeavor to show themselves worthy of their ancestors. These two races placed side by side, not by chance, we presume, but through the dispensations of a well-ordered Providence, are working together to make of this comparatively new country a great and glorious (I will not say Dominion) *but a great and glorious Empire.* This they will certainly achieve, if they remain true to their mission, and if they stand always united. For this they should understand each other well, communicate easily and freely with each other. And who can tell, that speaking the same languages would not contribute greatly to bring about this result. The pages of History would show how much truth there is in this enunciation, but time alone precludes me from doing anything more than to draw your attention to this fact.

It will not answer to have one party cry, "Come, give up your language and learn our own," for this would not be fair, as there are few things to which a nation is more attached than to its own language.

We would say, rather, let each one of our inhabitants learn these two languages. No one would be the worse for it. The very effort of doing it, if the work be long and painful, will be a good mental training which cannot fail in producing the best results. General prosperity would be the ultimate result; for, all things being equal, the man who can read and speak two languages and has been able to master them, is certainly superior to the one who has only one at his command. Charles the Fifth remarked, long ago, that, "*As many languages one can speak, so many times one is a man.*" The great utility of mastering these two means of communication can not be questioned. For, if we look at it in a utilitarian point of view, it can easily be shown how much a person may gain by mastering the French and English languages.

Let us suppose that we have two young men of equal abilities, and having nearly the same training, the only difference being, that the one has learned French, whilst the other does not know a word of it, and likely does not care much for it. They are both leaving school and are looking for a situation. They both see advertised in one of our newspapers (getting of daily occurrence in our town) that a boy or a young man speaking both languages is wanted; or that one speaking both languages would be preferred. Which of the two will have the preference? Are those boys any longer equal? Are their chances the same? Certainly not.

But, you may say, very few have the opportunity of learning French; very true, and why so? It is because our system of teaching French is deficient in most cases, it is because no pains is taken with it. It is the lack of time which is the excuse commonly given by those who are in favor of the present system, yet these same persons can spare the time to give the young a smattering of Latin, which may be good as training of the mind, but which, viewed in a practical point of view, cannot be compared to the French.

I would, for my part, much rather see them honestly confess that they don't value French much, and that they don't care for it.

If I had to give my opinion as to what course it would be best to pursue, and what system to follow, in acquiring the use of a spoken language, I would recommend that it should be begun in our schools almost simultaneously with the English; and for this, let the child learn and repeat, with the help of the teacher, easy words first, and short phrases, so as to get the exact and perfect pronounciation of every word he commits to memory. This, I think, is of the *utmost importance* and can not be too *carefully done*. Let him in this way, master a certain stock of words and phrases, which, by a little practice, he will be able to use as readily as his own language. This course may be pursued with great benefit for two or three years, and without meanwhile requiring him to spend much time in learning the rules of the French Grammar.

Then I would recommend, as a most excellent help in the proper acquisition of a foreign language, that some one or two of the regular studies of the school be taught in that language. If it is desirable, as I think it is in this country, that the child should know equally well both languages, then let us give an equal share of the subjects, and of the time, to each language.

I claim that this would, in no wise, be a loss to the scholar, for we have, in French, many school books that might be used with benefit, as text books, in our English schools.

One thing, Mr. President, I am altogether opposed to; it is that we should teach the French as though it were a dead language.

Another thing, in this respect, is truly remarkable in this country. It is the utter indifference of the great majority of the English population, in reference to the French language.

This is the more astonishing, as its utility is admitted by every body.

There is, in reference to this, a comparison which I cannot forbear making, and which is certainly not in favor of the English.

The French have shown themselves in this respect superior to the English. For their readiness in learning English and their success in doing so, deserve certainly the greatest credit. For we find among us, I will not say persons who can be classified among English scholars, but a great many who can speak English both fluently and correctly. On the contrary it is rather uncommon to find English persons who can converse in French, and, if they attempt it, it is generally with little success.

This fact is so evident, as to strike any stranger coming to live among us. This I consider a fault, very serious in our system of education. Let parents who send their children to school with the intention to qualify them either for trade or for a profession, ponder this well, and I think that they will feel the propriety of this suggestion. This granted, when should we have children learn this language?

Let us, in this respect, be guided by nature. For there is a time when a language can be learned almost without any effort. It is when the organs of speech, in the tender years of the child, are yet pliable, and when the sound and modulations of the voice are so easily mimicked and imitated.

I know the case of a boy who, a year ago, could hardly understand a single phrase of English, and who has been since exclusively to an English school. The result has been that he can now speak it nearly as well as his own mother tongue.

There is one thing, besides, which I do blame, in our manner of teaching French, it is that so much of the time is devoted to grammar, or to reading, and so little to speaking of the language. *Practice is what is wanted to learn conversation.*

I am sometimes surprised to see how some persons can say that they have studied French for several years, and yet if you ask them a question in that language they will stare at you as though you were speaking Chinese to them.

In the course of the past year I have met with one case tending to confirm me more than ever in my belief and in my mode of teaching. I will enter into no detail, and still less name the parties, but merely state the facts.

In one of the best schools of this city I have tried, for some time past, to introduce what I would call conversation in the class but this was thought a great innovation. I was asked if it was really possible that something like speaking could be learned in the school. This question I took to be as pertinent as to ask if one could learn to read in schools. And why, I pray, do we send our children to school, if not to learn whatever is useful and may qualify them for their calling in life? And, if this is not done in reference to the present subject, who is to blame for it? The fault must either be in the system of teaching, in the teacher, or in the community. A moment of reflection will, most likely, lead us to consider the three as more or less to blame in this respect.

1st.—The system is not perfect. Practice is too much neglected, as noticed above.

2nd.—The teacher himself often can read it, translate the language he is teaching, but he cannot speak it, and no wonder that the scholar will not be very proficient in it.

3rd.—The community is also to blame in not asking, as a right, that the *useful* should be studied and acquired before what is merely *fanciful*; or again, in not knowing the importance of learning in proper time—in youth—a language which will be found so necessary for business afterwards.

It is not my intention to enlarge on and speak of the vast field open to the student by the perusal of our French authors, because this is generally admitted by all, and does not therefore need any further remarks.

The only thing which, perhaps, has been overlooked by many, is that a thorough acquaintance with those authors would doubtless show that a great many beauties have escaped the superficial student.

Let the elements of the language be properly mastered in the school, and greater results will be obtained. Besides, there is no reason why the English population, so eminently practical in every other respect, should not, at once, consider this question.

I can count by the score the young men who have expressed repeatedly their sorrow at not having learned more French at school.

They had studied it, but were not aware of its importance. Let us ponder this well and see what, as teachers, we can do towards remedying this evil.

One thing I must say before closing. I feel bound to express my satisfaction at the change for the better which has taken place in some schools. In the Prospectus of the High School for the scholar's year 1870-1871, in the Preparatory Department, I find the following "the French language, during the whole period of the preparatory course, will receive, an equal share of attention with the English."

In our model schools connected with the McGill Normal School, more time is devoted to the study of the French than ever before. This is certainly a change for the better, and this should be imitated elsewhere.

Let us hope that, before long, justice will be done to this subject.

Principal HICKS then said he would offer a few remarks on the subject by way of stimulating discussion. He believed that children would never learn much French unless taught conversationally. They should first be taught words, then sounds, then sentences. The best way he considered was for English and French children to mix together and learn from one another the proper sound, and the names of articles. In this way they would learn much faster than when confined to rules of grammar and memory. He believed, also, with Prof. Duval that the study of French should be more introduced into the preparatory classes.

Mr. WILLIAMSON considered Professor Duval's paper an excellent one. A child, in learning the French language, should begin in a natural way with the objects around it; and, with the assistance of French children, learn two or three, or half a dozen words a day in a natural manner. Prof. Duval's book was an excellent one, as far as he could see. The words, he believed, should be taught first, and then the grammar; and all should be taught in this way, from the youngest to the oldest.

Principal GRAHAM also considered that the paper read by Prof. Duval was an excellent one, and indicated a very good system of teaching French, but the main question was how to carry it out. It was a fact that in this country there was a great scarcity of French teachers—a great scarcity of men competent to teach the French language. And, considering this, he thought that those who were available were not utilized as they might be. Professor Duval, for instance, could teach four, five, or half a dozen schools, in different parts of the city, or even at places a short distance out of the city which could be easily reached by railway; and, in this way, a great many more than at present could have the advantage of a teacher who had so good a system of teaching, and the French language could be more generally spread among children. For want of utilizing what teaching power we had, a great deal was lost to the country. He knew that, if this plan could be adopted in country parts, they would find it an immense benefit.

Prof. ROBINS said, it had been remarked that if an English child were put into a French school it would pick up a knowledge of the French language remarkably fast. The explanation of this was, he believed, that the French had good English masters, but the English had not good French masters. The youngest children, those who commenced without text books, learned French the fastest. French was required for either commercial, social, literary or scientific purposes. Those who studied it in this country wanted it almost altogether for the first two, viz., social and commercial purposes. Very few had time to learn it for the sake of studying the French literature, or as an aid to a knowledge of science. It could not therefore take the place of Latin. On this account, therefore, he believed it should be taught conversationally. The system of teaching it by rule was not good.

Prof. DUVAL explained that he did not say it could take the place of Latin, nor could a child commence to learn other branches of education in the French language, but after it had studied French for a few years it could commence to use it generally.

Prin. HICKS asked Mr. Duval if he thought it was possible to introduce the system of teaching English and French children together?

Prof. DUVAL considered that it was. He had tried it in some cases, and was surprised at the progress made by the English child in a knowledge of the French language. . . .

THE CHALLENGE OF IMMIGRATION

Report of the Superintendent of Education, N.W.T. for 1898, pp. 11-12, 24-6.

One of our most serious and pressing educational problems arises from the settlement among us of so many foreign nationalities in the block or "colony" system. There are colonies of Swedes, Finns, Bohemians, Hungarians, Jews, Austrians, Germans, Russians, Icelanders, Mennonites, Galicians, and Doukhobors.

In addition to the foreign colonies there are also exclusively French-speaking districts in Saskatchewan that, for a variety of reasons, have not been able to keep their schools in operation. In the interests of the children as well as of the country at large every means should be taken to encourage the opening and maintenance of schools among these non-English speaking communities.

It would be criminal to shut our eyes to the fact that this rapid increase of a foreign and relatively ignorant population is at once a challenge and invitation to our institutions. These "colonies" will add to our numbers, to our wealth in grain and cattle, to our material progress, but it will not be reasonable to expect them for many years to add much to that other wealth which is a nation's truest wealth—educated men with refined tastes, sound moral perceptions, a keen sense of civic responsibility and duty, and an adequate conception of the purposes of life. It is this latter wealth which determines the ranking of nations in the scale of civilization. It is a sordid ideal that makes what a man has of greater value than what he is. It is not the quantity but the quality of its manhood that determines the status of a nation.

To assimilate these different races, to secure the co-operation of these alien forces, are problems demanding for their solution, patience, tact and tolerant but firm legislation. Modes of life, customs, political forms, thoughts and ideals differing from ours have made these peoples what they are and have dowered them with an inaptitude for our political forms and a disregard of our social customs that tend to keep them apart from us. The older people will not give up the forms to which they have been accustomed, and the younger people cannot soon acquire ours, except perhaps where, at the edge of the "colony," they come into frequent contact with us. The block or colony system retards assimilation. Mr. Greenway, the Premier of Manitoba, speaking of the Mennonite colony there said: "Many of the latter though they have been here for twenty-five years do not know English and are not assimilated."

Only through our schools getting an early hold of the children of these settlers can we hope to train them to live according to our social system, and to understand and appreciate the institutions of the country which they are to form an integral part of. If in these respects we place these peoples two generations hence where their Anglo-Saxon neighbours now are we shall have done well. In the meantime the need for action is pressing. To delay undertaking the education of these children is but to increase the difficulty of assimilation; to undertake it at once demands large expenditures and skilled teachers with something of the missionary spirit actuating them.

A number of the smaller, older colonies have schools in operation. The Galicians near Yorkton and the Mennonites and Galicians near Rosthern are preparing to organise school districts. The seven thousand Doukhobors who are settling in north-eastern Assiniboia will require from forty to fifty new districts to supply their educational needs. If those French districts in Saskatchewan that have not succeeded in keeping their schools in operation are encouraged, as in the interests of their children they should be, to re-open them it is safe to say that $16,000.00 will hardly pay the grants earned next year by the schools referred to in this paragraph.

So far as I have been able to learn none of the foreign communities have among them persons with a knowledge of English and a general education sufficient for teaching purposes. It is to their advantage as well as to ours to have their children taught by those who, while having a sympathy for their customs, shall be Canadian in spirit, thought and language. If these children are to grow up as Canadian citizens they must be led to adopt our viewpoint and speak our speech. This does not imply that they shall cease to have a love for their mother land or mother tongue but that they shall be fitly prepared for the life they are to live in the land of their adoption. A common school and a common tongue are essential if we are to have a homogeneous citizenship. Strange as it may seem to some, it is nevertheless a fact that the most effective work in such schools has been done by Canadian teachers practically unacquainted with the language of the colony. The advantage of a knowledge of the language is more evident in the teacher's influence with the parents than in his work in the schoolroom. But it is difficult to get Canadian teachers to live in these recently formed colonies. The difference in modes of life and the lack of congenial society and comfortable boarding houses deter most of them. It has been suggested that for a time an addition to the salaries of such teachers, by way of "bonus," would tend to increase their numbers. . . .

In some of our "colonies" certain influences have been brought to bear upon the people to have them erect churches and use them or parts of them for school purposes. Recently it has become evident that there is a growing determination on the part of a number of these people to erect school buildings first and use them for church services until they are able to erect churches.

In outlying districts there are still some log buildings open to the rafters, "chinked" with clay, and banked with manure which is not always removed in the early spring. Dirty within and cheerless without, their effect upon the children is bad. Too frequently it is negligence, not poverty, that is the cause, and the inspector finds ample scope for missionary work in his visits to the trustees. There are still some villages and towns where the janitor thinks he has done his duty when he scrubs the floor and dusts the walls once in three to six months. There are trustees who deem it a sufficient reply to an inspector's complaint of lack of cleanliness at his spring visit to assure the department that their "schools were cleaned thoroughly last midsummer!" But there are also schools, and an increasing number of them, where cleanliness reigns and flowers in the windows and pictures on the walls give a happy home-like look to the rooms where the child spends so many of his formative hours.

Report of the Superintendent of Education, N.W.T. for 1900, pp. 25, 26.

In my report of 1898 I said: "One of our most serious and pressing educational problems arises from the settlement amongst us of so many foreign nationalities in the block or 'colony' system. There are colonies of Swedes,

Finns, Bohemians, Hungarians, Jews, Austrians, Germans, Russians, Icelanders, Mennonites, Galicians and Doukhobors."

That the educational progress made in some of the "colonies" is most encouraging is shown by the following extracts from the reports of inspectors. I call especial attention to the fact that the best work accomplished in these schools is done by English speaking teachers practically unacquainted with the language of the "colony." Each is a distinctly rural school.

ST. ISTVAN, No. 31. *Hungarians.* Inspector Hewgill reports:

READING Part I: They read intelligently in a "Hiawatha" primer—method correct, results excellent. Other classes in reading: Excellent mastery of words, meanings and thoughts. Each class is above the average in this subject.

ARITHMETIC: In all grades the work is fully up to the standard. The forms of solution are excellent.

WRITING: The general standing is above the average. Copy books excellent.

SPELLING: Very much above the average.

HISTORY AND GEOGRAPHY: Very good work in Standards II and III.

SCHOOL ROOM: Clean, neat; lavatory and fittings supplied.

PUPILS: Tidy, and particular about their appearance.

Note: Here in a school of Hungarians I find the course of studies carried out in all its details and the matter of it presenting no difficulty. Mr. O'Brien, the teacher in charge, does not know their language.

ROSE HILL, No. 459. Pupils all *Swedes.* Inspector Perrett reports:

READING: Work recognition good, articulation not very distinct; good grasp of thought, fair expression.

ARITHMETIC: Pupils make problems of good type, reasoning sound, statement of work complete and logical, advancement good.

COMPOSITION: Limited vocabulary but words used are generally correct and well chosen. Letter forms correct, contents natural and well arranged. Spelling weak.

GEOGRAPHY: They know land and water forms well and reason correctly.

NATURE STUDY: They observe closely, have a hearty appreciation of the purpose of the parts of a flower.

WRITING: Neat, careful, correct.

PUPILS: Cheerful, neat, orderly, prompt, interested. Miss Tunney, the teacher in charge, does not know their language.

STUCE GROVE, No. 450. Pupils, *Russians, Galicians and Germans.* Inspector Perrett reports:

Classes were examined in subjects of their standards and were found to have made considerable progress. They read clearly, distinctly and with good expression. Their work in calculation is rapid and accurate. Spelling is somewhat weak. The juniors compose good sentences and the seniors write creditable letters. Their writing is uniform, careful and neat. The children observe closely and are able to connect common phenomena. More time might be given to thought reading, statement of work in arithmetic and the use of prepositions in composition. The pupils sing well. The "role" songs they chose for themselves and sang for me were "God Save the Queen" and "The Land of the Maple." The pupils are clean, neat, well behaved, cheerful and interested. Miss Chegwin, the teacher in charge, does not know their language.

Many of the schools in these "colonies" rank far below these three. The cause is mainly their inability or unwillingness to secure and retain good teachers.

THE SCHOOLS' MISSION TO THE NATIVE PEOPLE

Report on the Affairs of the Indians in Canada, *Journal of Legislative Assembly of the Province of Canada* (1847), App. T.

It has been shown that, up to a recent period, the policy of the Government towards this race was directed rather to securing their services in time of war, than to reclaiming them from barbarism, and encouraging them in the adoption of the habits and arts of civilization. With this view, they were for many years placed under the superintendence of the military authorities in the Province.

Since 1830, a more enlightened policy has been pursued, under instructions of the Secretary of State, and much has been done in Upper Canada, both by the Government and various religious bodies, to promote their civilization, but the system, although improved, has had a tendency to keep the Indians in a state of isolation and tutelage, and materially to retard their progress.

The inquiries of your Commissioners, and their consideration of the numerous opinions submitted to them, have led them to the conclusion, that the true and only practicable policy of the Government, with reference to their interests, both of the Indians and the community at large, is to endeavour, gradually, to raise the Tribes within the British Territory to the level of their white neighbours; to prepare them to undertake the offices and duties of citizens; and, by degrees, to abolish the necessity for its farther interference in their affairs.

Experience has shown that Indians can no longer lead a wild and roving life, in the midst of a numerous and rapidly increasing white population. Their hunting grounds are broken up by settlements; the game is exhausted; their resources as hunters and trappers are cut off; want and disease spread rapidly among them, and gradually reduce their numbers. To escape these consequences, no choice is left, but to remove beyond the pale of civilization, or to settle and cultivate the land for a livelihood. From this cause, and under the influence of the Missionaries, few Indians remain unsettled in the inhabited parts of Canada.

But the settled and partially civilized Indians, when left to themselves, become exposed to a new class of evils. They hold large blocks of lands, generally of the most valuable description, which they can neither occupy nor protect against the encroachments of white squatters, with whom, in the vain attempt to guard their lands, they are brought into a state of constant hostility and collision. As they are exempt from any obligation to make or maintain roads through their lands, these reserves are serious obstacles to the settlement and improvement of the surrounding country, and their possessors become objects of jealousy and dislike to their neighbours; of these the more unprincipled are always on the alert, to take advantage of the weakness and ignorance of the Indians, and of their partiality for spirits, in order to plunder them of their improvements and other property; habits of intoxication are thus introduced and encouraged, destitution ensues, and general demoralization is the speedy consequence.

Against these latter evils, Christianity and religious instruction have been found both a prevention and a remedy. The several experiments which have been made with zeal, and followed up with perseverance, have proved eminently successful. The Indians have generally evinced much readiness to embrace the Christian religion, and to receive instruction.

But, in order to enable them to compete with the whites, and to take their position among them as fellow-citizens, some time and more comprehensive and active measures are necessary. Sir Francis Head despaired of ever being able to effect this object, and, therefore, he proposed to remove them to a distance, and to fortify them, as much as possible, against all communications with the whites. The evidence, also, which your Commissioners have received on this point, varies much, although they conceive that the isolation of the Indian Tribes has generally been recommended, on account of its convenience to the whites, and its supposed temporary advantage to the Indians, rather than from any enlarged or philanthropic views for the ultimate benefit of the latter. But all Sir F. Head's attempts to induce the Indians to abandon their old settlements, failed, and every similar attempt is likely to fail. The Indians have usually a strong veneration and affection for their old haunts, and consider it a disgrace to abandon the bones of their ancestors, while the faith of the Crown, and every principle of justice, are opposed to their compulsory removal.

Experience has also taught that, while they remain among whites, it is impossible to prevent the closest communication between them. Laws have been passed to prevent whites from settling in their villages, to protect them from squatters, to restrain the sale of liquors among them, but all these enactments have been disregarded or evaded, and if it were possible for the Government to devise a system of separation, the Indians would be the first to break through it.

There is, therefore, but the one course left, which has been pointed out—to endeavour to raise them to the level of the whites. To this there appears to be no insurmountable impediment. It is the universal testimony, that there is nothing in the character of the Indian race which is opposed to such a result. They possess all the higher attributes of the mind; their perceptions of religion and their sense of moral obligations are just; their imagination is fertile; their aptitude for instruction, and their powers for imitation are great; neither are they wanting in a desire to improve their condition; they are sensible of the superiority of the whites, and of the disadvantages under which they themselves labour, from their want of knowledge, and the converted Indians are generally very anxious for the education of their children. Many are acting as Missionaries and Interpreters among their brethren in Canada and the Territories of the Hudson's Bay Company, with credit to themselves, and infinite advantages to those under their charge. Most, if not all those who have received a good education, are equal, in every respect, to their white associates; some lads of the Upper Canada College have distinguished themselves highly. Among the Chiefs are many intelligent, well conducted, religious men, quite competent to manage their own affairs, and very shrewd in the protection of their own interests.

The chief obstacles to the advancement of the race are, their want of self-dependence, and their habits of indolence, which have been fostered, if not created, by the past policy of the Government; their ignorance or imperfect knowledge of the language, customs, and mode of traffic of the whites; and that feebleness of the reasoning powers, which is the necessary consequences of the entire absence of mental cultivation. None of these difficulties appear insuperable, and your Commissioners are of opinion, that all the measures of the Government should be directed to their removal, and to the development of those natural capacities which the Indian character exhibits. This may be a difficult task, as regards the majority of the adults, whose habits have been formed, with whom the time for instruction is passed, and who have become familiarized with their condition, but with the youth it will be otherwise.

They are represented to be very apt in acquiring knowledge, and the schools which have been established among them upon an efficient footing, have proved very successful. It is by their education mainly that your Commissioners look to the future elevation of the Indian race; but much may yet be done with a large portion of the adults, by instruction and encouragement. Their various recommendations will consequently have reference to these main objects.

GENERAL RECOMMENDATIONS

1. That as long as the Indian Tribes continue to require the special protection and guidance of the Government, they should remain under the immediate control of the Representative of the Crown within the Province and not under that of the Provincial Authorities. . . .

2. That measures should be adopted to introduce and confirm Christianity among all the Indians within the Province, and to establish them in Settlements.

3. That the efforts of the Government should be directed to educating the young, and to weaning those advanced in life from their feelings and habits of dependence.

4. That, for this purpose, Schools should be established, and Missionaries

and Teachers be supported at each Settlement, and that their efficiency should be carefully watched over.

5. That in addition to Common Schools, as many Manual Labour or Industrial Schools, should be established, as the funds applicable to such a purpose will admit.

Your Commissioners are satisfied, that if in England more elementary instruction in reading and writing be found ineffectual to form the minds and establish the character of the youth of the nation, the same difficulty presents itself, with much greater force, in dealing with the Indian youth. Their education must consist not merely of the training of the mind, but of a weaning from the habits and feelings of their ancestors, and the acquirements of the language, arts and customs of civilized life. Besides the ordinary routine of a primary School, the young men should be instructed in husbandry, gardening, the management of stock, and simple mechanical trades; the girls in domestic economy, the charge of a household and dairy, the use of the needle, &c; and both sexes should be familiarized with the mode of transacting business among the whites. It is by means of Industrial or Manual Labour Schools, in which the above branches of instruction are taught, that a material and extensive change among the Indians of the rising generation may be hoped for. . . .

The Chief Superintendent of Indian Affairs:—"I am of opinion that a general Education should be provided for the Indian youths, both male and female, on a uniform system, something similar to the New England Company's Establishment. The children should reside at the Establishment, and be placed under the constant supervision of a competent and attached Tutor, who should pay to their habits the same attention as to their minds. The course of Education should consist of reading, writing, and arithmetic, and religious instruction under the superintendence of the Minister of the church to which they belong; they should also be instructed in such mechanical arts as they display an aptitude to acquire, and in the theory and practice of husbandry; the more talented should be encouraged, by a more liberal education, to enter into Holy Orders, and become the resident Ministers among their Tribe.

The girls, besides a similar elementary Education, should be instructed in such useful acquirements as are possessed by white people of the inferior class. The proceeds of their labours, as well as of the boys, in the mechanical arts, might be profitably disposed of in the neighbouring towns and surrounding country. This constant employment of their intellectual and bodily faculties, will alone reserve the Indians from extinction, and elevate their condition." . . .

The Reverend Peter Jones:—"From the knowledge I have of the Indian character, and from personal observation I have come to the conclusion, that the system of education adopted in our Common Schools has been too inefficient. The children attend these Schools from the houses of their parents, a number of whom are good, pious Christians, but who, nevertheless, retain many of their old habits; consequently, the good instruction the children receive at the School is, in a great measure, neutralized at home.

It is a notorious fact, that the parents in general exercise little or no control over their children, allowing them to do as they please. Being thus left to follow their own wills, they too frequently wander about the woods with their bows and arrows, or accompany their parents in their hunting excursions.

Another evil arises from their not being trained to habits of industry whilst attending the Schools, so that by the time they leave they are greatly averse to work, and naturally adopt the same mode of life as their parents.

Under these circumstances, I am very anxious to see Manual Labour Schools established amongst our people, that the children may be properly trained and educated to habits of industry and usefulness.

I see nothing to hinder the entire success of such a plan, and, as the School in the Missouri country is answering the most sanguine expectations of its promoters, we may safely conclude, that the same success would attend the like operations amongst our Indians.

I am happy to inform you, that all the Indians with whom I have conversed, highly approve of the project, and are very anxious to see such a School in immediate operation. They are ready and willing to give up their children to the entire control and management of the Teachers.

I beg also to state, that, in my humble opinion, unless something be done in this way, the Indians will for ever remain in the half-civilized state, and continue to be a burden to the British Government and the Missionary Societies."

APP. 14. EXTRACTS FROM EVIDENCE OF MR. ROBERT M'NAB, FORMERLY OF
THE INDIAN DEPARTMENT (HAVING REFERENCE TO
THE TRIBES IN CANADA EAST)

From Memorandum shewing the present condition of the INDIANS OF CANADA EAST.

The Education of the Indians:—

I have now arrived at a point upon which depends the future happiness or misery of the different Indian Tribes. I mean Education. It is frequently said, even by those whose judgment on other matters is received as sound, that the Indians are not ripe for education; that a direct contradiction to the assertion can be at once given; I shall merely remark, that of the six Villages enumerated, containing together a population of about 3,000 souls, not 200 are pure Indians, the remainder either mixed or of pure European blood. To advance their moral improvement by means of education, what has been done? Nothing. The British Government continue to grant them bountifully annual presents of Clothing, &c., and pay a number of sinecure officers for issuing the presents, but at same time encourages a state of dependency that ought not to exist.

The amount voted by the House of Commons for a few years past for the Indians of Canada, amounted to £ 20,000, previously £ 50,000 and £ 100,000, even as much as £ 300,000, exclusive of other charges incurred in the Province. Say on an average since the conquest, £100,000 per annum for 80 years, would show the enormous expenditure of £8,000,000. And yet it is said the Indians are not ripe for education. Such, with some truth, might be said of the Tribes who inhabit the Rocky Mountains, or the shores of the Columbia River, being yet barbarians; not so of those residing in Canada East. I have known several half-breeds from the north-west Territory, educated at Montreal and in England, who were good scholars, and held situations of great responsibility; there exists not a shadow of a doubt but all the Tribes are now as ripe for education as ever they possibly can be; good English Schools only require to be established in every Village, and parents compelled, on pain of forfeiting the Government presents, to send their children to School, and thus educating the rising generation would, in my opinion, work a wonderful change in a short time, and incline them more to industry, at same time exercise a trade for literary and scientific pursuits. There have been a few natives of Caughnawaga and St. Regis educated at Dartmouth College, in the State of New Hampshire, richly endowed by Lord Dartmouth, in the early settlement of America, for the education of the Indians, who on returning to their native Villages after a long absence, and unaccustomed to Indian labor, became restless and unhappy, and eventually dissipated, and their minds not properly directed and employed, became in a short time for ever lost. But if education became general, a spirit of rivalry and a desire to excel each other in the pursuits of knowledge, would, in a short time, tend to rouse the Indian character and fit them for holding situations of usefulness and trust. The great stumbling block in the establishment of Schools among the Indians is placed and maintained by those whose duty it should rather be to encourage, I mean the Missionaries, who are openly and obstinately averse to English Schools. I would recommend that the Government adopt the plan of refusing the Indians their annual allowance, and informing them if they will not have English Schools, they shall not have English presents.

The State of Agriculture in the Indian Settlements:—
Proprietors in most cases of large tracts of waste lands, nothing has been done for them by instruction or even introducing the most simple forms of agriculture. I would suggest the immediate formation of Manual Labor Schools, similar to those now very general in the United States, in which various mechanical instructions might be taught, affording as it would, the youths an opportunity of acquiring a knowledge of the various trades common to the whites, but chiefly the introduction of agricultural instruction; the Indians generally are of an inquisitive disposition and desirous of obtaining information; for that reason, I would anticipate much good by the formation of such Schools in every Village; to commence with, say that a trial be first made at Caughnawaga, and the youths of other Villages be permitted to attend, and if found to answer, that similar institutions be then introduced amongst the other Tribes.

Had the Officers of the Indian Department been as industrious in instructing the Indians in useful knowledge as they have been in encouraging drunkenness and quarrelling, the Tribes would certainly at this day have presented a more pleasing picture than they now do. A reduction in the expenditure of the Indian Department might be safely made of about £500 per annum, which could be very beneficially applied towards the improvement of Agriculture, purchase of implements, awarding premiums for good ploughing, best crops, clean fields, &c.

Indian Mechanics

To the mechanical arts the Indians of Canada East lay no pretension, and so long as they are kept in their present uneducated and ignorant state, such knowledge cannot be expected or looked for; that they, under different circumstances, are competent to receive such knowledge, I may mention the fact of several half-breeds born in the north-west, but educated in Montreal, who served apprenticeships, and were first-rate mechanics, such as Coopers, Blacksmiths, Carpenters, Cabinet-makers, Tailors, Shoemakers, Watchmakers, &c.

All of which is humbly submitted.

(Signed,)   Robert M'Nab.

Caughnawaga, 9th September, 1843.

APP. 18.

No. 1.

Report of the Indian School at Colborne, in the Township of Carradoc, District of London, and under the tuition of Mr. Henry Jones.

STATE OF LEARNING

Number of Scholars.	Ages.	Primers.	Spelling.	Reading.	Writing.
17 boys	6 to 14	11	5	4	4
3 young men.					
18 girls	6 to 14	13	2	3	2
38					

Arithmetic.	Eng. Grammar.	Books used.
3	0	New London Primer, Mavor's Spelling, Richardson's Reading made easy, New
0	0	Testament, Angus' Arithmetic.

Remarks

The mode of teaching in this school is the same as the common schools established amongst the whites.

The school opens and closes with prayer, and is under the control of the Wesleyan Methodist Missionary Society in Carradoc; and the scholars belong to the Chippawa and Munsee Tribes.

(Signed,)	J. B. CLENCH,
	Supt. Ind. Affairs.

No. 2.

Report of the Indian School at Lower Munsee, in the Township of Carradoc, District of London, under the tuition of Mr. Henry C. Hogg.

STATE OF LEARNING

No. of Scholars.	Ages.	Primers.	Spelling.	Reading.	Writing.
21 boys	6 to 15	12	9	9	7
4 girls	6 to 10	2	2	2	1
25					

Arithmetic.	Eng. Grammar.	Books used.
3	0	Primer, Mavor's Spelling, New Testament, English
0	0	Reader, Murray's Grammar, Daball's Arithmetic.

Remarks

Spelling and reading taught in class; writing at the desk from copy lines, and occasionally from dictation.

A number of young men and women, some of the former of whom are learning Arithmetic and English Grammar, occasionally attend school, and are not included in the above Report.

The School opens and closes with prayer, and is under the control of the Missionary Society of the Church of England, and the scholars belong to the Chippawa and Munsee Tribes.

(Signed,)	J. B. CLENCH,
	Supt. Ind. Affairs.

No. 3.

Report of the Indian School at New Fairfield, in the Township of Oxford, Western District, and under the tuition of Mr. Lewis Kampinau.

STATE OF LEARNING

No. of Scholars.	Ages.	Primers.	Spelling.	Reading.	Writing.
23 boys	5 to 15	8	8	7	6
18 girls	6 to 14	8	5	5	5
41					

Arithmetic.	Eng. Grammar.	Books used.
3	0	The Union Primer, Webster's Spelling Book,
0	0	English Reader, Hutton's Arithmetic.

Remarks.

The children in their respective classes spell and read together, and then repeat their lessons individually.

The School opens and closes with prayer, and is under the control of the Moravian Missionary Society, and the children belong to the Delaware Tribe.

(Signed,)   J. B. CLENCH,
Supt. Ind. Affairs.

No. 4.

Report of the Indian School at New Oneida, in the Township of Delaware, District of London, and under the tuition of Mr. Abraham Sickles, an Indian of the Oneida Tribe.

STATE OF LEARNING

No. of Scholars.	Ages.	Primers.	Spelling.	Reading.	Writing.
16 boys	6 to 16	4	8	4	4
17 girls	5 to 15	1	10	6	4
33					

Arithmetic.	Eng. Grammar.	Books used.
0	0	Oneidas Spelling Book. Do. Testament.
0	0	English Testament.

Remarks

The children taught in their own languages learn very fast, but make slow progress in the English, and the teacher is not well qualified to instruct in the English language. I have recommended that the English language be altogether taught in this school, which is under the control of the Wesleyan Methodist Missionary Society in Canada, and the children belong to the Oneida Tribe.

(Signed,)   J. B. Clench,
Supt. Ind. Affairs.

INDIAN INDUSTRIAL SCHOOLS

Rev. Thompson Ferrier, *Indian Education in the North West* (Toronto, Dept. of Missionary Literature of the Methodist Church, n.d.), pp. 6-7, 9-13, 15-17, 25-9, 34-6.

... The commonest mistake made by his white well-wishers in dealing with the Indian is the assumption that he is simply a white man with a red skin. The next commonest is the assumption that because he is a non-Caucasian he is to be classed with other non-Caucasians, like the Negro, for instance. The truth is that the Indian has as distinct individuality as any type of man who ever lived, and will never be judged aright until we learn to measure him by his own standards, as we whites would wish to be measured if some more powerful race were to usurp dominion over us. If a century ago an absolutely alien people like the Chinese had invaded our shores and driven the white colonists before them to distant and more isolated territories, destroying the institutions on which they had always subsisted, and crowned all by disarming them and penning them on various tracts of land, where they could be partially clothed, fed and cared for at no cost to themselves, to what conditions would the white Canadians of to-day have been reduced in spite of their vigorous ancestry? They would surely have lapsed into barbarism and become pauperized. No race on earth could overcome, from forces evolved within themselves, the effect of such a treatment. That our red brethren have not been wholly ruined by it is the best proof we could ask of the sturdy traits of character inherent in them; but though not ruined they have suffered serious deterioration, and the problem now before us is to prevent it going any further. . . .

What is the effect of treaty on the general welfare of the Indian? The Indian is growing up with the idea firmly fixed in his head that the Government owes him a living, and that his happiness and prosperity depend in no degree upon his individual effort. Rations and treaty are all right for the aged, helpless and infirm. Strong and able-bodied Indians hang round for rations and treaty, neglecting other duties and the cultivation of their land in order to secure what in many cases could be earned several times over in the same length of time. The system destroys his energy, push and independence. It removes the necessity of compelling a man to labor for what he needs. The Indian massed in tribes is the problem; the Indian with individual opportunity is no problem.

To recognize the man as a unit and hold him responsible as such, train him for his place and then let him occupy it, is the true method of civilizing the Indian. We wonder why the Indian is so long in becoming a part of our national life. It is as if we had bound his ankles together with heavy chains and then express surprise that he has not learned to run. Our Indian policy pays more in dollars for the Indians to remain idle, unprogressive, dependent, than to become self-supporting, independent citizens. The inevitable result is discontent, lawlessness, unrest, laziness, debauchery and pauperism. As fast as our Indian, whether of mixed or full blood, is capable of taking care of himself, it is our duty to set him on his feet and sever forever the ties that bind him either to his tribe or to the Government. Break our treaties? By no means; it is not breaking a promise to go far beyond it and grant a hundred-fold more than was at first specified. One is justified in recalling what was given in good faith when a gift of rarer value is tendered instead. To be a free man in the enjoyment of life is vastly better than to be bound to an ignorant tribe. Both Church and State should have as a final goal the destruction and end of treaty and the reservation life. While the promises in these treaties are moderate, and have their origin in feelings that are most humane and philanthropic, backed up with the kindest and very best of intentions, yet in actual results they are proving to be the very best scheme that could have been devised for the purpose of debauching, demoralizing and pauperizing the poor Indian.

EDUCATION

Nothing can be done to change the Indian who has passed middle life. He will remain an Indian of the old school until the last. We should make his declining years as comfortable as possible. Anything to save the young; but as to the old it may be like putting the fire out of a rotten log—and if done the ash may be worth more than the log. With the younger adults we may do a little, but our main hope lies with the youthful generation. . . .

Of the 18,000 Indians of school age in Canada, at least two-thirds must settle down and draw a living out of the soil. Some will fish and hunt; a small part will enter the general labor market as lumbermen, canners, miners, freighters, sailors, railroad hands, ditchers and what not; only an odd one will enter the overcrowded trades and professions of to-day. Every Indian boy and girl ought to know how to speak and read simple English (the local newspaper), write a short letter, and enough of figures to discover if the storekeeper is cheating him. Beyond these scholastic accomplishments his time could be put to its best use by learning how to repair a broken harness, how to straighten a sprung tire on his waggon wheel, how to fasten a loose horseshoe without breaking the hoof, how to handle carpenter, garden and farm tools, how to care for horses, cattle, poultry, pigs, till the ground, produce a garden, learning the great possibilities of the soil.

The girl who has learned only the rudiments of reading, writing and ciphering, and knows also how to make and mend her clothing, wash and iron, make a good loaf of bread, cook a good dinner, keep her home neat and clean, will be worth vastly more as mistress of a log cabin than one who has given years of study to the ornamental branches alone. . . .

INDUSTRIAL SCHOOLS

There are no schools anywhere of any description better designed than our Government Industrial Schools for Indians. There is no system of schools kindlier of intent, more truly thoroughly educational, better adapted for the great work of unfolding and disentangling the warp and woof of the mysteries of life, more developing, expanding and comprehensive, than the present system of Government Industrial Schools. The chief aim of any education should be the fitting for self-support. Especially is this true of a dependent race. By self-support is meant the acquiring by honest labor of enough to eat and to wear, and a decent abode. It is not the duty of any Government or class of humanity, however favored, to do more than give this kind of education, but it is a duty, and a permanent one, to give this much.

The Indian must be educated along industrial lines. It should be along the line of the physical rather than the mental. In these schools at least half the time is given to this instruction. The industrial work should be adapted to the locality where the pupil may be expected to reside after leaving the school. In all cases the education should be adjusted to the paths of life they are likely to follow. The following will give an idea of what is usually taught, or at least ought to be taught, in an industrial school:

Housework, mending, sewing, darning, use of thimbles, needles, scissors, brooms, brushes, knives, forks and spoons. The cooking of meats and vegetables, the recipes for various dishes, bread making, buns, pies, materials used and quantity. Washing, ironing, bluing, what clothing should be boiled and what not, why white may be boiled and colored not, how to take stains from white clothing, how to wash colored clothes, the difference between hard and soft water. Dairying, milking, care of milk, cream, churning, house work. Sweeping, scrubbing, dusting, care of furniture, books, linen, etc. They should also be taught garden work. Our own women have to do a great deal of garden work, and it is of the greatest importance that the Indian girl should know how. Instruction should be given in the elements of physiology and hygiene, explaining particularly proper habits in eating and drinking, cleanliness, ventilation, the manner of treating emergency cases, such as hemorrhage, fainting, drowning, sunstroke, nursing and general care of the sick. Such an all-round training fits a girl to be mistress of her home very much better than if she spent her whole time in the class-room.

It is not worth while trying to teach them [boys] trades and professions, in fact such an education would begin after the boy leaves an industrial school, since the Department require the discharge at the age of eighteen. It is of the most importance that he should learn something of farming, gardening, care of stock and carpenter work. His agricultural training should be of an advanced character, covering stock raising, dairying, care and management of poultry, hogs, and horses. Fruit raising, especially in this western country, where he can find by actual experience that the small fruits they so often roam the country to find can be had at their own door with less labor and of superior quality. The manual training should be designed to teach the elementary portions of those trades most likely to prove most useful to the farmer.

The class-room work and the industrial work should be so merged as to give a thorough practical training with the aim of making the boy an all-round farmer, each of the employees in charge of particular lines of work giving lectures periodically on industrial topics. The farmer, for instance, on the rotation of crops, kinds of soil, use of fertilizers, methods of seeding, the manner of growth, the growing of wheat from the breaking of the ground to the storing and selling of the crop. After these lectures, which may be given the whole school, the teacher in the class-room should require compositions from all senior scholars. Gardening and farm work, thus blended with the class-room work, becomes one of the best methods of developing English in backward pupils, as the child when working with his hands unconsciously overcomes timidity and naturally endeavors to imitate all he sees done. His intellect is kindled, curiosity excited, and his mental faculties are thus aroused. Care should be taken that they are taught the use of the implements and machinery used in farm work, and yet such implements are to be used, as largely as possible, as will be within the reach of the boy when he leaves the school. . . .

WHAT ABOUT GRADUATES OF INDUSTRIAL SCHOOLS?

Reports of returned students show that most of them are doing well, showing themselves to be more neat, clean, thrifty and industrious, and exercising an influence for good upon their people. Many of the graduates never return to reserve life. Upon those who do not, especially the girls, a strong influence is brought to bear to induce them to return to reserve life. Efforts are being made to guard against this by training them in the habits of self-control, self-dependence, and to live up to the standard set and the instruction imparted at the school, so that as returned students they may become industrious, self-supporting women and men. Help to withstand the down-pull of reservation life should be given by agents, teachers, missionaries, and all others who have the opportunity. Even if all should return to the old life the remedy would not be to withhold the training from the one, but to send the other twenty-four to school. This tendency to degenerate would be greatly reduced if more of the children were educated, for the more enlightened the Indian becomes the more he conforms to the habits of civilized life. Another remedy would be in having a compulsory education, so that the day school could serve as a preparatory school for the more advanced reservation boarding school, and from the boarding school the best, physically, mentally and morally, should be graduated into the non-reservation school. If this were the enforced policy the recruits for industrial schools would be 100 per cent. better than at present, and so proportionately would be the graduates.

Those in charge of non-reservation schools should not be obliged to go after recruits. Such hurriedly collected children may not be the best for transferring, and great injustice may be done to the child and the receiving school.

A record of the pupils from the oldest institute, Carlyle, would show to be equally good. A careful observation of pupils from our own reservation boarding and industrial schools reveals that our graduates are endeavoring to overcome their environment and to prove themselves worthy of the education they have received. Their homes are neater and better cared for and more abundantly supplied with light and air. They have also more personal tidiness. They are beginning to help themselves and are becoming more industrious and self-supporting. They are filling nearly all the responsible positions with traders and others among their own people.

PETITIONS FOR SUPPORT FROM BLACK PEOPLE

Education Papers, RG 5, Series P, vol. 75 (1849-50), Public Archives of Nova Scotia.

To The Honourable The Speaker and the Members of the House of Assembly
The petition of the coloured Population of Port Latour
Humbly Sheweth

That your Petitioners are the coloured Population of Port Latour in the county of Shelburne. That your petitioners although possessing but a very small portion of education themselves are nonetheless anxious that their children should enjoy its benefit. That their is an eversion on the part of the white population around as to their children mixing with our children in school. That their is therefore no means for our children to obtain education but by the establishment of a school for their sole benefit.

That about three years ago their was such a school established in this place which still continues. That the number of children in this school has varied from fifteen to twenty-seven. That connected with this day school there was also a Sabbath school with scholars numbering from forty to forty five. That towards the support of the day school we have contributed twenty shillings per month towards the board of the master which was all that our humble circumstances enabled us to do.

That the first two years the board of school commissioners appropriated a sum which with the above the teacher accepted as an adequate remuneration. That the said board of commission has for the last five months appropriated to this school only the sum of seven pounds two shillings and six pence making the entire amount paid to the teacher for both salary and board the sum of twelve pounds two shillings and six pence for five months.

That your Petitioners have learnt with feelings of regret that the teacher intends to discontinue the school when his present term is expired unless he receives a more ample remuneration for his labours.

That your Petitioners deeply deplore closing the school against our children. That therefore your petitioners humbly pray your Honourable House to take the premises into consideration and to place a separate sum of money at the disposal of the school commissioners for the sole support of a common school for the education of the children of the coloured Population of this place.

Or to afford such other relief as Your Honourable House may deem meet.

And your Petitioners as in duty bound will ever pray.

John Tails his mark
Thomas Taska
John Sasko his mark
Tailor Ely his mark
John Keeling his mark
Tom Keeling his mark
James Barry
Moses Keeling
Augustus Keeling his mark
Joseph Keeling his mark
John E. James
Robert   his mark

> I have visited the above named coloured settlement
> together with their School, and can recommend the
> latter as an object of much interest, as well
> as much reqd. to be encouraged.
> J. Forsythe
> Missy Ch. Deoc. Socy
> at Barington
> I beg also to recommend the above school to the consideration of the
> Honourable the House of Assembly
> William [?]
> Wesleyan Missionary

To Mr James Fraser, Esq
House of Assembly
Township of Windsor 3 mile plains Hants County

We the Humble petitioners the coloured population of the 3 mile plains Humbly hoping that the Honourable Gentlemen of the House of assembly will be so good as to allow us a part of the provincial money to pay a Teacher as you have done these past 4 years   Hon Gentleman The Benevolent Gentlemen and Ladys and Mr. Gilpin all of Windsor has Built us a School house much to their credit and we have a very good Teacher of good morals to teach our children to our liking which Mr. J. Fraser and Mr. Songster members for Windsor and Talmouth can inform the Hon Gentlemen of the House of the

Needseysity of this School where they are above 70 or 80   Daily getting their instructions at that School of old and young By a careful Master

We Humbly hope that the Hon Gentlem of our assembly Will be so good as to allow us what will pay our Teacher as We are a poor Settlement of people having nothing But what we Receive from The N Subjects in this Country.

The Gentlemen and Ladys of Windsor has been very kind to us as regards how we are learning.

By paying attention to us We hope that God will bless your proceedings.

The Subscribers on the other Side

3 mile plains February 16th 1849

Edward Polate Trustee with Rev'd Mr. Gilpin

Davit Williams his X mark

Colonel Cooper his X mark

Nager Cooper	Do	Do
Colo Cooper	Do	Do
Pampi Johnston	Do	Do
Abraham Green	Do	Do
Jesoph Carter	Do	Do
Benjamin Mitchel	Do	Do
James Samson	Do	Do
Mark Teilor	Do	Do
Samuel Gardiner	Do	Do
Charles Upshaw	Do	Do
John Upshaw	Do	Do
—Alison	Do	Do
Miles Toeney	Do	Do
Danial Snide	Do	Do
Jacob Robeson	Do	Do
Widow Bone	Do	Do
John Lewry	Do	Do
Jacob Lewry	Do	Do
Bajs[?] Bone	Do	Do
Said [?] Walker	Do	Do
Pat Lawson	Do	Do
James W Johnston		

JUSTIFYING SEGREGATION

The *Leader*, December 12, 1862.

The Board of School Trustees of the neighbouring city of London is the first to take up a subject which has attracted more or less attention in different parts of the Province—the mingling together of coloured and white children in the Common Schools. The Board has not acted hastily in the matter. The subject has been under consideration for several months; and it is only within the last few days that the board came to a final determination. Their report is one which does them credit. It goes over the whole question, suggests difficulties and meets objections in a way which shows that they have not acted in a hasty manner or an ungenerous spirit; but on the contrary, that they have brought a careful study and calm deliberation to bear upon the various points which came before them. As the subject is one of provincial importance, we shall state as briefly as possible the views taken by the Board, and the recommendations they make in their report.

Let it be premised that the number of colored children of school age in London is 96. Of those 50 attended school on an average during the past year, and as many as 80 attended at various times. It is upon such *data* as this that the Board had to work. They set out by stating that a feeling exists in the community that from climatic reasons or organic causes, there is a repugnance in the minds of the white population to a close or intimate relation between their children and those of colored parents. The children themselves sympathize in this feeling or prejudice, whichever one may wish to call it; and the result is not unfrequently "a bandying of offensive epithets, embittered acrimonious feelings and juvenile quarrels. In these petty disputes the parents frequently take part, complaints are made, and will continue to be made by both parties, that their children have been insulted; and, by the colored parents, that theirs have been harshly and perhaps unjustly treated." The Board then touch upon another point, which they think a false delicacy should not prevent them from noticing; and this is, that during the summer months an "effluvium" arises from these children "which is highly offensive to many of the children, and still more so to many of the teachers." Then, there is naturally a want of sympathy between the colored children and the teachers. It is possible that the teachers endeavour to avoid the appearance of acting toward one scholar in a different manner from another; but there is nevertheless a want of sympathy, to use no harsher term, between the white teacher and the colored child, which the latter, with the natural shrewdness of its race, is not slow to perceive. This feeling of estrangement between teacher and scholar, the Board think cannot be the best means of elevating the negro, as the jealousy called into play in childhood must result in mutual dislike in later years. "When educated apart they will not be educated for evil; they will not have some of the worst passions of the human heart called daily into play and thus strengthened by exercise; they will have no taunts and insults to remember; and when they enter life as men, they will be enabled to meet their white fellow-citizens without a single acrimonious feeling, arising from the recollections of wrongs suffered or injuries retaliated."

This is the whole case as offered by the Board: these the arguments which they give for recommending that a separate school for the colored children should be established in London. Difficulties connected with the legal construction of the statute appeared to them at first in the way of carrying out their recommendation, but on looking into the different cases on which judgments have been given in the courts, they came to the conclusion that there is nothing in the Statute to prevent their establishing a separate school for the colored population. This is not the most serious point, however. The questions of a social or organic nature which the Board have ventured to touch upon, and handled in such a practical manner are those which are most likely to provoke discussion. Will the ultra advocates of the public schools denounce the recommendation of the London Board as an innovation upon our common school system? Will the ultra philanthropists, the firm believers in the doctrine that all men are born free and equal, independent of color or of race, direct their bitter shafts against the guardians of education in London the less? And last, though, to use an old expression, not least, how will the colored people themselves view the discussion of these London school trustees? We shall see.

In the meantime we have a little hesitancy in expressing our own opinion. We see no single reason for questioning the course which has been taken by the London Board. Physiological questions and questions of race may be thrown aside for the nonce and this subject viewed in the practical light of everyday experience. In those parts of the Province where there is a large colored population the difficulties arising out of the admixture of children of black and white parents give rise very often to unpleasant bickerings and creates a strong feeling of hostility between the two sections of the population. In some westerly parts of the Province the black children are entirely excluded from the common schools; and it was only the other day that an intelligent colored woman from that section of the country was in this city soliciting aid for the education of her race. Perhaps some person will say this ought not to be so. Such an argument is fully met by the fact as it exists. There is no use in trying to turn a stream against its head; and there is as little use in endeavouring to educate white and black children in the same school room. Natural causes, if no other, are opposed to it; but there is besides, an inbred feeling of repugnance in the breast of almost every white person at hybridism, which must to some extent be the result of a commingling of the races. We say this with no hard feeling toward the black population in our midst. They have received shelter here, and are safe under the protection of that flag which treats all men alike, no matter what their color, all other things being equal. But when a forcible and practical objection presents itself to an indiscriminate mingling together of black and white children in the same school rooms, we are sure to see a repetition of what has occurred in parts of the county of Essex, in London and other places west. There is but one way of meeting this difficulty. The children of black men are entitled to the benefits of education as well as those of the whites; but it does not necessarily follow that they both should be taught together. The conclusion of the London Board appears to be the only just way in which to meet the difficulty. It is hard to believe that the colored people will object to this. They prefer distinctive churches for themselves rather than to assemble together in the same edifices with their white brethren. This is not unnatural if they consider their own self-respect, which, whether rightly or wrongly is sure to be more or less hurt when they thrust themselves into positions which are not agreeable to them. And why should they not desire to receive education under similar circumstances? They ought to value rather than spurn a concession to a feeling which it is impossible to overcome or remove; and in this view it is to be hoped that the recommendation of the London Board of School Trustees will be carried out not only in that city, but in all other places where a similar difficulty arises.

A REPLY FROM THE BLACK COMMUNITY

Globe, January 3, 1863.

Sir,—I noticed lately in the *Leader* an editorial headed, "The Colored People and the Common Schools," and must say of all the aritcles that have appeared in that sheet against the colored people, it is the most despicable and malicious. The article commences by stating what the School Trustees of London are doing to degrade the colored people of that city, but it is only a pretext still further to pander to the prejudices of the "mudsills." As to the action of the London Trustees, their course is certainly most singular, for while the Americans, who were the first to establish separate schools and other institutions for colored people, are emerging from the dark ages of their prejudices, the enlightened school trustees and teachers of London are making a retrograde movement, and are relapsing into the slough of "Negrophobia." As it is in all cases where men espouse a bad cause, these trustees and teachers are obliged to descend to sophistry to make out their case. The *Leader* says: "They set out by stating that a feeling exists in the community that, from climatic reasons or other organic causes, there is a repugnance in the minds of the white population to a close or intimate relation between their children and those of colored parents." Now, that there are persons in London who are so tainted with "Negrophobia" as to object to colored children, however decent, going to the same school that they send theirs to, I have no doubt; and that these same persons instil these same feelings into their children and that there are teachers base enough to permit their prejudices to prevent them from discharging their duties to their scholars on account of their color; but I cannot believe that the people of Canada will at the caprice of such sycophants deprive us of our educational privileges. They say also that the result of the children being educated together, is not unfrequently a bandying of offensive epithets, embittered acrimonious feelings, and juvenile quarrels. In these petty disputes the parents frequently take part, complaints are made, and will continue to be made by both parents, that their children have been insulted; and by the colored people, that theirs have been harshly treated. Well, such may be the state of things in London, but it is a little singular that in Toronto, where we have a much larger population, and one, too, I have no doubt, quite as intelligent and refined as in London, the colored and white children go to the same schools together, and we hear of no such complaints and bickerings here. The very reverse is the case. The best feelings are cultivated among the scholars themselves and between scholars and teachers, as the following extract of a letter published in the *Globe* some time hence will prove:

"My mind has been led into the above reflections from the visits which I lately made to some of the common schools of this city in the discharge of a pleasing duty. Our old and worthy former fellow citizen, James Ketchum, senior, Esq., has, in the plenitude of his philanthropic and Christian feelings, devoted in perpetuity, the whole of the annual amount arising from the sale of the premise now owned and occupied by the Bible and Trust Societies, to "the benefit of the common Schools of Toronto, by furnishing books to be distributed from time to time among such of the scholars in each school division, whose standing and character may in the judgment of the school itself, best commend them to receive the gift." Mr. Ketchum being unable, because of the distance, to attend in person, was pleased to depute me to act for him. I found in several of the divisions, white and colored children seated in their respective classes, and intermixed throughout the school, and when I put it to the children to nominate those from among themselves whom they deemed the most worthy, there were not less than five, out of the comparatively few colored children present in the whole of the divisions, elected unanimously by their school mates, with the approval of their teachers. I need scarcely say, that the selection pleased, and in some measure surprised me; for I was not prepared to witness elections by whites so cordially and unanimously expressed in regard to a race against whom there has been fostered in America a prejudice founded on ideas of inferiority and incapacity. The grace and modesty evinced by those thus selected was also quite striking.

"By this comparatively small matter, as well as otherwise, I am the more confirmed in the opinion, that in point of intellect and formation of character, the African race, under just treatment, and with facilities for improvement, are in no wise inferior to others. Should any of our neighbours doubt this, I would merely say to them, *Come and see.*

"Yours respectfully,

James Richardson.

"Clover Hill, Toronto, Feb. 22, 1860."

Numerous cases might be cited to prove, that here, in many instances, the strongest ties of friendship exist betwixt the scholars and between the teachers and colored scholars; and we would particularly invite the London trustees and teachers, to pay our schools a visit during the examination, and at times when prizes and certifications are given, and they will see colored children receive both amidst the plaudits of the white scholars, and the parents and friends who attend on those occasions. Then, again, say the trustees, "an effluvium arises, during the warm weather, that is disagreeable to both teachers and scholars." Well, as to the children, they must have been trained by their parents, like the bloodhounds down South "in Dixie," to enable them to smell their colored schoolmates from the white ones. And as to the teachers, they must have extraordinary organs of scent to enable them to distinguish which of their scholars it is from whom the "disagreeable effluvium arises," without a personal scenting of each one separately. If they can, I, for one, would advise our city fathers to employ them to scent out the "pig nuisance" that is so much complained of in our city, for it is certainly an occupation more suited to them than common school teaching. And I would further recommend to the Teacher's Association, to expel all such members as being unfit to associate with them. And still further, they say, "When the colored people are educated apart, they will not be educated for evil; they will not have some of the worst passions of the human hearts called daily into play, and thus strengthened by exercise; they will have no taunts and insults to remember; and when they enter life as men, they will be enabled to meet their white fellow-citizens without a single acrimonious feeling, arising from the recollection of wrongs suffered or injuries retaliated." A gentleman, now a candidate for Mayor of this city, stated some years since, at the nomination when he was a candidate for Parliament, that while travelling in Europe he saw a man with a cage filled with all types of animals, both ferocious and harmless, fondling with each other in the best of friendship. He asked the man how did he manage to train them to treat each other so friendly; he replied by saying that he put them together when young, and they grew up as friends and remained so. Now, sir, I think the London trustees and teachers might learn a useful lesson from the man and his cage of animals.

Then, as to the law on the subject, it is evident that the trustees have no more right to establish separate schools for colored people than they have to establish them for Catholics, unless they ask for them; and according to the sixty-third chapter, section 1st, of the Consolidated Statutes for Upper Canada, the request must come from the twelve heads of families. It is said also, that the trustees feared that the law did not permit them to carry out their nefarious schemes, but that certain decisions will. Now, the only one that can with any color justify them, is the case of Dennis Hill against the trustees of Dresden. It seems the separate schools for colored people were very badly conducted, and Hill preferred to send his children to the schools other than the one for colored people. The trustees ejected them. He brought an action against them in the Court of Queen's Bench, Chief Justice Robinson presiding; and the judge decided that, as the colored people in that particular locality had asked for a separate school, they must send their children to it; and, consequently, the trustees had a right to exclude them from the other schools; and that the colored people must seek redress from the Legislature. This may be law, but it is certainly not justice; for if it is, then, upon the same principle, no Roman Catholic can send his children to any of the common schools of this city, because they have asked for and obtained separate schools. But suppose for argument's sake that they have the power to establish these separate schools for colored people, in consequence of the small number of colored children, they could not erect one in every ward, and, consequently, they would have to establish one in the centre of the city, and therefore the colored children would be obliged to travel a long distance past many common schools, however inclement the weather may be, to get to the separate school. See, then, how unjust such a course would be if it was generally adopted. The *Leader* asks how will the colored people view the discussion of these London school trustees. Well, sir, I will tell him how we view it. We will seek redress at the hands of the Legislature, by petition and otherwise, and we will never rest satisfied until it is out of the power of any set of school trustees to impose upon us separate schools against our will; and not only so, but we will agitate the subject for the purpose of getting those already established, abolished. And, sir, if the intelligent colored lady, or as the *Leader* has it, *woman*, was to exert herself to half the extent she does to beg money for a school "for the especial benefits of refugees and other colored people in Chatham," to get the school law so altered as to secure equal school privileges, she would not need to go round the country every year begging, but would do much to elevate her race, and less to put arguments in the mouths of their enemies to traduce them and build up barriers to their advancement.... The *Leader* says, "natural causes, if no other, are opposed to the admixture in the schools of the two races; but there is, besides, an in-bred feeling of repugnance in the breast of almost every white person at the hybridism which must to some extent be the result of their commingling." Now, sir, I must say, that if we look to the South, to the West Indies, and even to Canada, it does not appear that white people are so much opposed to hybridism after all, unless they practice one thing and believe another. It is further argued, that we should not object to the action of the London trustees, because colored people have separate churches. Well, the two cases are not at all analogous; for it would be absurd to say, because some few colored people in the exercise of their freedom choose to establish a Methodist or a Baptist Church, that all other colored people, whether they belong to any other denomination or not, must go to the colored churches, and be excluded from those of the white. I say, Mr. Editor, if this principle is to be carried out, a colored young man who headed his classes in the Upper Canada College while there, and now leads them in the Toronto University, and who never allows a convocation to pass without his name being mentioned in connection with some prize or mark of distinction, must be thrust from its halls, and driven into obscurity and degradation. Likewise other colored young men that are in the University, the Medical Schools, the Theological Seminaries and Colleges, those attending the law courts and lectures, and colored young ladies attending the public and private seminaries, all must be turned out to have their hopes blasted, and perhaps come to destruction. For while it might be possible to establish Separate Schools, it would not be to establish Separate Colleges. Mr. Editor, I must now conclude this already too lengthy communication, by appealing to an educated and Christian community, and ask is it right, is it according to the principles of freedom, is it in unison with the character of Britons, that, while the colored people are trying to elevate themselves in the scale of humanity, after having been brutalized by the white man for so many ages, and are both in the colleges and public schools, gaining so much distinction, a few obscure men in the community should try to pick flaws in the laws, and hunt up decisions to deprive us of our school privileges; and that newspapers, which should be the palladium of freedom and good order, should stoop so low as to stir up the prejudices of the white population against the colored? And, sir, to the colored people I will say that, while I am quite certain the school trustees of Toronto, as well as the local superintendent, are perfectly sound on the schools as they exist relative to the colored people, it becomes them to look well to their interest, and especially to the election of School Trustees, for their enemies are going about seeking how they may destroy their liberties. Nor need those colored people who do not identify themselves as such, think they will escape these disabilities on that account; for they may depend upon it, that whether they hail from either West or East Indies, it is as well known here who are colored as it is in the South where they came from, and the same rule that will exclude a child from the common schools because he is black, will exclude him because he is a mulatto or anything else but white.

I remain Sir,
Your obedient servant,
DIOGENES.

Toronto, Dec. 12, 1862

THE LEGALITY OF SEGREGATION, 1855

Francis G. Carter, *Judicial Decisions on Denominational Schools* (Toronto, Ontario Separate School Trustees' Association, 1962), pp. 132-5. Reprinted by permission.

IN RE DENNIS HILL V. THE SCHOOL TRUSTEES OF CAMDEN AND ZONE

DUCK obtained a rule nisi to shew cause why a writ of mandamus should not issue, to compel the defendants to admit to the common school of the school section No. 3, in the united townships of Camden and Zone, Francis and Rowland Hill, children of Dennis Hill.

Hill made affidavit that he is a negro, and an inhabitant and free-holder of the township of Camden, and liable to be assessed &c., and paying assessments; that he has continually resided in Camden for the last nineteen months, and still lives there with his family; that the children above named are his, Rowland being twelve years old, and Francis seven and upwards; that he lives with his children within school section No. 3, and has done so for nineteen months and "has applied" to the said trustees (naming them) for permission to have his children taught in the common school for the section, but that they have refused, and still refuse to permit either of his children to attend the said school; that on the 9th of April, 1853, he demanded of two of the three trustees (naming them) to allow his children to attend and be taught in the school, and that they then refused, though he took his children then with him to the said school for admission, and that the teacher also refused to teach or to receive the said children; that on the 17th of May, 1853, he demanded of the third trustee to permit his children to attend, and was refused; that all the trustees still persist in their refusal on account of his children being coloured or negro children; that there is no separate school for coloured children in the said section; and that the nearest school of that description is in sect. No. 12, distant four-and-a-half miles from his residence; that he has taken the oath of allegiance, and has been a resident in Upper Canada for the last eleven years.

This affidavit of Hill was confirmed in all material points by an affidavit of one George Carey.

In opposition to the application it was shewn, that since the 1st of January, 1852, there has been, and still is, a common school established and kept open at the British American Institute, in the Gore of Camden, in the united townships of Camden and Zone, for the exclusive benefit of the coloured population in the township of Camden, under a by-law passed by the municipal council of the gore of Camden on the 8th of February, 1850; and an affidavit was filed, made by the gentleman who was local superintendent of common schools for the united townships of Zone and Camden for 1850-1-2, to the effect that he received from the clerk of the council of the united townships a copy of the by-law passed for dividing the united townships into school sections; that early in 1850 he received the report of the chairman of the meeting convened to elect school trustees for the separate school sections, and stating who were the three trustees chosen; that he paid to their order the money apportioned to the school sections for 1851-2; and that, although he was not local superintendent for 1853, yet he had good reason to believe that a school was in operation for the said separate school sections for that year.

By the by-law passed on the 9th of February, 1850, dividing the township and gore of Camden into school sections (under the Act 12 Vic. chap. 83, then in force), it was provided as follows:—"And whereas according to the School Act 12 Vic. chap. 83, the establishment of separate schools for the education of the coloured population is authorized, be it enacted that one school for the education of the population of coloured persons in the said township and gore of Camden shall be, and the same is hereby established, and the site thereof directed to be fixed at or near the British American Institute in the said gore of Camden, and George Carey is hereby appointed and required to call the first school meeting of the coloured population of the said township and gore of Camden."

After this by-law was passed, the township and gore of Camden were united to the township of Zone, and all are now called the united townships of Camden and Zone; and it was sworn that school section No. 3, mentioned in this application, is the same school section No. 3 mentioned in the by-law as in the township and gore of Camden (being confined, however, to land in the gore).

It was stated in one of the affidavits that the deponent had no doubt that the establishment of the separate school in question was owing to the prejudice known by the council to exist among the white inhabitants against having their children attend in the same schools with the coloured children.

Read shewed cause.

ROBINSON, C. J., delivered the judgment of the court.

On examining the school acts, we have no doubt that it was intended by the Legislature, when they passed the statute 12 Vic. ch. 83, that if a separate school should be established for coloured people under the 69th, 70th and 71st clauses of that act, the children of people of colour residing within such section should be educated within such separate school. The reason recited for the enactment in the 69th clause leads strongly we think to that conclusion; and the provision in the 70th clause, respecting the paying over for the support of the teachers of such separate schools whatever amount of school rates may have been collected from coloured people, supports that construction. But in April, 1853, when Hill demanded to have his children admitted to the common school of school section No. 3 (within which section he resides) the statute 12 Vic. ch. 83 was no longer in force, though it was in force when the by-law was passed, and it was under the authority given by the ch. 83 that this separate school was established.

We must consider then whether any and what change had been made by the subsequent School Act 13 & 14 Vic. ch. 48, which was the law in force when the trustees refused, in April and May, 1853, to receive the children of Hill.

The first section of that act provides that the repeal of the former law—i.e., 12 Vic. ch. 83—shall not extend to "any act done" or any proceeding had under that law, and "that all school sections, or other school divisions, together with all elections and appointments to office, all agreements, contracts, assessments and rate bills, made under the authority of the said acts or of any preceding acts, and not annulled by the said acts or by this act, shall be valid and in full force, and binding upon all parties concerned, as if made under the authority of this act" (13 & 14 Vic. ch. 48), "and shall so continue until altered, modified, or suspended according to the provisions of this act."

It does not appear that since this act was passed anything has been done or enacted under it by the municipal council of the townships of Camden and Zone, or of Camden and Camden Gore, in relation to this separate school that had been already established; and the 19th clause of this statute, 13 & 14 Vic. ch. 48, is confined in its operation to such separate schools as might be established under that act, and does not affect separate schools that had been established under the former law of 12 Vic. ch. 83, and that were suffered, like this separate school, to continue without any special provision having been made under the new act respecting it.

But the 12th clause of this statute, 13 & 14 Vic. ch. 48, sub-sec. 13, has a strong bearing upon the question before us, for it provides that it "shall be the duty of the trustees of each school section to permit all residents in such section between the ages of five and twenty-one years to attend the school . . . provided always that this requirement shall not extend to the children of persons in whose behalf a separate school shall have been established according to the nineteenth section of that act." This shews that the Legislature did not intend at that time that separate schools should be resorted to or not, according to the choice of the persons in whose behalf they should be established, by which I understand not merely the applicants for the school, but those belonging to the class of persons in whose behalf the separate school had been established.

The last School Act, 16 Vic. ch. 185, being passed after the demand was made which gives rise to this application, can have no direct effect upon the question respecting the right of this applicant at the time of such demand, or at least not without express words giving it such operation; but we have referred to it to see whether it can assist in explaining what was probably intended by the former acts. It is the 4th clause of this last statute which relates to the subject of separate schools, and it seems to us that this clause relates only to separate schools established or intended to be established on account of a difference of religion. It makes no mention of separate schools for coloured people; but if it can be extended to them consistently with its language, still we do not see that it would affect the question now before us.

Upon a review of the several statutes, we are of opinion that the separate schools for coloured people were authorized, as the defendants have suggested, out of deference to the prejudices of the white population—prejudices which the Legislature evidently, from the language which they used, disapproved of and regretted, and which arise, perhaps, not so much from the mere fact of difference of colour, as from an apprehension that the children of the coloured people, many of whom have but lately escaped from a state of slavery, may be, in respect to morals and habits, unfortunately worse trained than the white children are in general, and that their children might suffer from the effects of bad example. It can hardly be supposed that the Legislature authorized such separate schools under the idea that it would be more beneficial or agreeable to the coloured people to have their children taught separately from the whites. They recite in the 69th clause that the ignorant prejudices of the whites had prevented the children of coloured parents being received in the common schools as the law stood; and in order that they might be educated, and without intending, as we think, to disregard and over-rule the objections of the whites, they provided that the municipal council of any township might in their discretion establish separate schools for the coloured population, and this too, it is material to remark without being moved to do so, as in the case of separate schools for Roman Catholics and Protestants by an application from the class of persons whose children were to be taught in such separate schools.

After the establishment of any such separate school in a division, we do not think a choice was intended by the Legislature to be left to the coloured people within that division to send their children nevertheless to the general common school, because that would defeat what we take to have been the intention of the provision, and it would besides have been inconsistent with the 70th clause of 12 Vic. ch. 83, which directed that the school rates raised upon the coloured population in any such division should go to the support of such separate school; and we think the 13th sub-sect. of the 12th section of 13 & 14 Vic. ch. 48 shews that the Legislature did not mean that it should be imperative on school trustees to receive in the general school for the division the children belonging to a class in whose behalf (or for whom) a separate school should have been established, nor do we see in any of the statutes an indication of a contrary intention.

We therefore abstain from issuing a mandamus, which can never be done in a doubtful case, and if it should be thought that we have misinterpreted the intention of the Legislature it will be easy so to modify the law in that respect as to make the point clear.

Rule discharged.

PLACES FOR GIRLS AND WOMEN

THE EDUCATION OF YOUNG LADIES

Address to Parents on the education of girls: by Mrs Holiwell, of 'Elm House' School for the Education of Young Ladies (Toronto, 1865).

The "Education of Girls" is a subject that in its various aspects resembles the mustard seed in the parable, a very small thing in tender youth, but far reaching, almost unlimited, in its mature influence. It would be difficult to point out the person, whether king or peasant, professional or mercantile, educated or ignorant, who is entirely free from female influence, through mother, wife, sister, or friend. We need not go to history to learn of kingdoms governed by women; society, we know by experience and observation, bends unresistingly to their sway, and we daily see numerous examples of feminine character and feminine will playing a conspicuous part in the domestic circle. When this subtle power is wielded by the virtuous and intelligent, it is a social reformer, it elevates and refines all within its reach; but unfortunately there are many sad proofs of this same fascination leading to ruin when exercised by the unprincipled and ignorant. We see parents who would be pious, led into amusements they look upon with distrust to please their daughters; we see men who would be honest and pay their debts, living far beyond their means to gratify their vain and pleasure-seeking families; we see girls who might be pure and intel-

lectual in their aspirations, following in the wake of a worldly minded mother, and frittering away time, the precious loan from God, in the most frivolous occupations. The beginning of evil in all these cases is in *education*. "Train up a child in the way he should go, and when he is old he will not depart from it."
... Education in its true sense, I take to be, that amount and direction of culture addressed to the intellect and heart which shall develop into fair proportions the finest talents and most generous impulses of the individual, which shall weed out evil inclinations and prune away rank luxuriance, which shall curb the extravagance of imagination and nurse into blossom the buds of native genius, and over all and through all impart, by God's assistance and blessing, that Christian spirit of love which is of greater price than any mere mental attainment. If such be a correct view of education, whence the contemptuous smile, almost a sneer, with which the mention of the subject is received with most people, as connected with a boarding school young lady? There must be something wrong; either its importance is not recognised, or there is an error in its practical application, for though a few ill-disposed persons may jest at what is good and worthy of reverence, we find that public opinion is mostly right; whatever is generally condemned needs careful examination at least, before it is accepted, and surely education as described above cannot be supposed to have much part in girls' schools usually, or why the almost universal distrust in its efficiency and results?

Having briefly noticed the significant bearing of female education on society and the world at large, I shall now proceed to examine more fully what is meant by the expression, as used by different classes of persons; then what it should mean; and lastly consider the best manner of applying our present improvements in the art of teaching to practical and beneficial use.

There are three distinct aims in educating a girl, varying according to the ability and aspirations of her parents—to render her useful, ornamental, or intellectual. To cultivate exclusively the useful or the intellectual is frequently the destiny of those who have to make their own way in the world; in such cases there is no attempt at perfection, no desire to combine those accomplishments and acquirements which are indispensable in forming the "Lady." Necessity is a hard master, often as cruel as the slave driver, and seldom vouchsafes leisure or opportunity for improvement in other walks than those prescribed by duty. I shall not dwell on these circumstances, they are foreign to my object just now, which is to treat of education as it presents itself to people in general, who entertain no particular views respecting their children beyond bringing them up in a style befitting their station in life. The ornamental is too often exclusively cultivated by those claiming the highest position in society, although types of the useful and intellectual woman are to be found among the most aristocratic circles.

Let us contemplate each of these characters, they are familiar to all, and each of them might be pronounced well educated by those who can grasp but one side of a subject or one view of a question.

Training up a girl to usefulness only has its failures as decided and fatal as the opposite course of educating only for show. Such a system recognizes no world, intellectually speaking, beyond the material one. Any instruction embracing the ornamental or intellectual, without direct reference to its utility, is regarded with jealousy, and thus the mind of the pupil is restricted to the humblest mental sphere. She must be a good arithmetician and disciplinarian, that will assist her in the practical duties of life, and will help her to economise money and time; she can thus keep accounts, shop advantageously, and will prove altogether a valuable machine in any household for saving or discreetly spending. The *menage* of a woman so reared is always a success, she can keep up appearances at less cost than other people, her servants and family are well regulated and orderly, and she has enough and to spare for charitable purposes, while her accomplished sister with the same means will be at her wits end to know how to supply the ordinary requirements of her household. We call such a person a good manager, and admire her domestic arrangements, but we do not often care to approach nearer. She is frequently arbitrary and narrow-minded, incapable of feeling an interest beyond her circumscribed world. She values her dumb possessions more than the enjoyment of her family, and abounds in luxuries too good for daily use, plate locked up and furniture and pictures too costly to gaze upon. This disposition has the art of distilling annoyance from every trifling domestic occurrence, and of spreading a cold unsympathetic atmosphere around, and although the inmates of the house are probably surrounded with more bodily comforts than others of their acquaintance, their enjoyment is marred from being reminded constantly of their cost and importance. The school-boy, ambitious of standing high in his class and of honorable distinction in his future career, values not his mother's admirable management for his health and comfort unless he can creep to her side in the twilight and whisper in her ear his youthful hopes and dreams, happy in her sympathy and faith. To be a model housekeeper is all very well, but is it the end and aim of an immortal spirit? Have we not minds to improve and pure tastes to cultivate? We meet with most amiable characters occasionally in this class, but even then intimate companionship can never be desired with minds limited to the daily cares and work and worries of life. We commend them, because they contrast favorably with the popular type of careless and extravagant women, and feel that their error is the safer, though an error still. However, in spite of all that can be said in disparagement of the exclusively useful as an end and object in education, we must hope that the style will not become quite extinct until a revolution takes place among its rivals, else I fear we shall be bankrupt in common sense, comfort and decency; for we can scarcely expect the fashionable *belle* and the blue-stocking to devote their superior minds to vulgar wants; and with many shortcomings, as congenial companions and friends, we must acknowledge that the thoroughly domestic woman is, after all, a blessing in her immediate sphere.

Many prize unduly manners and accomplishments—to bow gracefully, to enter a room with dignity, to dance well, to play and sing sufficiently to please the ordinary taste, to sketch or paint a little, to be skilful in fancy needlework, these are the ends and objects of some persons. Girls so reared are mere butterflies in prosperity, while adversity crushes them entirely. In cultivating accomplishments in the way young ladies are accustomed to do, there is no mental discipline or hard toil; and when trouble and anxiety come, as come they surely do in all lives, there is neither strength for the encounter, fortitude to bear, or intelligence to strike out a new path. Under such a training the intellect withers, absolutely withers; every subject is approached with frivolity and viewed on the surface only; and the most superficial criticisms are passed on men and women of the noblest aims and finest talents, if they fall short of the poor standard acknowledged by these shallow minds. I have endeavoured to show that the merely useful woman often proved a comfortless companion by the fire-side, but she is preferable to the frivolous one. The latter cannot manage her house or govern her children; she is treated as a child by her relations, because she is not fit for anything better; she cannot share the reflections of sensible people; her servants rule over her, and her children are openly rebellious; she may be spoiled and petted while young and pretty, but she will never feel herself an equal with father, husband, or brother; they may lavish gifts upon her and call her endearing names, but when care and thought sit on their brow, they will not seek her sympathy nor ask her counsel. Now, I consider confidence a higher compliment than presents or attentions. We make presents or pay attentions out of policy to indifferent persons, but our confidence is sacred to those whom we trust.

We have now only to consider that system which advocates the culture of the intellect to the neglect of the accomplishments. This course is pursued sometimes by fathers when left in charge of their daughters' education, through domestic bereavement. Annoyed at the want of cultivation and the frivolity of many of their lady friends, they resolve on a different result for their children, and certainly achieve it, though, perhaps, there is not much choice between them. I rather think no mistake in a girl's education has elicited more ridicule and condemnation than this; it is possible there may be a little jealousy in the matter. However, we know that in ordinary society a young lady, if pretty and lively, will receive admiration of some sort, even if she is severely criticised for her other deficiencies. But a young lady who can see the beautiful only in art and literature, and neglects it in her dress and her house; who can solve a mathematical problem easier than direct her cook's operations, and uses her needle more awkwardly than her pen, may make up her mind to be unappreciated and unpopular. I can fancy nothing more desolate than a home presided over by an unwomanly woman, nor anything more grating to a refined taste than contending for the mastery with man. Unless a woman is prepared to renounce every graceful feminine attribute, she assumes to be greatly man's superior, when she asserts herself capable of doing all he can do in the field of learning. Can she so entirely shake off the duties and renounce the pleasures of her position as mother, daughter, &c., as to place herself in an equally advantageous position as he? Possibly if she had the same rearing from the cradle she might compete successfully, though what benefit would be derived from such a course I am at a loss to know. Rivalry, then, where victory is denied, appears foolish and impolitic, and although a fine intellect adorns a woman in the eyes of all noble minded men, still it must not be cultivated to the prejudice of those graceful tastes and useful acquirements without which a lady loses her fascinations, and forfeits her natural and proper place in the social circle.

I think it will be agreed that a training, producing either of these types, would, to an enlightened and liberal mind, be inefficient and one sided. Yet we have here all the elements of a good education. The useful, the beautiful, and the intellectual. The error is in separating them; to render them valuable they must be combined, but what a task is this? . . . [I]f a woman is only useful, or ornamental, or intellectual, she must fail in playing a successful part in the drama of life; she is expected to live three existences; she must excel in household management, adorn the social circle and be capable of discussing the affairs of the nation, the tendencies of a new book, or listen intelligently to a political controversy, or a treatise on the midge. She must make an apt remark at the right place, or her companion will think her stupid, while at the same time she is manipulating a difficult piece of sewing, or perhaps speculating on the result of a new method of cooking oysters. This is a homely illustration of what is expected of a well bred and well educated lady, and yet this is the gigantic undertaking. No wonder then there are so many failures, no wonder that the becomingly dressed graceful girl often annoys and disappoints us with her silliness; the sensible well-read woman disgusts us with her ill arranged household and neglected children and the model house-keeper drives us away from her hearth by her sharp temper and twaddle about servants and management. Pause, ye who sit in condemnation, it is no trifle to do more than one thing well; is not society unjust in demanding so much from a young girl, and making so few provisions for educating her? . . .

Before we consider what education should be to form the "perfect lady," let me suggest a few ideas on the true meaning of the much abused word. I regard it as one of comprehensive signification; deficiency in one department is as detrimental to a claimant for the title as exclusive excellence in another. Should we see a person ignorant of the common usages of polite society, we should condemn her at once as unladylike, and justly; but would the individual who could pay and receive visits without any breaches of good manners be more entitled to the name if she occasionally tripped in her grammar and was incapable of making a single intellectual remark on the topics or questions of the day? The old proverb says, "Manners make the man," and the present age seems inclined to apply this in its most restricted sense to woman; yet, logically, the assertion will not stand. . . . To be a Lady, then, implies something more than the attainment of certain manners; there must be a higher standard than that of ordinary society; there must be the standard of the highly cultivated and the highly moral, as well as of the highly polished; and when education aims at meeting these requirements, and not till then, it has the right goal in view.

We are now somewhat prepared to answer the enquiry—What is expected from a young girl to render her a Lady, in the most comprehensive and proper sense of the term?

First, then, a fair acquaintance with the various departments and branches of knowledge, as combined in a thorough course of study.

Second,—Respectable attainments in the several accomplishments, or at least excellence in some.

Third,—An intimate knowledge of the requirements and usages of good society, and such refinement of manners as can be acquired only by mixing freely in it.

Fourth,—Such a knowlege of the practical duties of life as will enable her, when arrived at a proper age, to undertake with confidence and discharge with success the responsibilities of the household and the family

The two first qualifications are particularly the work of teachers and schools; the foundation of the third must be laid at the same time, but differs from the others, inasmuch as home co-operation is *indispensable*. Gentleness and refinement must prevail in the domestic circle, or school discipline and example are quickly forgotten. This department must be perfected, and the fourth entered upon, when the time comes for the usual routine of study to be dispensed with.

By the first qualification, I mean so much familiarity with History and Geography, Ancient and Modern, that she will readily understand most historical allusions, and the connexion of the present age in its politics and philosophy with the past, and I would have her acquire such a method of studying these subjects as would make it easy at any time to take up a particular history of a particular period or country, and master it with the least waste of time. Also such a knowledge of her own language that her correspondence may be correct and elegant; her diary, memorandum book, and album mirrors that reveal an educated mind. I would have her Arithmetic comprehensive, that in business transactions she could control results, and not feel herself at the mercy of the shopkeeper and the workman, as is often the case. I would add to these attainments, an acquaintance with the Sciences and Literature, that she may not look with an ignorant eye on the wonders of that world of which she forms a part, and when thrown among the learned and scientific she may follow the conversation with pleasure, even when forbidden to assist.

By the second:—A good knowledge of the Theory and Practice of Music, and such cultivation of the voice as the individual talent will permit. My own taste would lead me to desire no other accomplishment, if the musical talent were really superior, and very highly cultivated; should it, however, be only moderate, it would be as well to add Drawing or Painting, or both; and if musical taste were altogether wanting, I would prefer that a pupil devote herself altogether to Drawing, as the time spent over the Piano will be only wasted. The Modern Languages should never be neglected in a thorough course of education. French has a particular claim on us as Canadians, with half of our fellow-subjects speaking that tongue, and Italian and German might be added advantageously, especially if the young pupil showed no preference for art.

Dancing, and various kinds of Needle Work, are easily attainable by all, and should rather be looked upon as amusements, than matters requiring serious application.

The foundation of the third department of education should begin from the cradle, and depends more strictly on moral training than anything else. A perfect control of temper, a consideration for the feelings of others, respect for age and virtue, a modest estimate of self—these are the attributes of the true lady, and must be taught from infancy. The usages of the polite world—an easy and graceful demeanor—are readily gained by intercourse with good society, when the basis is constructed on Christian principles and Christian love. Without this, polish is a spurious coinage, detected from the genuine ore at a glance by those whose admiration and praise are an honor.

The fourth branch is altogether the mother's department, and should be entered upon as soon as the school routine is completed. Among the wealthy aristocracy of the European world, this branch of education might be dispensed with, without ill effect; but in this favored country, where few are so rich as not to be the happier and the better for excellence in domestic management, it should form an important part of a girl's training. Should the blind goddess lavish her favors on her, then will her efficiency in housekeeping add a charm to her *menage*, that wealth merely could not give; and money that would be ignorantly spent, without benefit to any one, would, under her administration, supply food for the hungry and clothes to the naked. If, on the contrary, comparative poverty should be her lot, what a jewel in her matron's crown would be economy! We need no magnifying glass to see the evils around us of bad management and extravagant housekeeping; families that might be respected are brought to beggary through it, and men that ought to enjoy competency and freedom from care are bowed down with the burden of supporting ill-ordered and spendthrift households. Mothers sometimes retain too tenaciously the reins of domestic government; if they would devolve some of their duties on their grown-up daughters, it would prove beneficial to both. A few errors must be overlooked at first; a few failures in marketing, a foolish investment now and then in shopping, must be expected, and cheerfully endured; but a little practice soon enables the tyro to choose and purchase with almost the success of her elders, while her mother has the happy consciousness that when the time comes for them to part, it is not as an inexperienced child she sends her away to learn her lesson in bitterness and alone, but hopeful and confident of the future.

It now remains for us to enquire what are the best means within our reach of providing this education for our daughters. Many persons, who estimate education highly, entertain a deep-rooted distrust, if not an aversion to schools. Much could be said on both sides of the question; and arguments in favour of home training, or school discipline, can be furnished in abundance by the advocates for either system: theoretically, I think, perhaps the admirers of home education have the best of it; but I believe the discipline of schools to have been crowned with the most practical success.

It is a beautiful picture that of a young girl reared in the pure atmosphere of the domestic circle, accustomed to live in the sunshine of parental love; to hear nothing but the refined conversation of her mother's select society, no reproof severer than *her* gentle admonitions, no word or sentiment but approved by her anxious censorship. With an amiable disposition, fair talents, and intellectual and refined parents, one can imagine a young girl bred up to womanhood in artless ignorance of all that is wicked and deceitful in the world, a charming study for those who are versed in its wiles, a creature to love and cherish, to watch and guide. . . . [But] the maiden that has never had an opportunity of comparing her mental and moral qualifications with those of others, is sure to enter life with false views, is likely to mistake specious vice for genuine virtue, and could never detect the gloss of superficial elegance from real worth. It might be asked, "How is this experience to be gained at school?" I would answer, that wisdom consists very much in forming a proper estimate of self, considered both absolutely and relatively, and in the power of applying that knowledge with discrimination to the various positions in which we may be placed; and that a school, from its very constitution, its numbers, and mixed character, affords a better opportunity for attaining the necessary information than the retirement of home. She can there compare her mental powers and standing with others of her age; she discovers her moral shortcomings; she cannot help finding out that she is peevish or passionate, and that the respect and love of her schoolfellows depend on overcoming her failings. In spite of the foolishness of youth, she will see that the popular and best liked are the truthful and independent; and if a high moral tone pervades the establishment, there will be the pressure of public opinion on a small scale which will work very beneficially on the character of the children. There is an atmosphere of impartiality about a school that is almost unattainable at home, which is admirably adapted to dissipate any false impression of superiority: . . . There is no doubt that submission and discipline might be taught at home, as well as at school; but are they, generally? It is good for a child to be so many hours of a day under control; she learns to govern her temper, and be forbearing; she has not the same inducements to idleness and disobedience, for all are busy and all obey; and youth cannot help moulding itself on the model offered for imitation. Now, this training is not to be arrived at in private tuition. . . . A child reared altogether under the paternal roof is somewhat similarly situated to a young Prince, in danger of never hearing the truth; it is the interest of those surrounding her to keep her self-satisfied; she is quite aware that her relations have a high opinion of her capacity and progress, she feels that she is an object of anxiety to her family: her efforts are magnified, her talents praised, and every step appreciated. The result of such a course must be disappointment.

So much in favor of schools. But school teaching often proves a miserable failure. Granted that the system of study is admirable, what is the cause of this failure? One of the most obvious reasons is the late age at which children are sent to school. They form low tastes, for dress and exciting amusements for instance; and not unfrequently, except in well regulated families, become disobedient as a rule, unless obedience is pleasing. After a while, at ten, twelve, thirteen, or even later, as the case may be, one parent, perhaps both, become aware that their little girl, who is the object of their tenderest affection, is growing up unmanageable and ignorant, and she is sent to school without one hour's preparatory discipline. Dislike for study is the consequence, and before the pupil's mind has had a chance of development, her age leads her into society more or less, and all hope of efficiently doing the work is over. This custom of permitting children to share the amusements of their elders, which is growing upon us daily no doubt from our proximity to the Americans, where girls have their beaux and boys their cigars when they should be in pinafores playing with dolls and kites, is obnoxious both to health and education. The aim of many young people, and of their parents for them, is to shine in society; and if they find they can attain their end, without further trouble and toil, why should they study? Various extraneous circumstances may give them temporary success in the social sphere—the position of their parents, their personal charms, the fascination of youth—and they naturally conclude they ought to be satisfied with themselves, since the world seems to smile so approvingly on them. . . . Thus, this early introduction into society deprives the young girl of a powerful incentive to study. How can any one be expected to pursue geography, history, and French with zeal, when the mind is occupied with the pleasures of the previous evening's entertainment, or the prospect of a future one? . . .

When we remember at how early an age many young women of the highest rank in Canadian society begin the serious duties of life, and that at twelve or thirteen they were ignorant of even the rudimentary branches of learning, should we be surprised at any want of culture or lack of information in young people so reared, or rebel at the contempt in which men in general hold the feminine mind, as it too often presents itself, after the usual fashionable routine of education has been completed. . . .

THE OFFICIAL OBJECTION TO GIRLS IN GRAMMAR SCHOOLS

Report of the Grammar School Inspector for 1865 [George Paxton Young]. *Documentary History of Education,* Vol. XIX, 96-8.

When the Bill, recently passed, was before Parliament, a cry was raised in favour of admitting non-classical Pupils to the Grammar Schools. To meet the views of those who did not wish to make the Grammar Schools purely classical Institutions, Girls have been allowed to take French, without Latin; and a Course of Study, extending over two years, has been provided for those Boys who, having already obtained such an English education as may be got in good Common Schools, desire to pursue the study of the higher English branches with French and Mathematics. From the first I was satisfied that there was no real demand in the Province for such a Course of Study as this Curriculum for Boys, and the event has proved the correctness of my opinion. In the Grammar Schools,—more than 80 in number,—in which, since the passing of the new Law, I have examined Pupils with a view to their admission according to the Regulations of the Council of Public Instruction, seven Boys in all have come forward to be examined for the course of higher English, French and Mathematics; and of these only three have passed the prescribed Entrance Examination.

I have been frequently asked whether I considered it desirable that Girls should study Latin in the Grammar Schools. It is, in my opinion, most undesirable; and I am at a loss to comprehend how any intelligent person, acquainted with the state of things in our Grammar Schools, can come to different conclusion. Those who advocate the study of Latin by Girls in the Grammar Schools, rest their case on the argument that, by the testimony of the most competent Judges, nothing is so fitting to develop fully the minds of Boys as classical study, and that the training which is best for developing the faculties of Boys must be best for developing the faculties of Girls. But this reasoning is plausible rather than solid. There is a very considerable diversity between the mind of a Girl and that of a boy; and it would be rash to conclude that, as a matter of course, the appliances which are best adapted for bringing the faculties of reflection and taste to their perfection in the one must be the best also in the case of the other. I do not doubt the capacity of Girls to learn Latin and Greek; nor do I doubt that if they did learn these languages, the exercises would be beneficial. But I am not sure that, for the proper development of their minds, a different Course of Study might not be preferable. The question, however, in this general form, is a difficult one; and for what I have in view at present it is not necessary that I should enter into the discussion of it. I look at the subject in the particular aspect in which it presents itself in our Canadian Grammar Schools. What we have to do with, practically, is the special enquiry: Is the study of classics, as pursued by the Girls attending our Grammar Schools, the best training which could be given them, in the time which they are able to devote to education? It seems to me that this question must be answered decidedly in the negative. The grand advantages of classical study are, first, the thorough insight which it affords into Languages generally, and into the modes of our thinking, as exemplified in Language; secondly, the special light which it sheds on the formation of the English and other modern languages; and thirdly, the cultivation of the taste. Now, as far as the last of these benefits is concerned, classical study, as pursued in our Grammar Schools, is of no advantage to Girls whatever. Since I became Inspector I have not met with half a dozen Girls in the Grammar Schools of Canada,—I cannot at present recall more than three,—by whom the study of Latin has been pursued far enough for the taste to be in the least degree influenced by what has been read. Aesthetically, the benefits of Grammar Schools to Girls are *nil*. With respect to the two other advantages of classical study which have been named, the same remark applies, to a very great extent. The mass of the Girls learning Latin in the Grammar Schools have scarcely the beginning of a perception of the relation between the Latin Language and their own Mother Tongue; and all the insight which they have obtained from their classical studies into the modes of our thinking, as exhibited in language, could have been equally well got from the English. It may, perhaps, be said that, although they have, for the most part, made but little progress in Latin up to the present time, a fair proportion of them may be expected to pursue the study to a point where its advantages can be reaped. I do not believe that three out of a hundred will. As a class, they have dipped the soles of their feet in the water, with no intention or likelihood, of wading deeper into it. They are not studying Latin with any definite object. They have taken it up under pressure, at the solicitation of the Teachers, or Trustees, to enable the Schools to maintain the requisite average attendance of ten classical Pupils, or to increase that part of the income of the Schools which is derived from Public Sources. In a short time they will leave School to enter on the practical work of life, without having either desired, or obtained, more than the merest smattering of Latin, and their places will be taken by another band of Girls who will go through the same routine. It may, perhaps, be urged that these remarks are as applicable to as large a number of the Grammar School Boys, as they are to the Girls. I admit that they are; and I draw the conclusion that such Boys, equally with the Girls in the Grammar Schools, are wasting their time, in keeping up the appearance of learning Latin. It would be unspeakably better to commit them to First Class Common School Teachers, under whose guidance they might have their reflective and aesthetic faculties cultivated through the study of English, and of those branches which are associated with English, in good Common Schools. This would, of course, diminish the number of the Grammar Schools in the Province; but that might not be a very grievous calamity,— especially if it led to the establishment of first class Common Schools in localities where inferior Teachers are now employed.

As far as I can see, no evil arises from having little Girls and little Boys taught in School together. But in many of our Canadian Grammar Schools, Girls of 15, 16, or 17 years of age are associated with Boys of the same ages. This feature in the Grammar School System has been often strongly objected to,—apart altogether from the questions, whether the studies most proper for grown up Girls are the same as those which are most proper for grown up Boys,—on the ground of its moral tendency. I think it right to state the impressions in regard to this subject, which have been left on my mind by what I have had an opportunity of observing.

In Schools conducted by Teachers possessing weight of character, I have no reason to believe that the general moral tone of the Pupils is injuriously affected by Boys and Girls being taught together. Perhaps, on the contrary, the result is beneficial. Schools of the kind described, partake somewhat of the character of families, or of well regulated social circles, within which the free intercourse of young persons of different sexes with one another is universally admitted to be salutary.

But out of a hundred Grammar School Teachers, there will necessarily be a few who do not possess weight of character; and, under their rule, there is a danger of grown up Girls suffering as respects the formation of their moral character, from attending School along with grown up Boys. In the rough sports of Boys, where not the slightest impropriety is intended, Girls are liable to be subjected to a familiarity of treatment, which is apt insensibly to blunt their instinctive feelings of delicate reserve. I remember one instance, in which, on entering the School unexpectedly, during the interval of recess, when the Teacher was not present, I saw some big Boys chasing, and even dragging, big Girls, about the Room, in simple innocent amusement, no doubt, but still in a manner which, probably the Parents of the Girls would not have been delighted to behold. And a far more serious thing is, that, under Teachers who are without due weight of character, Girls who may have enjoyed no domestic advantages and who do not understand the beauty of a "meek and quiet spirit," are in danger of being drawn, by the feeling that they are playing their part in the presence of Boys, into an unfeminine rudeness of behaviour towards their Teacher. To the credit of our Schools, I will say, that I found that this evil, manifesting itself in an extreme degree was observed in only a single instance, but shades of it appeared elsewhere. In the instance to which I refer, a class of Girls, about 14, or 15 years of age, when questioned by their Teacher, answered him with an undisguised carelessness, amounting to contempt. They were ignorant of their Lessons, but seemed to assume that they were young Ladies, he had no right to presume to be displeased with them; they were pert and bold. It may perhaps be said that this offensive vulgarity had not any connection with the presence of Boys in the School, but was a result simply of the incompetency of the Master, and of the absence of proper domestic training at home; but I am of a different opinion. A Girl, who is destitute of refinement of nature, more readily becomes insolent, or sullen, at having her self-love wounded in the presence of Boys, than she would if surrounded merely by Companions of her own sex. And, at any rate, the important practical point remains, that when a Girl does so far forget herself as to be disrespectful to a Teacher, this is a vastly greater evil in its permanent effects on her character, when the fault is committed before Boys, than it would be under other circumstances.

AN APPEAL TO REASON AND AMERICAN PRECEDENCE

Globe (Toronto), July 6, 1867.

HIGHER FEMALE EDUCATION

In a former article we drew attention to the peculiar views advocated, and now to a considerable extent carried into practice, by an influential body of American educationists, in reference to female education, and contrasted those with the results of the Rev. Inspector Young's experience of the results of combining young men and women in the same classes, in our Canadian Grammar Schools. The first question now practically claiming our consideration is this: —shall the well organized machinery already matured in our provincial system of University Colleges, and Grammar Schools, and supplemented by denominational and other collegiate institutions, for the education of boys, be rendered available for girls, and, as they advance in years, be made equally accessible for completing the education of young men and women?

If we are compelled to answer this in the negative the practical question will then remain: What other plan do we propose for higher female education, if we are not prepared to claim a masculine monopoly in all such intellectual privileges?

The more advanced school of American educationists strongly advocates "the system of mixed classes," as it is called, where boys and girls attend the same school, and young men and women the same colleges, not only in the Faculty of Arts, but in those of Law, Medicine, and even Theology. We may content ourselves, however, for the present, with the Arts course. Happily, our young Dominion is not yet ripe for throwing open the Bench and the Bar, the Pulpit, the Moderators, and the Episcopal chair, to the gentler sex, however well our fair Portias might become the Doctor's gown, or even the Episcopal silks and lawn.

"Within the last year," says the most recent advocate of mixed classes, for the United States, "I have visited the most conspicuous colleges in this country in which women are taught with men. I consider the system of mixed classes an immense advantage, as it secures the standard of scholarship, prevents all foolish hazing (i.e., practical jokes) and places personal character and moral deportment in their right relations to classical study. It prevents, also, such instruction in the classics as must necessarily deprave the estimate of women." Here the American educationalist starts with the assumption that the classical education is as necessary and as useful for women as men; as indeed follows from the prior assumption that the Pulpit, the Bar, Medicine, Surgery, &c., should be open to all, without distinction of sex. The Rev. Inspector Young, however, not having respect, we fear to such feminine aspirations, expresses a very different opinion. . . .

Accordingly, the latest action of our educational authorities has tended to shut the door of the grammar schools against girls. A recent opinion given by the Deputy Superintendent, followed by the action of the School Trustees, has practically excluded them from the Hamilton School.

Referring to our Provincial Grammar Schools, the Editor of the *Educational Journal* says:—

"It is the received opinion of all educationists—with very few exceptions—that however expedient it may be that children of both sexes should be associated together, while very young, in the study of the mere elementary branches, it is better, on various grounds, that their more advanced education should be conducted separately. The plan on which all private educational efforts for the higher branches are conducted, shows this to be the feeling of the community, and the experience of competent judges cannot in this matter be ignored. Nor should the public schools, which have been endowed by the forethought and patriotism of former sovereigns and statesmen, be allowed to suffer in consequence of neglect in adopting sound principles in their management."

While agreeing in the main with our contemporary, it must be admitted that his opening remark puts the case a little too strongly, when it is remembered that in the State of Ohio alone there are nine colleges for educating students of both sexes together. In Michigan, there are four:—one of them Hillside College with 609 pupils; another, Olivet College, with 308. Wisconsin has two such colleges; Indiana and Kentucky one each; Iowa two; and Kansas three. Oberlin, the parent of all these mixed colleges, now numbers eleven hundred and forty-five students of both sexes; . . .

It is thus apparent that the tendency of opinion in the newer States appears strongly to favour "the system of mixed classes." But the older states are not unaffected by it. Some of its keenest advocates are to be found among the "strong-minded women" of New England; while even New York has its Genesee and Elmira Colleges on the same footing. But if we are, for the most part, of one mind in Canada, as to the undesireableness of subjecting our daughters to the boisterous roughness and unsuitable rivalry of the boys' grammar school, and are still less likely to claim for them the right of mingling in the classes of University or Trinity College, we may still ask if "the forethought and patriotism of former sovereigns and statesmen" took no account of female education.

The need of some adequate provision for the higher education of girls, is pressing on us in many ways. Hamilton, already, has its Wesleyan Female College; Toronto has its scheme in progress for a Episcopal Institution, . . . if High and Low Churchmen can be got to agree on the details; while the want of some adequate economical provision for female education is complained of as the reason why many Protestant young ladies are now sent to complete their education at the nunneries of Toronto, as well as to those of Montreal and Quebec. But little more seems to be needed to supply this educational defect than an unanimity of purpose, and some adequate expression of public opinion . . .

It is not to be overlooked, in any comparison between the American educational system and our own, that an exclusive spirit of class and cast exists here, which is nearly unknown in the States. . . . It would lead to no good result to discuss the wisdom of such exclusiveness. The fact is indisputable, and cannot be overlooked in the estimate of any scheme for establishing Provincial higher schools for girls, as the feeling would operate even more strongly in their case; and thus the increased school-tax might prove an additional burden instead of help to many suffering already from the cost of educating their daughters. . . .

Among ourselves the common schools, in cities, are indisputably confined to the children of the industrious mechanic and tradesmen; exclusive, on the one hand, of the wealthier merchant and professional man, and, unfortunately, on the other hand to some degree, of the children of the poor and vagrant classes, who stand most in need of free education they supply. . . . An idea has been put forth in various forms for some years, of creating a Central High School, as an integral part of our present Common School system, in its application to large cities. . . . But to this must be added a distinct Central High School for girls, provided with an adequate staff of teachers, and guarded by a systematic matriculation examination of so severe a character that admission to it would be felt to be an honourable distinction. . . .

But the question still remains; can or should nothing be done to afford to our young women the same advantages which young men already enjoy in the University of Toronto and other kindred institutions? We confess, we see little difficulty in the way of accomplishing much, even with the machinery now in hand. As to placing young ladies in the same classes with the young men of our colleges, we shall propose to do so, when we see them joining the same boating and cricket clubs, asking admission to the military school, and enlisting in the university rifle corps. But is there anything unbecoming or really unacademic in the idea that our University College staff of professors should be called upon to deliver distinct courses of lectures especially and exclusively designed for classes of ladies; and that, following the example already set by Oxford and Cambridge, they should institute competitive examinations with prizes and certificates of honour? At the last competitive examination of the University of Cambridge, 118 passed the junior examination and 83 the senior one; and the effect of those examinations on the general system of the English education has been spoken of in many quarters in the strong terms of commendation. The machinery already exists among us in full force for effecting the same ends; and nothing is wanted to secure for the intelligent and studiously inclined, among the fair and gentle sex, intellectual advantages, such as the members of many communities of the old country might envy, than a clear expression of public opinion in its favour, and a readiness among the educated young ladies of our city and Province to avail themselves of the advantages when once placed in their reach.

HIGHER EDUCATION FOR WOMEN IN THE MARITIMES

'Educational Advantages for Girls in the Maritime Provinces', *The Educational Review*, I (New Brunswick, June, 1887), pp. 16-17.

In view of the great progress that has been made during the last few years in the matter of education for women, it is important to inquire what position is taken in this regard by the educational institutions of the Maritime Provinces.

The question of the higher education of women is no longer a disputed one, and the last half century has witnessed a great awakening both on the part of women themselves, and the foremost educators of our time, as regards the capabilities and needs of women in the matter of education. . . .

Victor Hugo has said that the "nineteenth century is woman's century," and, since education is the essential basis of all true progress, there is every reason to be assured that this prophecy is being fulfilled.

Upon inquiry into the attitude of the various institutions of learning in Nova Scotia, New Brunswick, and Prince Edward Island, with regard to this question, it is gratifying to find that these Provinces are no whit behind the leading nations of the world in recognizing the claim of women to full educational advantages, and in almost all the colleges and universities of these Provinces there exists no distinction on account of sex.

Dalhousie College, in Halifax, has for five years admitted ladies on exactly the same footing as male students, and of the five ladies who have been graduated there every one came off with honors, three winning the degree of B.A., one that of B.Sc., and one that of B.L. But beside these there have been about one hundred ladies who have taken special courses not leading to degrees. And in examinations in mathematics, philosophy, logic, political economy, history, English literature, and modern languages, the ladies have been first, and many of them are now to be found holding fellowships in the halls of learning in the neighboring Republic, while others are leaders in the didactic profession in these Provinces and in missionary lands. Beside those winning degrees, Miss Ritchie won distinction in philosophy, and Miss Stewart in mathematics.

There will be still further opportunities for collegiate training for young women afforded by the Ladies' College, of Halifax, which will be opened in September by the Presbyterian denomination. Connected with this college there will also be a preparatory department for students not far enough advanced to enter upon the collegiate course.

Pictou Academy is also co-educational, and furnishes an excellent curriculum extending over a four years' course.

Numbers of young ladies have been graduated from Acadia College, at Wolfville, which furnishes a fine preparatory department in the Acadia Seminary.

New Brunswick also offers the best advantages to women, both at Sackville and at the University of New Brunswick. Superior opportunities of education have always been afforded by Sackville College, which from its foundation has been open to ladies, and there have been numerous instances in which they have been graduated with honors. The first lady graduate in the Maritime Provinces was Miss Stewart, who claims Sackville as her *alma mater*; and Miss Narraway, of the same college, who graduated a few years ago, came off with high honors, being first in the graduating class. Miss Narraway also took the Grammar School License, and received the Lansdowne Medal, and, though still quite young, is filling the position of Chief Preceptress in the Wesleyan College, at St. John's, Newfoundland.

In the case of the University of New Brunswick it is, of course, too soon to pronounce judgment, as it has been so recently opened to women. The young lady who matriculated last year entered third in the class and is making good progress. In Fredericton there is a collegiate school, preparatory to the University, but in St. John such a school is not necessary, since the Young Ladies' High School offers sufficient training for entering University. The fact was demonstrated a year ago when nine young ladies, who had been instructed in the St. John High School, passed successfully the matriculation examination, though without any direct intention of entering the University.

These students had not undergone special training for the matriculation examination. They were not selected pupils, but were taken as an entire class to test the character of the work done in the higher schools. The result was entirely reassuring on that ground, and reflects great credit both upon the school system and upon the teachers in those grades.

Prince of Wales College, in Prince Edward Island, is also open to women, and the names of sixty-six ladies are on the list of students for last year, and very favorable reports are given of the character of the work done.

In view of all these facts it is certainly no fault of the powers that be if the girls of the Maritime Provinces do not show a great advancement in education in the future. There are now no hindrances to their progress, and it only remains for parents to direct their daughters in the pursuit of knowledge and encourage them to take advantage of their opportunities. There is no longer any need for parents to send their daughters from home to be educated. Our own institutions offer as good advantages as can be found elsewhere, and our own people should show their appreciation of these advantages by encouraging their children to remain at home and patronize our own schools and colleges.

When it is more generally acknowledged that education and enlarged interests can alone render girls less frivolous, we shall see greater numbers devoting their time to those studies and pursuits which have this influence; we shall see more of them in all our schools and colleges, and there will cease to exist any prejudice against the higher education of women.

St. John, N.B.   F.

FEMALE TEACHING IN NOVA SCOTIA

'Female Teaching', in Alexander Forrester, *The Teacher's Textbook* (Halifax, 1867).

Formerly, female teaching was confined to private families, or private schools, or matrons' village schools, but now it very generally prevails both in the Old and New World, especially in the more juvenile or primary departments. It is unnecessary here to refer to the prejudices that exist in the minds of some, and especially of those reared in Scotland, against female teaching. It is more to our purpose that we say a word or two in reference to the qualifications and position of female teachers. We do not here touch the controverted point, whether the mental energies of the female mind will, as a whole, suffer comparison with those of the male. It is sufficient for us to know that, both by the law of nature and revelation, there is a position of subordination and of dependence assigned to the former, and hence there may, and there ought to be, situations in educational establishments better adapted to the one sex than the other; and, accordingly, it is generally admitted, that the infant and primary departments are best fitted for the female, whilst the head masterships, and the more advanced sections, are for the male. This does not, and ought not to impose any restraint on the studies of the former, whether literary or professional. On the contrary, they ought to receive every possible encouragement to prosecute their studies and professional attainments with unabated ardor, seeing that the perfection of teaching is simplicity, and that the most profound erudition, and the most dexterous skill are required to make the most common things plain. Neither will this general rule put any impediment in the way of individual exceptions, for higher positions to be acknowledged either in the one case or other. The advice given by Stowe is, like himself, sound and solid, —"Let each sex copy the excellencies of the other, the female teacher, the firmness of the male, and the latter, the affection, kindness and entreaties of the former," and this will produce the best teaching.

'Female Teaching', *The Journal of Education for the Province of Nova Scotia*, 36, (April 1871).

There is a disposition to undervalue female teaching. To get a male teacher is a first consideration; if this cannot be, if the people are poor and humble, and if the trials that arise from such causes are to be endured, then only the people can think of a female teacher. Have the friends of right, and the keen discrimination of providential arrangements, considered these conclusions? What place does the women occupy in the family? Who does not know that in the most important institution in the world, Home, woman's mind is the governing power? Who does not know that all minds receive the first training, the first direction, the first noble, generous pulsation of future ambition, under the moulding and elevating authority of the female? Take from our homes this female training; take from society, generally, this element, and what are our homes, of what our country? There is a part of the great system of instruction in which woman towers immensely above man. The teacher's office is specially suited to women—who are natural educators. The question is often asked, Why this disparity in the number of the sexes who teach? The answer is obvious. Females in far larger proportions are suited to the work, and men, from a consciousness of their adaptation to the work they have assumed—not chosen—quit the profession for something more genial. The disparity between the salaries of male and female teachers, must often arrest the attention of thinking persons. When it is stated that, for the same labor, females receive less pay, though that labor may be as well, if not better performed, we are compelled to feel that an aspersion is cast upon our sex, from which our past history and present influence ought to save us, and if it has any meaning at all, is a sad commentary upon the Chivalry and gallantry of our countrymen.

Much of the work that is done in our school-rooms, is done better by women, simply because, from the constitution given by the All-wise Creator, she is better adapted to do it, and it would be well for the school system of our land, if the field of female labor, as teachers, were enlarged. I am quite sure that many of our County Academies and Superior Schools would receive a new and upward impulse if some of our active, energetic female teachers were placed over them. In other places, experiments in this direction have been made with eminent satisfaction. But, in any case, I contend that when the same work is done by females, and done well, they should have the same pay —anything short of this is unfair and unjust, for in the influence woman has exercised, she has assuredly won for herself this consideration. Her supremacy as teacher in the United States is felt and confessed in every State. It is growing in the parent country, and in this our native Province it is so apparent that we may justly draw the notice of the Government to the fact above stated, and inquire why, when we do the same work, and do it well, we should not receive the same generous consideration for our toil and influence in the great educational field.

These reflections have long been in my mind, and I had hoped to see some of the stronger sex find this same train of thought and present them to view. As yet I have waited in vain. And now, though it is uncongenial to my feelings, I send them, asking that they may have some spare corner of your excellent Journal, and by giving them such a place you will much oblige.

A FEMALE TEACHER.

THE REPRESENTATIVE OF A BRITISH CHARITY REPORTS ON GIRLS PLACED IN CANADIAN HOMES

Charlotte A. Alexander Papers, vol. 3, MG 29 B43, pp. 3-14, Public Archives of Canada.

Ada Frances Frost. Came to Coulsdon July 2nd 1885 b. Sep. 1877 . . . Went with me to Sutton Christmas 1886. I took her to Canada July 1886. Left her with Miss Bilbrough, Marchmont Home, Belleville. No satisfactory home offered. Came to me to Toronto September. Placed with Mr. & Mrs. David Stouffer, Stoufville. Mrs. S. great sufferer. Not sure whether could undertake charge, but wd like to have child at any rate till my return next year. After fortnight, wrote that were much pleased with her.

1887. Mrs. Stouffer much worse—in highly nervous state & could not keep Ada. Came back & spent summer with me 51 Northcote Avenue, Toronto. Spent some days with Mr. & Mrs. Coyne, senior, St. Thomas, who said she seemed "a child without a fault" & they would like to adopt her. Came back to me while I considered one or two other homes for her. Finally went to Mr. & Mrs. Coyne Oct 14.

1888. January 11. Very happy letter from Ada of this date. Later, one from Mr. Coyne dated April 4, saying she had died of Diptheria. Wrote "though she partook of our fallen nature like others, I can freely say that in all my experience I have not met with one with so little evil about her as Ada. She had no bad in her nature. It was all affection & love—all good." I went to St. Thomas August 24. Coynes away. Next door neighbour gave me many particulars of Ada. Devotedly nursed by Coynes. Took me to see her grave, beside those of Coynes 2 daughters in family Lot in Cemetery. . . .

Alice Maud Johnson b. January 1880. Came to Sutton January 1886. Brought by Miss Cole, Hintfield, Catecham. Came from Parish of Miss C's cousin, Camberwell. Father had small shop. Separated from wife who said he was so peculiar could not live with him. She thought out of his mind, but Lunacy Commissioners wd not give certificate. She took girls & went away leaving him boys. Could not maintain them. Very poor & often without food. Thankful to have Alice (youngest) provided for. Came to see her & said goodbye before she started for Canada. I took her to Canada July 1886. Left her with Miss Bilbrough, Marchmount Home, Belleville, whence she was placed by Miss B. with Mr. and Mrs. Featherstone, Arnprior, to be companion to their only child & to be treated as their own. They much pleased with her. I went to Arnprior & saw well & happy.

1887. Letter from Mrs. Bates, Arnprior, dated Jan. 5. Very satisfactory account of A.J. Later in year, Mrs. Featherstone wrote complaining of her temper & returned her to me to 51 Northcote Avenue, Toronto. After a little while adopted by Mr. & Mrs. Coyne, Ingersoll, who have two boys no girl— Much pleased with A. I spent a night with them after she had been there 1 or 3 weeks. Found her very happy & well.

1888. Letter from Mrs. I. Coyne saying one of her boys was very ill, irritable & jealous of A. &c. Consequently she wanted to be relieved of Alice. After some correspondence, placed her temporarily with Dr. & Mrs. D. W. Carroll, Ingersoll. Aug. 23rd. I called at Dr. C's. He out. Saw Mrs. C. Alice had been much teased by Coyne boys. Very ill just after she went to Dr. C. who nursed her day & night. Dr. C. will not sign agreement, but wd like to keep A. I agreed to leave her till next year. She goes to Church and Sunday School. Also day school. Made many enquiries about Carrolls. Heard nothing which made me think I ought to remove Alice, especially as she owed so much to Dr. C.

1889. July 29. Went to Ingersoll. Dr. C. away. Alice grown & looking well & happy, but Mrs. C. complained that she had been telling stories & had twice taken money. 1890. July 25. Went to Ingersoll. Mrs. C. away for 2 or 3 days. Dr. C. out. Servant said A. had been ill during winter. Also given trouble from untruthfulness &c. Had been troubled with sore eyes. August. Mrs. Carroll called. Said she could not keep Alice any longer. Disobedient, untruthful rude. September 16th. Alice J. came back to me 228 Cottingham Street Toronto. Behaved well. Was a very good child & liked by Matron & all in the house. Went Oct. to Mrs. Thomas Hambly, Nobleton P.O. nearest Ry St. Bolton.

1891. Mrs. Hambly wrote May 20th. "Alice is doing splendid. She has been going to school regularly since she came" &c. But owing to Mr. Hambly's death, probability of Farm being sold & of Mrs. H. going to live with her sister, A.J. could not remain permanently with Mrs. H. June 4th. Mrs. H. called & gave good account of A. July 14th A went direct from Mrs. H to Mrs. Q. Hayward, Kenilworth, on trial. Mrs. H. did not think her suitable & returned her to me July 22nd. Very good while with me. Went Aug 8th to Mr. Richard Rivers, Springhill farm, Walkerton. Aug. 13th. Miss Rivers wrote much pleased with her so far. Agreement signed Aug. 24. to keep her till Sep. 12, 1893.

1892. Received letter from Miss Rivers dated March 16. Mrs. Rivers had died. A. J. been very well except for occasional bilious attack. Eyes not been sore. . . .

O'Donnell Bridget Age 16. Came to Sutton early part of 1887 from Mrs. Ballantine, Ivy House Mission, Dalston Lane. No Father, bad Mother. Irish. Behaved well with me. Promising, capable girl. Went to Mrs. Seaton Gordon, 15 Isabella Street, Toronto, May 26. $5 a month. Aug 21 Mrs. G. wrote "I like her very much. She takes good care of the children & I really like the child." In October Mrs. G. complained much of her ungovernable temper & insolence & declined to keep her. She went to Mrs. Gibson, by Bloor Street.

1888. Found that B. had left Mrs. Gibson. Presented herself at Mrs. Lamond Smith's. said she was one of my girls & Mrs. S. took her in, but had found her so rude & troublesome feared that (she) could not keep her. I called & had long talk with B. who cried much & promised to do better. Improved —but after a time went back, and on Sep. 4 Mrs. S. wrote she was getting more & more rebellious & had left. Got herself a place at 26 Park Road.

1889. Heard from Mrs. Lamond Smith that she had changed her place. Was then in a respectable situation but did not wish her address known or that any-one should go and see her. Would not go into Mrs. Smith's house or have anything to do with her. Mrs. S. advised leaving her alone for a time. Later, after my return to England heard that she had died of Inflammation of the lungs. At the last seemed softened & wished to see Mrs. S. who went at once but was too late. Found she had died. . . .

Sarah Driscoll Age 16. Orphan. Came to Sutton early part of Spring 1887. From Miss Haddon's Home for girls, Dover. Passage paid by Uncle, Mr. Chappell, Bow Road, London. Superior sort of man. Guardian of the Poor & member of Committee for the East London Palace. Says he does not wish to give up all care for her & if she does not get on well, he will send for her home after 3 years, but impresses on her she is to stay 3 years. Went to Mrs.

Downes, 235 Wellesley Street, Toronto, May 26. $5 a month to begin. Woman to come in & do washing. Sarah to come into it by degrees & then receive more wages. July 12 called on Mrs. Downes. Sarah very happy & doing well. Likes Canada better than England. But Mrs. D. will not give her more than $4 a month because she is slow. Dec. 19. Miss Downes wrote good account of her.

1888. Received very nice & happy letter from S.D. early part of year. Saw Mrs. D. in summer. Says S. washes & bakes beautifully—but is very slow & so will not give her more than $4. S.D. does not wish to leave though I can get her much higher wages. Mr. Gordon advised leaving her.

1889. Saw Mrs. Downes in May. Gave S.D. good character but said she was slow & would not give her more wages. Sep. 23 called & saw S.D. Getting $4.50. but content & wishes to stay. Oct. 4. S.D. came to tea.

1890. June 2. Wrote to Mrs. Downes & asked for S. to come & see me. Said she ought now to be worth $8. S. replied June 3, too busy to come. Now getting $5 & some clothes (working). Prefers to stay with Mrs. Downes for that than go elsewhere for $8.

1891. May 15th. S.D. called with J. Collis and A. Scanlan. Looking well & improved in appearance. Still getting only $5 per month but Miss Downes makes her dresses & she has no wish to leave. July 20th S.D. came to tea.

1887. *Ann Olivia Scanlan* came to Sutton early part of April 1887, through Miss Lee, 34 Bryanston St, who wrote "nearly 13." Legitimate. Baptized. Father was boot maker for Parker 135 Oxford St. is in advanced state of consumption in North London Consumptive Hospital. Mother bears *very* bad character. Not known where she is. Has 2 sisters Mary 14, Margaret 7. Rev. Ernest Kevill Davies Senior Curate of St. Anne's, Soho, knows family. Says "Father is willing to sign Agreement to commit the girl wholly to the care of the Managers of the Home," (Ch. of England for Waifs & Strays) "to obey the rules in force, & to permit the said girl when fully trained to be sent to any situation in the United Kingdom or the Colonies, which may be obtained for her by the Committee." Later, Father signed a paper for Rev. E. Kevill Davies, giving his sanction to the child being sent to me to go to Canada. Was anxious that she should be out of reach of her mother. He died about a week before she came to me. A.S. came very ignorant & untrained but seemed warm hearted & willing. Placed in Canada with Mrs. Strangways, Pennville P.O. Becton by Station.

1888. Very unsatisfactory character from Miss [sic] Strangways. Violent temper & immoral tendencies. At same time kind & warmhearted. I took her to Home for Friendless Girls, corner Caroline & Duke Streets, Hamilton, Aug 29th. Mrs. McKellar, President, admitted her on condition Home should have control over her 3 years. Meantime in England action brought against Rev. E. K. Davies by Roman Catholics to get A.S. themselves on ground of her Mother being R.C. but as she was sent by Father's wish who was Protestant, judgment given against R.C.s.

1889. Saw A.S. July 11 at Mrs. Lockhart's, 61 Hannah Street West, Hamilton. She had been in another situation previously. Mrs. Lockhart's account better than that of last year. Has learned to cook & make pastry & has become much more capable, but still untruthful & unreliable, very self willed & disobedient. July 17. Sent from Home at Hamilton, to Haven, Seaton Street, Toronto. Could not be kept at Hamilton because of wicked things said to inmates about Mrs. Lockhart. Mrs. McKellar said she did not remember arrangement about keeping her 3 years. If she did make it, she exceeded her authority. July 19 I called at Haven. Mrs. More said Ann would be kept there for a time & then put out in situation. Called again end of Sep. or beginning Oct. Mrs. More (Matron) said A.S. had behaved well at "Haven"—been put out in situation where she was doing pretty well. Had been kind to child who had died during her illness—Mistress keeping her on for the present.

1890. Called in June at "Haven". Mrs. More could not see me. Sent message A.S. doing nicely when last heard of. Wrote June 21, re A.S.'s address. Mrs. More replied could not give it to me.

1891. A.S. called to see me with S. Driscoll & J. Collis May 15th. In service at 243 Wellesley Street, with Mrs. Lawrence as general servant. Small family $7. Been there 8 months. Place next door to Mrs. Downes & got for her by Mrs. Downes. July 15th. Matron went to see A.S. Found house shut up. Heard next door from Miss D. that family had gone into country for a month. A. wd not go with them—so had left & was staying with friends looking for another situation—Engaged to be married to a man who delivers ice. His wages $10 per week.

1892. Heard from Rev. E. Kevill Davies very unsatisfactory account A.S. had married very unsatisfactory man.

A VICTORIAN MOTHER'S DIARY OF HER CHILD'S LIFE

'Diary: 1886-1896', Merkeley Family Papers, MG 29E 29, Public Archives of Canada.

Dec 31/87

The last night of the old year. I wonder what my darling will be like at this time next year and if I will be here to look after her.

God help me to bring her up in fear and love.

She is not at all hard to get along with. She very often says "No No" when I tell her to do any thing but I tell her to run and sit in the corner until she is ready to do it, and in less than half a minute she jumps up and runs and does it.

She does not get whipped often but when she does she is heart broken over it, especially if it is from Fassie of whom she is very fond.

I wonder if our happy little family circle will be unbroken at the end of another year.

Jan. 8/88

She fell down or partly down stairs today and raised a bump on her forehead, the first mark from a fall she has ever had.

Jan. 22/88

Edith is up at her Aunt Minnie's today and it is so lonesome without her. How changed our home would be without her now.

Helen came from N. York yesterday where she had been with Dr. Rutherford... They met Aunt Hettie there where she has been for three months undergoing an operation in one of the Hospitals. She came part way home with the Maxwells, Helen brought Edith a silver thimble and a very pretty white embroidered dress to be worn over a colored dress. She never forgets Edith no matter where she goes.

Edith can put on her boots & stockings and dress and say her little prayer "Now I lay me Down to Sleep" all alone.

Feb. 15/88

Nothing worthy of note has transpired. Yesterday she was not well and we were very much frightened for we did not know what was the cause of it and she was so cross and wanted Missie to rock all the time, a thing she never wants when she is well.

Feb. 18/88

She does not seem to feel sick now only cross sometimes, and she has a terrible cold perhaps it was this coming on that made her so sick. She has gone to bed to night with her doggie (a toy one) and two dolls with her. I had to kiss "Nap" twice and say "Good Night Nap" and then I got down stairs I heard her getting doggie to say "Good Night". Oh she's a darling.

Oct 23/90

Edith has left her crib to-night and gone to sleep in a large bed all alone in another room. I do not know how she will get along for she often dreams in the night and her Father has to draw the crib up beside our bed and often have to take her into bed with us before she will get her nerves settled enough to sleep. The children on the street tell her stories that frighten her and she is getting so now that she loves to be on the street and she never tires playing. The children she gets to play with all get tired but she never tires. She is saving her money now... and she does very well and has got her four cents for this month ready. She is getting so now that she will argue with me and ask the why for every thing.

I hope I may be able to train her that she will grow up a good woman.

Nov 2/90

I have not anything very good to tell of my girl to night. I had to put her to bed today to punish her. She asked if she could go to some little girls house to play with them and I said "No" but when I went to look for her found she had been there. I did not want to whip her and thought putting her to bed would be better but I told her to get into bed as I was going out. I was gone half an hour and when I came back found she had never been into bed I then had to punish her and make her get into bed. When I told her I was going to put her into bed she was heart-broken and begged me to "spank" her and not put her to bed. She said "You make me feel so cross putting me to bed you make me feel like saying "The deuce"."

She is very heart broken and I hope will be subdued. She is up and determined to mind what I tell her and to obey me.

Nov. 2nd/90

The punishment was not effectual. This A.M. she wanted to go with us part way to Church I told her she could and when we got part way there sent her home and told her to come right along but when we got home found no Edith but in a few minutes Annie Hepburn came to see if she could stop over there for dinner. I of course said no and when she came in and got her dinner sent her to bed. She did not cry or make any fuss but played in bed for a couple of hours then asked if she could get up I said "Not in a good while", Then she said "I will be here and think if I will be good now". I said yes and in about an hour. She said she would be good.

Nov. 12/90

I have had no trouble since but she is very much afraid of being sent to bed. I think it a good punishment. Doe and Bell have been gone a month and she never forgets to pray for them. Tonight she said "God bless everybody and keep track of Doe and Bell while they are travelling so far".

Yesterday she wrote a letter to her Aunt Maggie I gave her a small envelope to put it in and told her to put it down for her father to post when he came in. Someone came in and she thought while I was busy she would post it herself so ran down to the P.O. and told the P. Master that it was for Aunt M. When her father went down he found it in his box.

Nov. 30/90

Today Edith went to S.S. and knew the first page in the Calvery Catechism. I wonder when she will know it all and I pray God her lessons in S.S. may not be in vain. She is up to every thing now that can be thought of.

March 1st/1891

Tomorrow my darling will be five years old. I thank God that he has spared her to us and such a healthy little girl as she is and has always been. She is to have a birthday party tomorrow and is full of it and talk of nothing else and the attraction is to be "A chocolate cake". She is no lover of cake and the only kind she eats is chocolate.

March 2nd/91

The party is over and has been a very happy day for Edith. . . . Her Papa and I gave her a silver spoon. One to be given her every year until she gets the dog. God only knows who or if any of us will live to see her get the dog, Nora Whitney gave her a new game called Tiddlely Winks. Bob Bradfield a cup & saucer. Jean Gibson a book. Aunt Maggie a work basket and Mrs. Rutherford of Lake City another set of dolls table napkins.

She ought to be good every one is so good to her and loves her so much. Oh that I may know how to train her to make a good true woman of her.

April 9/91

Edith has been good today all day as could be and has made up her mind to be a better girl. She got so that she would whine every time she did not have just what she wanted and scolding or punishing did not do her one bit of good.

To scold or punish her seems to bring out all the bad in her nature.

May 12

I am sorry to write that my little girl is not as good as I wish she is very disobedient and when I punish her by putting her to bed in the daytime she promises to be good and within half an hour forgets all about it. Today I have kept her in all day and will not let her out at all to play.

May 18/91

Edith is trying to be better. She went to Church yesterday and was very good she sat with Helen. It was hard work to keep quiet but she did very well. She wanted a bouncer ball and I told her when she made three dish-cloths she could have one. She finished the last one on Sat. night and her papa took her over and bought one for her but that is all it is just to have it she does not care so much for it when she does get it she does not.

June 6/91

Edith is just going down to Mr. Harpers to buy some wool to make an afgan for her dolls carriage.

March 1st/92

My little girl started to school today and I could not keep back the tears to see her go and she was so happy to think she was seven years old and "going to Miss Bakers school" I never intended to send her until she was seven but she could not wait until after her birthday tomorrow.

April 1st/93

Easter Monday

Edith is not going to school. She has been exposed to measles and by the way she acts & feels I think she is getting them. She complains a great deal of a pain in her knee and she is inclined to be a little lame. While we were on the island last summer she went in bathing and once when she came out she cried all night with pain in her knee and the inside of the right knee was swollen some. In A.M. we brought her over to Dr. Parry Chamberlain and he said it was rheumatism but ever since she cried out in the night often with the pain of it. I get up and go in to her and rub it only long enough to sooth her and she drops off to sleep. I am very sorry about it and very uneasy lest she should have trouble with her knee. I did not dream that going into the river in July or August would give it her but I think it did.

May 1st/93

Edith has been in the house just one month with measles but has started to school again today. She is very fond of school but she loves to play too. She is quick at figures but not so quick at reading and spelling. I hope she will learn easily. . . .

A DEFINITION OF DELINQUENCY

ALTERNATIVES TO IMPRISONMENT

Separate Report of E. A. Meredith. Annual Report of the Board of Inspectors of Asylums, Prisons etc. Province of Canada, *Sessional Papers*, No. 19 (1862).

The great object, as all admit, of penal legislation, and of penal institutions of every kind, is to diminish crime; and, I am persuaded, no class of institutions, penal or reformatory, is calculated to produce so large results in this way, and at so small a cost to the community as those institutions (whether styled "Ragged Schools," "Homes," or "Industrial Farms"), which, seeking out the neglected and perishing children, who otherwise would grow up in our midst in ignorance and vice—afford those unfortunate outcasts the necessary education and training, to enable them to earn an honest living for themselves.

Deeply impressed with the inestimable benefits resulting to society from such institutions, I submitted my views upon the subject to my colleagues and the Government, in a report presented to them in the early part of the year.

In that report, I advocated the establishment of institutions, under the name of "Homes" for the destitute and neglected children of the poorer classes; for those children, who, unless some such provision were made for them would, of necessity, grow up in ignorance and vice. It was recommended that the Circuit or County Judges, and the Recorders of cities, should, under certain restrictions and conditions, have authority to commit such children to "Homes" regularly established, for certain limited periods. That the managers of the "Homes" should give the children a suitable training and education, and afterwards apprentice them to some farmer or tradesman, or otherwise put them in the way of earning an honest living. It was recommended that the homes should be supported, mainly at least, by voluntary contributions, or by payment from the municipalities sending children to them, and that the aid of the Legislature should be invoked for the purposes, principally, of legalizing the establishments and of conferring the necessary power upon the magistrates to send the children to the "Homes," and on the managers to retain the children for the periods prescribed by law, and afterwards to apprentice them out. . . .

Canada boasts, and with reason, of the liberal provision which she makes for the education of her sons. She offers to all her children a good education, and offers it to them without charge. But yet it cannot be denied that a large proportion of the juvenile population, and especially of that class of the juvenile population who, from their circumstances and position in life, most stand in need of training and education, derive no benefit whatever from our admirable school system. It is, indeed, a matter of common remark that, in our large cities particularly, a great proportion of the children of the lower classes are utterly destitute and neglected, and grow up in our midst without receiving any education or training to fit them to act their part in life as honest and useful citizens.

The existence of this large and unfortunate class of the community is wholly ignored by society, until the wretched victims of neglect and cruelty present themselves before our magistrates, and become in due course the inmates of our jails and penitentiaries.

But imprisonment in jail tends only to complete the ruin of the unfortunate child. So far from checking the growth of juvenile crime, the imprisonment of the young in jail is, in fact, itself a fruitful source of crime. The indiscriminate herding together of the young and comparatively innocent with old and hardened criminals in our common jails, has here, as elsewhere, produced in too many cases its natural fruit,—the utter degradation and permanent ruin of the more youthful and innocent prisoners. We, in Canada, cannot indeed escape the conviction that we have been systematically manufacturing criminals in our jails, and that hitherto our prisons, instead of being reformatory institutions, have been simply nurseries of vice and hotbeds of crime. It may indeed be said with melancholy truth that we have provided a complete system of education for this portion of our population; but in that system the jails have been our normal schools, and the penitentiary our university.

True, indeed, we have not been singular in our neglect of these helpless and unfortunate children. Older and wealthier communities than ours, even England and France, the nations foremost in the van of civilization in Europe, have, until within the last few years, been as sinfully indifferent to the fate of the pauper children in their midst as we have been in Canada.

Within the last few years, however, a great change has come over the public mind in France and England on this great social question; and in these countries, and also in the neighboring States, institutions under the names of "Homes," "Industrial Farms," "Refuges," or "Reformatories," have been established, all intended, in a greater or less degree, to meet the wants of this large and unfortunate class.

In our own country, reformatories for juvenile offenders have, within the last few years, been established. These establishments go some way to meet the great social want. They afford an admirable moral, religious, and industrial training to the youths who enter them; but these youths are but a small fraction of the class to which they belong, who have need of such a training. To qualify himself for the reformatory, the boy must be a convict, he must have passed through a jail and undergone the disgrace of a trial. Reformatories are therefore not available for boys who have not entered upon a course of actual crime, and made themselves amenable to the law. They, in fact, are remedial, but not preventive; their object is to reform the boy who has become criminal, not to train and instruct the pauper boy while yet innocent of crime. This is, of all others, a case where prevention is better than cure. It is better, because it is more agreeable, more hopeful, more economical, more humane, and more christian.

Homes or refuges, such as I have briefly sketched, would form a kind of intermediate link between our common schools and our juvenile reformatories. While they partake, to some extent, of the character of both, they are entirely distinct, and properly distinct from both, and form in fact their natural and necessary supplement.

CLASSES OF CHILDREN FOR WHOM "HOMES" ARE INTENDED

From what has preceded, it is evident that "Homes" are intended for the benefit of destitute and neglected pauper children; for children who, but for the intervention of such extrinsic aid, would receive no training or education, and who, from the circumstances in which they are placed, would be drifted, as it were, into a career of vice and crime. This class of pauper children would be found to consist principally of

1. Vicious and incorrigible children.
2. Vagrants.
3. Children without parents or protectors, or children whose parents or natural protectors, from poverty or other causes, are unable or unwilling to afford them that education which they require, and to which they are entitled.

As it is my intention to present here an outline merely of the scheme which I have submitted for the consideration of the Board and of the Government, I do not think it necessary to discuss the objections which have been urged against such a scheme. Those objections I have endeavored to meet in the report submitted to the Government. Nor is it desirable that I should enter into any details as to the management and support of the "Homes." Upon these and all other matters of detail, much valuable information can be obtained from the reports of analagous institutions in other countries, and more particularly from the reports of the refuges, which have for upwards of twenty years been in successful operation in the neighboring States.

In concluding this brief memorandum, I am anxious to record my own strong conviction that it is not to our penitentiaries, nor yet to our jails, nor even to our admirable reformatories, but to homes or some such institutions that we must mainly look if we hope with God's blessing to "stand between the living and the dead and stay the plague" of immorality and vice around us.

A VERSION OF THE WAY IT WAS IN AN INDUSTRIAL SCHOOL

Report of the Halifax Protestant Industrial School, 1867 (Halifax, N.S., James Bower & Sons, 1867).

At the date of our last Report we had twenty-eight boys. We have received since twenty-one additional. Of these five were taken from the City Prison, where they were on the high road to degradation and destruction; and the rest with one or two exceptions were on the streets, and on the high road to crime. The father of one applied for him after he had been in the school for two or three months, and another left about the same time rather than submit to the regular discipline and restraints that are necessary. Eight of the old twenty-eight have left the school during the year; four of those, with the hearty consent of the committee, to go to good situations where they are now doing well; another to go to employment outside; two because their parents applied for them; and one expelled for insubordination. We have now with us 20 of the old 28; and 19 of the new 21; in all 39, their ages ranging from ten to twenty years.

It is easy to write or read those sentences, but it requires a good deal of imagination to conceive all that they imply. Any parent or teacher will confess that in bringing up to manhood boys naturally well disposed, all his patience, wisdom, and love are required; and notwithstanding the exertion of all those how many of our youths who have had every circumstance in their favour, go astray! Think then of the problem before us. Here are some lads, whose education has been on the streets, the wharves, the Police Station, Rockhead, the rumshop, the brothel. Here are boys young in years, but old in the ways of deceit, and hardened in depravity. Details as to thought, speech, and behaviour, we cannot give. He that knows what effect on the whole nature, habit and associations connected almost wholly with dirt, discomfort, rudeness, blaspheming, lewdness incredible, must have, he only can do justice to the difficulty of the work that has to be done before such natures can be redeemed from the power of evil. But though it were ten times as difficult, and the failures far more frequent, it must be attempted. How can any parent ask God's blessing on his boys, if he will not stretch out a hand to save those who are just as much God's dear children, as his own are? And poor fellows! It is but common justice to them to acknowledge that it is wonderfully easy to touch their better natures though the formation of good habits is necessarily a slow work. And though we have no wish to paint things rose-colour, and though we dare not boast, yet there are facts which encourage us and which we ought not to hide. Last April, nine of the bigger boys were confirmed at their own request, in St. Paul's Church, and five of those sat down at the Lord's table. And we get still greater encouragement from the manifest improvement in the tone and conduct, of the smaller boys. Mr. Grierson has often to sow in tears, but he sometimes is enabled to reap, and then it is with joy.

Why do the good Christians of Halifax take so little interest in this attempt that is being made to dry up the stream of crime in our city, by meeting it at the fountain head? Are they aware that now there is not a single Protestant boy in the City Prison, owing to our exertions? And in return for this, and for our saving the city revenues in hard cash thereby at least $900 a year, the Corporation has voted us for two years $100 annually. And the sum that we save the city indirectly is double the former amount; and as to the moral and christian gain we will not set that down in dollars. The public has generously supported us with money, but we wish that more of our friends would visit and inspect the Institution, and then they would take a greater interest in it. We are sure of this. If they go in the day time, it presents the aspect of a beehive. Enter the new workshop, and down stairs a squad of boys are busy at Cabinet-making. You hear from up stairs the hammering of the Shoemakers. Go into the nearest wing of the main building, and you come on a lot of little tailors, stitching away true tailor fashion, at flannel drawers, blue shirts for fishermen and lumbermen, and such like. At the other extremity of the building, in the new shed, you are pretty sure to find Mr. Grierson with the small boys, some of them just returned from errand-running, and all of them cheerily busy at splitting and making up kindling wood. Through the rest of the main building, you will come here and there on a boy, each one doing a special work, and knowing that it is his, and that he is responsible for its being done. The interior economy of so large an establishment must be complicated, but the work is so subdivided among the boys, that it is all done by themselves, and the whole machine is kept running smoothly. Offices are distributed among twenty-seven of the boys, and the weekly list is hung up where all can see it, and if anything is left undone, all know who is to blame. Thus there are six dormitories, the largest holding thirteen, the smallest five boys, and, in each, one of the inmates is responsible for the tidiness of the room. Every boy makes his own bed, but there is a head to the room every week. Then there are four workshops, and one boy in each sees that it is swept out, and that things are in their places. There are four waiters, one for each table, and four heads to the tables. Two boys to do kitchen work, two to do the washing, one in charge of the dressing room and hall; a dining room steward who has to kindle the fire in it, and sweep it out after each meal; a bread-cutter, librarian, &c. As to the looks of the boys, let visitors judge. We only wish that they were in a position to contrast what they are with what they were. Their general appearance now is, we believe, the best tribute to the Institution. They certainly are healthy. Dr. Hattie tells us that it is a rare thing for him to be called in nowadays; whereas when they come to us they are generally weak, sickly, and sometimes suffering from loathsome diseases. And the sound body indicates the sound mind.

If a visitor should go in the evening, he will find the entire rank and file assembled in the School-room. One or two of the young men who volunteered eighteen months ago to assist for an hour or two in the week in this department, still continue their services; but the burden of the work falls on Mr. Grierson, and we would be most grateful to any young gentlemen who could spare a little time in the evening, and who would volunteer assistance. One of the large boys is now so good a writer, that he takes charge of the writing department of the School. But some of our new comers need instruction from the beginning. . . . With forty boys to bring up we felt that it was unfair to them to have only one trade; and there were other reasons that made a broadening of our basis wise. So in February last we added tailoring; and then in June, Cabinet-making, and for each we have a well-qualified master who devotes his whole time to his trade and to instructing in it the boys who are assigned to him as apprentices. As to Shoemaking Mr. Lyons was obliged to return to Ontario in the spring on account of his health. We appointed then Mr. Samuel Ayres, as head of the shoe shop, and he has continued in it since, and has attended to it so faithfully that he has earned the esteem and confidence of all the committee. Mr. Ayres entered the Industrial School as a boy five years ago. He is now a young man one of our most valued assistants. This fact alone speaks loudly.

At present we have twelve boys engaged at shoemaking; ten at tailoring; four at cabinet making; and the rest act as errand boys and make up kindling wood. We do not intend to introduce any other trades, as those we have afford sufficient variety for selection; and we believe that in succeeding years they will prove to be paying. But every one must see that the ordinary income being sufficient only for the ordinary expenditure, the establishment of two new departments could not have been undertaken unless we had had faith that we were doing what was necessary and that there was wealth and willingness enough in Halifax to justify us. Besides, we had to put up a substantial fence around our grounds this year; to build a large wood shed, and make considerable repairs on our premises; and worst of all, we began the year in debt. The consequence is that we are now from $1,000 to $1,200 in debt. And if we do not get that amount soon, we shall be terribly crippled and hampered. We are confident that there are men and women in Halifax who will not let us make our appeal in vain. We are sure that if put in a sound financial condition now, our work will proceed prosperously. Hitherto the new trades have paid only the expenses we have been at in establishing them. We believe that another year will tell a different tale. . . .

THE TREASURER IN ACCOUNT WITH THE HALIFAX PROTESTANT
INDUSTRIAL SCHOOL.

1866.	DR.	
Sept. 30.	To Balance in hand	$ 187.95
	Received Subscriptions per list	1174.00
	Received Donations per list	662.70
	Received for boys admitted upon a guarantee of $40 per anm. per list	406.00
	Received for sale of Paper Bags	20.00
	Received proceeds Lecture by Capt Duncan	16.00
	Received proceeds Bazaar in Decr, 1866	479.32
	Received Special Donations, per list	200.50
	Received for sales of Shoe class Manufactory	784.92
	Received for sales of Cabinet-makers class manu.	78.86
	Received for earnings of Errand Boys . . . $259.14	
	Received for earnings of Errand Faggots . . 38.54	297.68
	Received for earnings of Tailors class	30.40
	To Balance due Treasurer 30th Sept, 1867	56.20
		$4394.53

CR.

Paid for Dietary	805.41
Paid for Clothing	306.13
Paid for Gas and Fuel	116.92
Paid for Water	12.00
Paid for Repairs and improvements	82.27
Paid for New Building	744.88
Paid for Incidental expenses	224.16
Paid for Superintendent	295.29
Paid for Shoemakers' class, materials & salaries	757.26
Paid for Cabinet-makers' class materials & salaries	278.87
Paid for Tailors class materials & salaries	164.29
Paid for Wood for Faggots	10.06
Paid for Sundry accounts for 1866 and 1867	596.99
	$4394.53

RICHARD TREMAIN, Treasurer.

Audited by Finance Committee,
Halifax, October, 1867.

ORGANIZED LABOUR PROTESTS; THE TESTIMONY OF D. J. O'DONOGHUE

Ontario, Legislative Assembly. *Report of the Commissioners appointed to enquire into the Prison and Reformatory System of Ontario, 1891*, pp. 738-44.

Mr. JURY.

Q. In reference to child crime, Mr. O'Donoghue has paid a great deal of attention to emigration, and I should like to ask him, first, what were the number of commitments in Toronto during the last year? A. For the last ten months I can give you the number of children who came before the police court. It was stated in some returns that 146 were committed to the county gaol. The casual reader would probably be under the impression that this was the whole number brought up. The chief of police furnished me with a statement showing the exact numbers brought before the police magistrate during the ten months. In January there were, males 26, females 1; February, males 39, females, 2; March, males 43, females 3; April, males 36, females 6; May, males 47, females 3; June, males 53, females 4; July, males 64, females 4; August, males 53; females 2; September, males 70, females 2; October, males 106, females 5; making a total of 569; that is, 537 males and 32 females.

Q. Of this number, how many received sentence? A. I assume that the 146 would come out of that. I am not in a position to say that, though.
Hon. Mr. ANGLIN.

Q. There is no doubt that many of these children appeared more than once; how many were re-commitments? A. I had that in my mind at the time, but I did not want to bother the chief of police very much. There is a phase of the subject that I desire to draw the attention of the Commission to. I cannot account for this increase month by month. Only in the last month the number of boys went up to 106; that is, the month of October, and with one exception the numbers increased in regular rotation.
The CHAIRMAN.

Q. Do you observe that they are more numerous in the summer than the winter months? A. The figures seem to point that way, but the greatest numbers are in September and October. The fruit is exposed more in the autumn months and this is a great temptation to children. In winter they are more willing to go to school than in the summer. I think it would be a good plan to get from the police a record of the nature of the offences.
Mr. JURY.

Q. What are your views, and the views of the labor people generally, on the question of manual training at the schools? A. Our labor bodies are unanimously opposed to manual training in the schools. . . . All we understand of it is that they give a very superficial knowledge of particular industries to these boys. . . . As regards the Industrial School, many who favor such institutions are under the impression that it would enable the children to be expert if more attention were given to subjects of a technical character; but as a matter of fact, this is a cause of great evil, for youths are sent out with a knowledge of the avocation in which they are engaged that is necessarily imperfect. They are not taught sufficient to enable them to enter into competition with men outside with any hope of success; the tendency is therefore to lower wages, for employers who are glad to get cheap workmen will not pay so much for an inferior as they would for a competent hand. Those who favor this manual training simply like to see one or two callings set up at such institutions, and they think that if children can pick up a smattering of any of these they are greatly benefited. Under short terms, or even under long terms of apprenticeship,they would necessarily be incompetent workmen, and the result inevitably is that a man who would be very useful on a farm is in this way turned out a very incompetent mechanic. He is an injury to himself and an injury most decidedly to the man who has served his time at the business.
Hon. Mr. DRURY.

Q. What in your opinion would be the effect of having a text-book on agriculture in the public schools? A. I think it would be decidedly advantageous, because everybody knows that we have not enough farmers in this country; and if instead of spending money importing them from abroad we were to expend money at home in fitting our young for occupations of this class, the result would be far better.

The CHAIRMAN.

Q. Is there any objection to such mechanical training as would make a man handy on a farm? A. I should think the attention of the youth would be more properly directed were it confined exclusively to matters relating to the farm.

Mr. JURY.

Q. The superintendent of the Industrial School says that he teaches boys rough carpentering and work of that kind for the purpose of qualifying them the better for agricultural pursuits. He says it makes a boy handy on the farm if he knows a little about carpentering in that way? A. A boy who is not taught anything of that kind at an institution, if he goes on a farm will not be so stupid that he cannot do anything that may be required of him. . . .

Hon. Mr. DRURY.

Q. Your objection to this is that it would have the effect of unduly increasing the number of artisans and mechanics? A. Yes, that would be the natural effect of it. . . .

Q. But how does this bear upon the question of crime? A. Well, I should think a congested labor market throws people out of employment, and when people are unable to find work they have got to live somehow. The moment you crowd any calling, the tendency must be to make the struggle for life keener for those who are in it. Men are thrown out of work, and the weakest go to the wall; thus people are led to do many things they would not do if they were in regular steady employment.

Dr. ROSEBRUGH.

Q. I visited several institutions in the New York State, one called the Roman Catholic Protectory, where they have from 1,000 to 1,100 boys. These boys are taught printing, bookbinding, engraving, making boots and shoes, knitting stockings by machinery, etc. In the city of Rochester, just across the lake, they have a large reformatory for boys and there they have training schools covering twelve or thirteen industries. In other parts of the State we found industries were taught, and I have yet to learn that they are objected to by the labor element. A. When there is such a demand, and everybody admits that there is a demand for labor on farms we should give attention to that. There is plenty of room for boys there, but now we are too apt to give boys a training that will keep them in the city where there are too many already. Why not turn attention more in the direction of the farms for the present at any rate. I contend that where the time is not sufficiently long to enable the teacher to make a competent workman there is an injury done to the boy himself, because he is turned upon the world incompetent to earn enough for his own support at the occupation to which he is put, and through the mere fact that he is not the equal of other men in the same calling, he is compelled to work for less wages. Thus you have men of this class working cheaply and they pull good men down to their own level.

Q. They say that they accomplish in one or two years at these technological schools what they cannot accomplish in three or four years in the regular trade; that the boy is taught the principles upon which the work of the industry

is carried on? A. He is made a theoretical mechanic but not a practical one. He is what, in plain English, we would call a "botch." . . .
Mr. JURY.

Q. There is a question arising out of emigration bearing upon pauperism and crime. What proportion of our criminal and lunatic population belong to the emigrant class? A. . . . We object to the emigration of children on this score, that we have in the institutions now about 4,000 children at a gross cost in 1889 of $800,000. We hold that we have children enough of our own to provide for without going to another land for them. In our reformatory for boys the total committals, since the establishment of the institution, have been 1,788. Of these there were 1,345 Canadians, and 443 foreign born. All but one under the age of 17 years. There were in residence there in 1889, 210; and the cost of the institution was $45,330.99. Now, turning to other institutions, to illustrate how largely we provide for the foreign born element in our charitable establishments, I will take the House of Industry in Toronto. Last year there were 9 Canadians and 126 foreign born, making a total of 135. In the House of Providence, Toronto, the Canadians numbered 123, and the foreign born 425; total 548. You find in the Home for Incurables, Toronto, Canadians 32, foreign born 98; total 130. St. John's Hospital, Toronto, Canadians 72, foreign born 72; House of Refuge, Hamilton, Canadians 15, foreign born 187; total 202. House of Industry, Kingston, Canadians, 20, foreign born 123; total 143. House of Providence, Kingston, out of a total of 153 inmates there were 30 Canadians and 123 foreign. Of the latter 102 were English; they were brought out by the Dominion government who paid a bonus of $2 per head upon them; 102 of this class are provided for by us in this public institution.

Q. What age were they? A. All under 16. I may say that about four years ago I drew attention to this fact, and I pointed out how injuriously and how prejudicially we were affected by this system of emigration. These facts I take from the public documents. I take these returns as the basis of my contention.
Hon. Mr. ANGLIN.

Q. It would be absurd to go to the asylums and pick out all those who were born in England, Ireland, and Scotland in order to prove what you allege. Many of these have been here nearly a lifetime, and it would be most unfair to charge their insanity or their infirmity against the country of their birth. It may be entirely due to the circumstances of their life here? A. We desire to be just to ourselves before we are generous to other people. We have 4,000 of our own orphans to provide for. Of course it is all very well to indulge in sentimentality. You are welcome to the sentiment so far as I am concerned. I represent the views of a very large section of the community upon this matter.

Q. In order to make out a strong case you have gone too far? A. That may be your opinion, and as I say you are welcome to it. Just think of the enormous proportion of foreign born in the House of Industry in Kingston. Out of 143, there are 123 foreign born as against 20 Canadians—123 English, Scotch and Irish. A catholic priest and protestant gentleman brought them out and they got $2 a head for them; and a most unfortunate thing it is they ever came

out here, for we have to provide for them. We object in the interests of the state and from a labor standpoint, to pay for the maintenance of such people. I will direct your attention now to the orphanages. The total number cared for in the orphanages in the year 1889 was 3,706; of these there were 2,466 Canadians, and 1,340 foreign born. You see there a very large proportion came from the old country. The cost of these institutions for the year was $16,336.52. I may say that I have had some experience in this matter. I was one of the directors of St. Patrick's Orphan Asylum, Ottawa, for years, an institution which by the way has 197 inmates—27 Canadians and 170 foreign born. I found that farmers got imported children in preference to the children out of the homes here. The reason is that we take good care to look after our own children. We see how they are treated, and insist upon their being cared for properly and not abused; but as regards children brought from the old country they can do with them as they please. In connection with the importation by Miss Rye, we made enquiries as to what subsequently became of the women who were brought out here and we found, so far as this institution was concerned, that if people want slaves they will take the children that nobody cares about. The persons who bring them takes the $2 a head and get rid of them, regardless in many instances of what may become of them.
Hon. Mr. DRURY.

Q. I think that we are all agreed that the system of granting aids to this class and of encouraging these persons to bring out a class of helpless people with a tendency to crime, is altogether wrong. These are not the people that we want in this country? A. I believe that the true policy of this country is to take care of our own and the more stringent measures we adopt to prevent an undesirable class of emigrants from coming here the better. Kingston has simply been a dumping place for these people, and that they should get a bonus of $2 per head for bringing the very people here that we do not want, the very class that fills our orphanages, our asylums, and charitable institutions, is perfectly monstrous.

EDUCATORS DEBATE THE MEANING OF INCORRIGIBILITY

Principal Millar, Dartmouth High School, 'A Provincial Reformatory for Incorrigible Pupils', *Nova Scotia Provincial Educational Association Report*, 1895, pp. 10-17.

When the boon of Free Public Schools was conferred upon the Province, it was naturally expected that all would thankfully hasten to avail themselves of its advantages.

A third of a century of Free Schools has demonstrated that this expectation has not been realized. Incredible as this statement may appear, it is unfortunately true, as every teacher and school official, especially in large villages, towns and cities, is painfully aware.

There are too many, not only grown people, but *young people*, growing up within sight of the thousand school houses that dot our Province, either without education altogether, or with the merest apology for it.

. . . there exists, underlying the superstructure of civilized life everywhere, but more especially in towns and cities, a vast substratum of humanity which is practically untouched by the influence of the Free School system.

This hotbed of ignorance and superstition constitutes a real and ever-present danger to society and good government—to life, property and prosperity. In it also is stored up immense potential energy, seething, restless, uncertain.

More frequently, as the years go by, can be heard the rumbling and muttering of the heaving mass. A more than usually brutal crime sends a shock of mild horror and alarm quivering through the calm indifference of the upper world; revolt, long slumbering, flashes out for a moment into open strife; blood is shed, and the aid of the military is called in to quell the disturbance. A day comes at length when a leader is found capable of organizing and directing the forces ready to his hand, the upper strata are shattered—a volcano bursts forth, chaos rules, and the "clang of the wooden shoe" is heard in the palace hall. From this class chiefly are evolved those who figure in the police court records and fill eventually the prisons. They have an education peculiarly their own. As infants they attend the Kindergarten in the slums and back alleys; later they study Geography and Astronomy about the street corners by day and the saloon doors by night; as youths they attend the sessions of the police court and receive object lessons in criminal jurisprudence; and finally, having completed their education, they graduate and are admitted behind the bars to be fed, clothed, and barbered at public expense.

This class furnishes the great majority of those who attain to eminence in the science of counters, jabs, uppercuts, right and left swings and knocks-out —knights of the short hair, square jaw, and broken nose—to whose brilliant achievements in the arena, even in this 19th century of civilization, and in this country of churches and school houses, the public press devotes half a column daily for the entertainment and instruction of its readers.

All the social vices and most of the crimes which shock and outrage society are here in embryo.

This class the Free School system has failed to reach to any considerable extent, and yet this is the very class to whom the restraining and refining influence of an education would be of the greatest benefit.

Victor Hugo has said that hunger breeds more revolutions than all other causes combined, and we know that mental starvation is usually found associated with and is quite as dangerous as physical starvation.

But this is not the only class which the Public Schools fail to reach.

It will probably be a matter of surprise to many, as it was to myself when I undertook to prepare a paper on this subject, to find that a large number of incorrigibles come from the homes of respectable, intelligent and well-to-do parents. . . .

In theory the State pays its debt by providing Free Schools for all—in practice the debt is but partially discharged, since many do not take advantage of the provision.

We already have on the statute book a compulsory school law, with elaborate provisions for the treatment of truants. It is a good law—so far as it goes. It is a step—a long one in the right direction. But it does not go quite far enough. It is incomplete and is therefore unworkable. Like the schools themselves, it fails to reach the very classes of boys for whom it was primarily designed—the habitual truants, the incorrigibles.

The compulsory law says that after having been "arrested and brought to school three times within three months, the offender shall be liable to imprisonment for such term as the Stipendiary Magistrate may adjudge, not exceeding one month."

The officers can easily arrest the offenders, but when we have them the question arises what to do with them. Where will the truant be imprisoned? In the County Jail? Well! let us think about that a little.

The truant is arrested, brought before the Magistrate, the offence proved and the offender sentenced to 30 days imprisonment in the County Jail. Now we have him safe. He won't play truant, annoy or defy his parents, furnish exercise for the police, or worry his teacher for 30 days anyhow. But, in the meantime, what about his education?

The primary object of all education is good citizenship—to make *men*—to turn them out intelligent, moral, law-abiding citizens; and one of the means by which this great work is to be prosecuted is—*the County Jail.*

The State owes an education to this child, and we are educating him— paying the debt—by shutting him up in jail, to transform a thoughtless, runaway pupil into a jail-bird; of a truant to make a criminal—to lock him up for a month and compel him to associate with crime and vice of every description; because he is bad and troublesome, to make him worse; to compel him at one plunge to cross the Rubicon that, as yet, separates him from degradation and disgrace; to strip off forcibly the cloak of respectability which, up to this time, has protected him, and to brand him—Jail-bird. It is horrible. But whose boy is this whom defective training has made a truant, and whom the law has made a criminal? Yours, perhaps, or mine. Think of it a little: the shame of the open court, of the public street, of the prison bars. It is an education in itself, certainly, but scarcely of that kind which the State owes to its children.

I may be, perhaps, too sensitive on this point, but I am quite sure of this— that I would as soon see my boy lying dead at my feet as behind the bars of the jail window. I can only suppose that those who framed that clause in the law did not stop to consider seriously the relations existing between Education and the Jail, or else they themselves had no sons upon whom the experiment was likely to be tried.

Every boy is born a communist. He believes instinctively in the great brotherhood of man. He unhesitatingly subscribes to the doctrines of Fraternity, Equality and Liberty. It follows naturally that he firmly believes everything to be his which is not beyond his reach. It is only by good training that he arrives at the distinction between *meum* and *tuum*—that it is wrong to consider "all things common."

Home and mother usually eradicate these traces of "original sin" during the first few years of existence, providing always that Home and Mother are of the right sort. In that case the school has but to build upon the solid foundation already prepared. But if the home training be defective or pernicious, then the school has a different and much more difficult task before it. It has to perform the home work, if wanting, or to counteract its teaching, if injurious, before it can enter on its legitimate functions.

The boy will dislike the confinement and restraint of the school and become a truant. He will covet his neighbor's property and will probably steal. He will soon be detected in wrong-doing, and, to shield himself, will very likely lie. But because he has stolen and lied to escape the consequences, it by no means follows that he is to be branded before the little world of the school-room as a thief or a liar. To do so might be logical, but would certainly be unreasonable. It would, moreover, hasten the average boy on the road to ruin, and subvert the very aims and purposes for which the school is designed.

The teacher, if she happen to be of the right kind, will frequently save this neglected waif by getting hold of his affections and winning his esteem and respect in some mysterious manner which I do not even pretend to explain. But, alas! these heaven-born teachers are few and far between. . . .

If the teacher be careless, unskilled, inexperienced; if her heart be not in her work; if her knowledge of child nature be deficient;—that boy is lost. His offences against law and order multiply; punishment follows rapidly each petty breach of rule or regulation; familiarity breeds contempt and indifference both for the punishment and the law which imposes it, and before very long the boy becomes an incorrigible.

He is arrested, tried and sentenced. We have already seen him behind the bars.

At the expiration of his term of imprisonment he is released and resumes his place among his fellows. Here one of two things is sure to happen—probably both. He will be despised by one class, the orthodox good boy, who will shun him like the plague. He will be admired by the ordinary every-day boy, whom he will contaminate as much as he is able. He will be a gilded hero of romance. His career while absent, his exploits—imaginary or otherwise—told in nervous English, ornamented and emphasized by choice and forcible expletives picked up during his residence at the public expense, will be listened to with breathless attention. Like all heroes, he will have imitators, and the numbers will increase.

Not good, but positive evil, has resulted from his arrest and imprisonment —evil to himself and to those with whom he is associated. He is in every respect a more dangerous companion for his fellows than before.

What we require to complete the compulsory law and to render it workable —to make it effective, is an institution where these unfortunates will be cared for, trained and reclaimed without subjecting them to the certain contamination of a public prison.

What we require is a place—not a jail—where our incorrigibles will be taught the subjects of a common school course; where they will, in addition, be trained to habits of obedience, self-restraint, industry; where they will be taught to use the ordinary tools of mechanical pursuits; and, in short, where they will be given a chance to develop into useful, respectable citizens.

"The State owes an education to its children," and to *all* of them.

DISCUSSION.—MR. WM. McKERRON, Commissioner of Schools for Halifax city, "rose to reply, and gave the basis on which the Industrial School was carried on, there was no criminal class in Nova Scotia, and he was clearly averse to any such institution, thinking it would be too rigid and jail-like. The Sunday-school, christian love, the churches, private subscriptions, etc., should deal with such children. He thought it clearly their duty, possibly with some assistance from the Government. He instanced the good work done by christian men and women in the courts, the slums, and wherever their good works were needed." . . .

A. McKAY, Supervisor of Halifax Schools.—There are in Halifax two establishments to which incorrigible truants are sentenced—St. Patrick's Home and the Industrial School. In the former the boys are taught the three R's for perhaps five hours a day. In the Industrial School several hours each day are devoted to splitting kindling wood and working in a shoe factory. In St. Patrick's Home the inmates include many respectable poor, besides truants and criminals. Much attention is given to farming and gardening. They are both excellent institutions, and both are doing much for the criminal classes, but truant children may be incorrigible truants and yet not criminals. They should not therefore be sent to associate with criminals.

Public sentiment and practice in every civilized country are against such treatment of those children who unfortunately cannot overcome their dislike for school.

Our Compulsory School Act, perhaps the best of its kind in the world, cannot be efficiently administered so long as we are without well-managed parental schools for such children. There are in Halifax and in all our large towns, as any unprejudiced person will at once admit, many boys who are growing up in illiteracy and crime, and who, instead of being trained as useful citizens, are fast drifting into the criminal classes to be a burden to the State. It would therefore be wise economy on the part of the Government to establish parental schools, to which unmanageable pupils could be sent, and where wise and kindly treatment would soon win them to better ways and industrious habits. . . .

It is vain to talk about leaving the work to societies and churches. They are to be praised for what they have done, but in spite of all their efforts the work is not half done. They have neither the money nor the legal status necessary. Experience everywhere proves that if education is to be general so as to safeguard the State, it must be in part compulsory, and if compulsion is to be effective there must be parental schools.

The following resolution was moved by Supervisor McKay:—

Resolved, That this Association endorse Principal Miller's arguments in favor of the establishment of a Reformatory for Incorrigible Truants, and that a committee be appointed by the Association to bring the subject before the Provincial Government.

E. T. McKEEN, Principal Sydney Academy.—Before putting this resolution, which, if carried, will definitely commit this Convention to the principle of establishing a reformatory for the incorrigibles of the Province, would it not be well for us to have a definite understanding of what is meant by the term "incorrigible?" If it refers exclusively to children of tender years who render themselves amenable to the laws of the land by the commission of some crime, I would strongly support any plan that would place them under such control that they could be properly trained in the duties of citizenship and kept from association with hardened criminals in the jails and penitentiaries. But if I understood Principal Miller aright and the "incorrigibles" are those who are specially disobedient and persistent truants, I am afraid that the establishment of either sectional or central reformatories will do more harm than good. The boy who is sentenced by process of law will always thereafter be under a cloud in his own community, and the taunts of his fellows would be conductive to anything but good in his after life. It would seem like an invasion of the liberty of the subject that a boy should be haled before a magistrate and condemned to a reformatory for a term at the caprice of somebody. I shall not presume to speak for Colchester or Halifax, or the western counties, but I firmly believe that in the section of the Province from which I come, no such law could be enforced. . . .

The following amendment to the resolution was then moved by Commissioner McKerron:—

Resolved, That the Superintendent of Education, through the Inspectors, collect statistics and information regarding the subject, and report at the next meeting of the Association.

G. J. MILLER, Principal High School, Dartmouth.—There seems to be a very general misunderstanding of the sense in which the word incorrigible was used in my paper. A great part of the adverse opinions expressed about the necessity of such an institution and the benefits to be derived from it, may be traced to that fact.

By incorrigible was not meant an utterly bad, vicious boy with whom nothing could be done, but generally speaking, a good *boy spoiled*,—a boy who plays truant and of whom it is impossible to get hold and keep hold.

To educate a boy, we must first be able to control him and we cannot control him unless we can place him where he cannot escape. Incorrigible boys are those who when brought to school by the truant officer, jump the fence as soon as his back is turned and play truant until caught again, when the farce is repeated.

It is to prevent those incorrigibles from becoming criminals that I advocate the founding of an institution where they may have at once the benefits of a home and a school training and if possible, the foundation of a trade.

The fact that over 1000 heads of families in Halifax were cited before the school Board for insufficient attendance during the school year just finished, is a complete reply to Comr. McKerron's statement "that there were not 25 incorrigibles" in that city. Further that none of those who spoke against the scheme were competent to judge except those in whose sections the compulsory law has been in operation, and those I think were very few. . . .

The resolution . . . passed unanimously.

THE ELUSIVE IMAGE OF 'HOME'

J.J. Kelso, 'Reforming Delinquent Children', *An address delivered at the Thirtieth National Conference of Charities and Correction, Atlanta, May 8, 1903.*

Few subjects are more important and none can more worthily occupy our attention than the proper care of neglected and dependent children, especially those who through petty delinquencies are in danger of drifting permanently into the criminal class. The destiny of children is controlled by early training and environment, and life with all its possibilities may be made or unmade by the circumstances surrounding the boy or girl when he or she is merging into manhood and womanhood. The superintendent of our Industrial School said not long ago that he very seldom received a thoroughly bad boy. There were mischievous boys and boys who from lack of proper advantages or from extra ebullition of spirits had got off the right track, but there was rarely a case where the boy was sufficiently bad to be classed as in any degree hopeless or incorrigible—and this has been my own experience. Children look to the future with eagerness and hope, and they are ready to respond to any call upon their faith or activity. Taken in the right way and by the right persons, the boy or girl who has gone astray, broken the law or given evidence of waywardness, can, if separated from hurtful environment and association, be reformed, or at least given an impetus toward reformation, almost instantaneously and without the necessity for years of special training and drilling in an institution. There is such a thing as an instantaneous awakening of the soul to the realization of higher and better things by the magnetic influence of one soul reacting upon another. If we earnestly desire the reformation of a child, and let the child feel and know that we have such a desire, the response will in almost every instance be prompt and sincere.

To illustrate what I mean let me tell the following incident: Years ago when I first entered upon philanthropic work I was conducting a Fresh Air excursion on the lake for some two or three hundred neglected children. There was one girl about fourteen years of age who had given a great deal of trouble; she was bold, defiant, profane and quarrelsome, and at last after a serious dispute with two or three of the workers, a request was made to me to have her put off the boat before it started. The girl, knowing that an appeal was being made, stood a short way off awaiting the decision with a hard, sullen look on her face. After hearing the complaints I told the ladies I wished to make an experiment and asked them to watch the result. I then went over to the girl and said to her: "Mary, we have just been talking about you, and we have decided that you are getting so big now that we will make you a member of the committee. See," I continued, "here is a badge which will show that you are one of the managers, and I will pin it on your dress." At first she could hardly grasp the new idea, but in a few minutes large tears came to her eyes and rolled down her cheeks. Without taking any notice of this, she was given a special work to do, namely, to distribute milk to the younger children, taking care that they were all served before the older boys and girls. This task she took hold of with zeal, and for the remainder of the day was a model of propriety. As the boat neared the wharf in the evening she came up with a beaming face, and, after being complimented on her good work, she said: "Do you know, Mr. Kelso, I did not get a drop of milk myself, although I was thirsty." "Well now," I replied, "I am glad of that." Looking up with surprise she wanted to know why I should be glad, and I explained I was glad because her forgetting herself showed that she was so busy helping the children that she had no time to think of her own needs. "And now, tell me," I said, "were you not happy doing that work to-day?" and she replied very heartily, "Yes, I never was so happy in my life before."

Finding this policy work so well with this particular girl, I tried the same plan with four or five large boys, who were causing much annoyance, appointing them caretakers of the supplies, with the result that they not only gave no further trouble, but were a decided help in many ways. Froebel's system of educating the child through his activities is the true solution for the waywardness of youth, and it will be found that success in child-saving work can be attained, and can only be attained, by making the children active agents in their own reformation. Show the children that you respect and trust them, and provide them with useful employment, especially giving them, where possible, work to do for others.

Some years later, when I accepted my present position as superintendent of neglected and dependent children of Ontario, an opportunity occurred for trying a simple plan. Word was sent me from a town, some fifty or sixty miles away, that there was a neglected boy, who had been arrested several times and sent to gaol, and that he should really be committed to the Industrial School, but the local authorities opposed this, because unwilling to pay for his maintenance. Finding that the boy had been driven to wrong-doing, as in the case of so many others, by defective home life, I requested that he be sent to me, and I would be responsible for his future. The boy came along in due time, closely guarded by a constable, whose parting remark when leaving the boy in the office was, "Better keep a sharp eye on him or he will get away from you." After waiting a few moments to allow the lad to collect his thoughts, I looked up and said, "Well, Joe, what do you think is going to become of you now?" He replied with pathetic indifference, "The reformatory, I guess." "No," I said, "not the reformatory, if I can do anything to keep you out of it;" and going over to him I said: "Joe, do you not think there is something better for you than the reformatory—don't you think if I will be your friend, and help you, that you can get along without either the gaol or the reformatory?" Then I explained exactly what I would do for him—that I would get him a boarding place, some good clothes, and after a time, when he was rested, would get him a home in the country, where the people would take a genuine interest in him. This was something new altogether, and more to his taste than his former treatment, and over his sullen countenance came that indefinable, indescribable glow of a soul awakening to high and noble aspirations. It happened that in the boarding home to which I sent him there was a girl about seventeen or eighteen, who was very sympathetic, and who found that Joe's feet were very sore from the constant friction of a pair of ill-fitting boots. She washed his feet and bound them up after getting him to promise that he would not try to walk for two or three days. This kindness completed his subjugation, and during the remainder of his stay he could not do enough to show his gratitude. In three or four weeks he went to a home in the country, and though now grown almost to manhood he has never been in any trouble, nor has he cost the community a dollar for his maintenance. Our whole attitude toward these children must be one of encouragement, showing them how good they may be rather than how bad they are. We must secure their good-will and co-operation in their own salvation, appealing to the soul, which exists in every child, however much he may have been neglected and mistrained. Institutional training which does not influence the spiritual nature may only serve to make a child more obdurate and expert in wrong-doing. . . .

This leads me to speak of the injustice of hastily committing children to reform schools for trivial offences. I remember once being in the police station when a mother came before the magistrate to ask that a fair-haired, innocent-looking boy of eleven should be committed to the Industrial School, because he was not only very bad and disobedient but because he had actually beaten her on several occasions! Enquiry, however, revealed the fact that she was about to be married again and one of the conditions was that the boy should be got rid of. Last year a case came to my notice in which a father had his son arrested, sent to gaol and ultimately committed to the reformatory for five years as a vagrant, vicious lad. His mother was dead and his step-mother did not want him. That the boy was not so very vicious may be judged from the fact that he was a regular attendant at Sunday school and his teacher regarded him as one of her best boys. Making enquiries concerning his absence she found him locked up in the gaol, where he had been taken on a warrant sworn out by his father. Second marriages mean much of misery for children of the first contract and they are a fruitful cause of the neglect and dependency of children that engages the attention of societies and institutions. Parents should not be lightly relieved of their responsibilities, but if the child is being so neglected and ill-treated as to make him a public charge or a menace to society, the solution is not a reform school, but a home in the true sense of the word, where he may receive free scope for his energy and something of kindness and affection.

There is a great lack of patience on the part of police officials with boys who have broken some of the numerous laws and ordinances that govern every well-regulated town. The reformatory is the easiest way to get rid of a troublesome lad, and often the spirit of revenge and punishment is given more weight than the consideration of the boy's future welfare. In the past hundreds of children have been hurried off to institutions who could have satisfactorily been tided over the danger point if only a different method had been pursued. I do not advocate by any means allowing such boys to go unmolested in their lawlessness, but the application of probation methods, such as procuring employment, transferring them to another home, or insisting upon parents exercising more control if they wish to retain the guardianship. Character cannot be developed so successfully in an institution as in the outside world, and like the forced plant that dies when exposed to the free air, the boy or girl who has been brought up in an institution is in great danger of falling when the institutional support is withdrawn. In too many instances also the children, after several years of careful training, are returned again to the degraded home surroundings from which they were rescued only to be dragged back by unworthy relatives to the misery and vice from which they were for a time delivered. The more popular a juvenile institution becomes the more dangerous it is, for it sets up a false standard, not only before slothful parents, but before municipal officers and magistrates who think they are doing the child a favor to commit him. Owing to their popularity some of the leading juvenile institutions in the United States have a roll call of from 500 to 800 boys. In Ontario we aim to keep the institution subordinate to the family home. No matter how earnest and zealous the superintendent may be he cannot avoid a certain routine in the institutional life that will have a deadening effect on the young people under his care. Even a child-saving society or charity organization, or any other kind of a philanthropic body, will gravitate toward a machine-like movement unless there is a frequent revival of interest and the constant introduction of fresh life and advanced methods. I can at this moment recall a very large and popular society the entire work of which is performed by two or three persons, while in the first year or two of its existence there were from fifty to seventy-five active volunteer participants. These have given up the work entirely, or have drifted into other enterprises, simply because they gradually realised that there were paid officers to do the work and these did not desire much volunteer help. Officialism is the bane of any good movement and any philanthropic organization that fails to utilize the great moral forces of the community, that like a mighty Niagara are only waiting for the call to usefulness, is simply acting as a buffer between the helper and the helped and would be better out of the way.

The juvenile court and the probation law going hand in hand are engaging public attention everywhere just now, and with wonderful unanimity of opinion they have been accepted all over this continent as among the greatest agencies for good yet devised. The movement is good because it is natural. It aims to employ the volunteer worker, to elevate and improve the home without breaking it up, to place the homeless child in a family home, and in every other way possible to follow the simple rule of friendly and brotherly cooperation. Children cannot be forced into goodness any more than a baby can be forced to go to sleep. They have to be led by gentler methods and gradually taught by their reason to appreciate the good and avoid the evil. Children should always be praised when they perform any meritorious act or have striven to accomplish anything. To be complimented and praised encourages them to persevere, and incites them to still greater and better things. There has been too much of scolding and punishment instead of the encouraging word and the helping hand. A mother one day told her little boy that he was to play in the front yard and was not to go outside the gate. The little fellow saw no hardship in this until he went outside and beheld his little companions playing some distance off. He walked to the gate and looked wistfully at them, but came back and tried to amuse himself alone; three times he went to the gate with the temptation growing stronger each time. At last he could resist no longer and sped away to join his play-fellows. On his return his mother called him in and said she would have to punish him for his disobedience, and explained to him that she had been sitting at the window and had seen him go to the gate two or three times and at last run off. The little fellow turned and said, "Mother, did you really see me go to the gate the first and the second and the third time?" "Yes," the mother replied, "I did." "Well mother," he said, "why didn't you tap on the window and help a fellow out." Was there not a cutting rebuke in this for the mother who was more anxious to punish the child for wrong-doing than to tenderly and lovingly prevent him from getting into trouble, and is there not something that each one of us can learn from the incident that will aid us in our work for the children.

We are all the product of our environment and live the life that is shaped and moulded for us in our early years. The boys and girls of our wealthy and prominent citizens, as well as the children of the poor, are made out of the same material, and it depends on the moulding they receive in youth what they will become later on. The children of the rich make mistakes and often transgress the law, but there is always sufficient influence at hand to save them from the error of their way, while the children of the poor have but few friends to take their part, otherwise they, like the others, might live down their wrong-doing and with names untarnished attain to positions of usefulness and honor.

BIBLIOGRAPHICAL NOTE

The study of the family, the child, and the school in history has been much enriched in recent years by the work of scholars coming to these subjects from a variety of vantage points. In the United States Bernard Bailyn and Lawrence Cremin, using traditional sources for cultural and social history, have inspired a generation of students to look beyond the development of schools and school systems, which had, until 1960, been the staple of most educational history. In their view a more complex picture of interweaving social, economic, and cultural forces was closer to the reality of education in the past. In the meantime the French historian, Philippe Ariès, drawing on a fascinating collection of iconographic and literary sources, provided an interpretive framework for looking at changing patterns of family life, child rearing, and school attendance that will stimulate historians for years to come. A quite different approach has been that of Michael B. Katz, who has brought quantitative sources such as the manuscript census and assessment rolls to bear on questions that educational historians previously either did not ask or thought unanswerable. The work of all of these historians rests on one common assumption: that to be properly understood, the history of schools must go beyond the pronouncements of pedagogues and educational administrators to the concerns of the people— the families, children, and teachers who used or did not use them. See Bernard Bailyn, *Education in the Forming of American Society: Needs and Opportunities for Study* (New York, Random House, 1960); Lawrence A. Cremin, *The Wonderful World of Ellwood Patterson Cubberly: An Essay on the Historiography of American Education* (New York, Bureau of Publications, Teachers' College, Columbia University, 1965) and *American Education: The Colonial Experience, 1607-1783* (New York, Harper & Row, 1970); Philippe Ariès, *Centuries of Childhood: A Social History of Family Life*, trans. Robert Baldick (New York, Random House, 1962); Michael B. Katz, *The Irony of Early School Reform: Educational Innovation in Mid-Nineteenth Century Massachusetts* (Cambridge, Mass., Harvard University Press, 1968). Other recent studies of American education in the nineteenth century that succeed in tying developing school systems to their economic and social context are: Carl F. Kaestle, *The Evolution of an Urban School System: New York City, 1750-1850* (Cambridge, Mass., Harvard University Press, 1973); David B. Tyack, *The One Best System: A History of American Urban Education* (Cambridge, Mass., Harvard University Press, 1974); and Marvin Lazerson, *Origins of the Urban School: Public Education in Massachusetts, 1870-1915* (Cambridge, Mass., Harvard University Press, 1971). For a stimulating collection of recent essays on children, families, and schools see also Michael B. Katz, ed., *Education in American History: Readings on the Social Issues* (New York, Praeger, 1973). A comparable collection of special interest to Canadian readers is Michael B. Katz and Paul Mattingly, eds , *Education and Social History: Themes from Ontario's Past* (New York, New York University Press, 1975).

Basic British and American works on the history of the child are Ivy Pinchbeck and Margaret Hewitt, *Children in English Society*, 2 vols (Toronto, University of

Toronto Press, 1969 and 1973), and Bernard Wishy, *The Child and the Republic: The Dawn of Modern American Child Nurture* (Philadelphia, University of Pennsylvania Press, 1968), while the psychohistorical approach to the subject may be examined in essays edited by Lloyd de Mause in *The History of Childhood* (New York, The Psychohistorical Press, 1974). From the growing literature on the history of the family from quantitative sources, Canadian readers should find the works of Peter Laslett and Michael B. Katz especially useful. See Peter Laslett, ed., *Household and Family in Past Time* (Cambridge, Cambridge University Press, 1972), and Michael B. Katz, *The People of Canada West: Family and Class in the Mid-Nineteenth Century* (Cambridge, Mass., Harvard University Press, 1975).

Most of the standard histories of Canadian education, unfortunately, focus rather narrowly on the institutional structures and as a result often pay too little attention to the broader social context and/or avoid many important questions. Nevertheless students will find much of interest in the general history of Canadian education by Charles E. Phillips and in F. Henry Johnson's shorter text on the same subject. The recent general history edited by J. Donald Wilson, Robert W. Stamp, and Louis-Philippe Audet treads the difficult ground between national and provincial educational history with great ingenuity and should be consulted. Volumes on the history of education in individual provinces vary in quality, but often contain useful insights or information. See Charles E. Phillips, *The Development of Education in Canada* (Toronto, Gage, 1957); F. Henry Johnson, *A Brief History of Canadian Education* (Toronto, McGraw-Hill, 1968); J. D. Wilson, R. M. Stamp, L.-P Audet, eds, *Canadian Education: A History* (Scarborough, Prentice-Hall, 1970); F. W. Rowe, *The Development of Education in Newfoundland* (Toronto, Ryerson Press, 1964); K. F. C. MacNaughton, *The Development of the Theory and Practice of Education in New Brunswick, 1784-1900* (Fredericton, University of New Brunswick Press, 1946); Louis-Philippe Audet, *Histoire de l'enseignement au Québec 1608-1971*, 2 vols (Toronto, Holt, Rinehart & Winston, 1972); John W. Chalmers, *Schools of the Foothills Province* (Toronto, University of Toronto Press, 1967), and F. Henry Johnson, *A History of Public Education in British Columbia* (Vancouver, U.B.C. Publications Centre, 1964).

The scantiness of the secondary literature on aspects of the social context of schooling that are explored in the documents underlines the newness of this approach to Canadian education. Much of the most innovative work is still entombed in doctoral theses or, at best, in various scholarly journals. A recent collection of articles dealing with aspects of the social history of Ontario, published in honour of J. J. Talman, contains two useful pieces that reflect well-established interests in early colonial education. The impact of Anglican bishops and Methodist ambitions on the establishment of institutions has been fairly well documented in the standard works frequently cited in bibliographies on educational and denominational history. In this vein David Onn's 1969 article on Egerton Ryerson's philosophy of education and Judith Fingard's monograph on the early work of the S.P.G. missionaries in Nova Scotia deserve special mention. The diversity of early colonial education has been highlighted in recent work by Professor Fingard and by R. D. Gidney, which departs significantly from the pattern of treating the first decades of the nineteenth century as the inevitable but inconsequential prelude to the mid-century creation of provincial educational systems. See F. A. Armstrong, H. A. Stevenson, and J. D. Wilson, eds., *Aspects of Nineteenth Century Ontario* (Toronto, McClelland & Stewart, 1974); David Onn, 'Egerton Ryerson's Philosophy of Education: Something Borrowed or Something New?' *Ontario History*, LXI (1969); Judith Fingard, *The Anglican Design in Loyalist Nova Scotia, 1783-1816* (London, S.P.C.K., 1972); Fingard, 'English Humanitarianism and the Colonial Mind', *Canadian Historical Review*, LIV (1973) and 'Attitudes towards the Education of the Poor in Colonial Halifax', *Acadiensis* (Spring 1973); R. D. Gidney, 'Elementary Education in Upper Canada, a Reassessment', *Ontario History*, LXV (1973).

The now fashionable interest in urban history is already reflected in the literature on education. Following the lead of American and British historians and geographers, Canadian scholars in the last five years have begun the systematic analysis of such problems as literacy, school attendance, and the relation of public education to urban-reform activity in general. Kenneth Lockridge's recent and controversial monograph on literacy in colonial New England effectively relates the historical study of literacy to modern anthropological and sociological theories of the impact of modernization on pre-industrial society. In this vein Harvey Graff's recent doctoral thesis analyses the social structure of literacy in nineteenth-century Ontario. See Kenneth Lockridge, *Literacy in Colonial New England* (New York, W. W. Norton, 1974); Harvey J. Graff, 'Literacy and Social Structure in the Nineteenth Century', Ph.D. Thesis, University of Toronto, 1975.

The pattern of school attendance in the newly free public schools of the nineteenth century is another important and, until recently, ignored aspect of urban education. For all that public schools have been touted as powerful agents of socialization, the impact of schooling on the social group for whose benefit it was promoted is only beginning to receive attention. Articles by Haley Bamman and Michael Katz, included in the anthology *Education and Social History* (cited above) have been followed by a methodological critique of Katz's Hamilton analysis by Frank Denton and Peter George, and Ian Davey's doctoral thesis on school attendance in Hamilton. See Frank Denton and Peter George, 'Socio-Economic Influences on School Attendance: A Study of a Canadian County in 1871', *History of Education Quarterly*, XIV (1974); Ian E. Davey, 'Educational Reform and the Working Class: School Attendance in Hamilton, Ontario, 1851-1891', Ph.D. Thesis, University of Toronto, 1975.

A picture of the reality of working-class life in nineteenth-century Canada—its transience and precarious dignity—is now slowly emerging. Judith Fingard's paper 'The Winter's Tale', given at the Canadian Historican Association meetings in 1974, Terry Copp's short monograph on Montreal at the turn of the century, and Greg Kealey's work on nineteenth-century trade unions and working-class activity are all significant contributions to this field. The role of urban schools in the 'progressive' response to the industrial city prior to the First World War have been critically treated in two doctoral studies by Terrence Morrison and Neil Sutherland. The relationship between employment opportunities for young men and women, school attendance, and the emergence of 'adolescence' as a universal stage in the life cycle has been dealt with in recent work by American and European historians; however, in the Canadian context, Michael Katz's monograph on Hamilton (cited above) is a pioneer. See Judith Fingard, 'A Winter's Tale: The Seasonal Contours of Poverty in Pre-Industrial Canada, 1815-1860', Canadian Historical Association *Annual Report* (1974); Terry Copp, *The Anatomy of Poverty* (Toronto, McClelland & Stewart, 1974); T. R. Morrison, 'The Child and Urban School Reform in Late Nineteenth Century Ontario, 1875-1900', Ph.D. Thesis, University of Toronto, 1970; Neil Sutherland, 'Children in English-Canadian Society: Framing the Twentieth Century Consensus', Ph.D. Thesis, University of Minnesota, 1974.

Minorities in Canada, both religious and ethnic, have received considerable attention from historians in the past. There is no space here to cite even the major works relating to education, although it should be noted that a forthcoming special issue of *Canadian Ethnic Studies*, the official organ of the Canadian Ethnic Studies Association at the University of Calgary, will be edited by Cornelius Jaenen on the theme, 'Ethnicity and Education'. Professor Jaenen's work on the history of education of minorities and Robin Winks' studies of the Blacks in Canada both require special mention. Current interest in women's studies, especially the history of women, has sparked work on neglected aspects of the traditional preserve of educational historians, as well as interest in the broader area of the history of childhood and family life. The feminization of the teaching professions and the higher education of women in the nineteenth century are two areas of particular note. See Robin Winks, *The Blacks in Canada, a History* (New Haven, Yale University Press, 1971); Winks, 'Negro School Segregation in Ontario and Nova Scotia', *Canadian Historical Review* (1969); Alison Prentice, 'The Feminization of Teaching in British North America and Canada, 1845-1875', *Histoire sociale/Social History*, XV (1975); Nancy Thompson, 'The Controversy over the Admission of Women to University College', M.A. Thesis, University of Toronto, 1974; D. A. Ronish, 'The Development of Higher Education for Women at McGill University from 1857 to 1899, with Specific Reference to the Role of Sir John William Dawson', M. Ed. Thesis, McGill University, 1972; Wendy Bryans, 'Virtuous Women at Half the Price: The Feminization of Teaching and Women Teachers' Organizations in Ontario', M.A. Thesis, University of Toronto, 1974.

Readers wishing to delve further into the sources for the history of the family, the child, and education in the nineteenth century will find other published collections of interest. For Canada, see the useful study edited by Douglas Lawr and Robert Gidney, *Educating Canadians: A Documentary History of Public Education* (Toronto, Van Nostrand Reinhold, 1973). Daniel Calhoun, ed., *The Educating of Americans: A Documentary History of Public Education* (Boston, Houghton Mifflin, 1969) and David B. Tyack, ed., *Turning Points in American Educational History* (Waltham, Mass., Blaisdell, 1967) are the most comprehensive of the American collections, while *School Reform: Past and Present*, edited by Michael B. Katz (Boston, Little, Brown, 1971) is an interesting juxtaposition of nineteenth-and twentieth-century documents. J. G. Hodgins, ed., *Documentary History of Education in Upper Canada* (Toronto, Warwick Bros. & Ritter, 1894-1910) is an older, multi-volume work that, in spite of its dated approach, is still very useful to students of Ontario educational history in the nineteenth century.

An exceptionally rich literature is available in Canadian archives and libraries. Pamphlet collections, family papers, correspondence, and diaries all contain material of interest, while old textbooks, school manuals, or even early novels like Ralph Connor's *Glengarry School Days* (Toronto, McClelland & Stewart, 1975) have much to offer the perceptive reader. The many and voluminous reports on schools and education that were produced by special committees of legislatures or municipal and provincial authorities from time to time, or in the latter case on an annual basis as school systems became firmly established, are of obvious importance. Equally valuable are the collections of correspondence of various government departments involved in education. Finally the attention of the reader is called to the great range of Victorian periodical literature that dealt with or touched on the subject. From short-lived magazines like *The Canadian Gem and Family Visitor* to official organs like *The Educational Record of the Province of Quebec*, Canadian periodical literature is full of commentary, advice, and information on the Canadian child and his or her education in the nineteenth century.